HOLMAN
New Testament Commentary

HOLMAN
New
Testament
Commentary

Hebrews
& James

GENERAL EDITOR

Max Anders

AUTHOR

Thomas D. Lea

**HOLMAN
REFERENCE**

NASHVILLE, TENNESSEE

Holman New Testament Commentary
© 1999 B&H Publishing Group
Nashville, Tennessee
All rights reserved

ISBN 978-0-8054-0211-7

Dewey Decimal Classification: 227.87
Subject Heading: BIBLE. NT. Hebrews
Library of Congress Card Catalog Number: 98-55979

Lea. Thomas D.
    Hebrews & James / Thomas Lea
        p.   cm. — (Holman New Testament commentary)
    Includes bibliographical references.
    ISBN 0-8054-0211-X (alk. paper)
    1. Bible. N.T. Hebrews—Commentaries. 2. Bible. N.T. James—Commentaries. I. Title. II. Title: Hebrews and James. III. Series
    BS2775.3.L43 1999   98.55979
    227'.87077—dc21   CIP

9 10 11 12 13   16 15 14 13 12

To my children,

Lisa, Marcie, and

Cliff, whose

support, encouragement,

and prayers have

sustained my life

and writing.

• *Thomas Lea* •

January 1999

Contents

Contents

Editorial Preface

Today's church hungers for Bible teaching, and Bible teachers hunger for resources to guide them in teaching God's Word. The Holman New Testament Commentary provides the church with the food to feed the spiritually hungry in an easily digestible format. The result: new spiritual vitality that the church can readily use.

Bible teaching should result in new interest in the Scriptures, expanded Bible knowledge, discovery of specific scriptural principles, relevant applications, and exciting living. The unique format of the Holman New Testament Commentary includes sections to achieve these results for every New Testament book.

Opening quotations from some of the church's best writers lead to an introductory illustration and discussion that draw individuals and study groups into the Word of God. "In a Nutshell" summarizes the content and teaching of the chapter. Verse-by-verse commentary answers the church's questions rather than raising issues scholars usually admit they cannot adequately solve. Bible principles and specific contemporary applications encourage students to move from Bible to contemporary times. A specific modern illustration then ties application vividly to present life. A brief prayer aids the student to commit his or her daily life to the principles and applications found in the Bible chapter being studied. For those still hungry for more, "Deeper Discoveries" take the student into a more personal, deeper study of the words, phrases, and themes of God's Word. Finally, a teaching outline provides transitional statements and conclusions along with an outline to assist the teacher in group Bible studies.

It is the editors' prayer that this new resource for local church Bible teaching will enrich the ministry of group, as well as individual, Bible study, and that it will lead God's people to truly be people of the Book, living out what God calls us to be.

Holman Old Testament Commentary Contributors

Holman New Testament Commentary Contributors

Holman New Testament Commentary

Twelve volumes designed for Bible study and teaching to enrich the local church and God's people.

Series Editor	Max Anders
Managing Editors	Trent C. Butler & Steve Bond
Project Editor	Lloyd W. Mullens
Marketing Manager	Greg Webster
Product Manager	David Shepherd
Page Composition	TF Designs, Mt. Juliet, TN

Introduction to

Hebrews

AUTHORSHIP

The book is anonymous. We find no name for a stated author. Best suggestion for authorship is that given by Origen, Christian leader in the third century, who said, "But as to who actually wrote the epistle, God knows the truth of the matter."

Eastern Christianity viewed Paul as the author, even though those who supported Pauline authorship knew that the language did not resemble Paul's other letters. Western Christianity did not accept Pauline authorship until the fourth century. They felt that the letter had great authority, but many saw it as anonymous and non-Pauline.

The writer of Hebrews held to the same basic apostolic teaching as Paul, but he wrote with a different style and quoted the Old Testament differently from the apostle.

Among possible authors suggested are Luke, Apollos (see Acts 18:24), Barnabas, Priscilla, and Aquila.

The author identified himself as a second-generation Christian (see Heb. 2:3), and he wrote with an excellent literary style and a vivid vocabulary.

The original readers of the book knew the writer's name, for he asked for prayers that he might be able to visit them (13:18–19) and expressed the hope that Timothy would come with him (13:23).

ORIGINAL READERS OF HEBREWS

The title "To the Hebrews, " though not original, can be traced back to the last quarter of the second century. The readers of this book were familiar with the Old Testament and knew the ritual of the Book of Leviticus and the details of the tabernacle. The intended audience was probably Jewish believers with a similar background to those Jews who wrote the Dead Sea Scrolls. They were not eyewitnesses to Jesus, but they had learned of him from those who were (Heb. 2:3–4).

They had faced persecution and endured abuse, imprisonment, and loss of property for their faith, but not martyrdom (Heb. 10:32–39; 12:4). They demonstrated their faith by serving fellow believers and particularly supported those who endured persecution (Heb. 6:10; 10:34).

They had ceased to grow as Christians and were falling away from the commitment they had known (Heb. 5:11–6:12). The writer rebuked them for not meeting together often enough (10:24–25). They were in danger of lapsing into sin (3:12–14).

The readers of Hebrews may have been in danger of returning to Judaism in order to avoid persecution. The author warned them against such apostasy (6:4–9; 10:26–31) and urged them to return to the mainstream of Christian fellowship.

Knowing where the intended audience lived is difficult to determine. Among locations suggested are Jerusalem, Alexandria, and Rome, with the latter being the best possibility.

DATE

Mention of Timothy in 13:23 suggests a date in his lifetime, some time in the first century. Their failure to suffer martyrdom (Heb. 12:4) rules out the Jerusalem church (see Acts 7:54–60) and suggests a date before Nero's persecution (A.D. 64). Rome was the intended destination.

The author wrote as if the Jerusalem Temple were still standing. The description of the ritual in 9:6–9 contains many usages of the Greek present tense, suggesting events still underway.

Mention of sacrifices in 10:2 implied that they were still being offered. Best suggestion is a date just before Nero's persecutions in A.D. 64.

CHARACTERISTICS OF HEBREWS

The Greek style of Hebrews is elegant and highly literary. It is one of the most difficult New Testament writings to translate from the Greek. The book also contains many Old Testament quotations and allusions. Most of the quotations were from the Greek version of the Old Testament—the Septuagint. Many of these references were taken from the Psalms, particularly Psalm 110:1,4.

The writer used the Old Testament sacrificial system as a background for the explanation of the superiority of the redemptive work of Jesus Christ.

The references to the person of Christ (Christology) are many and varied. There are more than twenty names and titles for Jesus (Son, Lord, High Priest, apostle, author and finisher of our faith, etc.). Although there is clear reference to the deity of Christ, the humanity of Christ is emphasized more than in most New Testament writings (Heb. 4:14–16).

Throughout Hebrews a series of warnings appear. These are injected into the argument of the epistle. The warnings urge the readers not to neglect salvation in Christ (2:1–4; 3:7–4:13; 5:11–6:20; 10:26–39; 12:15–29).

The form of Hebrews is unlike that of the typical Pauline letter of the New Testament. There are few personal references and greetings (cf. 6:9–10; 12:4). Some have suggested that Hebrews was an exhortation or sermon given to a specific congregation.

Hebrews 1

God's Son: Supreme over Prophets and Angels

I. **INTRODUCTION**
The Surprising Presidency of
George Washington

II. **COMMENTARY**
A verse-by-verse explanation of the chapter.

III. **CONCLUSION**
Portraits of Jesus
An overview of the principles and applications from
the chapter.

IV. **LIFE APPLICATION**
Jesus Will Not Be Moved
Melding the chapter to life.

V. **PRAYER**
Tying the chapter to life with God.

VI. **DEEPER DISCOVERIES**
Historical, geographical, and grammatical enrichment of the commentary.

VII. **TEACHING OUTLINE**
Suggested step-by-step group study of the chapter.

VIII. **ISSUES FOR DISCUSSION**
Zeroing the chapter in on daily life.

Quote

"*M*illions of angels are at God's command and at our service. The hosts of heaven stand at attention as we make our way from earth to glory, and Satan's BB guns are no match for God's heavy artillery."

B i l l y   G r a h a m

Hebrews

IN A NUTSHELL

*H*ebrews 1 shows that Jesus is superior to the prophets and to angels. God had spoken fully through his Son but only partially and imperfectly through the prophets. Jesus is superior to angels because he is God's Son, while angels are created spirits sent by God to minister to believers. As God's Son, Jesus is his heir, cocreator, and coruler of the universe, exercising authority over creation and over his enemies.

God's Son: Supreme over Prophets and Angels

I. INTRODUCTION

The Surprising Presidency of George Washington

*E*ven though today we call him the "Father of our Country," some of his contemporaries did not think that highly of George Washington. Washington's father died when he was eleven. He had almost no formal education because his family could not afford the expense of school in an era without public education. He never visited Europe. John Adams tersely remarked that Washington was "too illiterate, unlearned, unread for his station and reputation." He developed his mind through his own reading program.

This "unlearned" aristocrat surprised the country. He burst into the spotlight of leadership by commanding a frontier militia at twenty-one years of age. He delivered an ultimatum to French forces pushing into English lands in the Ohio Valley.

He was also a peacemaker. The followers of the brilliant politicians, Alexander Hamilton and Thomas Jefferson, often hotly debated their contrasting political views. With great skill and patience Washington brought unity and moderation to these unmanageable followers.

He had moral convictions. He provided freedom for his slaves after his wife's death and guaranteed their support in his will. In the 1830s these freedmen were still receiving payments from his estate.

He was unselfish. When Congress offered him command of the Continental armies, he refused a salary. He accepted only reimbursement for expenses. He made the same suggestion when he became President. Congress refused his suggestion and set the President's salary at $25,000, a large amount in those days.

Washington showed wisdom in what he expected for the country. He did not aim at power and expansion but at independence. In his farewell address he expressed the hope that the country would have the time "to settle and mature its yet recent institutions and to progress without interruption to that degree of strength and consistency which is necessary to give it, humanly speaking, the command of its own fortunes."

Many Americans did not expect greatness from President George Washington. His success surprised and impressed his critics.

Hebrews addresses readers who reverenced the Old Testament prophets and angels. When we think about Moses, Elijah, Isaiah, Jeremiah, and Amos, we must admit that the prophets were an impressive group. We aren't surprised that some believers admired them, perhaps a bit too much.

Some readers of Hebrews were also **carried away by all kinds of strange teachings** (Heb. 13:9). They may have become angel worshipers (Col. 2:18). Someone had to remind them how important Jesus was. That's when the author of Hebrews "sharpened his pencil" and started writing.

He emphasized that Jesus was better than the prophets (vv. 1–3). God had spoken through the prophets **at many times and in various ways.** When God spoke through Jesus, he revealed the Son as Creator, Sustainer, and Redeemer. Isaiah could not be compared with Jesus. God had spoken bits and pieces of truth through Isaiah, but God revealed all his truth when he spoke through Jesus.

Hebrews also emphasizes that Jesus is better than the angels (vv. 4–14). The very name **Son** made Jesus superior to angels (vv. 4–5). The angels' worship of Jesus (Luke 2:8–15) showed his majesty (vv. 6–7). Jesus has a throne and loves righteousness (vv. 8–9). He is eternal and unchanging (vv. 10–12).

A Son and Ruler who eternally loved righteousness was more important than an angel who attended the needs of believers. Angels had the important role of caring for God's servants (v. 14), but we can't compare their importance to that of Jesus.

Reading this chapter causes us to say, "We need to learn more about Jesus." Our writer's hope is that each day we will "grow in the grace and knowledge of our Lord and Savior Jesus Christ" (2 Pet. 3:18).

II. COMMENTARY

God's Son: Supreme over Prophets and Angels

> **MAIN IDEA:** *God has spoken through the Son more fully and authoritatively than through the prophets or the angels.*

A Better Than the Prophets (vv. 1–3)

> **SUPPORTING IDEA:** *The Son is more glorious than the prophets because God has spoken fully through him.*

1:1. The author of Hebrews did not record his name. We see no destination for the letter. We can only guess at both features. The writer tells us three things. First, God spoke. He has revealed himself. Second, God spoke to the **forefathers.** Our Old Testament contains this "Word of God" to our spiritual forefathers. Third, God did this speaking through the prophets. The words of Hosea, Ezekiel, Malachi, and the rest of the prophets were God's words to wandering human beings.

God spoke **at many times**. He spoke in fragments. He revealed a little here and a little there. God also spoke **in various ways**. He spoke through visions, angels, events, and people.

1:2–3. What God announced through the prophets was important. What he spoke through his Son was climactic, definitive, and superlative. We are living in the last days, not in a chronological sense but in a theological sense. Jesus' death, resurrection, and ascension showed that we have entered new territory in God's plans. In these final days God has spoken through his Son. God wants us to hear him. We had better listen. Anyone neglecting what Jesus says faces the spiritual danger of a driver crashing through road signs announcing, "Bridge out ahead!"

The overwhelming superiority of the Son is described with seven majestic phrases. The first two show the relationship of the Son to *creation*. Jesus is the **heir of all things** in that he will ultimately have control over all creation (Heb. 2:8). God worked through his Son to make the universe of time and space (Col. 1:16). The Son was God's intermediate agent in creation.

The next two phrases show the Son's relationship to the *Father*. As the **radiance of God's glory**, the Son reflects God's spotless purity; he shined into human hearts (John 1:9). As the **exact representation** of God's being, the Son has the divine substance of the Father. This was a bold proclamation of Jesus' deity. Jesus is God.

The fifth phrase shows something the Son is now doing in the *world*. God's creative word formed the world of time and space (Heb. 11:3). The sustaining word of the Son maintains it. As the sustainer of the world, the Son carries God's plan to its conclusion. With Jesus in charge we know that the world will not fall into utter chaos. God's plans will triumph.

The sixth and seventh phrases focus on the *redemptive work* of Christ. The Son brought us God's grace because his death removed the stain of sin. Jesus has provided **purification for sins** as an act of supreme grace without any merit on our part. After dealing with our sins, Jesus ascended the throne. In his resurrection and ascension he assumed a place of honor at God's right hand. Today we proclaim him as Lord.

The Son is a Prophet through whom God spoke his final word to human beings. The Son is a Priest who has removed the blot of sin from our ledger. He is a King exalted by God to a supreme place of honor.

Ⓑ Better Than the Angels (vv. 4–14)

> **SUPPORTING IDEA:** *The sonship, dignity, role, and authority of the Son show that he is better than the angels.*

1. Because He Is the Son (vv. 4–5)

1:4. The readers of Hebrews may have called Jesus Christ by the name, "angel." This title pictured him as a spiritual being carrying out a few errands for God. Hebrews calls Jesus Christ a Son and recognizes this as a superior title. A Son has a close, personal relationship with the Father. Jesus was much more than a supernatural creature who darted around on mercy missions for God.

1:5. To prove the exalted superiority of the Son, the first of seven Old Testament quotations is used. Christ is viewed as the ultimate aim and goal of all his Old Testament quotations. The first quotation came from Psalm 2:7. The psalm describes the coronation of an Israelite king. Paul referred to this verse in Acts 13:33 to explain Jesus' resurrection. Hebrews uses it to proclaim Jesus' royal dignity in his resurrection and ascension.

The second quotation came from 2 Samuel 7:14. The prophet Nathan passed these words from God to David. They contained a promise that Solomon would build a house for God after David's death. God promised that he would be David's father forever and that David would be his son. God did not exhaust these promises in Solomon. Later prophets looked for David to have a greater Son, the Messiah (Mic. 5:2). New Testament writers proclaimed Jesus as the descendant of David who fulfilled this verse (Rom. 1:3). No angel ever had a position as exalted as Jesus.

2. Because He Has Superior Dignity (vv. 6–7)

1:6. The Old Testament does not contain the exact words of this quotation. The idea appears in Psalm 97:7 and in the Greek Old Testament version of Deuteronomy 32:43. In the Old Testament the command involved the worship of God the Father. In Hebrews the Son is linked with the Father by receiving the worship due him. This provided powerful evidence for Jesus' deity.

This could be a reference to the angels worshiping Jesus at his birth. (Luke 2:8–15). Such angelic worship showed that the Son is superior to angels. He has greater dignity than they.

1:7. What do angels do? Psalm 104:4 is quoted to spotlight their subordinate role. Angels are compared to the natural elements of wind and fire. They did God's bidding and became his messengers. Angels fulfilled an important but inferior role. We will learn more about their actions in verse 14.

3. Because of His Important Role (vv. 8–9)

1:8–9. These words come from Psalm 45:6–7. The psalm originally celebrated a royal wedding. The words are so glorious that only God's messianic king can satisfy their meaning. These words tell us three facts about the role of the Son. Each fact proclaimed his superiority to angels. First, the Son has a throne and is a ruler. No one could say this of an angel. Second, this throne **will last for ever and ever.** It is eternal. Angels are not eternal, for God created them at a point in time (Ps. 148:2,5). Third, the Son loves righteousness. Nothing delights God more than for someone to love his righteousness (Ps. 1:1–6; Matt. 5:6).

4. Because He Is Unchanging (vv. 10–12)

1:10–12. This, the longest of the seven quotations, comes from Psalm 102:25–27. These words show that God will completely change the created order (2 Pet. 3:11–13). The psalmist was showing that only God provides stability and security. God is anchored like a rock, and we can anchor our lives to this mountain of immobility. Jesus is identified as the Lord who is to be praised.

5. Because He Has Authority (vv. 13–14)

1:13. The seventh quotation comes from Psalm 110:1. This verse shows that Christ's ascension lifted him to a place of authority and power at the Father's right hand. Jesus claimed that this verse referred to him (Mark 12:36). Although we live at a time when the Son's enemies are not yet a **footstool**, the New Testament promises the Son's complete victory at the end (1 Cor. 15:24–27).

1:14. In contrast to the authority of God's Son, angels have a servant role. They serve in God's behalf. He gives them orders which they carry out. Their primary duty is to care for believers. The Old Testament promised that angels would deliver believers (Ps. 34:7). The New Testament records angelic rescues (Acts 12:7–10).

> **MAIN IDEA REVIEW:** *God has spoken through the Son more fully and authoritatively than through the prophets or the angels.*

III. CONCLUSION

Portraits of Jesus

God has spoken! He has sent us a victorious E-mail message. He has not left us groping in the dark for spiritual direction. God has spoken in two ways. First, he has spoken in many different ways through the Old Testament prophets. Second, he has spoken gloriously and fully through Jesus Christ. We do not serve a silent God. Our God has spoken. We must search out the meaning of his message like one seeking directions to buried treasure.

What's so special about Jesus? First, he is the Creator. All things belong to him. All things began with him. Second, he is God. He is the radiant outburst of the Father's glory, and he unveils the divine nature. Third, he carries the Father's plans forward by his powerful word. Jesus is bringing the events of history to a God-honoring conclusion. Fourth, Jesus has met our spiritual needs. He has removed our sin. Today he is at God's right hand in heaven praying for us (Heb. 7:25).

What about angels? Why are they important? In comparison to Jesus, they are insignificant players in God's drama. We must show more commitment to Jesus than curiosity about angels. Five reasons explain why Jesus is more important than the angels. First, Jesus is more important because he is the Son of God and not merely a servant caring for believers. Second, Jesus is superior to the angels because they worship him. Third, Jesus is superior because he is a ruler before God, a ruler who loves righteousness. Fourth, Jesus is superior because he is unchanging. Fifth, he is superior because God has given him authority over his enemies.

These facts about Jesus show it is impossible to give too much attention to Jesus. Jesus is not merely a good example, a beautiful friend, a teacher of ethics, or a narrator of parables. He is the eternal God, worthy of our worship, and deserving of our constant obedience.

A noted New Testament scholar has said, "We should not disparage the founders of any of the great world-religions, but it is the simple truth that none of them is entitled to be called the Savior of the world. Jesus alone bears this designation, and 'there is salvation in no one else, for there is no other name under heaven given among men by which we must be saved'" (Acts 4:12) (F. F. Bruce).

Do angels fit into God's plan for Christians? Yes, God sends them on mission. God surrounds us with his constant love. Angels care for believers by protecting, guiding, and encouraging us.

PRINCIPLES

- God has spoken in fragments through the prophets.
- God has spoken in a grand finale through Jesus.
- Jesus is superior to angels because he is a Son with superior dignity and unchanging authority.
- God sends angels to protect and care for his children.

APPLICATIONS

- Look to the Old Testament prophets for genuine insights into God.
- Look to Jesus as God's final word to human beings.
- Look to Jesus for all the information God wants us to have. No more is coming. We must use what Jesus has given.
- Worship Jesus because he is righteous and kingly; love, adore, and serve him.
- Rest in God's protection through his angels.

IV. LIFE APPLICATION

Jesus Will Not Be Moved

One day in February the temperature reached the mid-90s. The next week we shivered in a sub-20s freeze. Even in mid-March we had weather extremes, alternating from a high in the 80s to a low in the 20s. My body finally said, "Enough!" By late March my allergies were in orbit. I had a raspy throat, and after a weekend of preaching I had no voice. "It's the weather," said my doctor, when I sought relief. "I can't do much to help you until it settles down." I took the medicine he offered, got a little better, but hacked, sputtered, and choked for ten days. Such are the weather variations in Texas.

Life changes like Texas weather. A trip to the doctor may bring a revelation of serious health problems. A phone call from a child or a friend brings information about a personal crisis. A pink slip from an employer starts a financial free fall. An unexpected resignation from a committee member saddles you with another job. A conversation with a friend informs you of someone who has decided to turn his back on Jesus. And the one who turned away used to be your prayer partner!

What do we do when life won't settle down? Hebrews points us to someone who does not change (vv. 10–12). Years on our mortal time clock tick away. Heaven and earth will perish. Only Jesus Christ **is the same yesterday and today and forever** (Heb. 13:8).

When the blustery storms of life blow your ship, Jesus will serve as your anchor.

The Tony Woods family serves as missionaries to Japan. In the early 1990s their teenage son Trevor fought a valiant battle with leukemia before dying at age fifteen. They had returned to America for treatment for Trevor, but they carried his ashes to Japan for burial. There in their field of ministry they tried to rebuild their lives.

In the weeks after their return, a Japanese lady came to them to say, "I also lost a son." They consoled one another and helped the woman develop a growing relationship with the Lord. Couple after couple came to visit the Woods, to console them but also to be consoled. Trevor's best friend, a Japanese boy named Katsuya, came to say, "I've watched how he [Trevor] lived and how he died. Now I want to give my life to the ministry."

In 1994 Tony Woods wrote in *The Commission:* "In the last year, a church has risen up from the ashes of our shared grief, a lighthouse of hope to this community we've loved so long but up until now have been seemingly unable to reach." He added, "God is working a miracle in our midst, not the physical healing that we wanted so desperately, but the eternal healing of life through Jesus."

The Woods are learning that Jesus does not change. Jesus will not be moved. He remains constant, provides strength for the journey, and new strength around every corner.

V. PRAYER

Dear Jesus, you are superior to all who would claim worship or honor. You are my Creator, Sustainer, Redeemer, and King. I bow in worship to you and to you alone. Amen.

VI. DEEPER DISCOVERIES

A. Last Days (v. 2)

When we read that God has spoken to us **in these last days**, we may immediately assume that the end of the age lies just around the corner. But you may also wonder, "Why has it taken so long for Jesus to come back and bring it to a close?"

The phrase **these last days** tells us more about the theological finality of Christ than the chronological time of his return. Note these facts:

1. Hebrews 1:2 says that God has already spoken to us in **these last days** through his Son. All of us, including the writer of Hebrews, have been living in these days.

2. The use of the term **end of the ages** in Hebrews 9:26 suggests that Jesus' first appearance concluded one age and began another. God really spoke through the prophets, but Jesus' coming began a new era. The curtain fell on the era of the prophets, and Jesus' coming began the final act. We are now in the last act.

3. All our talk about the last days shows us that Jesus' life, death, and resurrection announce the beginning of the end. God made his strongest move in Jesus. Since Jesus came, we have been living in the **last days**. We are surprised that concluding **these last days** has taken so long. We rejoice in the greatness of what God has already done in Jesus.

4. We face the challenge of keeping alive our hope in Jesus' final return while we preach that God has acted conclusively to save sinners through Jesus' death and resurrection.

Notice several other passages of Scripture which use the term **last days** (or a related idea):

> Acts 2:17: "In the last days, God says, I will pour out my Spirit on all people. Your sons and daughters will prophesy, your young men will see visions, your old men will dream dreams."

1 Peter 1:20: "He [Jesus] was chosen before the creation of the world, but was revealed in these last times for your sake."

1 John 2:18: "Dear children, this is the last hour; and as you have heard that the antichrist is coming, even now many antichrists have come. This is how we know it is the last hour."

You may ask, "If these are the last days, how can we know on which day Jesus is coming back?" We can't know that day with certainty. "Only the father" knows that day for sure (Mark 13:32). Events like wars, earthquakes, famines, and rebellion against God will take place before the end (Mark 13:3–8; 2 Thess. 2:3–4). We must not spend our time trying to decide whether contemporary events herald the return of Jesus.

Our job is to live obediently like alert, disciplined soldiers (1 Thess. 5:6–8). We must be ready so that whenever Jesus comes back we will be morally prepared. For disobedient people Jesus' return will hit like a night robbery (1 Thess. 5:2). Thieves don't announce their plans to their victims. Jesus wants us to wake up, live a life of faith, love our enemies, and hope for the time of his return (1 Thess. 5:8). We honor the Lord by living a life of moral commitment, not by wondering about the day of his return.

B. The Finality of Jesus (v. 2)

"Suppose God wanted to send a message to the world today. How would he do it?" A few years ago a friend asked me these words. He wanted me to listen to his explanation that God would speak today through the leaders of his church. I've had people provide me other answers to this question such as:

1. God is revealing his plans to prominent Christian leaders. Usually someone who believes this will supply me a name.

2. God is sending messages through angels. The angels are trying to protect us, guide us, or just get our attention.

These answers promote confusion for these reasons: (1) They often assume that God has not been speaking to people until recently. (2) They confuse a fresh understanding of God's will with an announcement of new truth never before disclosed. A lot of "insights" from God are really fresh discoveries of truths God revealed centuries ago. (3) They ignore the fact that in Jesus, God has spoken all the truth which he will ever communicate. Jesus is God's final word to human beings.

What do we mean when we say that in Jesus God acted with finality? We mean that in him God performed the definitive act which makes our salvation possible. The Bible tells the story of what God did through Jesus. God has nothing more to tell us, but we can read the Bible to increase our understanding of what he has said and done.

Because God has acted with finality in Jesus, we don't expect additional Scriptures to reveal more about God. It is all recorded in the Bible. We desperately need to understand more of what God has done, but all we need to understand, God has recorded already in Scripture.

The descriptions of Jesus in Hebrews 1:2–3 suggest a personality so overwhelming that we can't expect any later follow-up. The death, burial, resurrection, and exaltation are such climactic events that we need only expect a final return to consolidate Christ's accomplishments. God's actions in Jesus have been so magnificent that we can spend our time reflecting on and preaching about Jesus.

C. Use of the Old Testament in the New Testament

Hebrews 1:5–14 refers to seven Old Testament passages to prove that the Son of God is superior to the angels. Five of these quotations are from the Psalms; one from 2 Samuel 7:14, and another from Deuteronomy 32:43 in the Greek Old Testament.

Sometimes the writer of Hebrews took passages addressed to Old Testament kings and applied them to the Son of God (see 1:8–9 which quotes Ps. 45:6–7). Jewish writers felt that a descendant of David was a prince of God. They also saw nothing unusual in calling the Messiah, who was David's greater son, by the name of "God" (see Isa. 9:6 for the term "Mighty God").

On other occasions the writer of Hebrews took passages addressed to Yahweh, the God of Israel, in the Old Testament and applied them to Christ (see 1:10–12 which quotes Ps. 102:25–27). He felt that this was legitimate because the Son of God had an eternal throne (1:8). The Son was eternal just as the psalmist declared of the Father.

We also see several other principles in the use of the Old Testament in the Book of Hebrews:

1. The New Testament is the fulfillment of what God had begun in the Old Testament (Heb. 1:1–2). The two Testaments do not conflict but complement each other.

2. Old Testament authority is recognized by introducing the Old Testament quote with the formula, **he [God] says** (Heb. 1:7). Human beings wrote the words, but God was the source.

3. Sometimes an Old Testament passage is paraphrased without quoting it exactly. When you compare Psalm 104:4 with Hebrews 1:7, you will find the writer or Hebrews replaced "messengers" with **angels**. Perhaps this implies that angels carried out God's commands with the speed of wind and the power of fire.

D. Firstborn (v. 6)

This word is used three times in Hebrews (see also 11:28; 12:23). This is the only time in the book where the term refers to the Son of God. If we do not understand the meaning of this word correctly, we will have a first-class theological problem on our hands.

Some religious groups use the term to designate Jesus as the first of God's creatures. If we follow this meaning, then we see Jesus as a creation of God. If Jesus is created, then he is not eternal. But Hebrews describes God's Son as someone present at the beginning (1:10) with a throne lasting **for ever and ever** (Heb. 1:8). Clearly God's Son is eternal and not created.

The term **firstborn** had a specific meaning for Hebrew people. The firstborn son in a Jewish family had a special rank. He received special privileges and responsibilities. His inheritance included a double portion of the estate and family leadership after the father's death.

This term was used to show the supreme position of the Son of God. He was not the first of God's creations. The Son of God and the Father stand in contrast with the created order. The Son has created this order in the plan of the Father, but the Father and the Son have always existed. They are uncreated. The term **firstborn** shows the matchless superiority of God's Son.

Paul used the word in two key passages:

> Colossians 1:15: "He is the image of the invisible God, the firstborn over all creation."
>
> Colossians 1:18: "And he is the head of the body, the church; he is the beginning and the firstborn from among the dead, so that in everything he might have the supremacy."

In the first passage Paul placed God's Son in contrast with all creation. God had not created the Son. He had placed him over all creation. This showed his supremacy, not his order in creation. In the second passage Paul identified the Son as the first to rise bodily from the grave, never to die again.

Christ's superior rank and authority compel us to worship and obey him. Our response to him must be an obedient, "My Lord and my God" (John 20:28).

E. Angels (vv. 4–14)

The lengthy contrast in Hebrews 1:4–2:18 between God's Son and the angels raises some questions about the original audience of Hebrews. Did they view God's Son as one of the angels? Did they worship angels? Why put the reference to angels here?

We don't have answers to most of these questions. We know that Jews had curiosity and interest in angels. We know that angels appeared several times in the Gospels. They carry out God's will and are clearly supernatural beings. Our best guess is that the readers of Hebrews may have seen Jesus as just another angel. Our writer wanted to show how wrong they were. He started off by proving that God's Son was superior to angelic beings.

Who are angels? What relationship do we have to them today? Do we have guardian angels? Here are some facts we know about angels:

1. An angel is a divine messenger who protected Christians (Heb. 1:14), delivered a message to human beings (Luke 2:10–14), and provided guidance (Matt. 1:20).

2. Angels appear to be active today, but they often do their work invisibly (2 Kgs. 6:17). They still serve those who **will inherit salvation** (Heb. 1:14). They sometimes appear in human form (Judg. 6:11–24). Some of them appear as winged creatures (Isa. 6:2).

3. Jesus' comment in Matthew 18:10 has led some to feel that God assigns individual protective roles to angels. It is difficult to prove from this passage that each person has a "guardian" angel assigned by God.

4. Angels are created beings (Ps. 148:2,5), but they have superior intelligence and wisdom (2 Sam. 14:17). They do not know everything (1 Pet. 1:12). Because they are spiritual beings, they can move back and forth from the spiritual realm to the physical without hindrance.

5. God created angels holy (Gen. 1:31), but some angels later rebelled (Jude 6). Good angels are called "the holy angels" (Luke 9:26). They worship and serve God. God will cast evil angels "into the eternal fire, prepared for the devil and his angels" (Matt. 25:41).

The fact that God has given angels to protect us should give us much comfort. We praise God and not angels for protection, guidance, and understanding.

VII. TEACHING OUTLINE

A. INTRODUCTION

1. Lead Story: The Surprising Presidency of George Washington
2. Context: The readers of the Book of Hebrews were Jewish Christians who loved the Old Testament prophets and were curiously interested in angels. In fact, they were apparently more interested in the prophets and in angels than they were in Jesus. The writer of Hebrews fairly shouted that Christ was superior to both the prophets and angels.
   Better than the prophets (vv. 1–3). God spoke through the prophets in many different ways. Jesus is Creator of the world, Reflector of God's glory, Sustainer of God's plans, and our Redeemer in heaven. God has spoken in totality through Jesus.
   Better than the angels (vv. 4–14). Jesus is better than the angels because he is the Son of God. As the Son of God, he receives superior dignity and worship from angels. He functions as a ruler and loves

righteousness. He is unchanging. He has complete authority and power. Angels are important creatures, but they exist as servants who carry out God's will.

3. Transition: As we study this chapter, we will grow in our understanding of the greatness of Jesus Christ. Though we thank God for the role of the prophets and the actions of angels, we worship and praise only Jesus. Our worship and praise of Jesus should produce obedience, faith, hope, and stamina. R. E. Brown in his book *The Message of Hebrews* has said that "Hebrews introduces us to a Christ whose perfect sinless nature is a *unique revelation*, whose *sacrifice* is alone effective for our salvation, and whose *authority* in heaven and on earth is without rival."

We must live like people who know and practice that.

B. COMMENTARY

1. Better than the Prophets (vv. 1–3)
   a. The position of the prophets (v. 1)
   b. The position of the Son (vv. 2–3)
      (1) Creator (v. 2)
      (2) Reflector (v. 3)
      (3) Sustainer (v. 3)
      (4) Redeemer (v. 3)
2. Better than the Angels (vv. 4–14)
   a. Because he is a Son (vv. 4–5)
   b. Because he has superior dignity (vv. 6–7)
   c. Because of his important role (vv. 8–9)
   d. Because he is unchanging (vv. 10–12)
   e. Because he has authority (vv. 13–14)

C. CONCLUSION: JESUS WILL NOT BE MOVED

VIII. ISSUES FOR DISCUSSION

1. How do you describe Jesus to other Christians? to unbelievers?
2. How do you show Jesus that you believe He is the Son of God, Savior, King, Redeemer, superior to all created beings?
3. List specific acts of obedience you will take to demonstrate your awe and wonder at the majesty of who Jesus is.
4. Do you believe we are living in the last days? What does this mean to you? How does it affect your life?

Hebrews 2

Why We Should Listen to Jesus

I. **INTRODUCTION**
Doing It Our Way

II. **COMMENTARY**
A verse-by-verse explanation of the chapter.

III. **CONCLUSION**
Our Great Salvation

An overview of the principles and applications from the chapter.

IV. **LIFE APPLICATION**
Jesus Is a Wonderful Savior

Melding the chapter to life.

V. **PRAYER**
Tying the chapter to life with God.

VI. **DEEPER DISCOVERIES**
Historical, geographical, and grammatical enrichment of the commentary.

VII. **TEACHING OUTLINE**
Suggested step-by-step group study of the chapter.

VIII. **ISSUES FOR DISCUSSION**
Zeroing the chapter in on daily life.

"Before you try your way, read our instructions."

D i r e c t i o n s   o n   a   1 6   m m .   m o v i e
p r o j e c t o r ,   w a r n i n g   d o - i t -
y o u r s e l f   p r o j e c t i o n i s t s

Hebrews

 IN A NUTSHELL

Hebrews 2 tells us to listen to Jesus. Listen to Jesus because the penalties for ignoring him are too severe. If we ignore Jesus, we will miss out on his salvation (2:1–4). Listen to Jesus because he has begun a new stage in God's plan by tasting death for everyone, thus shattering the effects of death on those who listen to him (2:5–9).

Listen to Jesus because he is able to help us in temptation. His victorious experience in overcoming temptation allows us to receive help from him as we face temptation (2:10–18).

Why We Should Listen to Jesus

I. INTRODUCTION

Doing It Our Way

I was setting up a movie projector in the days before VCRs. Things weren't going very well. I had tried to force the 16 mm. strip of celluloid onto some sprockets which wouldn't hold it. My film was not ready for projection. My crowd was arriving. Success was not in sight. What could I do?

I had worked with the same projector before. Earlier I had shown a film to our young people. Surely, I reasoned, as I got it out to use it again, I could put the film into place. But my memory of how to do the job left me. Nothing I tried seemed to work. Then I discovered the warning which led me to burst out laughing.

Attached to a handle on the case of the projector was a cotton thread with a warning tag on it. The warning read, "Before you try your way, read about our way." I pulled the instruction book from the projector case. Quickly I found a diagram of the machine and learned how to thread it for projection. Doing it my way hadn't worked. The manufacturer knew better how to operate the machine.

In our religiously pluralistic society, people have many opinions about how to get to God. "Let every person worship his own god," someone will say. "Sincerity is all that matters," someone else advises. "Keep the Ten Commandments," a hard-working traditionalist might say. "God is inside you," we might hear from an advocate of personal potential.

Hebrews 2 gives us instructions which we must hear. These are directions from the Creator and Savior of the world. Reduced to a sentence, it says, "Listen to Jesus."

We will run into trouble if we try to come to God in our own way. If we try our way, we will be ignoring God's great salvation, missing the benefits of Christ's death, and losing the help of a sympathetic encourager. If we follow God's way through Jesus, we receive a great salvation, escape the pangs of eternal death, and experience in our lives the mercy and faithfulness of Jesus.

II. COMMENTARY

Why We Should Listen to Jesus

MAIN IDEA: *We must listen to Jesus because ignoring him leads to severe penalties, submitting to Jesus brings marvelous benefits, and Jesus' own suffering strengthens his ministry to sinners.*

A Because the Penalties for Neglecting Jesus Are Too Severe (vv. 1–4)

SUPPORTING IDEA: *Ignoring Jesus has horrible consequences.*

2:1. This verse introduces us to the plight of the readers. They had heard the gospel. They appeared ready to desert Jesus for some trifling replacement. The writer of Hebrews was horrified at this prospect!

Therefore reminded the people of the importance of the message about Jesus. The readers needed to listen because the truths of the gospel were too important to push aside. Issues of spiritual life and death were at stake. Whatever they did, the readers must hold fast to Jesus.

The idea of **drifting away** compared the audience to a boat sailing past warning signs to meet destruction and ruin on a rocky shore or in a raging rapid. The Hebrews needed to do something. They were listless while their situation demanded positive action. "Pay attention to your plight," said our writer, "lest you carelessly fall into ruin."

2:2. This verse moves from a truth of less importance to one of greater importance (v. 3). The fact of less importance is that violators of the Law received divine judgment for their disobedience. The **message spoken by angels** was the Old Testament Law. Jewish understanding associated the giving of the Law with the work of angels (Gal. 3:19). Our writer's word is that the Old Testament Law, despite its less impressive origin through angels, was still **binding**. God punished every violation of the Law. Violation of a single commandment brought a prescribed penalty. Those who deliberately disregarded God's Law faced death (Num. 15:30).

2:3. If even violators of the Law received punishment, how much more could those who ignored, rejected, and spurned the Lord from heaven expect judgment? Here is the more important issue. God's Son himself brought the gospel into view. Anyone neglecting to respond to its serious appeals could expect to receive God's severest displeasure.

The Lord himself had originally spoken the gospel to the first generation of believers. These are **those who heard him.** The writer of Hebrews received his understanding from that generation. Unlike Paul he had not received a direct revelation of the gospel from the Lord (see Gal. 1:12). Words like these lead many scholars to feel that Paul could not have written Hebrews.

This passage is the first of many warnings throughout Hebrews (3:7–19; 4:11–16; 5:11–6:12; 10:19–39). In each passage the author showed his concern for the readers. Spiritual pressure was about to make them stumble. They might renounce the gospel. They would not escape divine judgment if they rejected **such a great salvation.**

2:4. The proclamation of the gospel was powerful of itself. Along with that proclamation God also sent **signs, wonders, and various miracles** to verify the Christian message. The early church saw many of these signs and wonders (Acts 2:43; 4:30; 5:12; 6:8). Signs which Jesus demonstrated in John's Gospel led the disciples to believe in him (John 2:11). The signs pointed to the glory of Christ.

The awareness of the existence of the miracles must have been widespread. If that were not true, some critic could say, "I've never heard of these signs and wonders." A consideration of them would deepen the readers' faith that the gospel came as an authoritative message from God.

God not only sent miracles and signs with the gospel, but he also gave the Holy Spirit to believers. Peter's Pentecost sermon pointed to the activity of the Spirit as a chief indicator of God's work (Acts 2:14–18). The work of the Spirit showed that God's new plan had dawned. The miracles and the presence of the Spirit demonstrated the superiority of the Christian gospel. Drifting away from that truth would be a foolhardy stunt.

In the early 1990s my wife and I had the privilege of spending a year of sabbatical learning and writing in England. During the year a church graciously loaned us a car to drive while we ministered to them. We were responsible for gasoline and all upkeep. We soon learned that the English fined drivers one thousand dollars if the tread depth of their tires was less than one-quarter of an inch. In America I probably would have driven the tires longer, but in England I readily replaced worn tires whose depth neared that limit. The penalty for disobedience was too severe.

Why should we listen to Jesus? The penalty for ignoring or neglecting him has eternal consequences. After we die, we face the judgment (Heb. 9:27). Unless we have Jesus, we fail the judgment and the consequences are eternal. We must listen to Jesus and his message.

🅑 Because Jesus Is the Central Actor in God's New Plan (vv. 5–9)

> **SUPPORTING IDEA:** *Submitting to Jesus brings marvelous benefits.*

2:5. In this section we will meet the name of Jesus for the first time in Hebrews (v. 9). The readers of Hebrews knew that Jesus was a human being and that he had lived and then endured a disgraceful death. Why should they think that Jesus was superior to any other human being, much less to the angels? Some readers might think that Jesus, the human being, was far inferior to angels in might, position, and power. This verse now shows that Jesus was superior to angels despite his humanity.

Angels have an important role in this age. Some Old Testament verses suggested that God had assigned administrative chores over different countries to angelic powers (Dan. 10:20–21—note the terms **prince of Persia** and **prince of Greece**). Usually scholars interpeting the Old Testament passages in Daniel view these "princes" as evil angels because they oppose God's plans. But verse 5 implies that God had given some governing authority in this present age to angels. But what about the **world to come.** Who was in charge of this?

The term **world to come** (or "age to come") can refer either to the afterlife or to the new order of things which Jesus inaugurated. In this verse it had more reference to a new order of God's plans which Jesus introduced. God has enthroned Jesus at his right hand. Jesus' enthronement has begun a new world order over which he reigns. In Jesus, Christians already taste **the powers of the coming age** (Heb. 6:5). Jesus has already started this new age, but he has not completed it. In time he will bring his people into enjoyment of the final blessings of salvation (Heb. 9:28). Jesus is the central actor in God's new plan. He is far superior to angels. Even now he is God's messenger to us with a message of deliverance. If we listen to him, it can make the difference between eternal misery and eternal blessedness.

2:6–8a. These words represent a quotation of most of Psalm 8:4–6. Two observations will help us understand what the writer of Hebrews was doing. First, he attached great important to Scripture. His reference to Scripture settled the issue for him. Second, the psalmist talked about the insignificance of human beings, but the author of Hebrews pointed out the majesty of the **son of man,** Jesus Christ.

When the psalmist looked at God's majestic creation, human beings appeared puny and insignificant. Despite the lowliness of human beings, God had given them authority over creation. The opening question of verse 6, **What is man?** celebrated the dignity of human beings despite their insignificance.

The term **son of man** referred to the ideal man. Jesus frequently used this title to refer to himself (John 1:51). Since Jesus was the ideal man, this psalm was fulfilled in him. We start out thinking about human beings, but we quickly shift gears and think about Jesus, who is the ideal man. The use of the term **son of man** in reference to Jesus showed that he had true humanity. What happened to him affected and helped all human beings.

Once we see that the term **son of man** in verse 6 referred ultimately to Jesus, we can spot the reference to the incarnation and the exaltation in verse 7. The phrase **a little lower** actually means "lower for a little while." With this translation the opening words of verse 7 were suggesting that Jesus experienced a temporary humiliation in the incarnation. Now the Father has exalted him to his right hand and has given him glory and majesty while subjecting everything to him. What human beings lost because of sin, Jesus has regained by his obedience. We can experience God's fullness for us in Jesus' accomplishments.

2:8b–9. The subjection of all things to Jesus was still in the future, but it was certain to occur. The certainty that Jesus will experience future glory gives hope to us. This assurance leads to the introduction of Jesus by name in verse 9.

We find three statements about Jesus in verse 9. First, Jesus became a human being. He **was made a little lower than the angels.** Second, as a man he experienced suffering and death. The death of Jesus provided a marvelous display of divine grace. God permitted his Son to endure suffering, and the Son willingly offered himself. He tasted **death for everyone.** Third, the outcome of the suffering of Christ was that he was **crowned with glory and honor.**

Because Jesus Can Offer Help to the Tempted (vv. 10–18)

> **SUPPORTING IDEA:** *Jesus' own suffering strengthens his ministry to those who fall into sin.*

2:10. The death of Jesus on the cross was proper or **fitting.** Jews viewed the idea of a suffering Messiah as a horrible concept, but Jesus' death fitted in with the plans of a gracious God. Whatever God does is **fitting,** and Jesus' death is no exception to that principle.

God's goal was to bring **many sons to glory.** God wanted to bring lost, struggling humanity to sonship. He also wanted believers to experience his glory (2 Cor. 4:17). Jesus' death helped to accomplish this goal of sonship and glory.

God's method was to **make the author of their salvation perfect through suffering.** Jesus was the originator, founder, or trailblazer in securing salvation. If Jesus had not broken a new trail, no one else would have succeeded. Jesus' work was essential for God to make an offer of salvation to the world.

In what sense did Jesus become **perfect?** He was already **perfect** in a moral sense. Making Jesus **perfect** refers to qualifying him to become a perfect Savior by his death. By his death God qualified him to serve effectively as the priest of his people. This allowed him to accomplish his work of redemption. Only through the death on the cross could the world gain a perfectly qualified and effective Savior.

By dying on the cross Jesus experienced a perfection which resulted from having suffered. This type of suffering differs from a perfection which comes from being ready to suffer. By passing through the crucible of suffering, Jesus developed a perfection which qualified him fully to be a complete and effective Savior. He also demonstrated a perfect example of obedience to the Father's will. He failed at no point in obeying God. Jesus became **perfect** in that he learned sympathy through his own experience and practiced obedience without reservation.

2:11. Jesus, who makes us **holy**, is a human being just like the readers of Hebrews. The idea of sanctification (being made holy) means that Christ sets us apart for God's purpose. The fact that we are sanctified does not mean that we are without sin. It does mean that God has stamped his reservation on us. We are set aside to do his will.

Christ can sanctify us because of his close connnection with us. Christ is of the human family. He is fully one with us. He identified with us so that he was our brother. He has no shame in acknowledging us as his family. Because Christ is a human being, he can help us to grow in holiness. Three Old Testament quotations support the claim that Jesus is one with us.

2:12–13. Verse 12 comes from Psalm 22:22 which opened with the words Jesus quoted on the cross, **My God, my God, why have you forsaken me?** The first part of the psalm shows the suffering of Jesus on the cross. The second part, beginning in verse 22, shouted a conclusion of triumph.

The speaker was Jesus. He was lifting God's praises to other believers, **my brothers.** The word for "**congregation**" (*ekklesia*) is the term for "church." Jesus has shouted God's praises to fellow Christians, calling them **brothers**, thus showing that he was one with them. He suffered for them and was a part of them.

The second quotation (13a from Isa. 8:17) shows the attitude of Jesus in putting his trust in God the Father, demonstrating that he is like other human beings who must live by faith in the Father. Trusting and obeying represented the only principles for living life for Jesus and for us, his followers.

The final quote in Hebrews 2:13 came from Isaiah 8:18, the verse immediately following the preceding source. In the Old Testament Isaiah recognized that his own children were signs given by God. Hebrews understands Isaiah's words about his children as the words of Christ about his people. Jesus affirmed his closeness with his people by calling them **children**. In John 17:6, Jesus had described his disciples as "those whom you [God] gave me out of the world." Jesus was making a close identification with human beings.

His statement led naturally into a declaration that Jesus **shared in [our] humanity** in the next verse.

2:14. This verse is a theological watershed. It presents two facts about Christ and his death. First, it declares that Jesus shared the same humanity with human beings. Second, it presents the reason for his death.

Chapter 1 declared Jesus' superiority to angels. This verse states his equality with human beings in that he shared their humanity. In the incarnation at Bethlehem, Jesus became what he had not been before. He had always been God. He now also became a human being. We can call him the God-man.

Jesus entered his incarnate life on earth by birth. He departed this life by death. He did not merely appear to be a human being. He genuinely shared our humanity. No one who merely seemed to be human or who resembled human beings could meet our needs. Jesus was a real person. He can meet all of our needs.

Why did Jesus die? He died to **destroy . . . the devil.** Jesus' death was not a defeat. It was a triumph over sin and death. Sin always causes death (Rom. 5:12). Our sin, not his own sin, caused Jesus to die. His death snatched away our sin and guilt.

"Wait a minute," you may say. "Satan is pretty active in me today. How has he been destroyed?" Jesus triumphed over the devil at the cross (Col. 2:15), but we live in an interim period when we don't see the full effects of Jesus' death. Satan is still hanging around as a roaring lion (1 Pet. 5:8). He still has limited power in this age (Eph. 6:11; 1 Tim. 3:7). His future doom is sure (Rev. 20:10).

You might also ask, "How did Satan hold the power of death?" This statement raises a problem because Scripture asserts that God alone has charge of the issues of life and death (Luke 12:5). Satan took the lead in introducing sin into the world by his successful temptation of Adam (Rom. 5:12). Satan has "the power of death" because he introduced sin which causes death. Death is the fruit of sin (Rom. 5:21). The death and resurrection of Christ have rendered powerless the one who was formerly the master of death.

2:15. Jesus has destroyed our archenemy, but he has also liberated us from our chief fear. Death still occurs. We need no longer be afraid of it. Like Satan, death has a limited sovereignty. Its presence will conclude at the return of Christ with the resurrection of believers (1 Cor. 15:54). This hope sets us free from the nagging fear of death which can enslave us. Death cannot separate God's people from the love of God (Rom. 8:35–39). Satan no longer can use the fear of death to intimidate us or frighten us.

Notice that Christ has not yet abolished death. He has defeated the devil who had the power of death (Col. 2:15). We still face natural death. The removal of sin by the death of Jesus withdraws the sting of sin (1 Cor. 15:55–57). One day

Jesus will completely destroy death (1 Cor. 15:54). For Christians the fear of death is already gone.

Although this verse does not precisely mention the resurrection, we realize that the original readers would have understood the importance of the resurrection. Whenever we describe Jesus' death as a victory (Heb. 2:14), we point to his resurrection. Jesus' resurrection is the cornerstone of the victory over the fear of death which we have as believers.

2:16. This verse tells two facts about Christ's incarnation. First, Christ did not assume the nature of angels. He did not take angelic nature on himself. Probably some of the readers of Hebrews felt that an angelic deliverer would come to rescue them. Hebrews declares firmly that Jesus was not merely an angelic deliverer.

Second, Christ did assume human nature. The original language literally read that "he took on himself the seed of Abraham." As a human being, Christ descended from Abraham. He also showed by his obedience that he was a spiritual descendant of Abraham. All believers are spiritual descendants of Abraham (Gal. 3:29).

Christ became a human being to give help to us as sinners. When the Son of God humbled himself in his incarnation, he stooped lower than the position of an angel to become a human being. When he became a human being, he was able to provide for the salvation of human beings.

2:17. This verse restates the truth of verse 14 that Jesus had a complete, perfect humanity. We read two reasons for the incarnation of Christ. First, the incarnation allowed Christ **to become a merciful and faithful high priest in service to God.** Jesus' own suffering allowed him to be sympathetic to others and thus to show mercy. He demonstrated his faithfulness by remaining steadfast to the end without flinching. Jesus was completely trustworthy in everything God called him to do.

A second reason for the incarnation was that Jesus **might make atonement for the sins of the people.** Jesus' death handled the personal sins of all human beings. Jesus did in reality what the Old Testament sacrificial ritual could only do in symbols. It was not that Jesus' death satisfied the angry demands of a peevish God. The truth is that God himself provided the payment for our sins because of his ever-abiding love (Rom. 5:8).

2:18. This verse insists on the real humanity of Jesus. It also contains an important application of that real humanity. Because Jesus was a true human being and because he suffered, he can help us in our temptation.

This verse introduces several important questions. How could the sinless Jesus receive temptation? Was he tempted in the same way as human beings? These questions will be discussed further in 4:15.

Three important thoughts confront us here. First, Jesus suffered. He suffered as our Savior physically, emotionally, and spiritually. Second, this suffering became a source of temptation. The sufferings were so intense that Jesus could have decided that enduring them was not worth the pain which they inflicted. He never considered that, for he said, "Not as I will, but as you will" (Matt. 26:39). Third, enduring suffering allowed him to help us. His victory over temptation and sin allowed him to guide us through the dangerous rocks of temptation.

Jesus has great ability to help us. His ability is not based on his experience with sin. His ability is based on his experience of the temptation to sin. Only someone who is sinless can know this experience fully.

When my son was a child, I often took him swimming. He delighted in playing the game of holding his breath under water. We competed with one another to see who could outlast the other. His youth led to his defeat. At the first sign of pain and discomfort under water, he would surface for air. I stayed under until my lungs were heaving with pain. When I surfaced for air, I truly needed it. Jesus remained in the pool of temptation longer than any of us. He knew the pain more fully. He resisted to the end. He never sinned. His experience allows him to encourage us and lead us to victory as we face temptation.

MAIN IDEA REVIEW: *We must listen to Jesus because ignoring him leads to severe penalties, submitting to Jesus brings marvelous benefits, and his own suffering strengthens his ministry to sinners.*

III. CONCLUSION

Our Great Salvation

Why should we listen to the message about Jesus? We listen to Jesus because ignoring him causes serious consequences (vv. 1–4). When we neglect Jesus, we fall heir to severe penalties.

We listen to Jesus because obeying him leads to marvelous benefits (vv. 5–9). In God's plan, Jesus tasted death for everyone. Those who obey Jesus receive the joy of having their sins taken away.

We listen to Jesus because his own experience of suffering prepared him to strengthen us as we face temptation (vv. 10–18). Because Jesus has faced and overcome temptation, we can receive help from him as we face our own temptation.

When we listen obediently to Jesus, we receive a **great salvation.** This salvation has the power to produce holiness and godliness instead of evil and self-centeredness. Commentator William Barclay in *The Letter to the Hebrews* has said, "The proof of real Christianity is still the fact that it can change the lives of men. The moral miracles of Christianity are still plain for all to see."

When we listen to Jesus in continuous faith, we can receive from him salvation and an experience of holy living. We must not consider any other alternative.

PRINCIPLES

- God has performed miracles to show the greatness of his salvation.
- We face fearful judgment if we ignore Jesus' salvation.
- In Jesus' death he endured death for everyone.
- Jesus' own experience of temptation equipped him to help the tempted.

APPLICATIONS

- Pay careful attention to all that Jesus taught about how to come to God.
- Praise Jesus because he is Lord over all of God's creation.
- Live without fear of the future.
- Be grateful that Jesus' mercy allows him to encourage and help you.
- Be strong in Christ's power whenever you face temptation.

IV. LIFE APPLICATION

Jesus Is a Wonderful Savior

As a youth Tariri learned how to stalk and murder men on the trail. He then shrunk their heads to keep as trophies. He was a headhunter possessed by a spirit of Satan. He believed that the spirit of a jaguar could give him long life.

Then after Wycliffe Bible translators brought God's Word to his people, Tariri became the first among them to believe in Jesus. For Chief Tariri of the Shapra/Candoshi people in Peru, Jesus became a wonderful Savior. After his conversion he showed his people how to live in peace with one another and with their neighbors. His witness has been such that nearly half of his people have become believers. All of his children and many of his grandchildren and great-grandchildren serve Jesus.

In a trip to America in 1965 he promoted Bible translation at the New York World's Fair. He was a guest on the television program, "This Is Your Life." Tariri spent his final days warning others about the brevity of life on earth compared to eternity. His weakness confined him to a hammock; but lying in the hammock, he composed songs about the Lord he would soon meet. When he died at the age of eighty in August 1994, a news release bore the title "Chief Tariri Promoted." God promoted him from life on earth to fellowship in his presence in heaven.

Tariri's life change provides vivid proof that Jesus is a life-transforming Savior. Jesus' salvation has pardoned murderous tempers and wicked practices. His salvation has provided freedom for people who have lived as slaves. His encouraging help has furnished strength to resist compromise and willpower to demonstrate stamina. To people grieved by their own failure and disobedience, he has offered mercy and acceptance. Since Jesus is himself a human being, we can come to him with the confidence that he will understand us and provide realistic support. The transformation of the lives of such biblical personalities as Jacob, Moses, David, Paul, Peter, and John promises hope and victory to us.

V. PRAYER

Have you responded to Jesus as Savior and Lord? If not, you will find no time like the present to turn to him. You can become one of his children by praying sincerely the sinner's prayer: *Lord Jesus, I know that I am a sinner. I know that you have paid for my sin. I ask your forgiveness. I trust your death as the payment for my sin. Amen.*

Have you experienced Jesus' help and encouragement as you face trials and temptations? His own knowledge of hardship, suffering, and trial equips him to be a superior guide and source of strength moment by moment. You can receive his help by sincerely praying: *Jesus, my will is too weak to last long. I need your strength, help, and grace as I face this temptation. Give me wisdom to make the right choices. Give me the moral power to follow you completely. Keep me from destroying myself in compromise and disobedience. Amen.*

VI. DEEPER DISCOVERIES

A. Signs, Wonders, and Miracles (v. 4)

The New Testament often uses these three words to describe the supernatural actions of God in history (Acts 2:22; 6:8; Rom. 15:19; 2 Cor. 12:12; 2 Thess. 2:9; Heb. 2:4). Sometimes the phrase "signs and wonders" is used (Acts 2:43; 4:30; 6:8). Sometimes the two terms "signs and miracles" appear together (Acts 8:13). All three words describe God's powerful intervention in history, each with a slightly different emphasis.

"Sign" (*semeion*) refers to evidence of divine authority. John used this term as a general reference to all miraculous activity. In John the "signs" of Jesus pointed out something about God such as his glory (John 2:11), his authority (John 2:18), or his divine origin (John 3:2). The primary appeal of the sign was to the understanding.

"Wonder(s)" (*teras*) describes an unusual event which causes the viewer to marvel or admire. The wonder appeals chiefly to a person's imagination and arrests his attention. Wonders cause the viewers to be filled with awe (Acts 2:43) and to recognize clearly the powerful presence of God (Acts 4:30). The New Testament normally uses the term to refer to divine activity, but occasionally it is used to describe the work of Satan through human beings (Mark 13:22; 2 Thess. 2:9).

"Miracle" (*dunamis*) points to clear evidence of supernatural activity. The miracle spotlights the power or might of God. Mark uses the term to describe the actions of Jesus (Mark 6:2). Paul used the term to refer to supernatural actions which took place among the Galatians (Gal. 3:5).

Modern thinkers often force the supernatural element out of history. They assert that unchangeable natural laws govern the world and do not allow for the occurrence of miracles. Biblical writers felt that God created, sustained, and governed the universe. Christians from every century have continued to affirm the miraculous power of God in creating, caring for, and revealing himself in history.

B. The World to Come (v. 5)

The term **world to come** (or "age to come") refers to the new arrangement or plan which God began by enthroning Jesus at his right hand. It has both a present and a future aspect.

In the present Jesus has come to begin the age of fulfillment. In his life, death, and resurrection he has done everything needed to redeem us. The **signs, wonders and various miracles** (2:4) provide evidence that Jesus has started the age of fulfillment. God has given us the Holy Spirit as "a deposit guaranteeing our inheritance" (Eph. 1:14). We can live the life of heaven, even though we dwell on earth (Eph. 2:6).

Although Jesus has begun the new age, he has not brought it to completion. That event will occur in the future. We are still **looking for the city that is to come** (Heb. 13:14). Jesus will bring in the end and hand "over the kingdom to God the Father after he has destroyed all dominion, authority and power" (1 Cor. 15:24).

In the future Christ will return to bring the final blessings of his salvation to his people (Titus 2:12–13). For the present time we can experience the powers of this coming age in our relationship to our living Lord. If we listen to Jesus now, we can enjoy these benefits.

C. Son of Man (v. 6)

The words **man** and **son of man** (2:6) appear in a quotation from Psalm 8:4. The parallel terms referred to human beings. Hebrews marvels that God cared for mere human beings despite our insignificance and applies a psalm originally referring to human beings in general to emphasize that Jesus was a genuine human being.

Jesus applied the term **son of man** to himself eighty-four times in the Gospels, giving it a deeper meaning. Sometimes he used it to refer to the end times when he would come to earth to judge the unrighteous and rescue believers (Matt. 13:41). He also used it to describe his coming suffering, death, and resurrection (Mark 8:31) and to describe his ministry on earth (Luke 19:10). Jesus' usage in the Gospels showed a dependence on the Old Testament usage in Daniel 7:13, which Jews took as a reference to the Messiah.

I wear on my left hand a wedding band given me by my wife when we married. I can describe it physically as a white gold band weighing about an ounce and valued at about one hundred dollars. That description, however, does not accurately portray its meaning to me. The band represents my beloved wife's pledge of her love to me for a lifetime and is far more valuable than money can express.

In the same way, Jesus' special use of "son of man" makes us expect the term to mean more than appears on the surface. The words in Hebrews 2:6–8a find their deepest meaning in Jesus Christ, the God-man, who showed by his actions what God had in mind for human beings. The mere mention of the term **son of man** would lead the readers to reflect on images of Jesus as a true human being who suffered for sins and would return in glory to complete God's plan. His suffering had given him glory and honor. His return will complete our salvation.

D. Author of Their Salvation (v. 10)

Both the NIV and NASB translators of Hebrews 2:10 referred to Jesus as the **author of their salvation**. The word **author** appears three others times in the New Testament in reference to Jesus. In Hebrews 12:2 the NIV translates the term as **the author . . . of our faith.** In Acts 3:15 the NIV translators used the phrase "author of life," and in Acts 5:31 they use the term "Prince" to translate the word. Its two basic meanings involve either "Prince" or "originator."

Hebrews 2:10 presents Jesus as a pathfinder or pioneer of our salvation. It referred to someone who took action and then helped those for whom he acted to reach the intended goal. As a pioneer he has preceded us, cleared out a path leading to salvation, and is now leading believers along that path. We see Jesus in the role of an original settler in a wilderness who cleared out the land for additional inhabitants, invited others to join him, and assured that they would reach the destination.

E. Flesh and Blood (v. 14)

Flesh and blood in reference to human beings represents a figure of speech known as synecdoche. When Micah 4:3 said, "They will beat their swords into plowshares and their spears into pruning hooks," the prophet was using the surrender of two weapons to symbolize total disarmament. When the writer of Hebrews spoke of **flesh and blood,** he used these two terms to symbolize full humanity. Since Jesus shared the **flesh and blood** of all human beings, he was genuinely a man.

In the incarnation Jesus himself became truly man. Perhaps the writer of Hebrews was writing against an early heresy which came to be known as Docetism. This false teaching emphasized the deity of Christ but denied his humanity, teaching that Jesus only appeared to be a human being.

Jesus was a true human being. Because Jesus faced temptation as a real human being, he is able to give help to us as we face trials, hardships, and difficulties.

F. Devil (v. 14)

Devil and "Satan" are the two chief terms used to describe the supernatural enemy of God and his people. "Satan" means adversary. **Devil** means slanderer and describes someone who uses deception to mislead God's people. An example of the devil's deception appears in Genesis 3:5, where the serpent lied to Eve in suggesting that if she ate the fruit of the forbidden tree, she would be "like God, knowing good and evil."

The ministry, crucifixion, and triumph of Jesus (Luke 10:18; Col. 2:15) have combined to **destroy . . . the devil.** In principle Christ's work has defeated Satan, but he is not yet completely destroyed. In this age he continues to have real but limited power. The Bible describes the devil as "a roaring lion looking for someone to devour" (1 Pet. 5:8). Scripture promises us that if we "resist the devil . . . he will flee from" us (Jas. 4:7).

G. High Priest (v. 17)

The office of high priest was a hereditary office based on descent from Aaron. Usually the high priest served for life, but political reasons sometimes led to the removal of a high priest (1 Kgs. 2:27). Ideally, the high priest was someone fully committed to the Lord, ritually pure, and always ready to do the Lord's will.

Hebrews uses "high priest" seventeen times, and most of the references applied to Jesus. Its primary emphasis spoke of Jesus' sacrificial death (Heb. 7:26–28). The author of Hebrews pointed out that the role of the high priest was **to deal gently with those who are ignorant and are going astray** (Heb. 5:2). He also was appointed by God to the office (Heb. 5:4). As high priest, Christ encourages believers to remain firm (Heb. 4:14–16). He makes the **good things** of God relevant to believers today (Heb. 9:11). Other features about the high priesthood of Christ will appear as we study additional passages of Hebrews.

H. Atonement (v. 17)

The words **make atonement for the sins of the people** describe the work of Christ as our high priest. New Testament scholars debate the meaning of the term for **make atonement**.

One group suggests that the term means that God wipes away our sin, and they use the term *expiation* to describe this action. It is certainly true that the death of Christ wipes away our sin, but the terms **make atonement** in this verse speak of a feature of God's character which we must emphasize. The emphasis involves much more than the fact that God will wipe away our sins.

The Bible mentions holiness (Isa. 6:3) and love (Rom. 5:8) as important elements in God's character. God's holiness led him to show wrath against sin (Heb. 12:29). God's wrath was not his loss of temper, but his constant attitude of opposition to sin.

God's love is as constant as his wrath. God showed his love in that he took the initiative to send Christ as the atonement for our sins (1 John 4:10). The death of Christ makes it possible for sinners to be reconciled to a holy God (2 Cor. 5:18–21). The result is that God's love and holiness are satisfied in the death of Jesus.

The atonement of Christ is that action by which Jesus makes it possible for sinners to have fellowship with God. As our substitute, he received the suffering and death which each sinner deserves. The result of this loving offering is that we have the possibility of enjoying fellowship with the God who created us.

VII. TEACHING OUTLINE

A. INTRODUCTION

1. Lead Story: Doing It Our Way
2. Context: In chapter 1, Hebrews emphasized the superiority of Jesus to both the Old Testament prophets and to angels. God had spoken in bits and pieces through the prophets, but he has spoken with full clarity through Jesus. God had created angels to care for the needs of believers, but Jesus is God's Son, worthy of worship and ruling over God's creation.

As the writer began chapter 2, he still affirmed the superiority and finality of Jesus. He was pointing out that we needed to listen to the message of Jesus because of his important role in God's plan. Why should we listen to Jesus?

First, we should listen to Jesus because the penalties for ignoring him are too severe (2:1–4). Jesus' followers had preached the great salvation which he had made available. God had verified their message with **signs, wonders, and various miracles** (Heb. 2:4). The listeners could expect only divine judgment if they drifted carelessly past the gospel message without responding to it.

Second, we should listen to Jesus because he has begun a new phase of God's plan by tasting death for everyone (2:5–9). Jesus became a man and completely followed the will of God. God's will included Jesus' dying for the sins of the world (2:9). Jesus willingly followed God's plan, and God has crowned him **with glory and honor** (2:7) and has put all creation under him. Jesus will experience exaltation more fully in the future. In the present we see the glory of his death, burial, and resurrection. We can experience God's plan when we follow Jesus.

Third, we should listen to Jesus because he is able to help us in temptation (2:10–18). Jesus has the same traits of humanity which we have. In his death he has broken Satan's power (2:14). The fact that he is a human being allows him to provide mercy and encouragement for wandering believers. Who other than Jesus is qualified to help us when we face temptation? His experience and his shared humanity give him superb qualifications.

3. Transition: As we reflect on this chapter, we will grow in our understanding that Jesus is a wonderful Savior. We will develop a skill for listening to the commands of Jesus as we come to understand better his importance in God's plan. We will focus our lives on him more fully because of what he has done, who he is, and what he can do to strengthen and encourage us. Before we push ahead living life in our own way, we will learn his way and bring ourselves in line with that plan. As the tag on the projector warned me, "Before you try your way, read about our way." In Hebrews 2 we learn to listen to Jesus because he is God's way.

B. COMMENTARY

1. Because the Penalties for Neglecting Jesus Are Too Severe (vv. 1–4)
    a. The danger of drifting away (v. 1)
    b. The certainty of punishment (v. 2)
    c. The greatness of salvation in Jesus (vv. 3–4)

   (1) Announced by the Lord (v. 3a)
   (2) Confirmed by his hearers (v. 3b)
   (3) Proven by signs, wonders, and miracles (v. 4)
  2. Because Jesus Is the Central Actor in God's New Plan (vv. 5–9)
   a. In charge of the world to come (vv. 5–8a)
   b. Carrying out God's program (vv. 8b–9)
  3. Because Jesus Can Offer Help to the Tempted (vv. 10–18)
   a. Perfected by suffering (v. 10)
   b. Enjoying a family relationship with believers (vv. 11–13)
   c. Defeating the works of Satan (v. 14)
   d. Freeing those held in slavery (v. 15)
   e. Giving help to tempted believers (v. 16–18)

C. CONCLUSION: JESUS IS A WONDERFUL SAVIOR

VIII. ISSUES FOR DISCUSSION

1. What would happen to you if you turned your back on Jesus and ignored all that he has done to save you?
2. How can you claim that everything is subject to Jesus?
3. In what way was Jesus made perfect?
4. What power does the devil now have? How long will this last? Why?
5. How does Jesus help you when you are tempted?

Hebrews 3

First Things First

"*The* man-made excitements in which we persist in immersing ourselves . . . are reduced to the insignificance they deserve whenever nature decides to show us who is really in charge around here."

E d i t o r i a l i n *F t . W o r t h*

S t a r - T e l e g r a m a f t e r t h e 1 9 8 9

C a l i f o r n i a e a r t h q u a k e

Hebrews

I N A N U T S H E L L

How do we organize our lives to put first things first? How do we show that we know who is in charge of our lives and the events of history? We give top attention to Jesus. We fit everything else under that priority.

*In this chapter we see that Jesus is superior to Moses because Jesus served as a **son over God's house** while Moses was **a servant in . . . God's house** (Heb. 3:1–6). A son with authority is more significant than a servant without authority. Thus, rejecting Jesus is more serious than rejecting Moses (3:7–19). The generation of Israelites who wandered in the wilderness had rejected God's commands and paid a stiff price (Num. 14:20–38). Don't repeat their mistake.*

First Things First

I. INTRODUCTION

Setting Your Priorities

In the 1924 Olympics Eric Liddell of Scotland refused to run in Olympic trials when the trial came on Sunday. This committed Christian—the favorite in the race—thus sacrificed his opportunity to win a medal. He did participate in other events when trials were not on Sunday and eventually won the gold medal. Returning home to Britain, he found himself a national hero, admired for winning the medal and for maintaining his convictions.

Less than a year later, Liddell went to China as a missionary. He taught science at a college in Tientsin for some years. Then he committed himself to the more demanding task of rural evangelism, traveling many miles in rugged conditions on foot or by bicycle.

When the Japanese invaded China during World War II, they captured Liddell and sent him to a prison camp in August 1943. One of 1,800 prisoners packed into a tiny facility, he met the physical and spiritual needs of the camp. He organized athletic meets, taught hymns, and led Bible studies. On February 21, 1945, just a month before liberation, Liddell died of a brain tumor.

You can see that Liddell consistently organized his life around his commitment to serve Christ. He could have remained in Britain and enjoyed acclaim as a national hero. He could have enjoyed the relatively peaceful task of teaching in a Chinese college. He could have left China before Japan invaded. Each time he followed the priority he had set as a young man. He chose to follow the will of God.

The author of Hebrews penned this chapter to warn professing believers who did not have their priorities straight. Having made a commitment to Christ, they were considering returning to the empty rituals of Judaism. They thought highly of Moses as the founding figure of Judaism. But Jesus was superior to Moses.

Verses 1–6 compare and contrast Jesus and Moses. Both had been faithful to God's plan for them (3:1–2). Moses was presented as God's servant working in God's house for God's people (3:5). Jesus had fulfilled a higher calling. As God's Son, he stood over the house. Jesus was superior even to Moses, the giver of the Law.

A second warning is issued in verses 7–19. Rejecting Jesus was more serious than rejecting Moses. Psalm 95:7b–11 is quoted to show the stubbornness of the generation who died in the wilderness because of their unbelief (Num. 14:20–38). Hebrews seeks to prevent us from following the example of this faithless generation. We should endure in our commitment and share in Christ's blessings (3:14).

In short, we should get our priorities straight and produce obedience instead of disobedience. No matter how pressing our life demands, we must obey the commands and plans of Jesus. If we don't, we will stumble into ruin and unbelief just like the wilderness generation.

The quote at the beginning of this chapter warned us that we quickly focus on the wrong objects in life. Sometimes sudden shocks in life help us regain our focus. Earthquakes, job losses, sickness, and personal difficulty can help us to reassess our priorities and **come to share in Christ** (3:14). The original readers of Hebrews probably focused wrongly on the importance of Moses. We can also lose our way by focusing on some personal goal, aim, or plan which can take us away from God's best for us. Perhaps the words of this chapter of Hebrews can lead us to "put first things first."

II. COMMENTARY

First Things First

MAIN IDEA: *Jesus' sonship shows his superiority to Moses and reminds us that rejecting him has more serious consequences than rejecting Moses.*

A Comparison Between Jesus and Moses (vv. 1–6)

SUPPORTING IDEA: *Jesus is superior to Moses because he is God's Son serving over God's house.*

1. Faithful to the Divine Plan (vv. 1–2)

3:1. The opening words link this chapter with the preceding chapter. The **Therefore** tells us that not only is Christ superior to prophets and angels, but he is also superior to Moses.

The author of Hebrews used two designations of New Testament Christians. First, they are called "**holy brothers.**" This reminded them that God had set them apart to live in separation from sin. Second, he called them sharers **in the heavenly calling.** God had given them the task of helping to complete his spiritual purposes. They carried out their jobs on earth, but they lived as citizens of a heavenly kingdom.

The command to **fix your thoughts on Jesus** called them to reflect firmly on the true significance of Jesus in God's plan. They would then understand clearly that he was an **apostle and high priest. Apostle** presented Jesus as God's representative to human beings. **High priest** presented him as our representative before God. Jesus was God's perfect revelation to us. He also represented the perfect picture of our response to God.

3:2. A faithful representative does his job. Both Jesus and Moses were faithful (Num. 12:7; Heb. 2:17). For Moses, **God's house** was the people of Israel. Moses fully carried out all God's appointed duties with the chosen people. Jesus affirmed his own obedience in the task of representing God to human beings (John 17:4).

2. The Builder of God's House (vv. 3–4)

SUPPORTING IDEA: *Jesus received greater honor than Moses.*

3:3. The first two verses show a similarity between Jesus and Moses. This verse presents a contrast between them: God had chosen to give greater honor to Jesus than to Moses. Why?

Because **the builder of a house has greater honor than the house itself.** The **house** described the people of God, either the church for the New Testament or the people of Israel for the Old Testament. Christ was the builder of the house. Moses had an important role in God's plan, but he was only a part of the house. Moses was a person through whom God spoke, but Christ was the founder and heir of the household.

Jews and Christians alike recognize the greatness of Moses the lawgiver. How much more should they honor Jesus!

3:4. This verse backs up the claim of verse 3. Verse 3 describes Jesus as **the builder of a house.** Verse 4 introduces God as **the builder of everything.** Both the Father and the Son were involved in building the house. The Father clearly established his own house, but he worked through the Son to get the job done.

Hebrews deals with people who gave excessive respect to Moses for his role in giving the Law. No matter how important Moses was, God was still the lawgiver. God was the **builder of everything** in that he had established a new spiritual community with Christ as the head. (This affirmation does not deny the importance of those who worked with him in building.) The word **everything** may also refer to God's material creation as well as to the church.

God's role is exalted to show the greatness of the glory of Jesus. This God of such might and power appointed Jesus to the important office of apostle and high priest.

3. Because He Is a Son over God's House (vv. 5–6)

SUPPORTING IDEA: *Christ was faithful in his work with God's people.*

3:5. Here we find another argument to show the superior position of Christ over Moses: a son and a servant.

Moses was a servant. The word (*therapon*) for **servant** does not appear elsewhere in the New Testament. It pictures a person who willingly did the service expected of him. The term shows a certain tenderness in the service rendered without focusing on the low position of the servant.

Moses' field of service was **in all God's house.** He worked among God's people, Israel. His task was to testify of what was to follow. He pointed toward things which Christ would declare more clearly. Through Christ, God would give a clearer revelation than Moses had given.

Some Jewish Christians saw Jesus as a second Moses. The next verse proves that Jesus was greater than a second Moses.

3:6. Two features make Jesus superior to Moses. First, he was a Son, a position certainly worthy of more glory than that of a servant. Sonship carried a larger responsibility. Second, Jesus stood **over God's house.** Moses was **in all God's house,** but Jesus stood in authority over it. One who stood **over** something was superior to one who stood **in** it.

An **if** sentence warns readers. They needed to resist temptation and remain faithful to Jesus. Now the writer added: You are God's **house** only if you endure in your commitment. You cannot return to Moses and ignore Jesus. You need to hold fast to the confidence and hope with which you started. We prove the genuineness of our profession of faith by our endurance in Christian commitment.

Asbel Petrey served as a pioneer preacher in the Cumberland Mountains of eastern Kentucky in the early 1900s. One day an author, interested in writing about Petrey's spiritual adventures, visited him for an interview. He asked during the visit, "What is the greatest single thing that has happened to you during your long ministry in the Cumberlands?"

Petrey pointed to a white church clearly visible on a nearby hill. He said: "Two Sundays ago, I was guest of honor at services held at that church. As we entered the building, the ushers gave each person a red rose. When the services were almost over, the pastor asked me to stand. Then he said to the members of the congregation: 'If Brother Petrey was the one responsible for your finding Christ as your Saviour, come up and pin a rose on him.'"

Petrey said: "They started coming from every part of the room. They pinned roses all over my coat, down my pants legs, all over my back. I felt like a blooming idiot. But I would not trade those roses for all the hardwood in those hills nor all the coal beneath the surface of the land and all the gold in Fort Knox!"

Most Christians have never heard of Asbel Petrey. Thousands just like him have remained faithful to Jesus and his call during their lifetime. They have focused on the command of the Great Commission to make disciples (Matt. 28:19–20). We should follow their example.

B The Failure of God's People under Moses (vv. 7–19)

SUPPORTING IDEA: *Rejecting Jesus in unbelief is more serious than rejecting Moses, so God's people need encouragement to overcome sin and endure in their commitment to Christ.*

1. Hardened to God's Voice (vv. 7–11)

3:7. Verses 7–11 quote Psalm 95:7b–11 to compare the experience of Israel with that of the church. These believers faced a serious danger, and they needed to avoid repeating Israel's failures and experiencing Israel's fate.

Psalm 95 begins with praise (vv. 1–7a) and concludes with a warning (vv. 7b–11), based on the story recorded in Exodus 17:1–7. The judgment mentioned occurred in Numbers 14:20–38. The writer of Hebrews followed the psalmist in urging his readers not to imitate the folly of the generation of Jews who died in the wilderness under God's judgment.

Two words in verse 7 catch our attention. First, though a human author penned the words, the writer of Hebrews knew that the **Holy Spirit** was speaking. He recognized these words as a strong warning based on divine authority. Second, he used the psalmist's reference to **Today** to apply the words to his readers. He went back into the Old Testament history, but his mind was on his readers. He wanted them to hear the present voice of God in the ancient message.

3:8–9. Hardening the heart takes place whenever someone rejects God's call or instructions. Hardening is an action which we develop in ourselves by our own choice to disobey God. A constant response of resistance leads to a habit of disobedience and to a judicial sentence from God. The wilderness generation hardened their own hearts, and it was possible that the readers of Hebrews might do the same thing.

The term **rebellion** in Hebrews 3:8 is translated as **Meribah** in Psalm 95:8. The term **testing** in Hebrews 3:8 is translated as **Massah** in Psalm 95:8. The terms describe the attitudes of the Jewish people mentioned in Exodus 17:1–7 and above all in Numbers 14:20–38. Throughout the entire period from Exodus 17 to Numbers 14, the Jewish people had rebelled against the Lord. For forty years they resisted God's demands. They had hardened their hearts.

God was slow to anger, but forty years was too much even for him. Their rebellion developed into a settled habit of mind and led God to pronounce judgment. Hebrews warns against a repetition of rebellion against God.

The reference to **forty years** would have special significance if forty years had passed since the ministry of Jesus. Many scholars believe that the author penned Hebrews just before A.D. 70. God could have been warning the Christian readers that just as he had dealt with Israel for a probationary period of forty years, so now they, too, had arrived at the end of the same period of probation. They had a special reason to avoid the deceitfulness of sin (3:13).

3:10–11. Does God really become **angry?** We can answer "yes" to that question, but God's anger does not resemble human anger. We become angry when a sales clerk takes too long or when a slow car forces us to wait at a red light. God's anger always has a just cause, and it does not show a peevish nature in God but a consistent opposition to sin.

We often use human analogies to understand God. Whenever we attribute a human emotion such as anger to God, we produce many questions in understanding what happened. However, unless we express God in such human terms, we will find it hard to understand him. God does become angry, but he tempers his anger with justice and love.

Two actions of the Jews in the wilderness contributed to divine anger. First, the Jews habitually strayed from God. Second, they did not know God's ways. One sin reinforced the other.

This persistent practice of sin led God to deliver his verdict with an oath. The reference to an oath seems to reflect Numbers 14:21, where God supported his word with an oath. God used this oath when the spies returned to bring an unfavorable report of the prospects for entering the Promised Land. The people of Israel rebelled against trusting God and accused Moses of bringing them to the wilderness to die. God swore that such rebels would never experience his rest.

We will discuss **rest** more in chapter 4. For the present we can realize that all rebels place themselves outside of God's protection. These cantankerous people had to move ahead on their own resources. Dreadful failure lay ahead. Later the Jews would clearly learn that **it is a dreadful thing to fall into the hands of the living God** (Heb. 10:31).

All of us can learn from observing what has happened in the past. We can apply past experiences to the present. When we find hints of the past recurring in the present, we call that pattern typology. In this instance a typological interpretation of the Exodus is used to warn the readers of Hebrews not to imitate the actions of the wilderness generation. The present generation could also fall into the same pattern of unbelief. The warning message of the writer of Hebrews was quite clear. Readers could see what happened to those who fell in the wilderness. They could realize that they faced the same dangers. They must turn from their foolish disobedience before it was too late!

2. Deceived by Sin (vv. 12–13)

3:12–13. These verses begin a section of Hebrews which poses a troublesome issue in interpretation: Is the author discussing salvation or sanctification? Stated another way: Are the readers Christians or non–Christians?

If they were Christians, then they were being warned not to take steps to cause the loss of their rewards. If they were unsaved, they were being warned not to ignore God's warning so they would not be lost eternally.

Those who favor viewing the readers as Christians feel that the use of the term **brother** (3:12) or **holy brothers** (3:1) indicates that the readers were believers. These interpreters feel that the biblical text contains no hint that the writer felt that his audience contained anyone who was not a true Christian.

Some of those who favor viewing the readers as non-Christians feel that the term **brother(s)** refers to those who were racial brothers. These were unbelieving Jews of the same ethnic background as the writer and thus capable of being called **brothers**. In this view, the writer of Hebrews was warning the readers not to turn away from the gospel and thus become apostate.

Advocates for both of these positions can find support for their views in the biblical passage. This writer believes that the readers are being seen as non-Christians, but he does not follow all the interpretations of those who advocate this view. I find it hard to understand the term **brothers** as a statement that the readers were unbelieving Jews. I believe the writer used the term **brothers** to speak to his readers as professing believers and imply that they must demonstrate the reality of their faith by refusing to turn **away from the living God**. The readers were claiming to be Christians, and the writer wrote to them in that way. However, he could not know their inward condition. They needed to show the reality of their faith by enduring in their commitment and refusing to **be hardened by sin's deceitfulness**.

Paul used the term **brothers** to describe the Galatians in much the same way as the writer of Hebrews used it here. Paul addressed the Galatians as professing Christians despite the fact that some of them were holding on to doctrine which did not grasp the principles of grace (Gal. 3:15; 4:12; 5:13). His use of the term did not guarantee that all the readers were true believers. He warned them against turning away from the gospel they had professed.

Similarly, by using the term **brothers** the author of Hebrews did not guarantee that any or all of his readers were true believers. Each of them had to show his or her conversion by refusing to deny the faith they had professed. The writer issued such strong warnings because he observed that his readers were carelessly considering deserting Christ. If they actually turned from him, they would show that they were never Christians. The writer of Hebrews did not want them to be deceived by their own actions.

Two potential problems were then pinpointed among the readers. First, some were in danger of harboring **a sinful, unbelieving heart**. Second, they were in danger of turning **away from the living God**.

The main problem of these people was unbelief. They failed to take seriously God's commands and promises. This unbelief could lead to apostasy.

The God of Israel, the God of the Old Testament, the Father of Jesus Christ was a living God. Christians living in the pagan world found themselves thrown with people who worshiped idols, not the true God. He is alive. He stays in constant communication with his people through Scripture and the Holy Spirit.

Most scholars feel that the readers of Hebrews were considering turning from Christianity to Judaism. Those who practice the Jewish religion may worship the one true God, but they do not respond to Christ. All of God's fullness lives in Christ (Col. 1:19). For someone to turn from the full truth of God in Christ back to Judaism was open compromise. To turn from Christianity involved rejecting Christ. To reject Christ involved rejecting God. Even though Judaism has elements of spiritual truth, it was not God's final revelation. Only those who respond to God in Jesus have reached the final understanding of God's revelation. For the readers of Hebrews to turn back to Judaism after having professed Christ was a sin against the truth. It was outright rebellion. Such rebellion would show that they had never made a true commitment to Christ!

The words in verse 13 transferred the warning from the era of the wilderness wanderers to the **Today** of the readers. The psalm is relevant because of two features.

First, these believers were urged to provide mutual encouragement. They were to encourage one another. If the readers of Hebrews tried to live in isolation, subtle temptations would overwhelm them. If they came together for common worship, they could keep their hope and commitment burning brightly like charcoal embers warming one another. Christians grow better as a part of a fellowship (Heb. 10:25). If they live separately, they may retreat into halfheartedness and compromise and fail to realize their own lostness.

Second, these people were warned that sin deceived. In the parable of the sower, the deceitfulness of riches choked the seed (Matt. 13:22). Sin deceives by exaggerating the benefits of disobedience and hiding its consequences (Gen. 3:1–7). Sin may have deceived the readers of Hebrews by blinding them to the follies of their past life and giving them a nostalgic wish for returning to their previous lifestyle. A return to their previous practice of Judaism would demonstrate that they had never trusted Christ.

3. In Danger of Falling Away (v. 14)

3:14. Merely beginning the Christian life is not sufficient to assure its completion. We must continue in our commitment to **share in Christ**. The readers of Hebrews had started off with great confidence and hope. They must hold this hope firmly to the end, until Jesus returns or until their death. To do anything less would demonstrate that they had never experienced salvation.

The idea of sharing in Christ suggested that we would enjoy the benefits of family membership. We experience his presence on earth. We participate in his heavenly kingdom.

The concluding warning that we must **hold firmly** demanded vigorous effort. Commitment to Christ does not allow for halfheartedness. The term **confidence** (*hupostasis*) described the assurance a property owner had because he had the deeds to the land. Spiritually, this term carried an appeal for living faith. A property owner with the deeds had a claim to ownership. As believers in Christ, we have the title deed to heaven and its blessing. Believers with a steadfast faith demonstrate that they belong to Christ. These believers were encouraged to hold with firmness to their commitment.

4. Unbelieving (vv. 15–19)

3:15–17. So important was the quotation from Psalm 95 that the writer of Hebrews referred to it again in verse 17. Perhaps these believers knew the historical background of the psalm. The Jews had come through the waters of the Red Sea (Exod. 14:10–31). They had repeatedly rebelled against God's directions and leadership while they wandered in the wilderness (Exod. 16:1–3; 17:1–3; Num. 14:1–9). God had sentenced them to wander in the wilderness until the rebellious generation had died (Num. 14:29–35).

Five questions occur in verses 16–18. The second and the fourth question effectively answer the first and the third. The fifth question contains its own answer.

The first question in verse 16 concerned the extent of the rebellion. **Who were they who heard and rebelled?** The answer, given in the form of another question, pointed out what the readers of Hebrews already knew. The rebellion was total. All the Jews who came out of Egypt joined in the rebellion. The fact that Moses, Joshua, and Caleb were exceptions to this statement did not affect the truth of the application. The entire mass of Jewish people had proved faithless. How unbelievable!

The third question in verse 17 also showed the extent of the rebellion and drew attention to its duration of forty years. The rebellion lasted for the entire period of the Israelites' wanderings in the wilderness. The answer, also given in the form of a question, showed that God was angry with those who had sinned. Sin was the cause of the rebellion, and persistent sin led to judgment. Their **bodies fell in the desert.** They experienced God's judgment even as they were traveling to the Promised Land.

God's people had a wonderful beginning. God delivered them from Egypt with a display of majestic power (Exod. 12:31–51). With might God led them through the Red Sea (Exod. 14:10–31). He gave them manna and water as they traveled (Exod. 16:11–36; 17:5–7). Such privileged people still fell miserably into sin. Their good beginning did not keep them from later rebellion. What a tragedy to come to such ruin!

3:18–19. The fifth and final question in this passage appears in verse 18. The answer came as a part of the question. Those who were disobedient failed to enter God's rest. Three important ideas appear in these two verses.

First, God used an oath. This idea appears in Psalm 95:11, and oaths are later mentioned in Hebrews 4:3; 6:13,16 and 7:21–22. God's oath showed the complete truthfulness of his word. God used an oath to give undeniable evidence that his people could trust his promise.

Second, God promised **rest**. In this verse entering God's rest refers to the entrance into the Promised Land. Those who died in the wilderness failed to enter Canaan. The true rest which God designed for his people involved much more than possessing the land of Canaan. Chapter 4 shows that a true rest involved spiritual benefits.

Third, their failure to enter the Promised Land was caused by their **unbelief**. In verse 12 the people are warned against having **a sinful, unbelieving heart**. No reader of these words could escape the realization that the wilderness generation had failed to believe God. Despite the fact that God had given them mercy in the Exodus, the wilderness generation rebelled and died in the Sinai. These people faced the same danger.

The close link between disobedience and **unbelief** appears in the parallel mention of the two terms. The wilderness generation had **disobeyed**. They failed **to enter, because of their unbelief.** The result of unbelief was disobedience. The visible sign of unbelief was disobedience. The author of Hebrews was not so concerned about an intellectual grasp of truths about God as he was concerned over sinful behavior. What we believe about God will lead us to moral change. If we demonstrate only disobedience, we show that we have unbelief.

MAIN IDEA REVIEW: *Jesus' sonship shows his superiority to Moses and reminds us that rejecting him has more serious consequences than rejecting Moses.*

III. CONCLUSION

The Tiredest Night of the Week

Years ago I read a magazine article with a story that has remained with me. The writer related the story of his exhausting Saturdays. Saturday was his catch-up day. It was his day to mow the yard, repair leaky faucets, wash the car, plant the flower beds, and do a dozen other neglected chores. As his Saturday developed, his wife, children, or sudden emergencies added other duties to his plans. He was constantly reorganizing his day. At the end of the day, he had to live with a series of jobs half done, felt like a man who had worked three unbroken eight-hour shifts, and couldn't wait to get to bed, having endured "The Tiredest Night of the Week," as he entitled the article.

How could this man have handled his challenge in a better way? He could have made a prioritized list, including items that must be done, jobs that could be done if time allowed, and others for future performance. He could have concentrated on the "musts" and postponed the remainder.

How do we put first things first in our lives? We give top attention to God's work. We seek to follow the will of Jesus in all we do. We focus on those tasks which we must do for Jesus and neglect those things which do not fit in with his will.

This chapter of Hebrews contrasts the attention which we must give to Jesus with that attention which some had offered to Moses. The writer of Hebrews proclaimed, "Jesus is superior to Moses." Why was Jesus superior to Moses?

First, Jesus was superior to Moses because Jesus served as a **son over God's house** while Moses was **a servant in . . . God's house** (Heb. 3:5–6). It is more important for us to follow a son who has authority over God's people than to follow a servant who operates among God's people. It is more important to follow Jesus than to listen to Moses or any other competitor for our loyalty.

Second, because Jesus was so prominent in God's plan, neglecting Jesus was more serious than neglecting Moses (3:7–19). Those Israelites who wandered for forty years in the wilderness of Sinai had rejected God's commands (Num. 14:20–38). The same fate was possible for the readers of Hebrews. They were encouraged not to **be hardened by sin's deceitfulness.** Unbelief had prevented the wilderness generation from entering God's rest for them. The same thing could happen to these people.

I was standing with my son and grandson in front of a hospital when my grandson suddenly bolted away and ran toward a busy street. Although he was only a year and a half at the time, he quickly dashed so far away from us that he could have reached the street before we could stop him. My son cried out, "Nathan, stop!" And Nathan stopped. He had learned to obey his father's command. He wanted to explore the street. His curiosity could have produced deadly consequences. He had learned that disobeying Dad brought undesirable results. Doing what Dad said was important for him.

It is important for us to put Jesus first. He is more important than having fun, getting a promotion, making a million dollars, or completing any other personal goal. Nothing can compare with the joy of having him one day say to us, "Well done, good and faithful servant" (Matt. 25:21).

PRINCIPLES

- Jesus was faithful to follow every task which the Father delegated to him.
- Jesus deserves more honor than any other competitor for our attention.
- Jesus' commandments and promises in Scripture provide direction for victorious living.
- Jesus provides his blessings only if we endure in our obedience, faithful to the end.

APPLICATIONS

- Honor Jesus over all competitors for your commitment.
- Be careful not to substitute your own opinions for following the will of God.
- Encourage one another and avoid the deceitfulness of sin.
- Understand the consequences of hardening your hearts and falling into unbelief.
- Do not live in unbelief or you will miss God's rest.

IV. LIFE APPLICATION

Why Did We Do This Anyway?

Ninety years ago fishermen placed goats on Navy-owned San Clemente Island off the coast at San Diego. They wanted to maintain a ready supply of fresh meat. The goats consumed everything in sight and threatened three endangered species sharing the island with them. In 1976, the Navy hired private contractors to remove seventeen thousand goats.

One thousand of the goats defied all efforts at capture and removal. In three years this herd had increased to thirty-five hundred, was doubling every eighteen months, and posed an environmental threat to the island. Experts advised the Navy to shoot the animals from helicopters.

An organization called GOAT (Give Our Animals Time) formed to prevent the Navy from harming a single animal. One observer, feeling that the members of GOAT had become involved in a secondary campaign, said, "The goat people would be better off spending their time saving boat people" (a reference to people from deprived countries who try to escape hardship by putting out to sea in inadequate vessels and who often perish in the attempt.)

It is easy to lose perspective in doing life's work. We can get involved in doing good things instead of the very best things. We can maintain a routine just because we like following routines. We can let second-rate goals consume most of our energy. We can put our own ease and security ahead of venture for the sake of Christ. We can let the business of living, doing the necessary chores of life, and making a reputation for ourselves become our goals. We must put "first things first" and make our chief business that of following Jesus and doing his will.

Ask yourself, "What does Jesus really want me to do?" Then follow up with the answer to this question: How can I focus on those things which are God's will for me?

Responding to the answer of these questions will involve prayer, reflection, and an openness to God's will. Putting them into practice will cause a new arrangement of your schedules, a change in your daily priorities, and the addition and subtraction of some items from your schedule.

It is eternally important to put Jesus first. Do anything necessary to make that your goal.

V. PRAYER

Jesus, you are superior to all who would claim to be my Savior and rescue me from the trials and troubles I get myself into. Forgive me when I let you fall down to the bottom of my priority list. Forgive me for the foolish statement, "No, Lord," that my actions reveal I am so often making. From now on, let my life show that "Yes, Lord," is my permanent answer to you. Amen.

VI. DEEPER DISCOVERIES

A. Apostle (v. 1)

This is the first appearance of the word **apostle** in this letter and the only time the New Testament applies it to Christ. Most New Testament references to **apostle** apply to people called of God to proclaim the gospel with special authority. In Acts 1:21–22 Peter proposed the apostle who would replace Judas was to be "a witness . . . of his resurrection." In 1 Corinthians 9:1–2 Paul indicated that an apostle must have been a witness of the risen Lord and must have produced converts as evidence of his divine call. Apostles were God-called witnesses of the resurrected Lord who produced visible fruit in their widespread preaching.

Naming Jesus as an apostle showed him as one whom God sent into the world (John 17:18). Jesus fulfilled the duties of his office perfectly. Human beings called as apostles reflected his apostleship and served at his appointment.

B. Servant (v. 5)

The New Testament uses three words often translated as "servant." The most common term (*doulos*) refers to a bondservant. In John 13:16, it brings out the servile nature of the work the servant did. A second term (*oiketes*) denotes a household servant who did domestic duties (1 Pet. 2:18).

The third word (*therapon*), used here and nowhere else in the New Testament, is a tender word. It focuses on an attitude of obedient willingness to serve. This type of servant joyfully and cheerfully responds to a personal need for his master. The term shows the close personal relationship between God and Moses. Moses willingly gave himself unselfishly to do God's will. He was faithful to carry out the tasks which God gave him. This type of servant reflects an attitude of eager obedience which is a delight in all who serve the Lord.

C. Courage (v. 6)

This word (*parresia*) appears four times in Hebrews (3:6; 4:16; 10:19,35). Different versions use the translation "confidence," "boldness," or "courage." Outside the Book of Hebrews this word denotes the courageous attitude of someone who preached the gospel without fear: Peter's bold proclamation on the Day of Pentecost (Acts 2:29); the fearless proclamation of Spirit-filled believers who spread the gospel message (Acts 4:31).

In Hebrews its chief use was to describe the confidence or boldness with which Christians could approach God because of their new relationship to Jesus. In 4:16 Christians are to practice "confidence" in coming to the Lord for mercy and grace. In 10:19 Christians should be courageous in coming to God because of Christ's completed work.

In Hebrews 3:6 the word shows the assurance and certainty which Christians can have in coming to God. Because we are in Christ's family ("his house"), we have from God the strength to endure in obedience and commitment. Our hope in Christ gives us a solid basis for faithfulness in Christian living. We need not stumble and falter, but because of Jesus we can endure in faithful commitment. This is our confidence as Christians.

D. Perseverance (v. 6)

Hebrews 3:6 emphasizes that continuing in the Christian life provides evidence of real Christianity. Hebrews, perhaps more than any other New Testament book, raises questions about the perseverance of its readers. Hebrew 3:14 urges believers to **hold firmly till the end the confidence we had at first.** Hebrews 10:26 emphasizes the necessity of holding to the **knowledge of the truth** if we would experience the benefits of Christ's sacrifice for our sins. The writer of Hebrews feared that persecution or suffering (10:32–34) might lead his readers to abandon their Christian commitment. He inserted these warnings to encourage them to practice endurance. Though he was concerned about their commitment, he felt they were genuine believers, producing fruits which would **accompany salvation** (Heb. 6:9).

The New Testament emphasizes that God keeps believers secure in his love and protection (John 10:28–30; 1 Pet. 1:3–5). It also emphasizes the corollary truth, which we see here, that believers must persevere in their faith and commitment to Christ.

The result of these twin truths is that no Christian has a right to say, "I am a Christian because I made a commitment to Christ fifteen years ago, and God keeps me eternally secure." Our hope is not in some decision of the past which does not affect our lives today. Our hope for salvation comes from the fact that God will hold us in commitment to the hope and boldness which we received at the moment of our conversion. Those who have come to know Christ will endure in their commitment to him.

E. Rebellion (v. 8)

Hebrews 3:8 quotes Psalm 95:8 which refers to the unfortunate expression of discontent described in Exodus 17:1–7. The term **rebellion** in 3:8 is translated as *meribah* in the Hebrew text of Psalm 95:8. The term **testing** in 3:8 is translated as *massah* in the same verse. We can understand the meaning of the words only when we read the history behind the incident mentioned in Exodus 17:1–7.

During a stop in the wilderness at Rephidim, Moses confronted a nation of Israelites complaining because they had no water (Exod. 17:1). He accused the grumbling Jews of putting "the Lord to the test" (Exod. 17:2). The people continued to grumble against Moses and accused him of bringing them to the wilderness to die. In desperation Moses asked God, "What shall I do?" God directed Moses to strike the rock to produce water. He did this, and God supplied the water.

Nevertheless, because of the bitter experience in the location, Moses gave the names Massah ("testing") and Meribah ("quarreling" or "rebelling") to the place as a reminder of the people's disobedience and hardness of heart (Exod. 17:7). The writer of Hebrews feared that his readers might walk in the moral tracks of the Old Testament Jews. He was concerned that the rebellion of his own readers might cause them to forfeit the blessings which God had in store for them.

Christians today need to realize the danger of rebellion against the Lord through their own personal hardening. Those who listen to the warning of Moses can find the strength to maintain their initial hope, commitment, and courage to follow Christ. Those who ignore the warning will find that they have demonstrated that their profession of faith was an empty, meaningless promise, and they will experience divine judgment.

F. Wilderness Generation (vv. 7–11, 16–19)

In biblical thinking, "wilderness" referred to a rocky, dry wasteland. It resembled our desert if we think of craggy, rocky hills rather than flat, sandy stretches. Most of the wilderness areas in biblical lands had rainfall and some oases which could support human life.

The generation of Jews who escaped miraculously from Egypt wandered in the southern wilderness, including the area near the Sinai Peninsula. During their wandering God provided manna and quail to eat and water for drinking (Exod. 16:4–21; 17:1–7; Num. 11:31–35). He revealed himself to the Jews at Mount Sinai (Exod. 19–20). The dark side of these glorious events is that the Jews rebelled against the Lord and complained repeatedly against Moses.

Numbers 13–14 tells the story of Moses sending out the twelve spies to scout the land of Canaan. When these men returned, a majority of ten spies brought a fearful report emphasizing that "the people who live there are powerful, and the cities are fortified and very large" (Num. 13:28). Caleb, supported by Joshua, urged the people to "go up and take possession of the land" (Num. 13:30). The majority of the people accepted the unbelieving report of the ten spies rather than the faithful encouragement of Caleb and Joshua. God sentenced every member of that unbelieving generation except Caleb and Joshua to die in the wilderness before the land of promise was entered (Num. 14:26–35). This wilderness generation spent forty years of aimless wandering in the deserts of the Sinai region until they died. Their children entered the land of promise under Joshua.

This is the generation with which God **was angry** (Heb. 3:10). They rebelled against God, and their unbelief prevented their enjoying God's promises (Heb. 3:16–19).

G. The New Exodus (vv. 7–11)

In 3:7–11 the work of Christ is interpreted as a new Exodus. This method of interpretation has appeared in other passages of the New Testament. Luke called the death of Christ an "exodus" (Luke 9:31). The word "departure" in the NIV is the Greek term for "exodus." Paul described the death of Christ as a true passover (1 Cor. 5:7), and Peter pictured the sacrifice of Jesus as "a lamb without blemish or defect" (1 Pet. 1:19). Christ resembled the living rock leading his people through the wilderness (1 Cor. 10:4). Earthly Canaan was the goal of the wandering Israelites. The writer of Hebrews emphasized that his readers were moving toward a heavenly rest which Jesus would provide. This was the argument of Hebrews 3:7–4:11.

The point was that the readers of Hebrews must not imitate the disobedience of the Old Testament generation and receive the same judgment which they experienced. They must understand the seriousness of their rejection of Jesus.

This method of interpretation in which a writer finds a divinely intended correspondence between events in the Old Testament and those in the New Testament is called *typology*. Typology finds a similarity in some area between a person, event, or thing in the Old Testament and a person, event, or thing in the New Testament. The use of typology helps us to see the New Testament person, event, or institution as a fulfillment of that mentioned in the Old Testament.

The Exodus typology was an effort to give a serious warning to the readers of Hebrews. They could, if they were not careful, rush into the same experience of judgment which the Old Testament Israelites faced. We who live today must demonstrate our commitment to the Lord by a faith which is active, vigorous, and daring.

H. Sharing in Christ (v. 14)

Sharing in Christ translates a noun which the KJV renders as "partakers of Christ." A "partaker" was someone who participated with Christ, but in what did the partaker participate?

The partaker may be a partner with someone. The word was used this way in Luke 5:7 to describe those who were "partners" with Peter in a fishing business on the Sea of Galilee.

The partaker may also be a participant in or a sharer of something. This is probably the best understanding of the word in 3:14. The writer of Hebrews was saying that his readers could be sharers in Christ. They could receive the Holy Spirit, enjoy a close union with him, and share all the benefits which the Father had given to him. They could be "heirs of God and co-heirs with Christ" (Rom. 8:17). All of Christ's resources would be available to strengthen them. To experience these blessings, they needed to hold firmly to **the confidence** they had at the beginning of their experience.

Beginning well was not enough. God had provided in Christ the strength to endure, and they needed to receive it and take advantage of it. Only those who kept the course and dashed over the finish line could share in Christ's heavenly kingdom. Those who were considering dropping out needed to reconsider the effect of their halfheartedness. If they dropped out, they would show that they had not **come to share in Christ**. They would miss out on the salvation God had offered them.

I. Rest (vv. 11,18)

Rest appears in Hebrews 3:11–4:11 with several different emphases. The experience of the Israelites in seeking the rest of the Promised Land is a type of the rest which believers have in Christ. Three, perhaps even four, different usages of the term **rest** appears in this section of Hebrews.

First, the Israelites were seeking rest in attempting to enter the Promised Land (3:11,18). Their sin prevented their entering this rest. Some interpreters have called this "Canaan rest."

Second, on the Sabbath God rested from all his works (4:4). We may call this "Sabbath rest."

Third, God's people enjoy a present rest. This rest provided the strength of Christ for believers as they faced a variety of hardships and persecution (4:10). Christ himself promises this rest for those who follow him (Matt. 11:28–30). We may call this "present rest."

Even though this rest is available in the present, believers will enter into a more complete enjoyment of this rest in the future after our resurrection with Christ. This fact leads some interpreters to suggest that a fourth meaning of rest is that of an eternal rest for God's people. Believers can enjoy present benefits from their relationship to Christ, but these benefits will be intensified after the return of Christ and the resurrection of believers (1 Cor. 15:52–58). This would be called "eternal rest."

Each of these usages of **rest** refers to an experience of salvation which we enter by believing in Jesus Christ. The writer of Hebrews makes this clear when he insists on the necessity of faith in the gospel which the readers had received (v. 2). This faith demands a dependence on God's work instead of our own works (v. 10). Those who have begun the experience of faith in Jesus Christ demonstrate the reality of their commitment by continuing to enjoy the rest God has promised. Those who cease to enjoy that rest show by their failure that their profession of faith was false.

Not all interpreters view **rest** as a reference to an experience of salvation. Some see the rest as involving a life in unbroken fellowship with God. They feel that the issue discussed by the writer of Hebrews dealt with a loss of fellowship and not with an experience of salvation. Both the interpreters who see **rest** as a reference to fellowship and those who see the term as a reference to salvation make valid points. It is difficult to say that either viewpoint is completely in error. The preceding paragraphs attempt to show why the present writer feels that the experience of rest refers to salvation rather than to sanctification.

The quest for rest by the Israelites became a type of all the varieties of rests which God himself and his people could enjoy. Christians today can enjoy rest in Jesus.

J. Unbelief (v. 19)

Verse 19 warns us that the Israelites could not enter the Promised Land **because of their unbelief**. The preceding verse reminds us that God swore that **those who disobeyed** would never enter his rest. Placing these two terms so near reminds us of the close link between disobedience and unbelief. Unbelief led to disobedience. For the Jews, this experience was inexcusable because they had seen so much of God's love and power.

The author of Hebrews feared that the same "sinful, unbelieving heart" lay inside his readers (3:12). We have the same capacity for an evil heart today.

VII. TEACHING OUTLINE

A. INTRODUCTION

1. Lead Story: Setting Your Priorities

2. Context: Chapter 1 of Hebrews shows that Jesus was superior to both the Old Testament prophets and to angels. Chapter 2 begins by pointing out that we must listen to the message of Jesus because of his important role in God's plan. We must listen to Jesus because the penalties for ignoring him are too severe and because Jesus can help us as we face temptation.

   Chapter 3 emphasizes two facts about the superiority of Jesus. First, Jesus was superior to Moses (3:1–6). Both Jesus and Moses were faithful to God's plan. However, Jesus was superior to Moses because he was the builder of God's people and because he was a Son serving over God's people. Moses was only a servant working among God's people.

   Second, rejecting Jesus was more serious than rejecting Moses (3:7–19). God's people had failed under Moses because they did not listen to God's voice (3:7–11). They were also deceived by sin and needed encouragement (3:12–13). They needed to know that God expected them to endure in their commitment to Jesus Christ (3:14). They had hardened their hearts in unbelief, and they had reaped the consequences of their stubbornness (3:15–19).

3. Transition: We live in a time when it is easy to attach ourselves to talented human leaders who can claim the devotion that we would give to Jesus. Do you remember Jim Jones, Rev. Sun Myung Moon, or Herbert W. Armstrong? Each of these people attracted followers who gave energy, money, and commitment to their causes. We must always resist giving our commitment to human beings instead of rendering full allegiance to our Lord.

   Jesus is superior to any person whom we can follow. If we do not follow him, we reap serious consequences far worse than turning away from a human being. We must aim at nothing less than serving Jesus as Lord.

B. COMMENTARY
1. The Comparison between Jesus and Moses (vv. 1–6).
   a. Faithful to the divine plan (vv. 1–2).
   b. The builder of God's house (vv. 3–4).
   c. A Son over God's house (vv. 5–6).
2. The Failure of God's People under Moses (vv. 7–19)
   a. Hardened to God's voice (vv. 7–11)
   b. Deceived by sin (vv. 12–13)
   c. In danger of falling away (v. 14)
   d. Unbelieving (vv. 15–19)

C. CONCLUSION: WHY DID WE DO THIS ANYWAY?

VIII. ISSUES FOR DISCUSSION

1. Look at your daily planner or time schedule and your checkbook. What do they tell you about the priorities you are setting for your life? Where do they witness to Jesus' place in your life?
2. Describe the spiritual condition of the first recipients and readers of the Book of Hebrews.
3. How does this chapter support or modify your understanding of the doctrine of personal salvation?
4. What forces or people in the modern world tempt you to follow them and slacken or give up your commitment to Jesus?

Hebrews 4

Finishing the Job

Quote

"*S*ympathy with the sinner in his trial does not depend on the experience of sin but on the experience of the strength of the temptation to sin which only the sinless can know in its full intensity. He who falls yields before the last strain."

B . F .   W e s t c o t t ,   q u o t e d   i n
F . F .   B r u c e ,   *The Epistle to the Hebrews*

Hebrews

 IN A NUTSHELL

*C*hapter 4 shows Jesus is superior to Joshua. Joshua had tried to lead the Jews to rest in the Promised Land, but they did not reach their goal. Jesus can lead us to full rest, but his rest needs to be claimed. God's Word can diagnose spiritual needs and provide new life. His message can awaken stragglers and help them reach his goal, and Christ's mercy can help stumblers move forward with hope. Christ endured all the temptations we face and emerged triumphant. He knew the full experience of temptation to sin, but he never compromised. His triumph allows him to give us mercy and grace to complete the job of obeying God fully.

Finishing the Job

I. INTRODUCTION

Sealing the Driveway

*T*he mother of one of my friends lives in rural east Texas. Many weekends he drives four hours from his home to visit her, help with household repairs, and check on her physical condition. Some time ago they decided the rural home's driveway needed asphalt pavement. A local paver apparently did a good job, except for one detail. He did not apply the final sealer.

Sealing protects the asphalt from cracking due to moisture and other weather-related problems. Sealing guarantees you can use a driveway over a long period. The paver promised to get the sealer and come back to finish the task. Instead, he silently left town, leaving my friend with an unsealed driveway. All hope for long-term benefit was lost.

The readers of Hebrews had started well with the race of the Christian life. They had endured persecution (Heb. 10:32–35). They had labored with love to help meet the needs of suffering Christians (Heb. 6:9–10). Still they were immature (Heb. 5:11–14)—stumbling and faltering in their Christian walk. Like the paver, they had a job they needed to finish. If they did not, they stood to lose a great deal.

Our writer remembered the generation Joshua had attempted to lead into the Promised Land. They had heard a message of hope and deliverance from Joshua and Moses but had not responded with faith. They had entered the land, but they had not driven out all the pagan occupants (Judg. 1:16–36). God had promised rest in the Promised Land. They did not live in full obedience to the Lord and so never achieved rest in Canaan.

Fearing disobedience would squeeze the spiritual life from these people, the writer of Hebrews warned: "Do not follow the ways of the wilderness generation. Claim the rest which God has for his people."

Reading this chapter will fill us with hope. We do stumble. We sometimes wander in disobedience to God. Our waywardness and weakness threaten to overwhelm us! But we have a Savior who understood. He faced our temptations and overcame them. We can overcome them also if we come with boldness to claim God's mercy and grace.

II. COMMENTARY

Finishing the Job

> **MAIN IDEA:** *Jesus is superior to Joshua because he leads us to rest, provides a diagnosis of our needs, and supplies abundant grace and mercy.*

A A Superiority Promising Rest (vv. 1–10)

> **SUPPORTING IDEA:** *Jesus is superior because he provides spiritual rest, but believers must claim God's promised rest.*

1. A Rest Which Must Be Claimed (vv. 1–2)

4:1. Rest remains the subject under discussion. (For the various usages of this term in this section of Hebrews, see "Deeper Discoveries" on 3:11,18).

Wherever **rest** appears in 3:1 to 4:11, it refers to an experience of salvation we enter by faith in Jesus Christ. The writer of Hebrews makes this interpretation clear when he insists on the necessity of faith in the gospel the readers had received (v. 2). This faith demands a dependence on God's work instead of on our own works (v. 10). Those who have begun the Christian walk by an experience of faith in Jesus Christ demonstrate the reality of their commitment when they continue to enjoy the rest God has promised. Those who cease to share in that rest show by their spiritual failure that their profession of faith was false.

Some interpreters explain **rest** as a lifetime experience of unbroken fellowship with God. They feel that the issue discussed by the writer concerns a loss of fellowship rather than an experience of salvation. This interpretation, as the one in the previous paragraph, rests on valid points. It is difficult to accuse proponents of either viewpoint of being completely in error. Still, the present writer, as shown above, feels that the total evidence supports the interpretation of **rest** as related to salvation rather than to sanctification.

Rest appears in Hebrews 3:11–4:11 with several different emphases. Wherever the term appears, it refers to an experience of salvation with Christ, but the writer of Hebrews had different shades of meaning in mind as he referred to salvation. We will try to make these shades of meaning clear as we work our way through this chapter.

The NIV's **let us be careful** may be better translated, "let us fear." The writer of Hebrews feared his readers would live in disobedience, and he wanted to awaken them to repentance. What caused his concern?

Most of the wilderness generation died before reaching the Promised Land. Their death did not nullify the promise of God's rest. The children of this generation later entered the land. This entrance did not completely fulfill the promise of rest. The writer of Hebrews feared that his readers might stumble and falter just as those who left Egypt. They needed to be aware of the previous failure so that they might not make the same mistake.

These believers needed to rise up and claim the rest that God intended for his people. There is a typological relationship between the rest which God reserved for believers and that of Israel in the land of Canaan. (For a discussion of typology, see "Deeper Discoveries" on "The New Exodus" (3:7–11).

4:2. Gospel refers to a message of good news from God. For the refugees from Egypt, the gospel consisted of the promised rescue from Egypt and entrance into Canaan. It included also God's promises to Israel in Exodus 19:5–6. For the readers of Hebrews, it consisted of the message of Christ's atoning death and resurrection. God had spoken clearly to both groups.

The refugees from Egypt heard the message of deliverance, refused to believe it, and received no value from it. These believers must not imitate their Israelite forefathers. They needed to make a faith response so they might receive value, promise, and blessing from the declaration of the gospel.

Here is a practical truth: We get no benefit from merely hearing the gospel. We must believe it and act on it to receive its benefit. Faith involves a wholehearted trust in God's message. We must make a right response to the message about Jesus. *Faith* is a big word in Hebrews, and we will discuss it more fully in chapter 11. We already know that **without faith it is impossible to please him** (Heb. 11:6).

2. A Rest Patterned after God's Rest (vv. 3–5)

4:3. The rest the psalmist mentioned in Psalm 95:7–11 is still available. Those who put their faith in Jesus Christ enjoy that rest.

Those **who have believed enter that rest.** They enter that rest initially at the moment of conversion (see also 4:10) and will get a fuller experience of rest in the future. Those who truly experience God's rest share in his experience of salvation.

This claim for rest is supported by the divine oath of Psalm 95:11. The logic is something like this:

(1) The fact that God warned the readers to fear lest unbelief prevent entering his rest implied that the possibility of rest was still available (see Heb. 3:16–19).

(2) The Israelites did not experience the rest.

(3) God had someone else in mind who would experience it.

(4) The readers of Hebrews were among those people who could experience the rest.

Furthermore, this rest resembled God's sabbath rest. The final words of verse 3 refer to God's rest **since the creation of the world.** This was the rest that the Creator enjoyed when he had completed his work of creation. This means rest cannot be defined as inactivity; rather, it involves the sense of completion. The rest Christians can enjoy today comes when we willingly take on Jesus' yoke (Matt. 11:28–30). This sense of completion experienced in taking on Jesus' yoke is a benefit which comes to those who have experienced salvation through faith in Jesus Christ.

4:4–5. Two quotes affirmed that God's rest was real and that Israel failed to enjoy that rest. First, verse 4 quotes Genesis 2:2–3 to show that God's rest was a real event. God's rest occurred after the completion of creation and lasted indefinitely. God never returned to the work of creation, and we may understand that his rest still continues. Believers can share in that rest, in the sense of completion, today. Anyone who responds to God's message with faith and obedience assumes Christ's yoke and enters into a "rest" relationship with God. The idea of "rest" does not mean that we sit around sipping spiritual lemonades. It conveys the idea of our total acceptance by God and the blessing of his presence, leadership, and power in our lives.

When God rested on the seventh day, he celebrated the completion of his work of creation, but he did not just take a day off eternally. When we enter into rest with Jesus, we will find God's presence, blessing, and peace but not a cessation from labor. Our rest with God gives us new strength, but it does not introduce us into inactivity. God's salvation produces people who receive divine energy to serve, obey, and work for him.

This rest we enjoy as believers in Christ becomes a type of our rest in heaven after leaving earth. Our life in heaven is not merely an eternity of vacations but a new experience of face-to-face contact with God (1 John 3:2–3; Rev. 14:13). Heaven is a place of rest, but not of listless laziness. In heaven God will provide a new earth in which we can live, work, and glorify God (Rev. 21:1). Chief among our labors will be the privilege of offering praises to God (Rev. 5:12–13).

As I write these words, my father is living in a Mississippi nursing home and is approaching his mid-nineties. Throughout his adult life he was busy. He worked on numerous church and civic committees and served as a civil engineer in charge of track maintenance for a railroad. He never settled down to inactivity. Now the privilege of being busy is something he misses greatly. Physically he cannot do very much.

It will be an encouragement to him to know that heaven is not just a series of twenty-four-hour naps. He will be encouraged to know that God will give him something to do in heaven and the strength to do it. God gives rest to Christians both on earth and in heaven, but it is the rest of his presence which provides strength for activity.

A second quotation appearing in verse 5 shows that unbelievers fail to enter God's rest. This often-repeated quote (3:11; 4:3) comes from Psalm 95:11, and it reminds readers of Israel's failure to enter the rest. The fact the psalmist offered "rest" again shows that the idea of "rest" was not exhausted with the Israelites' occupation of Canaan. God still has a purpose of bringing believers into that rest, but hearers can forfeit this blessing by disobedience. These words become a fervent appeal not to disobey as the Jews of the Exodus had disobeyed. We have hope of experiencing rest if we follow in an obedience that shows itself by faith in God's gospel message.

3. A Rest Which Still Remained (4:6–10)

These verses reinforce truths of the previous verses. First, they emphasize that God intended for someone to enter his rest. No one could frustrate his purposes. Second, since the Jews of the Exodus did not enter this rest, the offer for experiencing rest is still available. Third, this rest far exceeds the physical promise of entrance into the Promised Land. It includes the rest of entering God's presence through Christ and experiencing peace with him.

4:6–7. The opening words in the Greek text of verse 6 contains the expression "Since therefore" which the NIV omits. This pair of words makes it clear that the statements of verses 6–7 are derived from the previous quotes of verses 4–5. Three thoughts are evident.

First, God intends for some people to enter the promised rest. If the Jews did not enter the rest, someone else must enter it, or God's promise of experiencing rest would be void and empty. Notice that the writer of Hebrews did not consider the fact that Joshua led the second generation of Israelites into Canaan. He was concerned only to contrast Moses, as the leader of the old covenant, and Christ, as the inaugurator of the new covenant.

Second, the first generation stumbled because of their disobedience or unbelief. They could blame only themselves for their failure. The **gospel** which this first generation received was a message of deliverance from Egypt and deliverance from sin. Although its message dealt with deliverance just as the message given to Christians, the first generation did not receive clear teaching about the work of Christ. We who live under the new covenant receive a clear statement about Christ.

Third, God's offer of rest is still open as shown by a repeated quotation of Psalm 95:7b–8a. **Today** emphasizes that God's invitation to enjoy rest with him finds fulfillment in the present. Many years had passed between Israel's fall in the wilderness and David's writing of Psalm 95. The fact that David expressed the truth as one available in his lifetime showed that the opportunity for enjoying rest was still present. The author of Hebrews warned his readers that both the blessing of rest and the fear of failure were as available to them as they were to the wilderness generation. They could harden their hearts and miss completely the opportunity for experiencing rest. The readers are encouraged to choose **rest.**

4:8. Here is a possible objection to this discussion about rest. Someone might say, "Moses could not lead the people to rest because of their unbelief. Joshua did lead them to rest." But Hebrews does not accept this argument.

The fact that David could speak to residents already living in Canaan about **another day** of rest suggested that Joshua had not led his people to rest. If so, followers of the Lord would have been enjoying rest for centuries, and David would have had no need to discuss the availability of rest. The fact that the writer of Hebrews could challenge his readers to experience **rest** suggested that the readers of Psalm 95 also failed to receive the promise. God must have had something more in mind for both generations.

Joshua had given **rest** to Israel in his day (Josh. 23:1), but God had more than political security in mind in the use of the term **rest**. Joshua gave his followers temporal rest by leading them to defeat their enemies. God has provided spiritual rest for those who approach him through faith in Jesus Christ as is made clear in verses 9–10.

4:9–10. These two verses provide a conclusion (v. 9) and the explanation of the conclusion (v. 10). **Then** introduces the conclusion: God's people enjoyed a rest patterned after God's own rest on the seventh day. **Sabbath-rest** is a new word, appearing only here in the New Testament. The author of Hebrews may have coined the word to express the special significance which he wanted to communicate. God's people will share in God's own rest. Those who enjoy this rest will be believers, those who have approached God through Jesus Christ.

Just what kind of rest can believers enjoy? When do they enjoy it—now, at death, or in the resurrection? This rest is not merely the entrance into Canaan. It is a present experience with Christ in which the Lord provides his presence, peace, and joy to replace the labor and heavy burdens of life (Matt. 11:28–30).

God's own rest (see 4:4) becomes the pattern of the rest of the believer. God's rest involved the completion of his work and not mere cessation of activity. Believers have become complete in Christ (Col. 2:10), and they can live in the light of a fulfilled relationship to Jesus as their exalted head.

The **work** from which believers have rested is perhaps a reference to the minute details of Jewish sacrificial ritual and purifying washings. Concern about these insignificant details was unnecessary. Christ's full work on the cross made it possible for believers to trust him instead of their own works.

When do we begin to enjoy this rest? We can live in those blessings here and now by faith. However, our present enjoyment of these blessings is not the whole story. We will receive more at the time of **the redemption of our bodies** (Rom. 8:23).

Let us summarize an involved idea: The writer of Hebrews called his readers to faith in Jesus and the enjoyment of the blessings which accompany that faith. Through faith in Jesus, believers today enjoy peace, joy, and fellowship with the living Lord as a part of their rest in him. This foretaste, which we now enjoy, will become a complete, unclouded experience of bliss at the time of the return of Jesus and the resurrection. As believers we can say, "Hallelujah!"

B A Superior Experience of Diagnosing Our Needs (4:11–13)

SUPPORTING IDEA: *God's message diagnoses the needs of our hearts and points us to a solution.*

4:11. This verse introduces an encouragement to seek God's rest because of the penetrating power of God's Word. Does it seem unusual to you that these believers are told to **make every effort to enter that rest?** This rest is a reality which believers must claim. The effort they must make involves obedience. The Jews of the Exodus generation had disobeyed. There was a clear possibility that these believers could also disobey and miss God's promised rest. Practicing obedience involves a determination on our part. Experiencing rest requires effort, but the blessing of rest makes the effort worth the cost.

Two additional features of this verse provide interesting insights. First, the writer of Hebrews included himself along with his readers when he said, **Let us . . . make every effort.** Second, the effort needed for reaching rest is not merely renewed willpower. Christ reminded his listeners that those who would bear fruit must abide in him (John 15:5–7). The effort calls for Christ power, not willpower. A confession of helplessness and an ardent trust in Christ is the beginning of the effort needed.

4:12. This vivid expression of the power of God's message provides the explanation for the strong warning of verse 11. Because God's message is alive, active, sharp, and discerning, those who listen to God's message can enter his rest. Two questions are important in this verse. First, what is **the word of God?** Second, what does this passage say about it?

Although the Bible sometimes refers to Christ as God's Word (John 1:14), the reference here is not speaking of Jesus Christ. Here we have a general reference to God's message to human beings. In the past God had spoken to human beings through dreams, angelic appearances, and miracles. He still can use those methods today, but our primary contact with God is through his written Word, the Bible. God's Word will include any method God uses to communicate with human beings.

This verse contains four statements about God's Word. First, it is **living.** God is a **living** God (Heb. 3:12). His message is dynamic and productive. It causes things to happen. It drives home warnings to the disobedient and promises to the believer. Second, God's Word is **active**, an emphasis virtually identical in meaning with the term **living**. God's Word is not something you passively hear and then ignore. It actively works in our lives, changes us, and sends us into action for God.

Third, God's Word penetrates the **soul and spirit.** To the Hebrew people, the body was a unity. We should not think of dividing the soul from the spirit. God's message is capable of penetrating the impenetrable. It can divide what is indivisible. Fourth, God's message is discerning. **It judges the thoughts and attitudes of the heart.** It passes judgment on our feelings and our thoughts. What we regard as secret and hidden, God brought out for inspection by the discerning power of his Word.

In 1995, Johnny Oates was managing the Texas Rangers baseball team when God spoke to him through the illness of his wife Gloria. Oates had become a Christian in 1983; but until the crisis in 1995, he had always lived as if baseball were his god. His wife was traveling to the spring training camp for the Rangers when she became ill in Savannah, Georgia. His daughter summoned him to Georgia with a phone call. Oates arrived to find his wife in a motel, despairing and defeated.

Oates said, "God got my attention and said, 'Johnny, it's not going to work this way.'" In the grief of the moment, Oates told God that he was ready to listen to anything he wanted to say. The next day Oates checked his wife out of the motel and headed for their home in Virginia. There he and his wife both participated in a Christian counseling program and learned how to communicate with one another. He learned that what he had worshiped was not God or his family, but the game of baseball. Both Oates and his wife moved closer, and Oates said, "As we get closer to God, . . . we get closer to each other."

God got his attention. Fortunately Oates listened. God's message to this baseball manager was life changing. It was also marriage saving.

4:13. This verse contains a general statement about the relationship between the Creator and the creation. The Greek text does not mention the name God, but it is clear that the writer of Hebrews was referring to God as the mighty Judge of the universe.

He stated the same truth both negatively and positively. Negatively, he said, **Nothing in all creation is hidden from God's sight.** Positively, he stated, **Everything is uncovered and laid bare before the eyes of him to whom we must give account.**

Laid bare (*tetraxelismena*) is a vivid term describing either the grip of a wrestler on the neck of an opponent or the grip on the neck of a sacrificial victim in preparation for sacrifice. The neck is about to be snapped, or the throat is about to be cut. The word picture reminds us that we cannot hide from God because he sees all our guilt.

Ending with this solemn thought causes us to ask, "Who can represent guilty sinners before a God who sees everything?" This leads to the next section on the high-priestly work of Christ and its provision of mercy and help for wandering sinners.

C A Superior Experience of Grace and Mercy (4:14–16)

SUPPORTING IDEA: *The transcendence, sinlessness, and grace of Christ encourage us to claim his mercy with confidence.*

4:14. This passage introduces the theme of Jesus' high priesthood. The epilogue for this section appears in 10:19–23. In between the superiority of Jesus to the priests of Aaron is explained. Three statements about Christ as our high priest appear in this verse.

First, Jesus is **a great high priest.** Perhaps some Jews were claiming that Christianity had no priesthood like that of Aaron. But Jesus was superior to the priests of Aaron. Both his character and his work are important.

Second, Jesus **has gone through the heavens.** This means that he had entered God's very presence. The priests of Aaron served in an earthly sanctuary. Jesus went far beyond all limits of time and space and reached into God's presence, where his work really mattered.

Third, Jesus is called **the Son of God.** This statement identifies the historical Jesus as our high priest. It also presents Jesus as one who perfectly combined humanity and divinity in his ministry for lost sinners. His human name was Jesus, but in reality he was the Son of God.

Because Jesus is our high priest, we can **hold firmly to the faith we profess.** Holding to the faith requires some determination on our part. The greatness of Jesus as our High Priest provides us an incentive to make the commitment to draw near to him.

Greatness, exaltation, humanity, and deity—all these traits of Christ encourage us to seek Jesus' help under testing. In the words of the hymn writer, we can say, "Man of sorrows, what a name for the Son of God who came. Ruined sinners to reclaim! Hallelujah! What a Saviour!"

4:15. How can we hold fast to our faith? Has God done anything to make this possible? This verse answers these questions. The writer of Hebrews had already declared the ability of Jesus to help the tempted (2:18). He now states negatively what he had earlier stated positively. Why would he change from a positive statement to a negative statement?

He may have tried to deal with some people who felt that Jesus Christ was too remote from human need. He stated three facts about Christ which would help readers know that Christ was no stranger in helping struggling human beings.

First, Jesus is able to **sympathize** with our weaknesses. **Weaknesses** is broad enough to include any form of human stumbling, bumbling, or failure. Christ has sympathy for the needy.

Second, Christ **has been tempted in every way, just as we are.** This statement may mean that he faced the full range of temptations we face. It need not mean that he met each specific type of temptation which we face. A sample of the entire range of options for sinning fell on Jesus. Because Jesus never yielded to sin, we know that he faced more intense temptation. Most of us say "yes" to sin before Satan has thrown all his weapons of temptation at us. Jesus said "no" as Satan hurled every arrow in his quiver. He resisted until he broke the power of Satan (Heb. 2:14).

Third, Christ was **without sin.** Jesus was completely a human being (Heb. 2:17), for he became **like his brothers in every way.** Must a person experience sin in order to be human? No! Jesus had no sin or deceit in his life (1 Pet. 2:22).

Jesus could have chosen to sin by giving in to hunger, desire for acclaim, or lust for power (Matt. 4:1–11). The fact that he chose not to do this shows that he lived out the condition of sinlessness. He battled constantly with Satan's temptations and claimed victory in the struggle with temptation.

If Jesus had sinned by surrendering to temptation, he would have needed an atonement. He would have been no better than the old priests who first had to offer sacrifice for their own sins (Heb. 7:27). He would have lacked the qualifications to secure redemption for us. Any sin in Jesus' life would have made his sacrifice unacceptable (1 Pet. 1:19).

Our sinless Savior provided for us a perfect redemption. His victorious experience with temptation provides sympathy, encouragement, and victory for us in our temptation.

4:16. Given the fact that we have a sinless Savior, what can we do? What should be our response?

First, we must **approach.** Worshipers used this verb (Heb. 7:25) in describing their movement into God's presence. We are to come to God with all the reverence and awe which his worship demands.

Second, we come to **the throne of grace.** This is a reverent reference to God's presence. It is the place where God gives out his free favor. The term describes an attitude more than a place. The seeking sinner will find this throne of grace (Luke 18:9–14).

Third, we come in an attitude of **confidence.** Although we must approach God with reverence, we can enter his presence with freedom and without fear. The term describes a boldness based on an awareness that God has all the grace we need. It is the attitude of customers coming to a store seeking an important item which they know is plentifully stocked.

Fourth, we come for the purpose of obtaining **mercy** and **grace**. God's mercy prescribes pardon for our many failures. God's grace provides strength for the demands of God's service.

> **MAIN IDEA REVIEW:** *Jesus is superior to Joshua because he leads us to rest, diagnoses our needs, and supplies abundant grace and mercy.*

III. CONCLUSION

The Bank Never Closes

At times I have raced with an empty wallet to a bank seeking money. Sometimes I have arrived just as the teller was locking the door. I couldn't get money that day. The bank was closed.

Now most cities have twenty-four-hour teller machines. With a card and a PIN number, you can withdraw the cash you need at any time. The bank never closes. It is always open.

In the same way God's throne of grace is always available to lead us to experience God's rest. We see no sign announcing, "Closed for the day." He makes his grace and mercy available around the clock. Come to God with boldness, an awareness of his majesty, and a willingness to claim his mercy and grace to reach his rest. Jesus will take you where Joshua never could.

PRINCIPLES

- God provides his people the rest of his presence.
- Faith in God's promises through Jesus is necessary to reach God's rest.
- Listening to God's message can help us understand the barriers to God's work in our lives.
- Jesus can sympathize with our weaknesses and failures.
- God offers his mercy and grace for those who boldly seek it.

APPLICATIONS

- Examine yourself to be certain that you are not failing to follow God's promises.
- Live with a conscious awareness of Jesus' presence in your life.
- Read God's message in the Bible to learn his diagnosis of your needs.
- Don't be timid about coming to God to confess your sin and claim his forgiveness.
- Tell Jesus your areas of weakness and ask him to lead you to understand his power.

IV. LIFE APPLICATION

Trust the One with Experience

On October 30, 1949, Harold Taft became the first television meteorologist west of the Mississippi, the third in the United States. He presented daily weather forecasts for what was then WBAP-TV, channel 5 in Fort Worth, Texas.

He served in his position for forty-one years and ten months, retiring after his broadcast at 6:00 P.M. Friday, August 30, 1991. His staying power, meteorological skill, and approachability made him a well-loved institution in Texas broadcasting. During a bout with cancer, which eventually took his life later in 1991, he received more than fifty thousand cards and letters, many of them addressed to the "World's Greatest Weatherman." Around the Channel 5 studios in Fort Worth, he was known as "the Chief."

In the 1980s a new station manager at Channel 5 threatened to terminate Taft. Protesters picketed the station, and advertisers threatened to cancel their commercials. Cars with bumper stickers reading "I BELIEVE HAROLD" were common for a time.

Taft had both friendliness and skill. This led the public to trust him. When he ate with his wife in a cafe, people would come by, pull up a chair, ask for an autograph, and stay to talk. When an airline crash occurred at D-FW airport during stormy weather in 1985, lawyers for both the airline and the plaintiffs sought out Taft for weather expertise. His openness and his experience led the public to trust him.

Taft was also a committed Christian. As a faithful member of St. John Lutheran Church in Grand Prairie, Texas, he played his trumpet in services each Sunday. He once told his pastor, "If you ever come across an atheist or an agnostic, send them in and let me show them the way the weather is formed, and they won't be an atheist very long."

You and I learn to rely on experience for weather forecasting. We also learn to rely on experience for guidance and strength in living the Christian life. The writer of Hebrews wanted us to know that Jesus was approachable. He was able **to sympathize with our weaknesses.** He understood, without condoning our easily-disturbed tempers, wavering commitment, fear of the future, and self-centeredness. When we come to Jesus with confession of our need and pleas for strength, we have the assurance that he identifies with us and understands our sorrows and griefs.

More important, however, is the fact that Jesus overcame sin. He faced the entire gamut of sinful temptation which comes to us. He faced hunger, desire for power, and an appeal to "show off" his powers. Each of these temptations (Matt. 4:1–11) provided an opportunity to compromise, but Jesus did not compromise. He faced the loneliness of the cross, the desertion of his disciples, and the opposition of his enemies (Matt. 26:36–46). He determined to follow only the will of God and never compromised his obedience to the Father's plan.

Jesus is approachable, and Jesus is experienced. He experienced the temptation to sin, and he overcame it. Because we have a Savior like this, we can come to him for help, encouragement, mercy, and grace. The concluding words of chapter 4 remind us to trust the one with experience: **Let us then approach the throne of grace with confidence, so that we may receive mercy and find grace to help us in our time of need** (Heb. 4:16).

V. PRAYER

Sinless Savior, thank you for providing rest for my soul. May I never take it as rest for my feet. Show me how I can represent your presence to do the work of your kingdom in your world. I trust in your promises and come to your throne seeking the grace and mercy I must have to live today and each day of my life. Amen.

VI. DEEPER DISCOVERIES

A. Gospel (vv. 2, 6)

Hebrews 4:2,6 describes two audiences as hearing God's gospel preached: the wilderness generation under Moses and his own generation after Jesus. What was the gospel the writer had heard? What was the gospel the wilderness generation had received?

The writer of Hebrews could use the term **gospel** because both his generation and the earlier generation received a message of deliverance. In both instances God was communicating his message to human beings. For the readers of Hebrews, the gospel concerned the death, burial, and resurrection of Jesus Christ. Paul outlined this gospel in 1 Corinthians 15:1–4.

For the refugees from Egypt, the gospel promised deliverance through the Exodus and a covenant of blessing at Sinai (Exod. 13–14; 19–20). These Jews learned that the God who had delivered them during the escape from Egypt would bring them safely to the Promised Land, allow them to possess it, and make them "a kingdom of priests and a holy nation" (Exod. 19:6).

Both messages contained good news. The refugees from Egypt heard the message, but they did not respond with faith. The writer of Hebrews wanted his readers to respond with faith to the message about Jesus so that they might claim mercy, grace, rest, and forgiveness of sin.

B. Disobedience (vv. 6, 11)

The act of disobedience is closely related to disbelief. Disbelief is a self-chosen unfaithfulness. Disbelief in attitude leads to disobedience in action. The disobedience of Hebrews 3:18 led to the disbelief of Hebrews 3:19. One act affected the other. Disbelief leads to disobedience. Disobedience leads to disbelief.

Hebrews 4:6 calls attention to the failure of the wilderness generation to receive God's promise and to enter his rest. The generation of the Exodus had received the good news of the gospel, but they disobeyed and disbelieved. Their disbelief excluded them from the land of promise.

Hebrews 4:11 warns believers not to play around with God's promise. They must receive his promise in faith and obey it in daily life. Those who wandered in the wilderness rejected God's promise. The readers of Hebrews must avoid imitating their evil example.

God gives his message readily to us in Scripture. We can choose to obey it, or we can ignore it and live our lives as if God's wishes do not matter. We must choose to live our lives with a faith commitment to Jesus as our Savior. Having chosen to follow him, we must take up our cross of obedience each day and live in whatever calling he has given us. To do anything less involves both disbelief and disobedience.

The challenge to obey is not merely a challenge limited to the generation who read Hebrews for the first time. It is a trumpet call we must continually obey as well.

C. The Authorship of Scripture (v. 7)

Hebrews 3:7 quotes Psalm 95:7b and cites the Holy Spirit as the author. Hebrews 4:7 refers to the same passage and names David as the author. Comparing these two quotations brings out the combination of the divine and human in producing Scripture. Ultimately God, speaking through the Holy Spirit, is the author of all Scripture. Because he is the author, he speaks to us through the content of Scripture.

To write Scripture, God worked through human beings. David may have spoken the words, but the authority of God lay behind them. The Hebrew Old Testament did not designate a human author for Psalm 95. The Greek Old Testament cited David as the author.

The important feature of the quote in 4:7, however, is that God still offered a rest to his people. God speaking through the Holy Spirit in David's writings was showing that the rest promised to those who fell in the wilderness was still available for the readers of Hebrews. This fact was not merely the opinion of the author of Hebrews; it was a statement from the Holy Spirit.

Sometimes people will respond to our use of Scripture with the accusation, "That is just your opinion." It is important for us to communicate that when we correctly interpret Scripture, we are not merely expressing our opinions. We are explaining the message of God (1 Thess. 2:13).

D. Joshua and Jesus (v. 8)

The KJV reading of 4:8 speaks about Jesus' giving rest to his people. The NIV translation of the same verse speaks about Joshua's giving rest to his people.

The Hebrew name *Joshua* and the Greek name *Jesus* both carry the meaning of "Savior." Whenever the New Testament refers to the great Old Testament leader Joshua, it uses the same Greek word as it uses to refer to Jesus. In Acts 7:45, Stephen was clearly describing Joshua and not Jesus. The term translated as **Joshua** uses the same Greek word as those passages which refer to Jesus.

Almost all interpreters agree that Hebrews 4:8 contrasts Joshua's failure to lead the Israelites to rest with Jesus' promise to provide rest for his people. Joshua tried to bring the Israelites to a temporal rest. Jesus provided his people with true rest.

Early Christians saw a typological relationship between Joshua, who tried to lead his people into earthly Canaan, and Jesus, who led his people into a heavenly inheritance. Typology finds a divinely intended relationship between the events of the Old Testament and those of the New Testament.

In Jesus we have a great high priest whose understanding and grace far exceed the abilities of the earthly Joshua. Jesus has a position in the presence of the Father in heaven. He can feel and understand our weaknesses. He overcame a barrage of temptations without falling into sin. Our great high priest Jesus gives us strength which Joshua could never have given to his people.

E. The Word of God (v. 12)

Word of God appears in Scripture with two meanings. First, it describes God's personal revelation in Jesus Christ. Both John 1:14 and Revelation 19:13 refer to Jesus as the "Word." The idea is that Jesus is God's personal message to human beings.

Second, the term also refers to the word which God spoke or communicated in some way. The idea probably was suggested by frequent references to a word or message from God appearing in 3:7,15,16; 4:2,7. God's message includes Scripture, but it is wider than Scripture. God has spoken to his people **at many times and in various ways** (Heb. 1:1). This would include the miracles (Exod. 14:13–14), visions (Exod. 33:11–23), and dreams (Matt. 1:20–25) of the Bible as well as its words.

God's Word is alive, powerful, and penetrating. It diagnoses our needs and points us to God's power. It discloses the condition of our hearts. It demands our obedient response.

Today God is still speaking to us through Scripture. We must turn to Scripture with a conviction that it contains a message from God to be obeyed and followed. Through Scripture God will offer comfort, provide insight, produce warnings, and present promises. Our experience with Scripture will show us that **the word of God is living and active.**

F. The Heavens (v. 14)

Does **the heavens** refer to the Jewish idea of a series of heavens? Paul spoke of "the third heaven" in 2 Corinthians 12:2. Some church fathers spoke of seven heavens. Jews thought in terms of a succession of heavens. However, this idea of a succession of heavens is not likely what Paul meant.

Both in the Old and the New Testaments the term for "heaven" is plural. The author of Hebrews was probably giving a general reference to the ascension and exaltation as events in Jesus' life by which he passed through the heavens to appear in God's presence. In his ascension and exaltation, Christ passed from the lower world (earth) through the middle world (the heavens) to the higher world (God's presence).

Hebrews 8:1–2 speaks of Christ as being seated at the **right hand of the throne of the Majesty in heaven.** This verse associates the **heavens** with Christ's priestly work. Hebrews 7:26 presents Christ as our **high priest . . . exalted above the heavens.** The heavenly position of Christ qualifies him to be our high priest.

Christ was exalted through the heavens to appear in God's presence. Earthly high priests entered the Holy of Holies of the tabernacle once a year to appear in God's presence for the sins of the people and for their own sins (Heb. 9:7). Christ is constantly in the presence of the Father dealing only with our sins because he himself had no sin. With a helper like Jesus representing us in God's presence, we stand a chance of holding **firmly to the faith we profess.**

G. The Temptations of Christ (v. 15)

Translations of verse 15 often differ on how to understand the temptations of Jesus. The NIV says that Jesus **has been tempted in every way, just as we are.** This means that Jesus experienced the full range of temptations we face. The NEB (New English Bible) speaks of Christ as one who **because of his likeness to us, has been tested every way, only without sin.** These translators understood that Jesus' nature was a human nature like our own.

This was one of those passages in which the uncertainty of the meaning of the Greek left translators with a question about their wording. The translators face a choice like the one in the following sentence: "GODIS-NOWHERE."

Does the statement mean that "God is now here," an affirmation of faith? Or does it mean that "God is nowhere," a hopeless affirmation of atheism?

Fortunately in Hebrews 4:15 we have some additional guidance. It seems more likely that the phrase **in every way** refers to Jesus' temptation and that the phrase **just as we are** picks up on that statement to affirm that Jesus was **tempted in every way, just as we are.** We find much comfort in being reminded that Jesus' experience of temptation matched our own. With an experienced Savior such as Jesus we are encouraged to come into his presence with boldness and **confidence** to claim the **mercy** and **grace** which we desperately need.

H. Throne of Grace (v. 16)

What is the **throne of grace**? Some see it as a reference to Jesus, who is our high priest. Those who follow this interpretation emphasize that God has exalted him to his right hand, and those who come to Jesus receive his help **in time of need.**

Others see this as a reference to the mercy seat of the earthly tabernacle. The writer of Hebrews mentions this object in 9:5 (NIV translation is **atonement cover**). In the act of offering sacrifice, Aaron sprinkled blood on the mercy seat (Lev. 16:14). The mercy seat was the location in the tabernacle before which God offered grace through the high priest to his people during the Old Testament era.

It is probably best to take the **throne of grace** as God's heavenly throne. Christ sits upon this throne at the right hand of the Father (Heb. 1:3). Christians who come before this throne enter into the very presence of God. Here God offers them all the mercy and strength which they need for making a timely response to life's crises and trials.

All three of the preceding interpretations emphasize the availability of God's grace for struggling Christians. The most straightforward interpretation is to see this as God's throne where he freely gives grace to wavering believers.

VII. TEACHING OUTLINE

A. INTRODUCTION

1. Lead Story: Sealing the Driveway
2. Context: The first three chapters of Hebrews show that Jesus was superior to the prophets, to angels, and to Moses. Chapter 4 shows that Christ was superior to Joshua.

First, Christ is superior to Joshua because he led his people to rest (vv. 1–10). Joshua tried to lead the Israelites to rest, but they did not follow his leadership in faith (vv. 1–2). God still offers rest to his people. Believers can enter that rest, and it remains for us who live today to claim this rest (vv. 3–5). Those who enter God's rest enjoy peace with God made possible by Christ's complete work on the cross (vv. 6–10). We can enjoy that rest now, and we can also expect more complete enjoyment in the life beyond with the Lord in heaven.

Second, Christ is superior to Joshua because his message provided a superior diagnosis (vv. 11–13). The message which God makes available through Christ is alive, powerful, and life giving. This message diagnoses our needs and points to a solution for our weakness and failure. God's message exposes our failures. What we need is an advocate with God who can bring pardon and mercy to us despite our failure.

Third, Christ is superior to Joshua because he offered a superior experience of grace and mercy (vv. 14–16). Christ has entered God's very presence. He has faced all the varieties of trials which believers experience. Jesus emerged victorious from everyone. We can enter God's presence and receive constant divine aid to meet our needs and to encourage our Christian walk.

3. Transition: Studying this chapter will provide access to God's help for three needs in our lives. First, we receive hope because God has given us a promise of rest. God has something ahead for us much greater than we now understand. Those who labor and are burdened with life can find rest in Jesus.

Second, we receive a diagnosis of our need. God's message clearly shows our weaknesses and his solutions. This leaves the choice for obedience up to us.

Third, we receive a superior experience of divine grace and mercy. God's mercy provides forgiveness for our sin. God's grace provides strength for our daily walk.

B. COMMENTARY

1. A Superiority Promising Rest (vv. 1–10)
   a. A rest which must be claimed (vv. 1–2)
   b. A rest patterned after God's rest (vv. 3–5)
   c. A rest which still remained (vv. 6–10)
2. A Superior Experience of Diagnosing Our Needs (vv. 11–13)
3. A Superior Experience of Grace and Mercy (vv. 14–16)

C. CONCLUSION: TRUST THE ONE WITH EXPERIENCE

VIII. ISSUES FOR DISCUSSION

1. How does the warning not to fall short of God's rest affect your life and your experience of salvation?
2. What benefits do you receive by entering in and experiencing God's rest in Christ?
3. What does it mean when a person who has made a public profession of Christ as Savior and has worked effectively in the church suddenly disobeys Christ and expresses disbelief in him?
4. Describe the rest that remains for you.

Hebrews 5

Jesus Christ—Supremely Qualified to Show Compassion

"*It* is by enduring the common weaknesses and temptations of man's lot, not by yielding to them, that He has established His power not only to sympathize with His people but to bring them help, deliverance and victory."

F. F. Bruce

IN A NUTSHELL

Hebrews 5 outlines the general qualifications for the office of high priest in Israel, shows that Jesus possessed those qualifications, and begins a warning, concluded in Hebrews 6, about spiritual immaturity.

The task of the high priest was to represent sinful human beings before God. The high priest needed compassion for sinners and a divine appointment to office (5:1–4). Jesus met these requirements for a high priest (5:5–10). His resurrection and ascension showed that God had appointed him to the job. His experience of suffering nurtured in him an incomparable capacity for sympathy to needy individuals.

Readers of Hebrews may fail to benefit from Jesus' compassion and strength (5:11–14) by being **slow to learn** *the importance of following Jesus. They may remain spiritual infants when they should stretch toward maturity. They may be untrained in choosing between good and evil.*

Jesus Christ—Supremely Qualified to Show Compassion

I. INTRODUCTION

The Healing Power of Compassion

In 1990, Betty Whitson was serving as a missionary in the African nation of Tanzania. The spread of AIDS had decimated and separated thousands of families in the country. Betty learned of a baby orphaned by the death of her mother with AIDS. The family and friends had virtually abandoned the infant from fear of contracting the disease.

Betty journeyed to the hospital in which the child had been born and found the ten-month-old girl abandoned and weighing barely two pounds. She and other members from her church in Bukoba took the child, cared for her, and held a funeral when she died three days later.

A woman in the same ward watched this demonstration of compassion and approached Betty with the question, "Would you care for my baby if I die?" Betty and the church accepted this plea for help. They cared for the weakened mother, who was virtually starving to death. African hospitals often do not supply food to patients, and family members must bring it to them. This woman's family was so afraid of developing AIDS that they had not brought her food. Church members brought her food and comfort. They later buried first the baby and then the mother.

Word of what Betty and the church had done reached the home village of the second woman. A group of men visited the Baptist church at Bukoba to say, "We've never seen such love. Would you come to our village and start a church to teach us about this kind of love?"

Compassion met the needs of sick, weakened victims of AIDS. In so doing, Christian compassion pried open a door for the gospel. Such compassion follows the example of Jesus.

The author of Hebrews began this chapter by describing the office of high priest in Israel. He pointed out that the task of the high priest was to act for human beings **in matters related to God** (v.1). Each high priest of Israel received a divine appointment to office. The office required that he show compassion for wandering sinners and offer sacrifices for sins.

Jesus demonstrated his qualifications to serve as High Priest for his people. Jesus did not follow the steps of the imperfect priesthood of Aaron. He became a priest after the order of Melchizedek.

Even with Jesus as their High Priest, all was not well with the readers of Hebrews. There were three elements to their spiritual immaturity. First, they were **slow to learn** (v. 11). Second, they had failed to rise to the level of instructing others (v. 12), needing again to learn the **elementary truths of God's word** (v. 12). Third, they needed to develop the skills to distinguish good from bad and to follow the good (v. 14). They had dabbled so long in mediocrity that they had become content with this level.

Reading this chapter will give us a broader picture of Jesus' marvelous ability to show compassion to wandering, weary sinners. It will also provide a warning against spiritual dullness and careless living.

II. COMMENTARY

Jesus Christ—Supremely Qualified to Show Compassion

MAIN IDEA: *Christ has supreme qualifications to serve as our high priest.*

A The Office of the High Priest (vv. 1–4)

SUPPORTING IDEA: *God called the high priest to offer sacrifices for sinful human beings.*

5:1. The work of Christ in 4:14–16 involved providing grace and mercy to struggling sinners. This was the work of a high priest. This verse explains how a high priest functioned.

First, the high priest represented people before God. No angel could do this job. No superhuman need apply. This job required a man who could understand and feel the pain and guilt of sinners.

Second, the high priest was **selected.** God made the choice. God never intended that the office of high priest be filled by democratic selection. He designated his own person. Sadly, in the time of Christ the high priesthood had become a political prize, often going to the highest bidder. This description was of the work of the high priest in its Old Testament intention.

Third, the high priest served **in matters related to God.** He was a mediator who represented God to men and men to God.

Fourth, he offered **gifts and sacrifices for sins.** The terms **gifts** and **sacrifices** refers to the full range of offerings which the high priest presented to God. This included both meal offerings and the blood sacrifices. The high priest officiated in relation to human sins. He dealt with any hindrance which separated human beings from God. The special time in which he did this was annually on the Day of Atonement.

5:2. This verse moves from a general discussion of the qualifications of the high priest to a focus on the personal dimension. The high priest needed an ability to **deal gently with those who are ignorant and are going astray.** The verb **deal gently** (*metriopathein*) describes one who found a middle course between indifference to need and anger at sin. A true high priest was not harsh toward sinners or calloused toward moral lapses.

The high priests in the line of Aaron had a feeling for sinners because they were **subject to weakness.** The high priest was clothed with the weaknesses of his people. Although Jesus was a human being, he was not surrounded with weakness. Jesus himself was never **ignorant** or **going astray,** but he understood those who were.

The special objects of the high priest's concern were those who were nuisances in most societies. Most societies make no provision to care for those who stray through their ignorance. These straying people were very conscious of their need. The high priest had a special ministry with them.

Consider the weakness of Aaron, who gave a feeble excuse to Moses for yielding to the people's demands for a visible god to worship. His words were, "They gave me the gold, and I threw it into the fire, and out came this calf" (Exod. 32:24). A man like this could certainly understand human weakness, for he was weak himself. However, it required a Savior like Jesus Christ to deal effectively with human sinfulness.

Some years ago I was associate pastor at a church when the pastor became ill on Saturday evening and called to tell me, "You'll be preaching tomorrow." I quickly pulled together some thoughts and ideas from recent seminary classes and fed the congregation the next day with a sermon orthodox in theology but lacking in application.

On the Monday after my sermon, the recently retired pastor of the church—still a member of the congregation—made a special visit to my office. "Young man," he said, "preach to their needs." His advice was sound. God's Word speaks to the needs of people who stumble and bungle through life. We must not omit practical application for struggling Christians as we expound the theology of Scripture.

5:3. A high priest with a weakness like Aaron had to present a sin offering first for himself and then for the people to whom he ministered. Leviticus 16:6 prescribed Aaron's offering of a bull for his own sins before he proceeded to the rituals for the people.

Christ shared with the high priests a common human nature and an experience of physical pain and hardship. The cross itself showed that physical pain.

Christ stood in contrast with the high priests in that his physical weakness did not produce sin. Since he had no sin, he did not need to offer a sacrifice for himself. When he did make an offering, he did not offer an animal, but he gave himself. He was able to focus entirely on dealing with **the sins of the people.**

5:4. Another important qualification for the office of high priest is the call of God to the office. No human being could assume the office of high priest. The Bible records disasters in those instances when human beings assumed the right to perform priestly duties (see Saul in 1 Sam. 13:8–15; Uzziah in 2 Chr. 26:16–21).

Aaron had received a call to the office of high priest (Exod. 28:1–4). His successors received a divine appointment to office (Num. 20:22–29). God called Christ **to be high priest in the order of Melchizedek** (v. 10).

Jews who read these words would know that for centuries the office of high priest in Judaism had been filled by the whim of human rulers. The will of God and descent from Aaron were no longer concerns to the kings who made these appointments. The writer of Hebrews did not mention this issue, but he focused on the ideal role of the high priest. Many a Jew reading these words could agree that the succession of greedy, immoral high priests they knew had brought the nation to spiritual ruin. They could long for the kind of high priest which the writer of Hebrews described.

B Christ's Qualifications for High Priest (vv. 5–10)

SUPPORTING IDEA: *Christ's ability to sympathize with sinners and his call from God qualify him to be our high priest.*

1. Called by God (vv. 5–6)

5:5. This is the first of six verses explaining the relationship between Christ and the order of Aaron and introducing the priesthood of Melchizedek.

The use of the name **Christ** instead of **Jesus** may emphasize that as Messiah, Jesus did not take the glory of the high priesthood on himself but received a divine call to the office (John 8:54). Psalm 2:7 is quoted to confirm Christ's appointment to the office of high priest. This psalm has already appeared in Hebrews 1:5 to present Christ's coronation. Paul used this same verse in Acts 13:33 to support the resurrection of Christ.

The psalm presents an exalted view of Christ. It narrates the coronation of a Jewish king. The psalm affirms that God had appointed Christ as a king. The act of the resurrection showed that God had orchestrated this event.

Christ had made it clear on earth that he regarded his work as a divine appointment (John 17:4). He had not sought out the job of high priest, nor had he refused it when God called him to this task. His assumption of the function came from a divine appointment. We can say, "Christ was performing the will of God."

5:6. This verse contains a quotation from Psalm 110:4, to establish the priestly role of Christ. Three features of this quotation are significant.

First, it contains a general formula. **In another place** refers generally to Scripture and shows that God spoke the words and uttered the appointment to office. Jesus found the authority for his words in Scripture.

Second, the priesthood of Christ differed from that of Aaron in that it was **forever.** Nothing about Christ's priesthood required improvement or change. It would last always.

Third, the priesthood of Christ was according to **the order of Melchizedek.** The significance of this order is explained in chapter 7.

Melchizedek was a mysterious Old Testament figure who appears only in Genesis 14:18–20. Abraham accepted the priestly ministry of this unusual leader. Melchizedek possessed a certain aura which seemed fitting for the exalted role which he represented. He was both a king and a priest (Gen. 14:18). Since Jesus was both king and priest, he had a likeness to Melchizedek. Although Jesus' role as Son was eternal, his function as high priest could not begin until his incarnation. Christ's priesthood served to reconcile sinners to a holy God.

Jesus belonged to the tribe of Judah, not the tribe of Levi from which priests descended (Heb. 7:14). If Jesus were to serve as high priest, it became necessary for him to serve as representative of a different order from that of Aaron. We will later learn more about the significance of the role of Melchizedek.

2. Demonstrating sympathy (vv. 7–10)

5:7. This and the following three verses show that Christ developed his ability to sympathize as he passed through testing and suffering. This happened during his days on earth and guaranteed that our Savior could identify with the weaknesses and problems of human beings. Christ himself was no stranger to hardship and affliction.

Some facts in this verse go beyond the statements of the rest of Scripture such as the reference to **loud cries and tears.** This was probably a description of Jesus' experience in Gethsemane (Matt. 26:36–46).

The two words used to describe prayer demonstrate Jesus' identification with his people. **Prayers** (*deeseis*) is the most general New Testament term for prayer. **Petitions** (*iketerias*) appears only here in the New Testament. It shows a strong element of entreating God. Still, we should be careful not to find too much difference in meaning between the two terms.

Jesus prayed to God, who was able deliver him out of death. Since Jesus did die, we find ourselves asking, "In what sense did God hear his prayers?"

Scholars have supplied two answers to this question. Some say that God heard the prayers of his Son in that Jesus fully accepted the divine will and pursued it (Matt. 26:42). In this interpretation God delivered Jesus from the fear of death. Another possible interpretation is that his prayer was not to be spared from dying but to be delivered from the consequences of death. This deliverance from death occurred in the resurrection. Either interpretation offers a biblical solution to the problem.

The fact that Jesus **was heard because of his reverent submission** may suggest that the Father heard Jesus' prayers because of his devotion to God's will. Because Jesus submitted himself to God's will, his prayer was heard in a far greater way than we would ever have imagined. God raised him from the dead in the glorious event of the resurrection and established him as Lord and Christ (Acts 2:36).

The fact that Jesus experienced the cup of death qualified him to sympathize with human beings all the better. In the wilderness temptations (Matt. 4:1–11), Jesus refused to appeal to angelic forces to rescue him. He saw the road of the Father's will and followed it without flinching. This caused him great suffering. It also enabled him to identify with the suffering of human beings. We have a merciful, sympathetic Savior.

Several years ago one of my relatives developed serious health problems that led me to grapple with some issues about prolonging life. What do you do to preserve quality of life in people with deteriorating health? As I considered this complex problem, I did not want advice from a teenager. Neither did I want someone in their early twenties who had never faced life and death issues in the family. I turned to a friend who had recently lost a loved one and who had grappled with issues of life and death. I wanted someone with experience. His own experience provided me insight, help, and encouragement.

We turn to Jesus for the same reason. He has experienced our trials, overcome them, and has the compassion to help us. It is a great blessing to have him as our Savior.

5:8. It would not be unusual for a son to learn obedience by suffering, but Jesus was no ordinary son. He was a perfect Son, and we could wonder why he needed to learn obedience. Certainly, he did not need to learn obedience in the sense that he learned the unpleasant consequences of disobedience. Jesus never disobeyed.

The connection of Jesus as subject of a verb involving learning raises a theological issue we must explore. Jesus shared in God's omniscience, that is, the ability to know everything. Why would the Omniscient One need to learn anything?

Luke explored a similar idea about Jesus in his youth: "And Jesus grew in wisdom and stature, and in favor with God and men" (Luke 2:52). Again we must ask, Why would the Omniscient One need to grow in wisdom? This question of how we could understand development, change, and learning in an omniscient deity has long troubled theologians.

One effort to deal with this issue has followed a special interpretation of Philippians 2:7, saying Jesus "emptied Himself, taking the form of a bond-servant" (NASB). These theologians, emphasizing the *kenosis* or self-emptying of Christ, have said that during his time on earth Jesus surrendered his attributes of omniscience, omnipotence (all power), and omnipresence (being everywhere at once). Opposing this interpretation is the recognition that if Jesus gave up the attributes of deity, he would cease to be God. Others have suggested that Jesus did not surrender the possession of the attributes, but he surrendered the right to use them independently. This feature of interpretation would explain why at times Jesus indicated that he did not know some things (Mark 13:32) but at other times claimed a knowledge which reflects omniscience (John 6:64). Jesus used his attribute of omniscience only when it was the Father's will for him to do so.

We should probably recognize that a divine mystery is involved in Jesus' learning obedience in Hebrews 5:8. It is difficult to understand why the divine Son would need to learn. It is understandable that one who was the God-man might grow in wisdom, understanding, and in a grasp of the importance of obedience. In a sense that we cannot fully comprehend, the incarnate son of God acquired knowledge through suffering that allowed him to learn the value of obedience.

Jesus always possessed the attitude of obedience, but by practicing obedience he learned the value and importance of obeying. By making a response of obedience to his testing, he acquired the experimental knowledge of obedience. He learned what was involved in following obedience. Learning this trait equipped him to understand better the struggles and weaknesses of human beings. It added to Jesus' skills in showing sympathy with wandering sinners.

This is the sole New Testament verse in which Jesus is the subject of the verb **learn**. Jesus came with a commitment to obey, but in obeying he learned a new level of experience in obedience. His example and experience encouraged both the readers of Hebrews and today's readers to persevere. We cannot experience a hardship in which he fails to identify with us.

Jerry Bedsole served for twenty-five years as a missionary veterinarian in Ethiopia. During his time in this famine-ravaged, politically unstable country, Bedsole saw loving Christians develop from former atheists. He saw God use a communist government to build his church. He watched in amazement as a Christian response to a famine in Ethiopia opened opportunities for spreading the gospel.

Bedsole saw an entire church, parents and children, imprisoned on one occasion for several weeks. That imprisoned church grew in love, fellowship, and eagerness to learn the Bible. He saw believers disowned by families, and persecuted by their friends and families, but they remained solid in their commitment. Bedsole said, "Their families may have turned their backs on them, but they never turned their backs on Jesus." These Christians learned the value of obeying God by their exposure to suffering. The encouragement from other believers and the strength of God taught them the importance of commitment. Jesus learned in the same way.

5:9. The fact that Jesus **learned obedience** perfected him. Jesus was perfect in that he possessed every qualification to be our High Priest. He also was perfect in that God glorified him with exaltation to his right hand.

Made perfect (*teleiotheis*) describes perfection in the sense of completeness or fulfillment. Jesus was obedient to God's will in that he endured suffering and death. In doing this Jesus brought God's redemptive purposes to their fulfillment or completion. By enduring suffering Jesus attained the goal the Father had for him. This enabled him to become a perfectly equipped high priest.

To say that Jesus was perfect does not suggest that he was imperfect before he suffered. During his human life Jesus' perfection endured severe testing. None of this testing blackened a single feature of his perfection. Jesus' perfection was the completion of someone who had faced trials, endured them, and learned to trust God through them. Jesus' perfection developed in an atmosphere in which he had his obedience tested and strengthened by the trials he faced.

After passing victoriously through suffering, Jesus became the **source of eternal salvation**. This phrase carries a meaning similar to **author of their salvation** in 2:10. Jesus' salvation is eternal because Christ accomplished salvation through a sacrifice which was thorough, effective, permanently valid, and never to be repeated or superseded.

Jesus' salvation applies only to those who obey him. The practice of obedience does not mean that only the morally perfect receive salvation. We obey the Lord when we accept his provisions for our salvation. Obedience is our acceptance of God's will. This response to salvation allows the privilege to be available to rich and poor, important and unimportant, Jews and Gentiles, and learned and uneducated. God's gift of salvation is open to all. The one who learned to obey made salvation available to all who obey.

5:10. This section closes with the announcement that God had designated Jesus to be a high priest in a new order, **the order of Melchizedek.** This statement added additional confirmation to the emphasis that Jesus served in this position through a divine appointment.

Several features of this order differed from the order of Aaron. First, the order of Melchizedek had no hereditary succession. This feature stood in contrast to the Aaronic order, which saw wave after wave of priests succeeding one another.

Second, it was a unique order because only Christ belonged to it. It was an order which was fit for Christ because it placed him in an entirely different order from that of Aaron.

We might expect the writer of Hebrews to plunge immediately into a discussion of the theme of Melchizedek, but instead he paused to consider some problems among his readers. Their spiritual immaturity was a serious concern to him, and he spent the final four verses of this chapter and most of the following chapter warning them of the dangers of their present attitude. When he finished this warning, he returned to explain more about the significance of Melchizedek in chapter 7.

C Giving Help to Fickle Followers (vv. 11–14)

> **SUPPORTING IDEA:** *Spiritual immaturity hinders effectiveness in serving Jesus.*

5:11 This verse explains the subject of Melchizedek's relationship to Christ as an issue which **is hard to explain.** This was not because it was an unfamiliar subject. It was because they were **slow to learn.** This phrase highlights their slackness and dullness.

The fact they were slow learners was their own fault. They were no longer capable of receiving solid instruction. They had closed their ears to God's message. Jeremiah's descriptions applied to them: "The word of the LORD is offensive to them; they find no pleasure in it" (Jer. 6:10).

Verses 12–13 describe the results of this dullness. Verse 14 outlines a solution ready and available if they will follow it.

5:12. The writer of Hebrews had spoken strong words against his readers. He now justified his weighty challenges.

First, he said, "You've been Christians long enough to be teachers, but you still need instruction in the ABCs." They should have been able to pass on their basic understanding of the Christian message to others. Instead, they needed a good review of the elementary matters themselves. Not only had they failed to move forward in their understanding; they had lost their grasp of the **elementary truths of God's word.** "If the dark things do not become plain then the plain things will become dark" (Thomas Hewitt).

Second, these believers were in need of **milk, not solid food!** The term *milk* represents a beginning level of instruction for Christians. The term solid food describes advanced instruction. Both the milk phase and the solid food phase were important and essential. However, someone who never reached the solid food stage was seriously defective.

As I write these words to you, I am looking forward to going home tonight and finding my two-month-old granddaughter in our house. She is spending her first night alone with us. She likes motion, varied colors, soft words, and milk. She can't walk, roll over, or talk. She can give heart-stealing glances at adoring grandparents. If she skipped this stage and bounced into this world as a rollicking teenager, something would be out of place. If fifteen years from now, she still could not walk, roll, or talk, we would be quite concerned. For now she is quite normal in her development.

The writer of Hebrews was concerned that his readers should be showing signs of Christian maturity. They were still caught up in issues only "baby" Christians found to be important.

5:13. This verse explains the meaning of the "milk" metaphor in verse 12. Three important features are mentioned.

First, those who lived on milk are called infants. The child should appear before the man, but grown men should not meet their nutritional needs on a diet of milk. No one should remain a child forever. Paul explained in 1 Corinthians 13:11 that "when I became a man, I put childish ways behind me." These believers needed to move out of spiritual infancy.

Second, those who lived on milk were described as **not acquainted with the teaching about righteousness.** The phrase **"not acquainted"** (*apeiros*) describes someone who lacked experience. They lacked this experience because they had failed to develop the skills which their conversion made available to them. The readers themselves were to blame for this stunted growth.

Third, commentators differ in their understanding of the **teaching about righteousness.** The term may be a general reference to the gospel. It may also take righteousness in the sense of that standing with God which faith in Christ brings (Rom. 3:21–26). The term may also refer to a lifestyle of upright behavior. A teaching which produces righteous behavior may have been intended. It may be best to combine all of these understandings and suggest that the intention was to describe a teaching about Jesus which produced right standing with God and caused upright living in daily behavior.

The hearts of these people were dull and disinterested. Their intellects were preoccupied and uninformed. "The intellect is not over-ready to entertain an idea that the heart finds unpalatable" (F. F. Bruce).

5:14. Babies must have milk. Their stomachs have not yet adjusted to the digestion required of solid food. Mature adults need the varied nutrition which solid food gives.

The readers of Hebrews were compared to babies who needed to learn again the elementary truths of God's Word. These truths involved the basic teachings of the gospel, particularly as seen in the Old Testament. The readers did not know and understand these truths because they had not applied themselves to them. The solution to this dilemma lay in developing their spiritual senses through practice.

The training they needed involved a steady application of spiritual discipline. Spiritual maturity would not develop primarily from a sudden burst of insight. It would come from dogged usage of spiritual resources.

God has given believers faculties to make spiritual judgments and to develop understanding. God gives Christians training in understanding (Heb. 12:11) so that it can produce **a harvest of righteousness and peace for those who have been trained by it** (Heb. 12:11).

Christians are able to distinguish between good and evil. The terms **good** and **evil** may have both a moral sense and a theological sense. Christians are those who can spot moral evil and avoid it. They can see moral good and attach themselves to it. Christians also can distinguish between true and false doctrine. They will turn aside from the false and faithfully follow the true. Living the Christian life demands the spiritual skills of stamina seen physically in a long-distance runner. Unswerving, relentless applications of Christian truth and practice will equip us for a lifetime of usefulness which will continue into eternity.

> **MAIN IDEA REVIEW:** *Christ has supreme qualifications to serve as our high priest.*

III. CONCLUSION

Someone to Show Me the Way

A few years ago a pastor friend brought me a manuscript describing a discipleship program for his church. He entitled it: "Someone to Show Me the Way." His belief was that we needed teachers who could show others how to share their faith in Christ.

God knew that we needed someone to show us the way to himself and to take us to him. What we needed was a high priest

What did an Old Testament high priest do? He represented human beings before God. He could deal compassionately with weak, struggling sinners who had lost their way. God gave him a special call to undertake this task.

Christ has all the qualifications to serve as our High Priest. God called him to the task by exalting him to his right hand in heaven. He put Jesus in enough places of suffering and hardship to develop in him an appreciation for the value of obedience. A High Priest like Jesus becomes the perfect source of God's salvation.

Sometimes, however, we simply do not use God's resources. We slip backward instead of marching forward. We ought to be able to teach others, but we need to receive new teaching ourselves. We ought to be mature followers of Christ, but we live like spiritual babies.

The solution is for us to come to Jesus; admit our faint, feeble efforts; and set our sights on the solid food of spiritual understanding and commitment. Once we start this path, we must endure on it. Those who develop spiritual stamina find that they will be "mature and complete, not lacking anything" (Jas. 1:4).

PRINCIPLES

- Jesus offers compassionate understanding to bungling believers.
- Jesus learned the value of obedience by enduring suffering.
- Jesus received a divine call to represent us before God.
- Christians who do not grow toward God slip backward into sin and ignorance.

APPLICATIONS

- Come to Jesus for the strength to overcome your weakness.
- Look to Jesus' example of obedience in suffering for inspiration and hope as you face hardship.
- Give Jesus your full obedience and attention because of his importance in God's plan.
- Stay constantly alert to distinguish good actions and beliefs from bad practices and teachings.

IV. LIFE APPLICATION

An Example Gives Us Courage

During the opening years of the Second World War, the superior military resources and surprise movements of the German armies almost succeeded in defeating the British and forcing them to surrender. British military and civilian forces found courage and strength to continue the fight as they listened to the eloquent, courageous speeches by Prime Minister Winston Churchill. In May 1940, just after becoming prime minister, Churchill told his countrymen: "I have nothing to offer but blood, toil, tears, and sweat."

In June 1940, the Royal Navy rescued 335,000 French and British soldiers from a triangular trap in Dunkirk, France. The army left behind all its equipment and saw 30,000 soldiers killed, wounded, or missing. In such a dark day, the British found courage when Churchill challenged them over the radio: "We shall not flag nor fail. We shall go on to the end. We shall fight in France and on the seas and oceans; we shall fight with growing confidence and growing strength in the air. We shall defend our island whatever the cost may be; we shall fight on beaches, landing grounds, in fields, in streets and on the hills. We shall never surrender."

Churchill's courage provided an example for his countrymen to imitate. It gave them an incentive to show more discipline and to work harder at the goal of stopping the German advance and preserving their country. It produced in them a stamina which they needed to resist the attacks of the enemy.

As Christians we need the courage to face the trials, sufferings, and difficulties of the Christian life. One source of help to provide us discipline and stamina is Jesus' own example and encouragement as he faced life's sufferings. On earth Jesus faced trials, misunderstandings, threats, rejections, and death. He faced these challenges with prayer, concern, submission, and unflinching commitment to God's will. **He learned obedience from what he suffered** (Heb. 5:8). Jesus' sterling example of stamina provides us a living picture to study and imitate.

Not only do we find help from Jesus' example, but we also have the reality of his encouragement. He can understand our weaknesses. He provides grace and strength to enable us to obey him. He is the **source of eternal salvation for all who obey him**. In a way in which Churchill could never provide encouragement for the British, Jesus lives to provide power, stamina, and discipline to his people.

As we face the challenge of Christian living, we must not imagine that all our difficulties will vanish if we become committed Christians. We can't pin our hopes on an anticipation that God will suddenly destroy all difficulties in our path and give us an easy road to follow. God will supply through Jesus the grace for us to travel the path he chooses for us to follow.

We need to commit ourselves to depend on Jesus for endurance in the Christian life. We can follow Jesus' example. We can experience his encouragement. As we respond to him, he can produce in us the stamina and steadfast commitment we will need to face the trials and sufferings of life.

Our need is to demonstrate discipline and tough-minded obedience. Jesus' example can enable us to develop this type of stamina.

V. PRAYER

Jesus, I want to face life with courage, faith, and stamina. I cannot do it alone. I trust you as my High Priest who has paid the price for my sins. I want to follow your example even if it means enduring suffering and shame. Help me endure faithfully through all life's trials. Thank you for your presence with me each day. Amen.

VI. DEEPER DISCOVERIES

A. Gifts and Sacrifices (v. 1)

Gifts (*dora*) is a general term used to describe the gifts offered to Jesus in Matthew 2:11 or sacrifices offered to God in Hebrews 9:9. **Sacrifices** (*thusias*) could describe a life offered to God in obedience (Rom. 12:1) or an offering given to God in worship (Heb. 7:27). Sometimes the two words occurred together (Heb. 8:3; 9:9).

Bible scholars differ in answering the question, "Do the words in Hebrews 5:1 refer to different types of sacrifices?" Some feel that the term **gifts** refers to meal offerings (Lev. 6:14–23) and the word **sacrifices** to blood offerings (Lev. 6:24–30). Others feel that the two terms make a general reference to all types of sacrifices offered to God, including both animal sacrifices and inanimate sacrifices.

In the original language, the writer of Hebrews spoke of offering **both gifts and sacrifices for sins.** The linking of these two terms with the conjunctions "both" and "and" suggests that the writer wanted to distinguish between them. When we find both words used together, it is likely that the first word describes meal, oil, or incense offered to God. The second word refers to animal sacrifices.

The emphasis was on the fact that a high priest dealt with all kinds of offerings to God for human sin. The fact that the high priest made these offerings repeatedly showed that their sacrifices were ineffective (Heb. 10:1–4). Jesus, however, offered one sacrifice, and **he has made perfect forever those who are being made holy** (Heb. 10:14).

B. Sins of Ignorance (v. 2)

The Old Testament made a distinction between a sin committed in ignorance and one done "defiantly" (Num. 15:28,30). When an individual sinned without knowing it, God imputed guilt, but he prescribed an offering through which the sinner could receive forgiveness (Lev. 5:17–19). The Old Testament made no provision for supplying mercy to the willful sinner.

The high priest had a special ministry of gentleness and concern for those who knew their weakness and failure. For those wanderers who wanted a way back to fellowship with God, a godly high priest could provide encouragement and strength.

The New Testament does not distinguish clearly between sins of ignorance and sins committed willfully. Hesitant, fearful sinners as well as stubborn, hard-headed sinners can find forgiveness in Jesus by repentance and faith. The promise that God "will forgive us our sins and purify us from all unrighteousness" (1 John 1:9) is available for all who confess their sins.

C. The High Priesthood (v. 4)

The hereditary office of the high priest was limited to descendants from Aaron (Exod. 29:29–30). Normally, the high priest served for life, but strong rulers sometimes deposed a high priest for political reasons (1 Kgs. 2:27).

The office of high priest required a special degree of holiness in the occupant (Lev. 21:10–15). He was to be totally dedicated to the Lord's service, ritually pure, and ready to do the Lord's bidding.

The high priest carried out general priestly duties, but he alone could enter the section of the Temple known as the Holy of Holies. He did this only on the Day of Atonement (Lev. 16:1–25).

The work of a priest also involved those known only as "priests" and the servants known as Levites. The priests were in charge of sacrifice and offering at the tabernacle and in the Temple. Unlike the high priest they could not enter the Holy of Holies. The Levites were primarily Temple personnel who assisted the priests in their work. They prepared the sacrifices and offerings, performed general maintenance in the Temple, and led in singing praises to the Lord during the time of the morning and evening offerings.

The office of high priest became increasingly a political plum in the years when the Syrian ruler Antiochus Epiphanes ruled Palestine (175–163 B.C.). Strong rulers made appointments to the office as part of political strategy. At times the office of high priest was combined with that of military commander or political leader. The Romans continued this practice when they controlled Palestine. The high priests Annas and Caiaphas, whose names appear in the Gospel accounts, held their offices by political appointment from the Roman government.

D. Melchizedek (v. 6)

This is the personal name of an Old Testament king mentioned in Genesis 14:18–20. His name means "king of righteousness." While returning from a battle against enemy kings, Abraham met Melchizedek. Abraham received blessings from Melchizedek and offered him tithes of all the goods he had captured in battle. Both men worshiped the one true God. Abraham also recognized Melchizedek's role as a priest.

Psalm 110:4 refers to one who would serve forever as a priest after the order of Melchizedek. This psalm teaches that the leader of God's people would reflect the role of both a king and a priest.

The priests descended from Aaron were of the tribe of Levi. Since this priesthood had not met the spiritual needs of the nation, God designated Christ as a priest after a new order, the order of Melchizedek. As a priest after this order, Jesus remained a priest continually (7:3), offered compassion and understanding to sinners, and offered himself as a sacrifice for sin (5:1–4).

E. Elementary Truths (v. 12)

The writer of Hebrews explained that his readers needed someone to explain for them the **elementary truths** (*stoixeia tes arxes*) of God's message. This term probably referred to the basic teaching of the gospel. It was sometimes used to denote the basic foundation of a thing or to describe the "elements" composing the earth (2 Pet. 3:10,12) or the "basic principles" of the world (Gal. 4:3,9) which bring human beings into bondage and sin.

These **elementary truths** may refer to the Old Testament background of the Christian message. The items of faith and belief mentioned as **elementary teachings** in 6:1 seem to refer more to Old Testament items which the readers failed to understand.

Believers who have known Christ for a time have the responsibility to pass on Christian truths to others. The writer of Hebrews was concerned that his readers not only were not teaching others but even needed to learn the basic truths again for themselves.

F. God's Word (v. 12)

God's Word (*logion tou theou*) literally means "the oracles of God." Often it refers to the Old Testament. In Acts 7:38 it describes the revelation given to Moses at Sinai. In Romans 3:2 it serves as a general reference to the Old Testament Scriptures. The term here refers to those general principles of the gospel which the Old Testament contained. These truths the readers had not mastered.

G. Teachers (v. 12)

The New Testament refers to "teachers" (*didaskaloi*) as a special office in the church (1 Cor. 12:28), limited to those who had the spiritual gift of teaching. The appearance of the term in this verse is probably not a reference to a special office but to a duty which all Christians should follow.

All Christians have a command from the Lord to assist in teaching the basic truths of Christianity to young believers (2 Tim. 2:2). Such teaching was not a formal type of communicating truth but may have taken place in private meetings, in homes, and in personal contacts which involve discipleship.

H. Infants (v. 13)

Many readers will remember the KJV translation—"a babe." Here the term (*nepios*) has a figurative use to describe anyone who is immature in Christian growth and development. The same word appears in 1 Corinthians 3:1 to describe worldly believers who quarreled, were slaves to jealousy, and followed human beings instead of Jesus.

In our passage **infant** stands in contrast to those who are **mature**. The mature (*teleion*) had developed their understanding so that they could distinguish between truth and error and between righteous living and ungodly living.

The **milk** the **infant** needed for development was the elementary teaching mentioned in verse 12. An example of this **milk** appears in 6:1–2. The writer counts the discussion about the priesthood of Melchizedek as **solid food**, which his readers desperately needed to understand in order to grow spiritually.

I. The Warning Passages (v. 11–14)

These verses begin the strongest warning passage we have yet found in Hebrews. Earlier passages in 2:1–4; 3:7–19; and 4:11–16 contained preliminary warnings to the readers. The warning in this section continues through 6:12. A final warning appears in 10:19–39.

The readers of Hebrews were exhorted to pay close attention to the voice of the living God. They were in danger of neglecting the salvation available in Christ or missing out on it because of unbelief, apostasy, or compromise.

This passage prods believers to pass from spiritual infancy to maturity (5:11–12; 6:1–2). They had produced fruit showing their salvation, but they needed to avoid laziness or carelessness in their Christian living (6:7–12).

These verses confront the question, Can believers lose their salvation? It is certainly true that professing believers can appear to lose their salvation. However, those who profess Christ and turn away from him show that their faith was never real. The distinctive evidence of vital Christianity is endurance (Heb. 3:14).

VII. TEACHING OUTLINE

A. INTRODUCTION

1. Lead Story: The Healing Power of Compassion
2. Context: Chapter 4 concludes with a reminder that Jesus is our high priest, tempted but victorious, sinless, and approachable. But what did a high priest do? How could Jesus serve effectively as our High Priest?

   The Office of High Priest (vv. 1–4). These verses describe the work and qualifications of the high priest (vv. 1–4). The task of the high priest was to represent human beings before God by dealing with their sin. To accomplish this job, the high priest needed a sense of compassion and a divine call to his job.

Christ as our High Priest (vv. 5–10). Christ had the two qualifications which every high priest needed. First, he had the divine call (vv. 5–6). God had named him a high priest **in the order of Melchizedek.** Second, his experience with suffering gave him a compassion for suffering sinners (vv. 7–10).

A Warning about Spiritual Immaturity (vv. 11–14). Although the readers of Hebrews desperately needed the priestly ministry of Christ, their spiritual condition made them **slow to learn.** They were able only to receive elementary teaching about spiritual truths. What they really needed was **solid food.** They needed to make a fresh commitment to grow from infancy to maturity.

3. Transition: Our study of this chapter reminds us of Christ's position in God's plan and of his compassion for us. We will find his understanding a source of strength in applying God's grace to our lives. As we face suffering and trials, the knowledge of his obedience can carry us forward in commitment. As we learn more about Christ's ability to garnish our lives with mercy and grace, we can grow from spiritual infancy to maturity in Christ. We can develop a discernment between beliefs and practices which are good and those which are evil.

B. COMMENTARY

1. The Office of the High Priest (vv. 1–4)
2. Christ's Qualifications for High Priest (vv. 5–10)
   a. Called by God (vv. 5–6)
   b. Demonstrating sympathy (vv. 7–10)
3. Giving Help to Fickle Followers (vv. 11–14)

C. CONCLUSION: AN EXAMPLE GIVES US COURAGE

VIII. ISSUES FOR DISCUSSION

1. Write a job description for the Jewish high priest. How did Jesus meet the qualifications? In what way did he surpass them?
2. What high priestly functions does Jesus perform for you now? Where would you be if Jesus did not function as high priest?
3. Are you teaching others the basic truths of the faith? Why? Why not?
4. What warnings does this passage set forth before your life? How do you respond?

Hebrews 6

The Urgency of Enduring

Quote

"*T*rue Christian faith . . . is manifested when apostasy does not occur. True Christians do not (i.e., cannot) apostatize. This is the urgent message of the author for his readers."

D o n a l d   A .   H a g n e r

Hebrews

I N   A   N U T S H E L L

*C*hapter 6 shows the urgency of enduring with faith in Jesus. It warns us not to claim allegiance to Christ without actually possessing this allegiance, urging us to repent of actions which lead to death (vv. 1–8). It points out evidence of real salvation, calling us to continue in our commitment (vv. 9–12). It provides encouragement to those who genuinely profess faith in Christ, encouraging us to endure patiently in receiving the promises just as Abraham had (vv. 13–20).

The Urgency of Enduring

I. INTRODUCTION

Hope for the Hopeless

In 1972, Tom Bentley's main goals in life were drinking and gambling. His alcohol abuse and compulsive gambling led to a nervous breakdown at twenty-nine. For three weeks he remained in a psychiatric ward of a North Carolina hospital. He faced a hopeless situation. One night in the depths of depression, Tom Bentley cried out, "God, if you'll let my mind come out of this, I'll get my life straight." Unknown to him, his wife of ten years, Muriel, had already been praying, "God, save Tom, whatever it takes."

Tom Bentley's change produced an attitude of hope to replace the cloud of hopelessness which had enveloped his life. Tom became a new creature in Christ Jesus. He became an effective employee. From 1978 to 1996, he worked faithfully as a maintainer of critical care equipment at a general hospital in North Carolina.

He helped others. He and his wife developed a strong ability to help young people battling alcohol and drugs. He transmitted his faith. Tom and Muriel passed their faith to their son, the Rev. Tim Bentley, who serves as a missionary to Kenya.

In 1996, Tom, at age fifty-three, resigned his hospital position to go to Accra, Ghana, where he and Muriel will serve as house parents for a youth hostel. They will care for children whose parents serve as missionaries elsewhere in Africa. When Tom announced his plans to leave the hospital, coworkers responded with a reception to show their affection for him. One fellow worker, security guard Alvin Houck, pulled out his handcuffs in a mock attempt to keep Bentley from leaving. "I want to keep him here," said Houck. "I'll miss Tom. He's my buddy."

Tom Bentley says, "My main motive is to go to people who have never heard his love and evangelize for Jesus Christ." He added, "Jesus gave his all for me, and I should try to share some of his love back to other folks."

Bentley's experience presents dramatic evidence of the hope which Jesus Christ can bring into a life. In Tom Bentley's life Jesus Christ produced changed character, a new purpose, and enduring stamina. Bentley's life now radiates ample evidence that Jesus lives within him. God has provided hope to replace the hopelessness which threatened to make ruin of his gifts and abilities.

The writer of Hebrews penned words of concern to friends who claimed to know Christ, but were retreating spiritually and falling into a deadly routine. He commended their past actions and called them to "imitate those who through faith and patience inherit what has been promised" (v. 12).

As we read this chapter, we will find strong warnings, words of encouragement, and a renewal of hope. These words encourage us to endure with faith in Jesus.

II. COMMENTARY

The Urgency of Enduring

MAIN IDEA: *God provides hope to help us endure in our faith commitment to Jesus.*

A The Danger of Profession without Possession (vv. 1–8)

SUPPORTING IDEA: *Believers must move beyond immature practices which lead to spiritual defeat.*

1. Profession of Faith and "Dead" Works (vv. 1–3)

6:1. Chapter 5 of Hebrews concludes by pointing out the immaturity of the readers. This verse describes what a mature believer must leave behind in growing beyond immaturity.

First, the verse presents an appeal with both a forward and a backward look. They were to **leave the elementary teachings about Christ**. These believers were to move beyond the initial understanding of Christianity with some similarities to Judaism. They were also to **go on to maturity**. They must desire the growth which only God could ultimately give them. They must escape from the doldrums of halfhearted commitment.

Second, six statements about elementary doctrine are presented. These statements called the readers to move courageously through them. The doctrines are grouped into three couplets. The first couplet included repentance and faith. The hearers were called to progress beyond teaching the need to repent of works which **lead to death**. Instead of involving themselves in dead works, they must respond in faith to God's provision in Christ.

We must settle forever the fact that we come to God by relying on the provision of Jesus. We cannot remain in a life of sin and disobedience. The readers of Hebrews may have dallied around with sin and may have avoided full commitment to Christ.

6:2. The next couplet of doctrines described external rituals. **Instruction about baptisms** referred to teaching about the importance of baptism or other types of washings familiar to Jews. Hebrew people often used ritual washings as a part of their spiritual routine. Perhaps the readers of Hebrews had lingered too long in reflecting on the importance of ritual washings in living the Christian life. **The laying on of hands** in the New Testament often related to the conferring of special gifts (see Acts 8:17; 13:3). The writer may have called his readers away from being absorbed in ritual matters with little spiritual impact for their lives.

He also called them to progress beyond such doctrinal matters as **the resurrection of the dead and eternal judgment.** Both the future resurrection and judgment are important Christian doctrines, but they should not be emphasized to the exclusion of further biblical understanding.

The six issues mentioned above contained important truths which Christians must understand. However, they were elementary truths. The writer of Hebrews wanted his readers to move beyond the elementary truths. Judaism had some of these same doctrines, and probably the readers did not differ greatly in their beliefs from non-Christian Jews. They were called to a mature understanding of Christian distinctives. They may have tried to live with a minimal Christian commitment to avoid alienating their friends. They needed to leap into the deep water of obedience and understanding.

6:3. The coming of Christ had provided a fresh understanding of some truths contained in the Old Testament. Doubtless the readers of Hebrews knew some of these truths. They could have yielded gradually to pressures to compromise out of fear of persecution. They could have surrendered Christian distinctives and yet have retained an interest in repentance, faith, religious washings, laying on of hands, the coming resurrection, and eternal judgment. If they abandoned Christ and mouthed an allegiance to the teachings of verses 1–2, they could expect no help from Christ. They needed to remain committed Christians and move toward maturity in teachings with a Christian distinctive. God wanted the maturity of his people. They needed God's help because this maturity would not come automatically. They must follow God's conditions. They were called to consider those conditions carefully.

2. A Warning to Those Who Merely Profess Their Faith (vv. 4–5)

6:4–5. Debates on these verses between Calvinists and Arminians have often produced more flame than insight. Many different interpretations of this passage appeal for your acceptance. Among these are:

(1) Some feel the passage teaches that a true Christian can become lost. Opposing this interpretation are those passages of Scripture which assure believers that God will keep them in security (John 6:39,40; 10:27–29; Rom. 11:29; Phil. 1:6; 1 Pet. 1:5). The writer of Hebrews did not attempt to write an essay on the security of the believer, but certainly he was not contradicting other inspired Scripture. Thus, we can conclude that he did not assert that Christians can lose their salvation.

(2) Others think the case discussed is purely hypothetical. The writer of Hebrews never says that this happened. Some interpreters feel that expressing the warning as a hypothetical case makes it more impressive. The urgent tone here makes it unlikely that the writer dealt only in hypothetical but unrealizable situations. The repetition of a similar warning in 10:26–31 seems to oppose any attempt to interpret this passage as hypothetical.

(3) Still others see the threat as consisting of a loss of rewards rather than a loss of salvation. They see the readers as disobedient Christians who might lose their reward and escape with a bare retention of salvation (1 Cor. 3:12–15). Against this interpretation is the recognition that the warnings in 6:7–8; 10:27 promise divine judgment. This seems to involve more than loss of rewards.

(4) Some feel that the readers of Hebrews were near Christians and not true Christians. They feel that the reference to tasting **the heavenly gift** and sharing **in the Holy Spirit** refer to some activities of "common grace" which both Christians and non-Christians could experience. They feel that tasting **the goodness of the word of God** can refer to an experience common to both Christians and non-Christians. They feel that repentance is an impossibility because their resistance to the gospel has built immunity against it.

(5) This writer feels that the author of Hebrews addressed his words to those who profess to be Christians and urges them to show their genuine profession by their refusal to apostatize. The writer spoke to the readers as Christians. He could not clearly evaluate their inward condition. If the readers turned from Christ to Judaism, they would show their profession of faith in Christ had been false. Not all his readers were alike. It would be possible for some of the readers to have true professions and for some to have had false professions. The writer of Hebrews spoke to all of them as if they were true Christians, not wanting to make the judgment himself. He urged them to show their real faith by endurance in their commitment.

Some professing believers seemed to be toying with the idea of a return to Judaism. The writer of Hebrews assumed that continuance in commitment to Christ demonstrated real Christianity. The readers had professed some experiences with Christ. If they turned away from him after this initial start, their desertion would show that they were not real Christians. They needed to understand the seriousness of what they were considering.

It was impossible to renew those who had enjoyed the experiences of verses 4–5 if they fell into apostasy. These were people who claimed to have real experiences with Jesus. They might have received an inoculation of something which resembled Christianity but was not the real thing. Only their endurance with Jesus would demonstrate that they had the real thing.

What experiences had the readers enjoyed? Verses 4–5 outline four events in their lives.

First, the readers claimed to have been **enlightened**. They had some revelation of Jesus Christ. The idea of enlightenment appears in 2 Corinthians 4:4, where unbelievers fail to see in Jesus "the light of the gospel."

Second, they had also **tasted the heavenly gift**. Probably this referred to the readers as people who claimed to have experienced a vital relationship with Jesus Christ (Ps. 34:8). They claimed to have faith in Christ. They were urged to demonstrate their faith by their works (v. 12).

Third, the readers had **shared in the Holy Spirit**. They had experienced some gifts, influences, and tugs from the Holy Spirit.

Fourth, they had **tasted the goodness of the word of God and the powers of the coming age**. Jesus himself had spoken of the day when some of his professing followers would say to him, "Lord, Lord, did we not prophesy in your name, and in your name drive out demons and perform many miracles?" (Matt. 7:22). Jesus would reply to these startled disciples, "I never knew you. Away from me, you evildoers" (Matt. 7:23). The readers enjoyed a sample of Christian experience, including a knowledge of the Christian message and some powerful experiences which seemed to be linked to the Holy Spirit.

The Scriptures offer encouragement to the weakest believer, but they declare alarming warnings to those who carelessly presume that they are on God's side. It is possible for an individual to approach the Word of God without any relish for its message. It is possible for a person to have something resembling Christian experience without genuinely knowing Christ. The readers of Hebrews were looking, sounding, and seeming to be like believers; but they were urged to show the reality of their faith by enduring in their commitment to Jesus.

3. The Consequences of Mere Profession of Faith (v. 6)

6:6. The severe warnings of this verse apply only to those who commit apostasy from Christ after having experienced an understanding of the gospel and some influences from Christ. The impossibility of restoration comes because those who turn away from Christ are guilty of **crucifying the Son of God all over again**. They also hold Jesus up for public contempt. The rejection of Christ after confessing him is an act of relentless hostility. The author of Hebrews condemned it as a condition from which a participant could not return to fellowship with God.

God will pardon all who truly repent. It is possible for human beings so to resist the grace of God that they arrive at a state of heart in which repentance is an impossibility. It is not impossible because God would not be willing to bring them to repentance, but it is impossible because the person is so hardened he will not repent. This condition is described in Romans 1:28.

People become so completely sinful that God gives them up to a reprobate heart.

The Bible promises that God will keep those who truly know him (John 10:28–29). It also reminds us that "man looks at the outward appearance, but the Lord looks at the heart" (1 Sam. 16:7). Those who claim to have known God but who finally turn away from him demonstrate that they never knew him. Hebrews 6:6 presents a strong warning to willful sinners that they cannot expect restoration to God after their adamant rejection of his mercy. No person with an attitude as contemptuous as the descriptions of these verses (vv. 4–6) need expect repentance. The self-hardening has produced "an impenetrable casing which removes all sensitivity to the pleadings of the Spirit" (Donald Guthrie).

4. A Comparison for Those Who Merely Profess Their Faith (vv. 7–8)

6:7–8. These verses use an agricultural illustration to present a spiritual truth. A farmer naturally expects that, given the right conditions of moisture and fertility, the land he cultivates will produce a crop. The fruitful ground responds to the conditions which God provides and produces useful results. The "thorny" ground shows that it is unworthy of God's blessings and produces thickets and briers. A harvest of weeds, thorns, and thistles is fit only for burning. This is a picture of final destruction.

This agricultural analogy also applies to the spiritual realm. Those people or groups who produce no "good fruit" demonstrate their barrenness. The image of "burning" suggests that divine judgment lay ahead for them. Those who produce fruit give evidence that they are receiving God's blessings. God will increase their productivity. Believers who persevere in faith are like fertile land and can expect further blessing from God. Those who profess Christ but turn from him and never produce credible evidence of commitment need the reminder that **God is a consuming fire** (Heb. 12:29).

B Evidences of Endurance (vv. 9–12)

SUPPORTING IDEA: *The Christian labor and love of the readers prove their genuine commitment to Christ.*

6:9. This verse moves from warning to encouragement. The writer of Hebrews offered a stern warning, but he hastened to assure the readers that he did not consider that his extreme description applied to them. He called them **dear friends** as an additional indication of his warmth and genuine hope for them. His statement **we are confident** used a Greek perfect tense which showed that his decision was not a "snap" judgment. He had reflected on his words, and he gave them with measured purpose. They needed to listen to his warning, but he was confident that their lives demonstrated **things that accompany salvation.**

His reference to **better things** as coming from them indicated that he expected them to enjoy a productive spiritual life. He was not looking for spiritual thorns and briers from them. He will name some of these **better things** in the next verse.

6:10. What had the readers of Hebrews done to make the writer **confident** that they were believers? The readers' works and God's justice convinced him that his friends had given a demonstration of divine grace.

First, he mentioned the **work** of the readers. They had labored in Jesus' name. Their works included concern for others, righteous living, and other Christian virtues. Hebrews 10:32–36 points out additional details of righteous living.

Second, he pointed out the **love** of the readers. They had ministered to other Christians in the past. They continued to follow this ministry. We see a past and a present participation in their ministry.

Third, he cited the justice of God. In the face of such overwhelming moral evidence, it seemed inconceivable to the writer that God would overlook the works and the love which were evident products of divine grace.

We should be careful not to see this verse as offering support for any doctrine of salvation by works. God had no obligation to the readers, nor did they have any claim on him. Their works were the normal fruit which we should expect from believers. We would expect that God would look with favor upon the evidence of transformed lives which they put out.

In 1979, Vladimir Bojev, a tough, hard-drinking Russian unbeliever, barged into a Baptist service in Russia and blustered, "I'm going to destroy you all. You are just religious fanatics." To his surprise a beautiful young lady suggested that the believers gather around him and pray for him. Bojev said, "The next thing I knew, I was the center of a prayer circle. I had never before known such love." The Baptists invited him back, and Vladimir returned to meet with the Baptists daily for two months. He received Christ, married the young lady, and became pastor of a Baptist church in Lipetsk, four hundred kilometers southwest of Moscow. Vladimir said, "Their love won me to Christ and I was converted." Transformed lives convince others that our Christianity is genuine. Transformed lives attract others to Jesus.

6:11–12. Having commended his readers for their good works and love, the writer of Hebrews now described what he wanted them to continue to do and not to do. He encouraged, and he warned.

First, he asked them to continue to show **this same diligence** so that they might make their **hope sure** (v. 11). The strong urging here to certify their hope suggests that at the moment they lacked assurance. They may have had love for other believers and yet lacked assurance for themselves. The writer made his wish personal by emphasizing that he wanted each of them to experience this assurance.

He made another positive emphasis in urging them to **imitate those who through faith and patience** inherit God's promises (v. 12). They needed to emerge from their spiritual doldrums and become followers of the heroes of the faith such as we find mentioned in chapter 11. To reach these goals, they needed to demonstrate a faith in God's provision to them and a patience which refused to quit under pressure. In Galatians 5:22 Paul listed both of these traits as fruits of the Spirit.

As a young Christian I had the privilege of being thrown in with several more mature Christians who wanted to help me in my Christian growth. These friends provided me with visible examples of faith in God, service to others, boldness in Christian witness, and stamina in the face of hardship. The friends we choose can make us or break us spiritually. The writer of Hebrews wanted his friends to imitate the right examples.

Second, he warned them not **to become lazy.** He used the same word which appeared in 5:11 with the translation of **slow to learn.** He wanted them to check their movement toward sluggishness. If they did not put a halt to their spiritual drifting, they would never reach full maturity. Even though the author of Hebrews thought well of his friends, he gave them warnings and encouragements to hasten their progress toward the goal of full maturity in Jesus.

Ⓒ Encouragement for Those Who Profess Christ (vv. 13–20)

> **SUPPORTING IDEA:** *God's steadfast promises encourage us to hold our Christian hope.*

6:13. Abraham is mentioned here to show the reliability of God's promises. If God's promises were reliable, then his followers can claim the hope which he promises.

God had confirmed his promise to Abraham with an oath. Genesis 22:16 claimed that God made a promise and supported it with his own personal oath. God found no one greater than himself to whom he could appeal in an oath. God's Word itself was a foundation strong enough for our trust and confidence. When God added an oath to his Word, the addition made the promise even more certain.

6:14–15. In Genesis 12:2–3 and again in 17:6–8 God had promised Abraham that his blessing would come on the patriarch and his descendants. Since Isaac was the child of promise, Abraham surely was startled at God's command to offer Isaac in sacrifice. After Abraham responded with obedience to the command, God reinforced the earlier promise with an oath (Gen. 22:17–18).

The promise to Abraham involved the multiplication of his offspring and the blessing of the nations of the world through his offspring. Abraham saw the multiplication of his offspring. The blessing of the world was accomplished in the redemptive work of Christ on the cross.

Abraham endured the challenges of the trial concerning Isaac. He became an outstanding example of someone who obtained his inheritance by faith and patience (see 6:12). Abraham himself provided a pattern which the readers of Hebrews could profitably imitate.

6:16–17. Human beings use oaths to back up their statements because the promise of a human being is not reliable enough for trust. Jesus urged his followers to be so truthful that human beings could trust their "yes" and "no" (Matt. 5:37). The writer of Hebrews followed normal human conventions of requiring an oath to support a promise. People who make official promises need to swear an oath by someone in order to settle the issue.

Why did God make an oath? A mere statement of his intentions was sufficient to provide a foundation for our trust. Human beings, however, respect the value of an oath. Catering to the needs of the human beings who heard his promise, God supported his word with an oath to **make the unchanging nature of his purpose very clear.** God's use of an oath supplied evidence no one could doubt.

Whenever human beings offer oaths, they swear **by someone greater than themselves.** Since God had no one greater than himself, he swore by himself. He based his oath on his own great name, guaranteeing he would accomplish his purpose.

Some Jewish opponents of Christianity may have suggested that Christian teaching was a departure from the promises that Israel anticipated. The Christian hope was a fulfillment of the promises God had earlier offered to Israel. What God had done through Christ was a necessary step for both Jews and Gentiles to make. The work of Christ was not a change from God's previously announced plans for Israel. It was the confirmation of the hope of blessing the nations which he had earlier given to Abraham (Gen. 22:17–18). The heirs of that promise were the writer and his readers, who experienced in the gospel the reality of the oath God swore to Abraham.

6:18–20. The strength of God's promise provided hope and encouragement for the readers of Hebrews. Where did they find this hope?

First, they found it in the complete trustworthiness of God's Word. When God—who cannot lie—supports his statement with an oath, his followers find hope and encouragement.

Second, they could find it through their own tenacity in seizing the hope that was available. Retaining hope demanded strong action. The readers had drifted along aimlessly. They needed to understand and grasp the promises the Father had offered them. They should flee to Christ for security and protection from the uncertainty of the world.

Third, they found it in a safe and secure anchor—Jesus, our High Priest. We have a firm basis for our hope because Jesus finished his work on earth and continues that work in heaven as our High Priest, carrying us into God's very presence. He has gone before us as a forerunner and is the assurance of our admission into God's presence. His prayers for his people guard the church (Heb. 7:25) and give believers the hope of future glorification. Christians find a basis for hope in the completed and continuing work of Jesus.

Fourth, they found it because Christ is our High Priest *forever*. The fact that we have access to God's presence **forever** gives us a firmness for our hope. This is a new idea. The next chapter of Hebrews develops the relationship of Christ as a priest to the priest Melchizedek.

In the summer of 1996, electric power outages twice hit the western United States when high demand and unfortunate accidents combined to trigger massive blackouts. The first failure affected two million customers in fourteen states on July 2. The second blackout affected four million homes in ten states. One spokesman for the power industry said, "Under no circumstance should this [a blackout] happen, let alone twice in one summer." But it happened. Customers wondered if they could trust their power suppliers when they could not provide uninterrupted service.

Jesus provides uninterrupted access to God's presence for his children. We will never have an outage of divine power. His presence before God fills us with hope, encouragement, and stamina. With the strength we receive from him we can find the staying power to endure in our Christian commitment. Let us rise up and claim our heritage!

MAIN IDEA REVIEW: *God provides hope to help us endure in our faith commitment to Jesus.*

III. CONCLUSION

Warning with Hope

Some years ago as a younger pastor I became impatient with what I saw as halfhearted commitment by active members of a church I pastored. My impatience reached a crescendo near Easter and led me to push aside a proposed Easter sermon to fashion a new message for my people. I pointed out their disobedience, the need for repentance, and a call for commitment. The message came over to most of my people as a strong denunciation with little hope of grace, mercy, and divine love. One of my members wrote me a letter implying that "you tore us down, but you didn't lift us up."

She was right! I had attacked, but I had not provided a solution. I had warned, but I had not pointed to mercy. I had censured, but I had not encouraged. The writer of Hebrews did not make this same mistake. He began with a strong, necessary warning to a band of lackadaisical, wavering believers. He called them to move beyond "dead" works to genuine stamina in their discipleship (vv. 1–3). He warned those who had merely "professed" their allegiance to Christ and were not demonstrating works (vv. 4–6). He compared those who had received divine blessings without producing fruit to worthless land which faced burning (vv. 7–8).

Then he provided words of encouragement. He commended the labor and love of his readers. He reminded them of a God who would **not forget your work** (v. 10), and he complimented their past and present assistance to troubled believers. What the readers truly needed was to continue **to show this same diligence** (v. 11).

He ended on a high note of hope. He encouraged them to produce fruits patiently by presenting Abraham as an example of patience and service (v. 15). He reminded them that God had both extended his word with the promise of a blessing and had sworn an oath to support his word. These expressions from a God who could not lie provided comfort, relief, and strength for the struggling readers (v. 18).

The author of Hebrews challenged the readers to take hold of the divine hope offered them and enter into God's very presence. Jesus was already there as their high priest, and he would provide them unlimited access to divine strength and power.

Sometimes people become so careless in their spiritual lives that only a shocking warning will get their attention. Anyone who turns away from Christ has no hope of entering God's presence. However, it is equally important to provide hope for those who will listen to this reprimand and turn to God. Jesus is able to save us completely **because he always lives to intercede for us** (7:25). He is able to keep us on a path of obedience. Which path are you traveling?

PRINCIPLES

- Professing believers who produce no evidence of conversion face God's judgment.
- God provides strength to lead us beyond elementary teaching to maturity.
- It is impossible to rekindle faith in those who deliberately turn from Christ.
- Good works provide a clear proof of genuine Christianity.
- We must imitate the lives of those who believed God's promises.
- God has promised his blessings to those who follow the hope he offers.

APPLICATIONS

- Do not linger on elementary issues of the Christian life.
- Resist all temptations to push Jesus back to a secondary place in your life.
- Provide an example of faithfulness for others to imitate.
- Enter God's very presence by claiming the hope we have in Jesus.

IV. LIFE APPLICATION

I Sure Could Use Some Hope

Several years ago Alice Pierce, a Christian language arts teacher at a California school, was traveling from Burbank to Sacramento. She had just spent three days with other women in a Bible conference. She was excited about rereading her notes and absorbing the truths in her material. As she read on the airplane, a man in his thirties sitting next to her asked, "What do you do?"

She answered, "I'm a speaker."

"What do you speak about?" came the question.

She answered, "Hope. I am a Christian, and I speak about the hope that Christians have in Christ Jesus."

The man looked Ms. Pierce in the face and said, "Lady, I sure could use some hope! My wife has left me for another man; my mother has been diagnosed with Alzheimer's disease; and I have just filed for bankruptcy in my business. Why don't you speak to me about hope?"

From Sacramento to Burbank, Alice Pierce told the inquiring stranger about the hope that Christians have in Jesus Christ, whatever their circumstances may be. Two things happened that day. First, a man heard a witness about Christ's power to inspire and provide hope. Second, a Christian woman came away thrilled with the opportunity to share with hungry people the hope which Jesus can give.

The writer of Hebrews had spoken firmly and trenchantly. He had told his readers how serious their problems were. He didn't leave his explanation there. He also encouraged his readers by presenting the eternal hope they have in Jesus. Jesus gives us entrance into God's very presence. Jesus prays for us. Jesus gives us fellowship with the Father. We can come to Jesus for mercy and grace to face life's needs. We all can use hope, day after day after day. Jesus is our only sure source of that hope.

V. PRAYER

Jesus, my High Priest, I come to your presence because I need God's presence. So many things lure me away from you. So many promise success. I inch along their path, then look back to you. You alone possess true hope. You alone understand my trials and troubles. You alone have eternal answers. I come to you. I trust in you. I will travel no other path. You are my anchor forever.

VI. DEEPER DISCOVERIES

A. Repentance (v. 1)

In the popular mind, repentance describes sorrow for sin. We can, however, be sorry for sin for the wrong reason. Our sorrow can come because someone caught us in the act of sin or because we feel humiliated by what we have done. True repentance is deeper than mere sorrow for sin.

Repentance is a spiritual and moral change of attitude toward God which turns an individual from sin to God. The act of repentance may cause sorrow, but it must cause a turning from sin. John the Baptist called his hearers to turn from sin to the true God (Matt. 3:7–12). The prodigal son repented when he abandoned the course which he had followed and returned to his father (Luke 15:17–19).

The **acts that lead to death** ("dead works") are evil deeds which leave an individual "dead in . . . transgressions and sins" (Eph. 2:1). For most Gentiles these works consist of immorality and idolatry. For Jews these works consist of self-righteous actions to gain favor with God. All such works call us to repentance, to trust in God to change our lifestyle.

B. Faith (v. 1)

Faith in God describes the positive act of reliance on divine promises which balances and accompanies the negative act of repentance. The two complementary acts form a unity, resembling the two faces of a coin. Both must be present in the experience of salvation. In this context faith is an act of turning toward God to receive new life in Jesus Christ. Faith in Christ is identical with faith in God.

C. Baptisms (v. 2)

Scholars struggle to understand whether the reference to **baptisms** discussed Christian baptism or Jewish ceremonial washings. In favor of regarding the reference as a discussion of Jewish practices is the fact that the word used for **baptisms** (*baptismon*) is not the common word used in the New Testament for the practice. In two other New Testament appearances, the term refers to Jewish ceremonial washings (Mark 7:4; Heb. 9:10). The Old Testament used the act of sprinkling with water as a symbol of the spiritual cleansing of God's people (Ezek. 36:25). Language similar to that of Ezekiel provided Jewish groups interested in spiritual washings the biblical authority to support their practices. The Qumran community from the Dead Sea observed ritual cleansings, but the practice was not common among early Christians.

The author of Hebrews may have been discussing instruction which contrasted Christian baptism with Jewish ritual washings. He may have been denying that his readers needed additional focus on these basic Christian practices.

D. Laying on of Hands (v. 2)

The act of laying on hands appeared in the Old Testament to commission someone for public office (Num. 27:18,23) or as part of a sacrificial ritual (Lev. 1:4). Jewish rabbis used the term to describe the ordination of someone to office.

Among Christians the practice referred to the laying on of hands to symbolize the giving of the Holy Spirit and the bestowal of gifts for ministry (Acts 8:17; 13:3; 19:6; 1 Tim. 4:14). Probably the reference in Hebrews described the giving of a blessing for all classes of Christians. Occasionally the laying on of hands symbolized the experience of healing (Acts 9:12; 28:8).

The readers of Hebrews were warned that instructions about the laying on of hands were of an elementary nature. Although the act symbolized truth important to Christians, these believers needed to move beyond the act and sample the reality of commitment to Jesus.

E. Resurrection of the Dead (v. 2)

Pharisees accepted the resurrection of the dead, but Sadducees rejected the idea. The discussion of this subject in Hebrews suggested that the readers were not Sadducees. For Christians the subject of the resurrection included also the resurrection of Jesus.

The doctrine of resurrection appeared in the Old Testament (Isa. 26:19; Dan. 12:2). The resurrection of Christ made the subject of special importance to Christians (1 Cor. 15:1–11). Paul regarded the subject of the resurrection of Christ as an issue of vital importance, and the writer of Hebrews was probably not suggesting that his readers needed to move beyond a concern about the resurrection of Christ.

Paul wrote that Christians in Thessalonica suffered confusion about the order of events related to the resurrection of believers (1 Thess. 4:13–18). He also mentioned false teaching on the issue given by a pair of heretics who troubled the church in Ephesus (2 Tim. 2:17–19).

Probably the readers of Hebrews had engaged in speculation about the timing of the event or the participants in the resurrection of the dead. They were urged to move beyond this immature preoccupation with divisive issues.

F. Eternal Judgment (v. 2)

Both Jews and Christians affirmed that the God of Israel was also the judge of all the earth (Gen. 18:25; Acts 17:31). Christians accepted the agent of God's judgment as "one like a son of man" (Dan. 7:13), whom they identified with Jesus (John 5:22,27). The reality of a final judgment was an important part of early Christian doctrine. A belief in future judgment made Christians aware of God's demands and became a factor in encouraging holy living (1 Cor. 15:29–34).

The writer of Hebrews warned his readers against remaining embroiled in debates about **eternal judgment.** They needed to move on to full commitment to Jesus. Contemporary Christians find it easy to become bogged down in debates about the number, timing, and significance of the events of judgment mentioned in the New Testament. The warning of Hebrews has great present relevance.

E. Tasting the Goodness of the Word of God (v. 5)

Probably the most important New Testament example to help us in understanding the experience of "tasting" is 1 Peter 2:3, which quotes Psalm 34:8. Peter's reference in that passage described an individual who had the experience of knowing and living with God's goodness. To taste **the goodness of the word of God** involved a profession of experiencing God in conversion. It suggested that the readers of Hebrews had claimed that they had responded to the gospel and knew the goodness that God showed to sinners.

Some commentators of Hebrews have tried to suggest that the experience of "tasting" comes short of claiming a full experience of God's grace in salvation. This term seems to be used to describe people who claimed that they had truly shared in God's blessings of acceptance and forgiveness. If these professing Christians should turn their backs on Jesus, this would demonstrate that their earlier profession was false.

H. Worthless (v. 8)

The author of Hebrews compared those believers who endure in their faith and produce fruit to fertile land which bears abundant crops. Those who never produce the evidence of righteousness are compared to land which never grew anything but weeds and thorns and is therefore **worthless.** The KJV translates the term **worthless** as "rejected."

The word translated **worthless** (*adokimos*) also appears in 1 Corinthians 9:27, where it describes someone disqualified from obtaining a prize or reward. In 2 Corinthians 13:5, the same word identifies someone who failed a test.

The word is used to picture those who claimed to be believers but presented no evidence. They could expect to confront the God who was a **consuming fire** (Heb. 12:29) in a future judgment.

I. Hope (vv. 18–19)

Hope represents an interest or desire in seeing a cherished goal fulfilled. Those who have strong hope have a better basis for expecting the fulfillment of a desire than those who have weak hope. Christians have a strong hope that they will receive the same blessings promised to Abraham (v. 14).

Three comments about hope appear in these verses. These believers needed to **take hold of . . . hope.** This represented an appeal to turn away from discouragement and halfheartedness. They needed to show urgency in clinging to Christ and avoiding apostasy.

Second, hope is compared to **an anchor.** An anchor was to remain fixed in the bed of the sea to hold a ship stable whatever the conditions of the sea. Their hope was **firm and secure,** and this fact would give confidence to wavering followers of Christ.

Third, our hope depends on Christ's priestly work. We have unlimited access to God's presence guaranteed by God's own servant who has entered God's presence on our behalf (v. 20). Christ's work as a perpetual High Priest provides us the hope that we also will receive divine blessings from God's presence.

VII. TEACHING OUTLINE

A. INTRODUCTION

1. Lead Story: Hope for the Hopeless
2. Context: Chapter 5 concludes with a warning about immaturity. These believers are described as **slow to learn,** with the implication that they were **infants.** They needed the **solid food** of strong doctrine and renewed commitment. They were urged to use their spiritual senses to **distinguish good from evil.** Chapter 6 expands upon this message and concludes with a description of Jesus as our **high priest.** *The Danger of Profession without Possession (vv. 1–8).* The author of Hebrews called on his readers to abandon their practice of works which **lead to death.** He gave one of the New Testament's strongest warnings to those who professed their faith in Christ without any

other evidence. He used an agricultural illustration to clarify the future expectation for those who produced no fruit in their spiritual lives.

Evidences of Enduring with Faith in Jesus (vv. 9–12). Despite his tough talk, the writer of Hebews assured his readers that he saw evidences of genuine Christianity in their lives. Their past and present practice of ministry to God's people provided evidence of their faith. He warned them against spiritual laziness and appealed for them to follow the examples of believers who endured in their faith.

Encouragement for Those who Profess Faith in Christ (vv. 13–20). Abraham patiently endured to receive God's promise of blessing. God had both offered his Word and supported it with an oath and promise to bless those who followed Abraham's faith. God's promise provides an anchor for our hope. Christ enters God's presence as our forerunner to nail down our experience of fellowship.

3. Transition: This chapter provided a vivid warning of the importance of demonstrating our faith with works which continue, endure, last. The God who saves us provides **faith and patience** so that we can inherit God's promises. Christ himself enters God's presence to offer effective prayer and ministry for us. With such powerful resources, we have no excuse for spiritual failure. Thank God for this strong warning against spiritual deception and laziness.

B. COMMENTARY

1. The Danger of Profession without Possession (vv. 1–8)
   a. Profession of faith and "dead" works (vv. 1–3)
   b. A warning to those who merely profess their faith (vv. 4–5)
   c. The consequences of mere profession of faith (v. 6)
   d. A comparison for those who merely profess their faith (vv. 7–8)
2. Evidences of Endurance (vv. 9–12)
3. Encouragement for Those Who Profess Christ (vv. 13–20)

C. CONCLUSION: I SURE COULD USE SOME HOPE

VIII. ISSUES FOR DISCUSSION

1. What elementary teachings do you and your church repeatedly discuss without advancing to the deeper things of the gospel? How do the warnings of Hebrews 6 apply to you?
2. Do you agree with this writer's description of the original audience of Hebrews? How would you modify or change that description? Does that description fit you and your church? How?

3. Describe your hope in Christ. How can that hope be strengthened? How does a strong hope affect your daily life?
4. What is required before a person reaches the state of not being able to be brought back to repentance? Can you know if a person has reached this state?

Hebrews 7

Safe in Jesus' Praying Hands

"*H*is once-completed self-offering is utterly acceptable. . . . His contact with the Father is immediate and unbroken; His priestly ministry on His people's behalf is never-ending, and therefore the salvation which He secures to them is absolute."

F . F . B r u c e

Hebrews

IN A NUTSHELL

*C*hapter 7 unpacks the significance of Jesus' priesthood and shows that Jesus' prayers for stumbling sinners guaranteed their complete salvation in his hands. Melchizedek (Gen. 14:18–20) was greater than Abraham and a type of a more effective priest than that of the Levites which had failed to provide for the spiritual needs of the people. God thus created an entirely new priesthood with new provisions to meet the needs of struggling sinners (vv. 12–14). Jesus' priesthood was superior because God's oath established Jesus' priesthood on an immovable foundation, because Jesus' priesthood lasted forever, and because Jesus' character provided purity and perfection for his people. With a high priest like Jesus praying carefully for us, we can enjoy complete salvation and acceptance with God.

Safe in Jesus'
Praying Hands

I. INTRODUCTION

Living in Real Safety

A firm in Arlington, Texas, offers a new product for protection from tornadoes known as "Safe-N-Side," a huge steel cocoon that promises to prevent the mayhem of a tornado from hurting you. It serves as an emergency in-home shelter for someone trying to hide from a storm.

Alan Weaver, manufacturer and promoter of the half-inch-thick steel boxes, was running a landscaping business in Lancaster, Texas, in 1994 when a tornado devastated the town. Debris tossed about like paper toys crashed down on helpless human beings. Many suffered serious injuries.

Weaver reasoned that people would be willing to pay for a steel box that could protect them from hard-hitting storms. The shelter comes with a light and a telephone jack. Each box is forty inches high and twenty-seven inches deep. His smallest model is twenty-seven inches long and holds a single adult. A forty-eight-inch long jumbo box holds two adults and two children. A burglar can't get inside the box. Laboratory tests show that a bullet from most handguns can't penetrate the steel. A two-by-four moving at one hundred mph can't make a hole in the box.

Obtaining this peace of mind is not cheap. The small model sells for $1,678. The large model goes for $1,985. That would be a small price, indeed, if it saved you from one of nature's most terrifying dangers.

As we face the storms of life, we need protection from harm, affliction, and compromise. We need help, encouragement, and stamina. We need to know that though we stumble, we "will not fall, for the LORD upholds" us "with his hand" (Ps. 37:24).

For the storms of nature, Weaver's box offers a great deal more protection than most homes have. For the storms of life, your deepest need is for the protection of a Savior who prays for you and loves you despite your sin and need. The Lord Jesus **is able to save completely those who come to God through him, because he always lives to intercede for them** (Heb. 7:25).

We desperately need spiritual safety. In Jesus we have a High Priest who takes us into God's presence. Jesus himself provides holiness and purity. He persistently prays for us. His ministry to us is permanent. His character operating for us is without sin or blemish. We could not be in better hands than to be in the praying hands of Jesus. With Jesus as our Savior and Lord, we can live in real safety.

II. COMMENTARY

Safe in Jesus' Praying Hands

MAIN IDEA: *In Jesus God has provided struggling sinners better access to him than Old Testament believers ever had.*

A A Biblical Example of a Perfect High Priest (vv. 1–10)

SUPPORTING IDEA: *Believers have a priest who gives us constant access to God.*

1. Evidence from Scripture (vv. 1–3)

7:1. Hebrews 5:6 quotes Psalm 110:4 to introduce the idea of Jesus' priesthood patterned after Melchizedek. Now 7:1 refers to Genesis 14:18–20, the only other Old Testament passage using the name Melchizedek. After a victory over four invading kings from the east (Gen. 14:1–16), Abraham headed home with his nephew Lot, whom he had rescued from a kidnapping. They carried the plunder received as the rewards of battle. The king of Sodom came out to propose that Abraham might return the captured people to him but retain the spoils of battle. Abraham refused to retain anything because he had just sworn an oath to "God Most High, Creator of heaven and earth" (Gen. 14:22).

Just before the king of Sodom offered his proposal to Abraham, Melchizedek had come out to meet Abraham. He brought Abraham bread and wine and blessed him. In response to Melchizedek's blessing, Abraham offered him tithes of all his spoils.

Melchizedek **was king of Salem**, which the author will interpret in verse 2, and **priest of God Most High** (see Gen. 14:18). Nations outside of Israel often combined the roles of king and priest in a single person. Among the Jews the role of king remained separate from the office of priest. The combination of kingship and priesthood in one person becomes important in the interpretations of verses 2–3.

Like Abraham, Melchizedek worshiped the one true God. In Melchizedek, Abraham met face-to-face with his superior, and Melchizedek blessed Abraham in a way which only a greater person could do.

7:2. Abraham's tithe was a form of thank offering to God for victory in battle (Gen. 28:22). Abraham's offering of a tithe showed the superiority of Melchizedek and his right to receive it.

Melchizedek's name carried the meaning, **king of righteousness**. Jews attached great importance to the meaning of names and would find this type of exegesis of special interest. The idea of "righteousness" would also be an appropriate description of the nature of Jesus as our High Priest.

Salem was another name for Jerusalem in Psalm 76:2. Salem is related to the Hebrew *shalom* and refers to "peace," so Melchizedek is **king of peace**. In Ephesians 2:14 Paul designated Christ as **our peace**. Hebrews shows the significance of peace in Christ's work. Jesus' work introduced positive blessing for lost, struggling human beings. As a priest, Jesus justifies all who trust in his atoning sacrifice (Rom. 3:26).

7:3. The insights of this verse are based on the silence of Scripture rather than on its explicit statements. Because the Scripture did not mention the birth or death of Melchizedek, he was **without father or mother, without genealogy**. This trait of Melchizedek resembled Jesus who, because he lived eternally, had **a permanent priesthood** (Heb. 7:24). Melchizedek was **without beginning of days or end of life**.

If we take the statements literally, we might conclude that Melchizedek was a heavenly being. The entire argument of Hebrews concerning Melchizedek assumed that he was a human being who resembled Christ in several ways. To the writer of Hebrews, the silences of Scripture were inspired as well as its direct statements. This verse does not claim that the priest-king Melchizedek appeared on earth without parents or a family. Melchizedek was a mortal human being. The silence of Scripture about his birth, death, and genealogy was a type which resembled the eternal priesthood of Christ.

The information about Melchizedek is presented in such an unusual way that it has led scholars to view him as something besides a normal human being. Some view him as an angelic being. Others see him as a preincarnate form of Jesus Christ appearing during Abraham's lifetime. Since the role of angels is prominent in Hebrews (1:5–14), the author of Hebrews probably would have designated Melchizedek as an angel if he had been one. Hebrews 7:3 describes him as **like the Son of God**, a statement the author would not have made if Melchizedek were Jesus Christ in a preincarnate state. Melchizedek was simply a mortal man who in many ways resembled and prefigured the Son of God.

Historically, Melchizedek appears to have belonged to a succession of priest-kings and had both predecessors and successors. In comparing the priesthood of Melchizedek to that of the Son of God, Hebrews makes the priesthood of Jesus the standard. Melchizedek is like Jesus, the Son of God. The record about Melchizedek was arranged so that it demonstrated some truths which applied more fully to Jesus than to Melchizedek. Melchizedek was a figure of Christ, but Christ was the reality.

In his humanity Jesus Christ had a human mother and a human genealogy and birth. As the Son of God, he remains the same eternally, and his years will never end (Heb. 1:12).

The silence of Scripture about the succession to Melchizedek suggested that he had a permanent priesthood. In the timelessness of his priesthood, Melchizedek resembled the Son of God. In the case of Christ, his nature guaranteed his perpetuity. The fulfillment in Jesus was more glorious than the type in Melchizedek.

The text of Hebrews uses typological exegesis in explaining the significance of Jesus' priesthood. For an earlier usage of typological exegesis in Hebrews, see the discussion under Deeper Discoveries in chapter 3 entitled "The New Exodus." Since Melchizedek was king of righteousness and king of peace, he is described as a type of Christ. Melchizedek anticipated or represented beforehand the broader peace and greater righteousness Christ would provide for his people.

2. The Proof of His Greatness (vv. 4–10)

SUPPORTING IDEA: *The greatness of Melchizedek provided a symbol of our great access to God.*

7:4. This verse repeats his emphasis on Melchizedek's greatness, this strange priest-king from Salem. No one could dispute the greatness of Abraham. Jews saw him as the father of Israel. Christians saw him as the "father of all who believe" (Rom. 4:11). The writer of Hebrews designated Abraham as **the patriarch.** In the original language the word for "patriarch" ended the verse, a position of emphasis. The text declares, "It was our patriarch Abraham himself who gave the tithe." The great Abraham gave his tithe to the even greater Melchizedek.

7:5–6a. The Law provided that the people should pay tithes to the Levites (Num. 18:21,24). The Levites paid tithes to the priests, so that we could actually say that the people paid tithes to the priests (Num. 18:26–32). The people who paid the tithes in the Old Testament and the priests who received them were **brothers.** The priests receiving the tithes were not superior to the payees. They were kin to them. Their ability to collect tithes did not come from any inherent superiority but from the commandment in the Law.

Melchizedek, however, was different. He did not receive tithes from any special commandment in the Law but from his inherent superiority. Abraham's spontaneous action implied Melchizedek's superiority.

Melchizedek did not trace his lineage from Levi. He was not a brother to the Levites. He stood out as a lonely figure of grandeur. He did not receive tithes from his brothers, but from Abraham. Abraham's willing surrender of a tenth of his spoils to Melchizedek further revealed the majesty of this mysterious priest.

7:6b–7. Melchizedek not only received tithes from Abraham, but he also blessed the patriarch. The act of blessing showed the acceptance of the implied superiority. Anyone who read the account in the Old Testament would see this principle without additional explanation. Abraham acknowledged the greatness of Melchizedek by accepting the blessing from him. Jewish readers would perceive that **the lesser person is blessed by the greater.**

7:8. This verse draws from the silence of Scripture to undergird Melchizedek's greatness. The Levitical priesthood is contrasted with the priesthood of Melchizedek. The Old Testament priests were mortal men. After a few years of service to God, they would die. Melchizedek, however, served in a priesthood which enjoyed a continual existence. Records show the death of generation after generation of Levitical priests, but not of Melchizedek. Levites transferred their position and duties to their heirs. Israelites paid tithes to these mortals. Abraham paid his tithes to one whom Scripture never showed to be anything except a living person. Scripture's silence could thus be seen as a type representing the eternal priesthood of Christ.

Hebrews will show that Jesus lived forever by his statements in 7:16,24. The Bible recorded that Christ died and rose again from the dead. He is now alive for eternity. The doctrine is made practical with the observations of 7:23–25.

7:9–10. One final piece of evidence testifies to the superiority of Melchizedek to that of the Levitical priests. In one sense we might say that even Levi paid tithes to Melchizedek. The writer of Hebrews prepared his readers that his argument would take an unusual twist with his statement, **One might even say.** It is almost as if he said, "Do not press this too literally." His argument would carry more force to a Jew familiar with the concept of solidarity or unity of purpose and interest than to a twentieth-century American emphasizing individuality. The idea is that neither the father nor the children would be independent of one another. Levi here is more than an individual. He served as ancestor and representative of the Jewish priesthood.

Since Levi was Abraham's great-grandson and was unborn when Abraham met Melchizedek, he could be described as already in Abraham's loins. Biblical thought accepted the idea that an ancestor contained within himself all of his descendants.

Although Levi had not yet been born when Abraham paid the tithes, we could view him as paying tithes to Melchizedek by this manner of reckoning. The payment of tithes by Abraham could be transferred to his offspring Levi and to all the priesthood. If we view the statement from the standpoint of solidarity, the payment of tithes by Levi through Abraham becomes more evident than Levi's right to receive tithes from others. If Levi paid the tithes to Melchizedek, this demonstrates even more clearly the superiority of Melchizedek.

In these seven verses are listed four evidences of the greatness of the priesthood of Melchizedek:

1. Abraham gave him tithes.
2. Melchizedek blessed Abraham.
3. Melchizedek had an eternal priesthood.
4. Levi paid tithes to Melchizedek through Abraham.

B The Necessity of a New Priesthood (vv. 11–14)

> **SUPPORTING IDEA:** *The Old Testament methods of providing for God's people did not produce holiness in them.*

1. The Failure of the Levitical Priesthood (v. 11)

7:11. While Melchizedek was a superior personality, this would not establish him as a successor to Aaron. Someone could object that the priesthood of Aaron was established and respected. Aaron's priesthood had to be replaced because it could not produce godly character in its followers. The Levitical priesthood could not lead sinners to their God. Such a poor product demanded a complete new order of priesthood.

Psalm 110:4 showed the inability of the Levitical priesthood. They were so inept that God established another order of priesthood to replace them. Jews would understand this argument well, and the type of thought presented here suggests that Hebrews was written primarily for Jewish people.

Perfection here contains two assumptions. First, it assumes that **perfection** is a desirable experience with God. The longings of God's people in Hebrews 11:13–16 showed that the Old Testament saints had longed to know God. Second, it assumes that the Levitical priesthood could not lead its participants to produce this perfection. The Levitical system provided a means for imperfect people to approach God, but it could not provide them victory over their sin. At best, it could only expose the sin (Heb. 10:3).

2. The Change of Priesthood (7:12–14)

7:12. Our writer saw that a different priesthood demanded a different law. God's designation of the order of priesthood after Melchizedek abolished the meaningless ceremonies of the Levitical priests. Even with a change in the law, Christianity stands in continuity with what God had long ago promised to do. We cannot understand the significance of Christ and his work unless we see the temporary status of the Law.

A **change of the priesthood** describes more than the transfer of the office from one person to another. An entirely new kind of priesthood was appearing, disclosing a fundamental difference between the priesthood of Melchizedek and that of Aaron and the Levites.

The priesthood of Aaron and the Levites developed under the Mosaic Law. If the Levitical priesthood were temporary, then the Law supporting it must also be temporary. Paul also felt that the Law was a temporary provision (Gal. 3:24–25). The designation of the Messiah as a High Priest after the order of Melchizedek implied that the new priestly order had replaced the old order of Aaron.

7:13. Anticipating that someone would say, "Jesus can't be superior to Aaron because he did not come from a priestly tribe," Hebrews designated Jesus as a priest even though no one who served as a priest had ever come from Jesus' tribe, the tribe of Judah. Jews would surely feel that the ministry of Christ could never take place at Jewish altars because he did not belong to a priestly tribe.

David and Solomon came from the royal tribe of Judah and offered sacrifices (2 Sam. 6:12–13; 1 Kgs. 3:4), but their offering was occasional and not their regular function. Only the tribe of Levi provided priests for serving at the altars during the Old Testament period. This sets the stage for declaring that Jesus became the High Priest of an entirely new order of priesthood despite his genealogical failure to descend from a priestly tribe.

7:14. Revelation 5:5 designates Jesus as a descendant of the tribe of Judah. The narrative in Matthew 2:6 assumes the same fact. The descent of Jesus from Judah was an acknowledged part of tradition. The genealogies in Matthew and Luke provide support for this.

Psalm 110:4 addresses the Messiah (see Matt. 22:41–46). Clearly the words of this psalm refer to Jesus. The psalm declares Jesus to be a priest after the order of Melchizedek. The writer of Hebrews found no precedent for this turn of events. He saw that the Levitical priesthood had been replaced by another order. Nothing that Moses had said in the Pentateuch had prepared for this change of events. This produced amazement at the uniqueness of the divine plan.

The greatness of Jesus' priesthood appeared in at least two features. First, Jesus was an eternal High Priest (7:8,16,24). Because Jesus was eternal, he always lived to pray for his people. Second, Jesus' high priestly ministry was effective not merely for earthly ordinances but also for heavenly realities. Jesus entered into heaven itself and carried on his work for us in God's presence (Heb. 9:24).

An eternal High Priest who can bring us to God! That is what we need. In Jesus that is what we have.

C The Superiority of the New Priesthood (vv. 15–28)

> **SUPPORTING IDEA:** *God's divine oath and Jesus' permanent priestly ministry and character provide a superior priesthood for believers today.*

1. Superior Because of God's Oath (vv. 15–22)

7:15. The failure of the old has established the necessity of a new priesthood. Verse 15 is based on two assumptions. First, the priesthood of Christ is accepted without dispute. Despite his origins from the tribe of Judah, Jesus had a right to the priestly office, a right transcending tribal qualifications.

Second, it is assumed that in Melchizedek we have evidence for an earlier priestly order accommodating the ministry of Christ. The priesthood of Melchizedek foreshadowed the priestly ministry of Christ in a way that Aaron's successors never did. Psalm 110 provides clear evidence that God had planned for another priestly order which had no connection with the laws of Moses. The spiritual ineffectiveness and temporary nature of the Levitical priesthood made the initiation of another priestly order a necessity.

7:16. This verse gives two contrasts between the priesthood of Aaron's successors and that of Christ in the order of Melchizedek. First, Christ became a priest through his personal moral power. A legal requirement established the successors of Aaron. This legal requirement could not guarantee that the individuals were morally worthy of assuming the office. Many of them demonstrated no inward personal power toward holiness. This was not true of Jesus Christ. His life, death, burial, resurrection, and ascension were a magnificent demonstration of vital power. No fleshly ordinance had established Christ as a priest, but he assumed the office due to his own personal power.

Second, Christ became a priest not because of genealogy or **ancestry**, but on the basis of a life which could never be destroyed. No mere regulation had installed Jesus in his position. The Law which established the Levitical priesthood was a system of earthly rules and only amounted to a **regulation as to his ancestry**. Death removed the descendants of Aaron from serving. Jesus continued forever because he was alive eternally. The Aaronic priesthood was temporary and ineffective, but the priesthood of Jesus was permanent and effective.

Jesus did experience death, but his resurrection presented him as indestructible. Jesus is able to continue his priestly ministry because of his resurrection and ascension into God's presence. Death could not restrain Jesus, nor did it destroy his priesthood. Jesus discharged his ministry for his people with a life which knew no destruction.

7:17. A renewed quotation of Psalm 110:4 (see 5:6) comes here because the word **forever** in the quotation supported the claim in verse 16 that a priest after the order of Melchizedek had **an indestructible life.** The priesthood of Aaron might continue throughout all generations (Exod. 40:15), but no individual priest lasted forever.

The fact that Psalm 110:4 was an oath provided a foundation for permanent security of Christ's priesthood. No oath from God will ever be revoked. We find nowhere a greater evidence of security. Jesus became the priest mentioned in Psalm 110:4 because he was the person described in Psalm 110:1. Jesus' own use of the psalm indicated his belief that it spoke of him (see Matt. 22:41–46).

7:18–19. Verse 18 shows the weakness of the Law, while verse 19 describes the new hope which Christ's priesthood provides. Verse 18 makes three statements about the Law and the priesthood connected with it: (1) weak, (2) useless, (3) annulled. The Law provided a standard by which a person could evaluate moral condition, but in its weakness it could not provide life and spiritual vigor to anyone. It was merely a diagnostic tool. It was useless because it could not provide a constant means of access to God. These two deficiencies made it necessary to set the Law aside.

This does not mean that the Law was annulled in that it no longer had any use. It served the function of revealing sin (Rom. 3:20), but it could not bring perfection. It could only demonstrate imperfection. It reminded sinners of their sin. The establishment of a new priesthood meant that the old Levitical priesthood no longer had divine authority. A new priesthood which could give power over sin had come into operation.

Verse 19 introduces a theme of hope (cf. 6:19). The hope Christ provided was better than the empty regulations of the Levitical priesthood and the commandments which produced it. Christ's priesthood made it possible for sinners to **draw near to God** (see 10:22 and often in Hebrews).

Wandering sinners seeking for God find much hope in Hebrews. The new priesthood of Melchizedek provided a foundation for such optimism. Believers can draw near to God even though **God is a consuming fire** (Heb. 12:29). Seekers can actually find God.

7:20–21. Hebrews 6:16–20 emphasizes the importance of God's oath in providing a more secure foundation for the divine promise to Abraham, while 7:20–22 emphasizes that God's oath provided a basis for a more secure covenant.

An important difference between the Aaronic priests and the priestly order of Melchizedek was God's oath that established the priesthood of Melchizedek. The Levitical order which Aaronic priests followed was based on the Law, but it did not include an oath. In establishing Aaron as a priest, God had simply commanded Aaron to assume the office (Exod. 28:1). The presence of an oath made the security and clear superiority of Melchizedek's priesthood doubly certain.

Verse 21b returns to Psalm 110:4 after verse 17 had quoted the oath there. Verse 21b refers to the first half of Psalm 110:4 to show that God's unchanging plan lay behind the priesthood of Melchizedek. Whenever God made a divine oath, he did not change his mind. Anyone who questioned the reality of this priesthood would have to contend with the mighty authority of God who had established the order.

7:22. This verse summarizes the discussion of the superiority of Jesus' priesthood. The oath God offered guaranteed that Jesus would provide a better and more secure covenant for his people.

The name *Jesus* appears last in the sentence, a position of emphasis clearly stating the importance of Jesus.

Jesus' character, his sacrifice, and the power of his resurrection pledge the strength of the new covenant. This is the first appearance of the term **covenant** in Hebrews. The word will play an important role in the discussions in coming chapters. The covenant was an arrangement by which God's purpose to save human beings became a reality. This new covenant depended on the saving work of Christ to accomplish its purpose.

The word **guarantee** appears nowhere else in the New Testament. Outside the New Testament it carried the meaning of a pledge or security for bail. Jesus himself provided a guarantee that God had provided a better covenant with a better hope.

The following chapter will discuss the content of the new covenant Jesus has introduced. The old covenant had links with the Law and the Levitical order. It had proven to be a failure in producing people of godly character. Because Jesus was a better High Priest, this new covenant introduced a better hope. Jesus' life provided strength for turning weak people into spiritual champions (see chapter 11). His death provided a basis for the acceptance by God of sinners into his family.

2. Superior Because of its Permanence (vv. 23–25)

7:23–24. The permanence of Jesus' high priesthood appears again (v. 17), this time emphasizing the contrast between the Levitical priests and Jesus. Aaron's line of priests had a multitude of members because **death prevented them from continuing in office.** For the Aaronic priests the office continued, but the person changed. The law of heredity guaranteed that some descendant of Aaron would fill the office. The successor, however, might lack the qualifications to intercede effectively with God for the people. A change in office might introduce an unqualified replacement. Not so with Jesus. He continued to fill the same office. In his holy hands the office of High Priest was permanently secure.

Jesus holds his priesthood without change. Although Jesus has died, his priesthood has continued to function. Jesus' death was not his cessation of being. His resurrection allowed him to live forever. His permanence stands in contrast with the transience of other priests. With Jesus nothing has changed. He still holds his office of priesthood. For eternity he knows and helps his people.

7:25. Jesus has a permanent high priesthood. As High Priest he prays always for his people. He pleads the cause of his people. The result of this priestly prayer is the salvation of his people. Because Jesus lives forever, he is able to save forever.

The word **completely** may mean that Jesus can save with totality or that he can save permanently. Either possibility supplies good meaning, but most commentators feel that here the emphasis is that Christ is able to save people entirely. Anyone who comes to God for salvation must come through Jesus, for salvation comes only through Christ.

3. Superior Because of Christ's Character (vv. 26–28)

7:26. This verse summarizes the qualities of an ideal high priest clearly seen in Jesus. Only those who come to God through Jesus can experience these qualities.

First, three personal traits describe the ideal high priest. The first refers to personal holiness. Jesus was a perfect accomplishment of all God required. No one could find in Jesus any deficiency or failure. The second word **blameless** describes Christ as innocent or without guilt. Jesus had no craftiness or malice. The third word **pure** refers to Jesus as having no moral contamination. These three words describe Jesus as having holiness by nature and also as remaining pure in all his contacts with sinful human beings.

Second, in relationship to human beings Jesus was **set apart from sinners.** Jesus was sinless, and this fact set him apart from sinful human beings. Jesus' service in the office of high priest also set him apart from other human beings. The holy High Priest can perfectly serve the needs of a sinful person to come to the holy God for salvation.

Third, despite Jesus' likeness to human beings, he nevertheless stands above them, for he was **exalted above the heavens.** Many New Testament passages, such as Philippians 2:9, underscore the exalted nature of Jesus. His exalted standing should cause us to appreciate more deeply the glory of his ministry.

A high priest like this fits our condition. He has experienced the complete force of temptation, and he has yielded to none of it. He has the perfect fitness to represent us before God and to secure our acceptance with God.

7:27. Jesus' superiority also appeared in that he did not need daily sacrifices for himself. The Aaronic high priests offered sacrifices first for themselves and then for the people. Since he was sinless, Christ did not need to offer any sacrifice for himself. He needed only to offer a single sacrifice once for all (Heb. 10:10). He offered himself for sinful human beings, and he needed to offer no repetition.

It may have been shocking at this point to introduce the idea that Jesus offered himself. No high priest offered himself. He offered a substitute animal sacrifice. The total unselfishness and commitment of Jesus appeared in his offering up of **himself.** Jesus had said that he came to offer his life a ransom for many (Mark 10:45). All who have come to Jesus for salvation have found him to be a powerful and sufficient Savior.

7:28. This verse summarizes the previous two verses concerning the appointment of the Levitical priests and the Melchizedek order. The Levitical order was appointed by the Law. The order of Melchizedek came by an oath. The difference between the two orders appeared in the character of the priest.

The Levitical order contained **men who are weak.** Priests did not come from any super race. They came from among ordinary people with all the weaknesses of human beings. The order of Melchizedek had as priest **the Son, who has been made perfect forever.** With a perfect High Priest like Jesus, Christians may approach God with confidence. Jesus' character guarantees our access.

The idea is not that Jesus first became perfect and then became High Priest. Jesus' nature was perfect from the beginning. He came to earth as a perfect High Priest. His earthly life was an exhibition of the moral perfection he always possessed. It is true that his suffering developed in him an ability to understand our needs and to become an even more effective Savior (Heb. 2:10). His eternal perfection allowed him to meet the needs of sinful, wandering human beings.

MAIN IDEA REVIEW: *In Jesus God provided struggling sinners better access to him than Old Testament believers ever had.*

III. CONCLUSION

Purity, Permanence, and Predominance

Purity, permanence, and predominance! These three features make Jesus a perfect representative for stumbling sinners. We need someone of spotless character and superior position to represent us before God with stability. Thank God. We have this in Jesus.

God appointed the house of Aaron from the tribe of Levi to represent his Old Testament people before him. The laws that Aaron and his priests administered could point out mistakes and sins, but they could not provide power for holy living. The priests who followed Aaron became greedy, immoral, self-centered, and powerless to help others. They could not help the people to practice godliness because they were not godly.

God saw this problem and gave us an entirely new representative. He established Jesus in a new priestly order patterned after an Old Testament priest-king named Melchizedek. In serving as our High Priest, Christ brought with him to the position a prominence and power enabling him to do a superb job. He assumed a position of predominance. He was God's Son. Just as the Old Testament priest-king Melchizedek received honor and recognition from Abraham (7:4–10), Christ received honor and glory from God's angels (Heb. 1:6). Jesus' greatness qualified him to be a great representative for us before God.

In serving as our High Priest, Christ also served permanently. The Aaronic high priests died generation after generation. Often the replacement for a priest was less godly than his predecessor. Just as Melchizedek remained a **priest forever,** Jesus serves us as priest forever. He has assumed a permanent priesthood, and he will never require a replacement. His permanent priesthood allowed him to give us the complete salvation we desperately need (Heb. 7:25). His permanent priesthood allows him to present himself one time for the sins of his people. His single sacrifice permanently accomplishes the job of bringing us to God.

In serving as our High Priest, Christ also brought with him purity. No one could uncover sin in Jesus. His own friends witnessed of him, "He committed no sin, and no deceit was found in his mouth" (1 Pet. 2:22). Even his enemies remained silent when he challenged them to point out sin in his life (John 8:46). Those who found fault with Jesus accused him of associating with sinners (Mark 2:15–17). We glory in Jesus' ability to heal people who are morally sick and make them righteous. In Jesus we have a Savior who is **holy, blameless, pure, set apart from sinners, exalted above the heavens** (Heb. 7:26).

Purity, permanence, predominance! These are the traits which we have in Jesus. This is the kind of high priest God gives us in Jesus. This is the kind of representative who can bring us into God's presence. This is the type of high priest who can produce other holy people.

PRINCIPLES

- In Jesus God has given us a great and powerful representative in his presence.
- The ministry of Old Testament priests did not produce godly people.
- Jesus' ministry for us is effective because it is permanent.
- Jesus' ministry for us is effective because Jesus has spotless character.

APPLICATIONS

- Offer praise and thanksgiving to God for the greatness of the ministry which Christ has for you.
- Find hope in the fact that Christ is able to save you completely (Heb. 7:25).
- Cast the burden of your failures on Christ because his sacrifice has paid for all your sins.
- Make no excuses for your own failures but claim strength and forgiveness from Christ to move forward in obedience.

IV. LIFE APPLICATION

Perfecting Imperfect People

"Nobody's perfect, preacher!" How many times have you heard this excuse? People use this excuse to cover up halfhearted commitment. They use it to explain their own lack of character or integrity. The excuse contains both truth and error.

It contains truth because the Bible reminds us that "there is no one righteous, not even one" (Rom. 3:10). All people, including both believers and nonbelievers, have a sinful nature and will fall into sin. There is much self-seeking in the best among us. There is meanness and dishonesty even in God's saints!

The statement contains error because we use it to cover up our own failure to obey. Instead of admitting our sins, confessing them to God, and repenting of them, we claim, "Nobody's perfect!" Somehow we think that this excuses our moral lameness.

Jesus is in the business of perfecting imperfect people. That's what his high priesthood is all about. Jesus' death has paid for all our sins. In God's presence he is praying for us. When we confess our failures and repent of our sin, God offers us forgiveness through Jesus. Confession, forgiveness, and repentance are processes through which God perfects imperfect people. The perfect sacrifice of Christ, his godly character, and his permanent prayers can take weak people and move them toward God.

Prison Fellowship is a ministry working among prison inmates and parolees to provide a service of Christian encouragement and challenge. Several years ago this ministry sponsored a dedication service for a chapel in a prison in Georgetown, Delaware. Local churches had contributed funds to build the chapel, and volunteers and inmates had done the work.

The chapel seated two hundred and seventy-five people and stood in the center of the prison yard. Surrounding it were drab cell blocks and razor wire.

The chapel represented God's invasion of a prison for the purpose of righteousness. It was an outpost of righteousness squarely in the middle of a place of punishment for lawlessness.

The lieutenant governor of Delaware attended the dedication of the chapel. Dignitaries from Georgetown, Delaware, participated. The prison chaplain introduced several prisoners who had already received help from the ministry. One of the most touching prisoner testimonies came from an inmate named Jim, who was serving life without parole.

Jim explained that volunteers had cared for him. He shared movingly what Jesus meant to him, and how he and his brothers were free, even in prison (John 8:31–36). He tried to control his emotions as he thanked local churches for supporting the building of the chapel.

Later the group adjourned to a local Methodist church for a supper meal and an evening service. The service celebrated a new community service project in which five prisoners were furloughed to restore a senior citizens' center and the home of an elderly retired couple. These inmates had lived in the homes of community people during a two-week period of work.

During the service the inmates spoke movingly about their experiences of living in community homes. The commissioner of corrections for Delaware's prisons sat wide-eyed as he listened to the testimonies. Hardened men, who would not dare weep in prison, choked up as they explained how much it meant to them to live with Christian families outside the prison.

At the end of the service the chaplain asked each of the host families to stand at the altar with their guest inmate. A little girl, six or seven years old, took the hand of the prisoner who had lived in her home. During the concluding prayer she looked up into his misty eyes. Others in the audience were touched by the significance of the evening.

The inmates in Delaware's prison were not perfect people. Their imperfections had landed them in the facility. Many of them had found Christ, and he was changing their lives. Christ was taking them as they were and changing them into what they could be.

The people who hosted the inmates were not perfect people. They were just ordinary Christian families willing to risk some privacy to give moral encouragement to prisoners. Christ had given them compassion. He was changing them into people who had love even for society's outcasts.

We have in Christ a Savior and High Priest who can take imperfect people and lead them to holiness. Christ prays for us. He offers forgiveness when we come to him with confession and repentance. He is eternally available to offer his encouragement and support. We have in Jesus a priest who can take us in our imperfections and make us what we should be.

V. PRAYER

Father, thank you again for Jesus, our perfect priest. Jesus, I confess my sins before you. I am imperfect. I need forgiveness. I depend on your prayers before the Father and on your death on the cross to atone for my sins. Now unholy as I am, I can draw near my holy God because you are my holy intercessor. Thank you, Jesus. Amen.

VI. DEEPER DISCOVERIES

A. Eternal Priesthood (v. 3)

This is the first of several verses in this chapter discussing the uninterrupted priesthood of Christ (see also vv. 16,21,23–25). This verse does not claim that the priest-king Melchizedek had no parents or family. He was a mortal human being. Our author took the silence of Scripture about his birth, death, and genealogy to be a type which resembled the eternal priesthood of Christ.

Levitical priests died and were replaced. Often the successor was not as godly as the predecessor. The successor did an inadequate job of representing the people before God. Not so with Jesus!

Jesus possessed **an indestructible life** (v. 16). He had an unending priesthood. He continually represented his people before God. Jesus has presented to God a perfect sacrifice for sins (v. 27). He brought to God a pure, spotless character. We could have no better representative before God.

With Jesus as our representative, we have a secure salvation. Jesus' prayers guarantee our growth, development, and complete salvation (v. 25). In Jesus we have a perfect representative before God, who without interruption serves as our representative and helper.

B. Tithes (v. 4)

The Old Testament laws commanded the practice of tithing for all the people of Israel except the tribe of Levi. The Levites received these tithes, whether they came from crops or livestock (Lev. 27:30,32; Num. 18:21–24). The special religious function of the Levites disqualified them from receiving any inheritance of territory (Deut. 10:8–9; 12:12).

Among the Levites the priestly office belonged to the descendants of Aaron. The remainder of the Levites assisted in maintaining the tabernacle and participating in its services. They also passed on a tithe of their income to the Aaronic priests for their needs (Num. 3:5–10; 18:1–7,25–32).

The first mention of tithing in Scripture occurred when Abraham gave a tithe of his spoils from battle to Melchizedek (Gen. 14:18–20). The writer of Hebrews understood this action as a display of respect by Abraham for

Melchizedek. He also took the action as an indication that the priesthood of Melchizedek was superior to that of Aaron.

C. Levi (vv. 5–7)

Levi was the third son of Jacob and Leah and the ancestor of the tribe of Israel bearing his name (Gen. 29:34; 35:23). He and his brother Simeon led out in violence against Shechem, the Hivite who assaulted their sister Dinah. They avenged the crime by killing all the males and spoiling the city of Shechem (Gen. 34:25–31). In his final blessing on his sons, Jacob mentioned this act of cruelty (Gen. 49:5–7). The descendants of Levi displayed this tribal characteristic by killing three thousand rebellious Israelites at Moses' order in the episode of the golden calf (Exod. 32:25–29).

All the Aaronic priests were descendants of Levi. The Law gave these priests the right to take a tithe from the people (Num. 18:26–30). Melchizedek, who had no right to receive tithes, received them spontaneously from Abraham. The text of Hebrews offers no explanation for Abraham's action, but it understands the action to be proof of the superiority of Melchizedek.

The Levites were descended from Abraham, but Melchizedek had no descent from Abraham and hence no connection with Levi. It was amazing that this obscure priest-king offered a blessing (v. 6) to a man like Abraham, who received promises from God. The greater person was the one who offered blessings to the less. The greatness of Melchizedek offered a suitable type of the greatness of Jesus as our eternal high priest (vv. 15–16).

D. Solidarity (vv. 9–10)

Americans live in a society which emphasizes individuality and personal rights. The biblical writers lived in a world which emphasized the idea of solidarity, the unity of individuals into groups with similar purpose, interest, and feelings.

The writer of Hebrews seized upon the idea of solidarity when he explained the relationship between Abraham and Levi. Jews would recognize that Levi was a descendant of Abraham. The payment of tithes to Melchizedek by Abraham could be transferred to his descendant Levi and to the entire order of priesthood.

Levi's payment of tithes carried more importance than his right to receive the tithes. The statement about Levi's payment of tithes carried weight only if we accept the idea of solidarity between Levi and Abraham.

Accepting the idea of solidarity is important today because we know that the actions of ancestors do have an influence on their descendants. We are not merely the product of our own choices, but we have also a linkage with the past. It is important for us to maintain an appreciation for our debt to the past and a sense of responsibility for our choices in the present. Accepting the concept of solidarity will help us appreciate our debt to the past.

E. Perfection (v. 11)

Perfection (*teleiosis*) appears only here in Hebrews, but it also appears in Luke 1:45. In Hebrews the term describes arriving at the goal God intended. The idea does not involve moral or ethical sinlessness, but refers to being brought to a place of completeness in connection with God's plan. The work of the Levitical priests aimed at bringing human beings into a position of acceptability with God. The Levitical priests failed; they did not bring God's plan to completion by their priestly ministries.

F. Aaron (v. 11)

Aaron was the oldest son of Amram and Jochebed (Exod. 6:20; 7:7). The genealogy in Exodus 6 suggested that Amram was a son of Kohath and thus a grandson of Levi (Exod. 6:18). Aaron's wife was Elisheba, sister of Naashon. They had four sons—Abihu, Nadab, Eleazar, and Ithamar (Exod. 6:23).

Aaron received no mention in God's plan until God brought him forward as someone who could speak for Moses (Exod. 4:14). He became associated with Moses in performing the powerful acts of the Exodus, but he had no part in receiving the Law from God. In establishing the priesthood in Israel, God decreed that the priests must be descendants of the family of Aaron (Exod. 29:29; Num. 20:25–28).

Aaron owed his important position in the life of the Israelites to his quick tongue and to his kinship with Moses. His compromise at the incident of the golden calf (Exod. 32:22–24) and in his disloyalty to Moses (Num. 12:1–8) showed him to be an untrustworthy leader who needed the support of his brother to accomplish his office.

G. Function of the Law (vv. 18–19)

These verses picture the Law as a weak and ineffective instrument. It could provide a standard for moral measurement, but it could not provide spiritual life to accomplish that standard. The Law could only draw attention to human imperfection. A priesthood emphasizing the Law carried with it the weaknesses which the Law contained. If the Law could not provide perfection and the power to approach God, what was its purpose?

Its purpose in God's plan of salvation was to make sinners conscious of their sin (Rom. 3:20). It could not make people righteous in God's sight, but listening to the Law could make sinners aware of their need. Those who understand their need and lostness will learn to turn to Christ for a solution (Gal. 3:22–24). A right understanding of the Law will prevent a person from trying to obtain right standing before God in any other way than by faith in the redeeming work of Jesus Christ.

H. Guarantee (v. 22)

Guarantee (*egguos*) appears only here in the New Testament. Outside the New Testament it appears in legal documents to describe a pledge or to refer to money deposited for bail. A father who agreed to the marriage of his daughter provided a pledge of his intention to permit the marriage in the form of a marriage dowry.

This verse discusses the covenant that God had instituted with man. Jesus himself was the guarantee that God would honor that covenant. The greatness of Jesus' person, the purity of his character, the thoroughness of his sacrifice, the power of his resurrection, and the superiority of his priestly work provided solid assurance that God would completely save sinners. The old covenant had Moses to serve as a mediator (Gal. 3:19), but it had no one to guarantee a fulfillment for sinners. Jesus became that guarantee. The new covenant offered a better hope, and because of Jesus it had a better High Priest.

I. Covenant (v. 22)

This is the first appearance of the term **covenant** or "testament" (*diatheke*) in Hebrews. It will become an important term in the following chapters. It is used more often in Hebrews (seventeen times) than in all the rest of the New Testament (sixteen times). Sometimes the word is used with the legal meaning of "testament" or "will" (see Heb. 9:16). The chief reference of the word is to an arrangement by which God carried out his saving work.

At Sinai the Israelites experienced an old covenant which aimed at redemption. This covenant did not make anything **perfect** (Heb. 7:19), and God inaugurated a new state of affairs (see Jer. 31:31–34). The new covenant (mentioned in Heb. 9:15) has now appeared in God's plan. It depended on Christ's saving work to carry out its promises. Because God based this new covenant on a better foundation, it would succeed where the old covenant had failed.

"Covenant" (*diatheke*) emphasized that God was in absolute control of the agreement. God has established the terms, and human beings cannot bargain or argue with him. God's sovereignty, however, is not a careless exercise of power. God established the new covenant because he wanted a method of guaranteeing the full salvation of sinners. Only a covenant grounded in Christ can provide such a guarantee.

J. Jesus' Intercession (v. 25)

Hebrews has already mentioned the sympathy and understanding of Jesus (2:18; 4:14–16). This verse states more clearly than other verses the active involvement of Christ in praying for his people.

The word used to describe Christ's prayers (*entugxainein*) appears only here in Hebrews, but four other times in the New Testament. It means to "turn to" or "to appeal." In Romans 8:27 the term refers to the Spirit's intercession for believers. In Romans 8:34 it refers to Christ's intercession for us. In Romans 11:2 Elijah appealed to God for help against an Israel that wanted to kill him. In Acts 25:24 the Jewish nation petitioned Festus for action against Paul.

Christ's ministry of intercession for his people is an outgrowth of the effectiveness of his earthly ministry. It also is an indication of his present activity for believers. In Luke 22:32 Jesus came to Simon Peter to say, "I have prayed for you, Simon, that your faith may not fail." Those words provide a sample of Jesus' prayers for believers during his time on earth. I believe that they also help us to understand how Jesus prays for us today. Jesus' prayers for Peter helped him endure the failure of denying Jesus and find usefulness as a leader in the early church. We have this same resource available for us today in Jesus' prayers for us.

As Christ prays for believers in heaven today, he presents himself on behalf of believers who have approached God through him. With such an introduction to God as this, believers will not fail to receive God's grace and help in their times of need. They will remain eternally safe in God's strong hands. Christ's intercession for us gives us secure hope.

VII. TEACHING OUTLINE

A. INTRODUCTION

1. Lead Story: Living in Real Safety
2. Context: Chapter 6 concludes by mentioning our need for a high priest and by presenting the obscure priest-king Melchizedek as a pattern for a high priest. Chapter 7 explains the typological meaning of Melchizedek's priesthood and shows how Christ has become our High Priest to bring us triumphantly into God's presence. Because Jesus exercises a constant ministry of prayer for us, we have hope, encouragement, and the assurance of reaching God.

   A Biblical Example of a Perfect High Priest (7:1–10). Melchizedek is presented as a high priest who continually remained to minister to his people. His name carried with it the suggestion of righteousness, and his receiving tithes from and offering blessings to Abraham showed his greatness.

The Necessity of a New Priesthood (7:11–14). Why did God's people require a new high priest? The Levitical priesthood could not bring the people to God (v. 11). This sad condition led God to establish Jesus as High Priest in a new order which could genuinely relate people to God (vv. 12–14).

The Superiority of the New Priesthood (7:15–28). Why was Jesus' priesthood for his people so important? God's oath to establish Jesus as a High Priest gave this office a stronger foundation (vv. 15–22). What God supported with an oath would become a reality. In Jesus we have a permanent priesthood, not one subject to change with the death of the priest (vv. 23–25). Finally, we have in Jesus a High Priest of superior character (vv. 26–28). Jesus is **holy, blameless, pure, and set apart from sinners**. With a high priest of this quality, believers have an unfailing supply of divine grace.

3. Transition: Some years ago my father was at the edge of a swimming pool teaching me how to jump from a small diving board into the pool. When a vigorous jump from the board sent me plunging toward the concrete bank, my father reached up, grabbed me with his strong hands, and set me gently down into the water. I was safe in his hands.

With Jesus as our High Priest, we have a strong, effective representative in God's presence. He is praying for us. He is pure and spotless in his character. He can pray for us in our weakness. He can pick us up when we stumble. We can always have access to his strength. As believers we find ourselves constantly safe in Jesus' praying hands.

B. COMMENTARY

1. A Biblical Example of a Perfect High Priest (vv. 1–10)
   a. Evidence from Scripture (vv. 1–3)
   b. The proof of his greatness (vv. 4–10)
2. The Necessity of a New Priesthood (vv. 11–14)
   a. The failure of the Levitical priesthood (v. 11)
   b. The change of priesthood (vv. 12–14)
3. The Superiority of the New Priesthood (vv. 15–28)
   a. Superior because of God's oath (vv. 15–22)
   b. Superior because of its permanence (vv. 23–25)
   c. Superior because of Christ's character (vv. 26–28)

C. CONCLUSION: PERFECTING IMPERFECT PEOPLE

VIII. ISSUES FOR DISCUSSION

1. How do you understand the nature of Melchizedek's priesthood? Why is it superior to Levi's or Aaron's? How is it suitable as a precursor of Jesus' high priesthood?
2. What kind of person do you need to pray for you before God? In what way does Jesus meet the qualifications?
3. What does Jesus need to pray for you? Have you asked him to do it?
4. Why were a new priesthood and a new covenant needed? Describe the new covenant.

Hebrews 8

A New Leader, a New Agreement—New Hope!

"*No* condemnation now I dread; Jesus, and all in Him is mine! Alive in Him, my living Head, and clothed in righteousness divine, Bold I approach th' eternal throne, and claim the crown, thro' Christ my own. Amazing love! how can it be that Thou, my God, should die for me!"

Charles Wesley

Hebrews

 I N   A   N U T S H E L L

In Jesus we have a High Priest who has offered an effective sacrifice for sin. In contrast with the earthly priests Jesus demonstrated effective service and provided a better covenant or agreement with God. God instituted the new covenant because the old was ineffective. The new covenant promised a new nature to obey God's law, a new knowledge of God, and the forgiveness of sin. The ineffectiveness of the old covenant rendered it useless, fit only to decay and disappear.

A New Leader, a New Agreement—New Hope!

I. INTRODUCTION

Hoping in God's Mercy

*J*ohn Wesley, founder of the Methodist Church, searched for many years to find assurance that God had forgiven and accepted him. He met people who had this experience, but he lacked it. He had sought assurance of forgiveness by working, praying, reading the Bible, attending church, and sacrificing. A stint as a missionary in Georgia in the 1730s brought him disillusionment. He returned from the trip with the observation, "I went to America to convert the Indians; but, oh, who shall convert me?"

After his return from Georgia, he continued to search for peace with God. Gradually it dawned on him that God would not be pleased with these feeble efforts to gain divine love. He began to spend time in the company of a group of earnest Christians known as Moravians. During his travels across the Atlantic Ocean, their devotion had challenged him.

On Wednesday, May 24, 1738, during a Bible study in London the light of gospel truth broke upon him. He explained his experience:

> In the evening I went very unwillingly to a society in Aldersgate Street, where one was reading Luther's preface to the *Epistle to the Romans*. About a quarter before nine, while he was describing the change which God works in the heart through faith in Christ, I felt my heart strangely warmed. I felt I did trust in Christ, Christ alone for salvation; and an assurance was given me that He had taken away *my* sins, even *mine*, and saved *me* from the law of sin and death.

Wesley was rejoicing in the forgiveness of his sins. He had tried for years to find forgiveness. Wesley found God's mercy through faith in Christ. He learned what the writer of Hebrews meant when he promised that God **will forgive their wickedness and will remember their sins no more.** He had placed his hope in God's mercy.

One of the greatest joys believers find is the assurance of forgiven sin. We do not discover it by trusting in our goodness, church attendance, efforts to keep the Ten Commandments, or any other feature of self-effort. The apostle Paul himself acknowledged that he was the worst of sinners and rejoiced that God had shown him mercy "so that in me, the worst of sinners, Christ Jesus might display his unlimited patience as an example for those who would believe on him and receive eternal life" (1 Tim. 1:16).

We find new hope when we live each day knowing God has forgiven our sins. Hebrews presents Christ as a new leader, a High Priest, who can give all wanderers this type of hope.

II. COMMENTARY

A New Leader, a New Agreement—New Hope!

MAIN IDEA: *Through Jesus, God has established a new covenant which provides believers new power, new knowledge of God, and new assurance of sins forgiven.*

A A New Leader (vv. 1–6)

SUPPORTING IDEA: *Christ provides effective service for his people by giving an effective sacrifice for sin.*

1. Service, Sanctuary, Sacrifice (vv. 1–3)

8:1. Several chapters of Hebrews have been devoted to discussing the work of Christ as our high priest. Now we come to this succinct summary: Christ serves his people before God by offering a sacrifice for sin.

Christ had **sat down at the right hand of the throne of the Majesty in heaven.** This repeats a point already established in 1:3 but now with a clear application to the role of Christ as High Priest. The idea that Christ was seated comes from Psalm 110:1. The act of sitting down suggested that Jesus' task was done. He had finished his job. By contrast, the priests of Aaron's line always stood in God's presence without sitting (see Heb. 10:11). Their act of standing suggested an incomplete task. Jesus had accomplished the work whose completion the priests could only anticipate.

Majesty is a reverent reference to God the Father. The word showed that Christ had assumed a position of dignity, power, and excellence as a result of his faithful work.

8:2. Christ was a priest who served in the **true tabernacle, set up by the Lord, not by man.** Christ had a real and spiritual ministry in God's presence. Aaron's priests could only go through the motions of pursuing a symbolic ministry in an earthly tabernacle. The work of Christ was successful where it really counted. The Lord himself had established the work of Christ.

The ministry of priests in the earthly tabernacle presented pictures and symbols of the forgiveness of sin. Christ came actually to accomplish the job. He did not deal with pictures and symbols but with reality. He obtained forgiveness by offering himself in God's presence. Believers can find hope by living in the light of the fulfillment Jesus made available.

Christ's ministry for believers in heaven does not consist of his offering his sacrifice for sin. He has already completed that (see John 19:30). His sacrificial ministry reached completion when he offered himself on the cross. The present ministry of Christ is to pray for his people before God.

The **true tabernacle** in which Christ carries on his service for sinners is located in heaven. Verse 1 assumes that Christ is **at the right hand of the throne of the Majesty in heaven**. The same point appears in 1:3. The heavenly location means God is the source of strength to support and enable Christ's work. This certifies that Christ will be successful and effective in his heavenly labors.

8:3. Earthly priests came to present offerings for human sinfulness. This is a reminder of the ritual of the Day of Atonement in Leviticus 16. Our High Priest Jesus also came with an offering for sin. Jesus offered himself for sin in a single, effective act. This theme will be treated in greater detail in chapter 9.

The offering of the earthly priests was expressed with a present tense which focused on the continual nature of their offering. They kept on offering sacrifices for sins. Jesus, our High Priest, offered a single sacrifice, an event expressed in a tense which suggests a single act in the past. Jesus' single offering never needed repetition.

2. Contrast in Effectiveness (vv. 4–6)

8:4. Christ's ministry is more effective both because of who he is and what he does. Verse 4 emphasizes his effective work as a priest. Jesus' effective work as a priest did not occur on earth. According to the Mosaic Law, Jesus was not descended from the proper tribe for serving as an earthly priest (see 7:14). Jesus would find no place for serving as a priest on earth. but he serves effectively as a priest in heaven. His effective ministry on earth was his offering up of himself as a sacrifice for sins.

The ministry he exercised on earth was a preparation for his ministry in heaven. Jesus' heavenly high priesthood depended on the offering of a perfect earthly sacrifice followed by his ascension to be seated before God in heaven. In heaven Jesus carried on a far greater priestly ministry than any earthly priest enjoyed.

8:5. This verse makes two emphases about the ministry on earth by Levitical priests. First, the priestly ministry on earth represented only a shadow of the truly effective priestly ministry Jesus performed in heaven. A shadow is a reflection of another object. It resembles the other object, but it contains some distortion. A copy of a work of art only gives a general idea of what the original work is like. The earthly ministry of Jesus served only as a shadow and copy of his real priestly ministry in heaven. The work of the Levitical priests only served as a preview of the atoning work of Christ.

Second, even though the earthly ministry was only a copy of the heavenly reality, God had still designed this earthly priestly ministry in detail. Quoting Exodus 25:40, the author reminds his readers that God had provided precise instructions about the details of the tabernacle. Even the small details of the earthly tabernacle were in God's hands. If this were true, then the heavenly sanctuary in which Jesus served with such effectiveness must be more glorious and significant.

Do these verses suggest that heaven contained a literal counterpart of the earthly tabernacle? The Jews often discussed this subject, but it is important for us to avoid making our view of a heavenly temple too materialistic. The priestly activity on earth pointed not to a physical temple in heaven but to the cross of Christ. It was on the cross that Jesus accomplished the real activity which affected our relationship with God.

8:6. Jesus' ministry was more effective in its service than the work of the descendants of Aaron because God had established Jesus' ministry on **better promises.** What these better promises involve will be explained in verses 10–12. Better promises produce a better covenant.

Christ was the **mediator** of the new covenant. We will see a more complete explanation of this idea in 9:15–22. The mediator had the job of keeping two parties linked in fellowship. As mediator, Christ rescued the perishing and flawlessly carried out God's will (John 17:4).

🅑 A New Agreement (vv. 7–13)

> **SUPPORTING IDEA:** *Christ has established a new agreement which promises inner power, personal knowledge, and forgiveness of sins.*

1. The Reason for the New Agreement (v. 7)

8:7. The failure of the **first covenant** at Sinai demanded the institution of a second covenant. This did not suggest that the Law itself had flaws, but that the experience of human beings under the Law was faulty. The Law had not met the needs of sinful human beings. The Law could reveal sin, but it could not remove it. It could not justify or save sinners. The problem was with the people who lacked the power to obey the Law (see Rom. 7:7–12).

Therefore, God introduced a new agreement or covenant. This statement became the signal for the author of Hebrews to use Jeremiah (ch. 31) to explain the new covenant which God had begun.

2. The Content of the New Agreement (vv. 8–12)

8:8. The **new covenant** promises new moral power, personal knowledge, and forgiveness of sin. This verse begins a quotation from Jeremiah 31:31–34.

It explicitly identifies Jeremiah's words as God's Word to establish that divine authority lay behind his quote. God had spoken something, and this verse makes his message clear.

Jeremiah had spoken these words as God was restoring the Jews after the captivity. The new experience of return demanded a new approach in God's dealing with his people. The demands of the time called for a new covenant.

Centuries passed after Jeremiah's words before God inaugurated the new covenant with the coming of the Messiah. Jeremiah's words referred ultimately to the coming of Jesus and to his provision for helping sinners.

Jeremiah lived at a time when a separation had occurred between Israel and Judah. The proclamation of the covenant involved healing the breach which had occurred between these tribes of God's people. The promise of healing the breach between rival groups of Jews symbolized the reconciliation of all nations and people in Christ. Through Christ God accomplished the reconciliation of the world to himself (2 Cor. 5:19).

8:9. This verse contrasts the old covenant with the new by describing the historical circumstances in which God had begun the old. God had initiated the first covenant in sovereignly leading his people from captivity in Egypt. God's people were helpless until God took the initiative. Even though God took the initiative, the covenant did not last. God's people failed. The covenant became invalidated. The Jews broke the conditions of the covenant.

In response to this disobedience, God ceased to pay attention to them. God was not acting recklessly in turning away from his people. His response was to be expected after his people turned their backs on him. He had provided for their needs, but they had rejected his provision. God's turning away from them was an act of judgment.

The word of hope was that God had promised a new **covenant**. It would not do to patch up the old covenant. God established an entirely new covenant with new benefits for his people, benefits discussed in the following verse.

8:10. Three features stand out in this verse. First, the covenant applied to **the house of Israel.** This expression included the entire people of God. Although Jeremiah had spoken of a covenant which had applied to ethnic Jews, this verse focuses on all of God's people, both Jews and Gentiles. This statement is in line with Paul's observations in Galatians 3:29 that all believers "are Abraham's seed."

Second, the covenant would be inward. God would write its content in the minds and hearts of his people. The old covenant could reveal the paths of good and evil, but it could not supply power to walk in righteousness. The power which enabled believers to follow these laws was none other than the power of the Holy Spirit, who frees believers from the law of sin and death (Rom. 8:2–3). The words **mind** and **heart** apply to the whole person.

The entire life of the believer experienced the effects of the presence of God's laws.

Third, the new covenant would produce intimacy, creating a relationship in which Israel's God would become the God of his followers, and they would become his people. We will read more about this intimacy and closeness with God in the next verse. God had promised his Old Testament people that he would guard and love them (Exod. 6:7). His actions for believers through the life, death, resurrection, and ascension of Jesus meant that God had acted even more vigorously to redeem his people.

8:11. Fellowship with God would be direct and immediate. God would not appoint any privileged class of priests to teach others, but **all** would **know** him. All distinctions of rank and importance in the new community would disappear. The knowledge of God would be spread **from the least of them to the greatest.** The Holy Spirit, who teaches all things, will introduce all believers to a close walk with God (John 14:26). God would not confine the knowledge of him to a privileged few. All those under the new covenant would enjoy a walk of deep fellowship with God.

8:12. God had promised new power to fulfill his laws and a new closeness to know and understand him. His third promise offered forgiveness to sinners. A literal translation of verse 12 has God promising, "I will be merciful to their deeds of unrighteousness." God had always been merciful. The new covenant gave more open expression to God's mercy.

The parallel statement that God would **remember their sins no more** reassured sinners that God's forgiveness was complete. God, unlike human beings, does not say, "I will forgive, but I will not forget." God promises to forget our sins.

The ground of forgiveness was not human repentance but Jesus' sacrificial death. Only the death of Jesus could provide full assurance that God has wiped away sins and made believers righteous in his sight. God took the initiative to give sinners his grace and mercy. Because God really dealt with sins, the blessings of knowing him and serving him with power become possible.

3. The Result of the New Agreement (v. 13)

8:13. People are born, grow, age, and die. Life is transient. Jeremiah had announced the demise of the old covenant six hundred years earlier, but its death took time. When these words in Hebrews were written, the Jerusalem Temple was likely still standing. Day after day its priests offered sacrifices, but **it is impossible for the blood of bulls and goats to take away sins** (Heb. 10:4).

The old covenant came, served the purpose of informing sinners of their need, grew old, and has died. It was viewed as already **obsolete.** The old covenant had done its job. It had pointed to, prepared the way for, and was now giving way to the new covenant. The new covenant offered such superior benefits to needy sinners that the old gave way to it.

The new covenant promised inward power, an intimate knowledge of God, and forgiveness of sin. Nothing in the past could equal the provisions of this new covenant. We who live today as believers can rejoice in God's lavish provisions for our spiritual needs.

MAIN IDEA REVIEW: *Through Jesus God has established a new covenant which provides believers new power, new knowledge of God, and new assurance of sins forgiven.*

III. CONCLUSION

Love Doesn't Leave You Hanging

When my first child was born, the hospital presented me with a bill for the birth which I could not pay. Their instructions were: "Pay this bill before we release your wife and daughter." I called my father. As a family member I felt free to ask for help. My father loved me, his daughter-in-law, and his new granddaughter too much to leave us hanging. We were family! Dad would help!

By faith in Jesus you and I become members of God's family. We have urgent and desperate needs. Because God is now our heavenly Father, he loves us too much to leave us hanging. We are family. God will help.

You and I desperately need to know that God will accept us. Whenever we are honest about it, we must admit that we have broken God's laws, lived selfishly, forgotten to seek God's will, and lived as if there were no life beyond. We need to know that someone will represent us before God. We need someone who can say for us, "God, I present my life as a sacrifice for their sins. Let them enjoy your blessing."

That's where Jesus fits in. He is the new leader who gives us hope. Through faith in Jesus, we become children of God (John 1:12). Through following Jesus, we experience abundant life (John 10:10). Because of Jesus, we can find mercy and grace for our every need (Heb. 4:16). Thank God for Jesus!

Knowing these truths produces three responses in our lives. First, we have gratitude. We can say, "Thank you, God, for your great provisions for me." We can live as thankful people. Second, we have encouragement. We can feel, "God has given us a good agreement. He supplies all we need." When our load becomes heavy and our future confused, we find hope simply to keep plodding on in God's strength. Third, we find fear and respect for

God. We must say, "A God this gracious deserves our obedience." Then we must live as if we mean it.

PRINCIPLES

- Jesus serves as our High Priest in God's presence.
- Jesus offered an effective sacrifice for our sins.
- God has given us the Holy Spirit to enable us to obey his laws.
- God has given us the privilege of knowing him and calling him our Father.
- Through Jesus we have our sins forgiven.

APPLICATIONS

- Come confidently to God through Jesus with your needs.
- Follow the strength of the Holy Spirit as you do God's will.
- Rejoice that you personally know the God who made heaven and earth.
- Believe that God will forgive your sins.
- Find hope, joy, and reverence for God as he forgives and helps you.

IV. LIFE APPLICATION

Forgiveness Brings Freedom

Mark hosted a bachelor party for his friend Jon, who was about to marry. As the group sat on a swimming dock with Mark's family boat below them, Jon casually requested a pocket knife. Mark's father reached into the boat, pulled out a plastic container, and found a brown, three-bladed pocketknife. He tossed it to Jon with the question, "That good enough?"

Mark looked at the knife and felt a twinge of horror. The knife had once belonged to Jon. Mark had stolen it from him years ago. He had forgotten it until his Dad pulled it out.

Just two days earlier Mark had become a Christian. For the first time in life he had experienced forgiveness. Years of guilt, fear, dread, and self-hatred were gone. Christ had brought freedom.

Mark asked Jon, "Do you recognize that knife?"

Jon responded, "I'm not sure."

Mark continued, "You should. It's yours. I stole it from you when we were kids."

The group gathered on the dock fell silent. All eyes focused on Mark, who continued, "I'm sorry I did that. It was wrong. You can have the knife back."

Jon waved away the idea, saying, "It's all right. Don't worry about it." Then he addressed Mark directly, "Man, Littleton, you are a little too honest!" Before Mark could respond, Jon again added, "Hey, it's good. I wish I could be that way."

That incident became a time for Mark to reflect on God's forgiveness. He realized that God's forgiveness offered him two marvelous benefits. First, it wiped the slate clean with God. Guilt for past disobedience was gone "as far as the east is from the west" (Ps. 103:12). Second, it sets us free to understand and accept ourselves. Because Jesus has accepted us, we don't fear exposure before others. People delight in pointing the finger at Christians and saying, "You live like that and call yourself a Christian? You are a hypocrite!" Forgiven Christians can say, "Yes, I have sinned. I can't hide it. God has forgiven me. Will you also forgive me?"

Christians alone can accept pardon for sins in the past, mistakes of the future, and embarrassments in the present. Only Christians have the resources to accept themselves when others accuse them. God's forgiveness is a wonderful gift.

V. PRAYER

Father, thank you for knowing our needs and providing a new covenant in Jesus. Thank you that he died for my sins. Thank you that you have forgiven my sins and made me part of your family. Thank you for the joy and hope I find in belonging to your family. I will reverence you and obey you. Amen.

VI. DEEPER DISCOVERIES

A. The Heavenly Sanctuary (vv. 2,5)

References to the sanctuary, the true tabernacle, and the shadow of what is in heaven have led some Bible interpreters to feel that Hebrews is discussing a heavenly temple in which God actually lived. Was the author saying that the earthly tabernacle in which Aaron and his descendants served was a copy of such a heavenly reality? Was there a real temple in heaven in which Jesus carried out his high-priestly ministry?

Most probably, the text does not try to describe a real tabernacle in heaven. Symbolic language built on earthly reality is used to emphasize that Jesus' atonement for our sins was totally effective for removing them. The work in the earthly tabernacle pointed forward to Jesus' own sacrifice. The ritual of sacrificing animals in the tabernacle was a picture and a symbol of what actually happened when Jesus died. It was not so much that the earthly tabernacle symbolized a heavenly reality as that the work of Aaron's priests pointed forward to what Christ would do perfectly. Christ actually secured our pardon with God. The tabernacle presented a reflection, but Jesus brought in the reality.

B. Mediator (v. 6)

This is the first appearance of a word (*mesites*) which appears also in 9:15 and 12:24 (see also Gal. 3:19–20; 1 Tim. 2:5). The mediator was an arbitrator or a go-between for two parties. As the mediator of a covenant between God and human beings, Jesus showed a concern to preserve the honor of God from all stain. He also looked with unrelenting zeal for sinners whom he could rescue and reclaim.

To say Jesus is our **mediator** means more than that he was our middle-man. His service as our mediator guaranteed our salvation. Since his priesthood endures forever (7:22–25), the covenant he established will last eternally. Christ both stands with and between God and lost human beings, guaranteeing that lost sinners can find God.

C. The House of Israel (v. 8)

Although God will make the new covenant with the house of Israel and Judah, the ultimate recipients are the people of Christ, the church. The Old Testament people of God experienced none of the benefits of this covenant—new power, new knowledge of God, and a new experience of forgiveness. Only the death of Christ provided these benefits for those who came under the protection of his shed blood.

D. Minds and Hearts (v. 10)

Whenever the term **mind** is used alone, it refers to the understanding or intellect (Eph. 2:3). Whenever the term **heart** is used alone, it describes the will and the emotions (Rom. 2:15). Used together, the words denote the human personality as a unity. God has placed his laws on the intellect, emotions, and will of his people. This expression serves as a picture of the inward effect of the new covenant. This new covenant does not affect people superficially, but it reaches to the very core of their being. The new covenant affects all that we think, feel, and choose.

VII. TEACHING OUTLINE

A. INTRODUCTION

1. Lead Story: Hoping in God's Mercy

2. Context: Chapter 7 of Hebrews emphasizes the prayers and perfect character of Jesus our High Priest. Chapter 8 summarizes the significance of these truths. These chapters serve as a foundation for new hope because Jesus was a new leader who authored a new covenant.

   A New Leader (vv. 1–6). Jesus was a new leader who worked in heaven at God's right hand and offered an effective sacrifice for sin (vv. 1–3). The priestly service of Jesus was effective in supporting a new covenant (vv. 4–6).

   A New Agreement (vv. 7–13). Jesus produced a new agreement for his people because the old agreement was ineffective (v. 7). This new agreement promised new power, new closeness to God, and a fresh experience of forgiveness (vv. 8–12). The result of this covenant was the disappearance of the old covenant (v. 13).

3. Transition: As we study this chapter, we will appreciate the effectiveness of Jesus' sacrifice for our sin. We will gain hope from knowing that we have a representative in God's very presence. We will learn to claim this new power, new intimacy with God, and new experience of forgiveness which Christ makes available.

B. COMMENTARY

1. A New Leader (vv. 1–6)
   a. Service, sanctuary, sacrifice (vv. 1–3)
   b. Contrast in effectiveness (vv. 4–6)
2. A New Agreement (vv. 7–13)
   a. The reason for the new agreement (v. 7)
   b. The content of the new agreement (vv. 8–12)
   c. The result of the new agreement (v. 13)

C. CONCLUSION: FORGIVENESS BRINGS FREEDOM

VIII. ISSUES FOR DISCUSSION

1. What is the current priestly ministry of Jesus?
2. Describe the differences between the old and new covenants.
3. How is Jesus' ministry superior to that of the Old Testament priests?
4. What is the relationship between the covenant work of Christ and your obedience?

Hebrews 9

The Superior Sacrifice of Christ

I. INTRODUCTION
A Lesson from an Easy-Bake Oven

II. COMMENTARY
A verse-by-verse explanation of the chapter.

III. CONCLUSION
A Serious Ritual

An overview of the principles and applications from the chapter.

IV. LIFE APPLICATION
Sacrifice—Effective but Deadly

Melding the chapter to life.

V. PRAYER
Tying the chapter to life with God.

VI. DEEPER DISCOVERIES
Historical, geographical, and grammatical enrichment of the commentary.

VII. TEACHING OUTLINE
Suggested step-by-step group study of the chapter.

VIII. ISSUES FOR DISCUSSION
Zeroing the chapter in on daily life.

"*I* never made a sacrifice. We ought not to talk of sacrifice when we remember the great sacrifice that he made who left his father's throne on high to give himself for us."

David Livingstone

Hebrews

IN A NUTSHELL

The old sanctuary and ceremonies of the Levitical ritual offered no effective remedy for sin (9:1–10). The ceremonies of the Day of Atonement offered impressive pageantry, but left the conscience untouched. The work of Christ affected the conscience, provided forgiveness, and needed no repetition. His work left his followers looking with hope for his return to complete their salvation.

The Superior Sacrifice of Christ

I. INTRODUCTION

A Lesson from an Easy-Bake Oven

One Christmas my younger daughter put an easy-bake oven at the top of her Christmas gift list. She squealed with delight when she found it among her gifts on Christmas Day. The oven came equipped with a cupcake mixture to which you added water. It had a small metal baking pan and used the heat of a lightbulb.

She couldn't wait to try it out. We opened the mixture, added water, poured it into the pan, switched on the lightbulb, and waited with anticipation. As the minutes ticked by, we saw the cupcake rise, brown, and reach an "almost edible" appearance.

When it was ready, we removed it from the oven, cut it into several small pieces, and munched on it as a family. The best thing about the cupcake was that it was warm. Its taste was bland, and it had a sticky, half-baked texture.

No one expected prize-winning baking to emerge from the oven. This was a "play" oven intended to prepare children to graduate upward to the real oven in the kitchen. The "easy-bake" oven was a copy of a real oven, and its food was a pale imitation of baked goods from the kitchen. Real food came from the kitchen, not from a child's play oven.

The sacrifices and offerings of the earthly tabernacle were like an easy-bake oven. They are not the real thing. They could never remove the stain of sin. They could make an offerer ritually pure before God. They provided an instructive picture of the perfect sacrifice which Christ would one day offer. Still, activities in the tabernacle represented only a copy of what Christ could effectively do in heaven. Real forgiveness came from Christ's death, not from the impressive offerings repeatedly given in the tabernacle. Only the death of Jesus could overcome sin once and for all.

Reading this chapter will introduce us to Christ's remedy for sin which affects the conscience, provides forgiveness, and never needs repetition.

II. COMMENTARY

The Superior Sacrifice of Christ

MAIN IDEA: *Through Jesus, God has acted with finality to destroy the effects of sin.*

A An Ineffective Antidote for Sin (vv. 1–10)

SUPPORTING IDEA: *The ceremonies and sacrifices of the tabernacle did not destroy the effects of sin.*

1. An Ineffective Sanctuary (vv. 1–5)

9:1. This verse summarizes the glories of the old tabernacle, showing its orderliness The components of the earthly tabernacle showed that it was temporary. The intent of this verse is not to ridicule the past but to prepare the readers to appreciate the superior glories of Christ's new work.

The **first covenant** provided both regulations for worship and a place for worship. The place for worship was **an earthly sanctuary.** Earthly did not suggest any feature displeasing to God. It pointed out that the tabernacle was material, imperfect, and temporary. The earthly tabernacle belonged to this world, but Jesus ministered in heaven (v. 24).

9:2. The old **tabernacle** had two parts. **First** indicated the room closer to the entrance from the outer courtyard—**the Holy Place.** It was approximately thirty feet long, fifteen feet wide, and fifteen feet high. This room contained a lampstand, a table, and the bread of the presence (Exod. 35:10–29). The lampstand illuminated the first tent. The glorious presence of God illuminated the second tent. The table contained the bread placed there every Sabbath. Only priests ate the bread (Exod. 25:23–30; Lev. 24:5–9).

9:3. A curtain separated the Holy Place from the second part of the old tabernacle—**the Most Holy Place** (see 6:19). **Second** distinguished this curtain from the curtain between the outer court and the Holy Place (Exod. 26:36–37). Once a year on the Day of Atonement the high priest passed through this curtain into God's presence. This veil symbolized the barrier between a holy God and sinful people. At the death of Christ this veil was torn "from top to bottom" (Matt. 27:51).

9:4. The golden altar of incense was located in front of the curtain (Exod. 30:1–6) so that it actually stood in the Holy Place. This incense altar was vital for the burning of incense on the Day of Atonement (Lev. 16:13), so it is associated it with the Holy of Holies.

The **gold-covered ark of the covenant** was a box or chest about four feet long and two and one-half feet high and broad (Exod. 25:10–22), covered with gold on every side. The ark contained three treasures. "The gold jar of manna" (Exod. 16:32–34) was a reminder of God's faithful provision during the wilderness wanderings. **Aaron's staff that had budded** (Num. 17:1–11) reminded readers of God's powerful warning against complaint and faultfinding. **The stone tablets of the covenant** (Exod. 25:21–22) reminded them of God's expectations, and pointed, as we will soon see, to the ministry of Christ.

9:5. The cherubim (Exod. 25:18–22) situated above the ark symbolized the presence of God. They were probably winged creatures. They overshadowed **the atonement cover**, also called the mercy seat. The high priest sprinkled this part of the ark with blood on the Day of Atonement (Lev. 16:14).

2. Ineffective Ceremonies (vv. 6–10)

9:6. The priests regularly came into the Holy Place to carry out their ministry. They lighted the lamps daily (Exod. 27:20–21), replaced the loaves of bread every Sabbath (Lev. 24:5–8), and burned incense on the golden altar (Exod. 30:7–8). The daily repetition of these ministries showed that they never resulted in access to God.

9:7. Only the **high priest** could enter the Most Holy Place, and he could enter only on the Day of Atonement. Leviticus 16:12–16 suggests that he entered twice on that day, once with blood for his own sin and again with blood for the sins of the people. The use of blood showed that the priest had offered a sacrifice for sin, but the ceremonies of the Day of Atonement did not bring access to God. This prepares us for the importance of the shed blood of Christ in providing sacrifice for our sins (Eph. 1:7).

Under the old covenant, the high priest could only atone for **sins . . . committed in ignorance** (Heb. 9:7; see also Num. 15:29–30). No atonement was available for sins committed willfully. The fact that the priest offered this sacrifice annually showed that it never succeeded in completely removing sin.

9:8. What did these details of verses 6–7 mean? The existence of the outer sanctuary showed that the Old Testament ceremonies limited access to God's presence. Once a year the high priest alone could enter the inner sanctuary. But how limited and incomplete all of this was! Ordinary people had no access to God. Under the new covenant, *all* believers could enter into the Most Holy Place by the blood of Jesus. Jesus opened access to God. Now all believers at all times had the right to come to God. What a privilege!

9:9–10. If the old sacrifices could not bring common people to God, what good were they? These **gifts and sacrifices** were imperfect and temporary. They were imperfect because they **were not able to clear the conscience of the worshiper.** Some Old Testament saints had clear consciences, but they did not get them through the sacrificial system.

The sacrifices were temporary because they applied only **until the time of the new order.** Even though the sacrifices could not cleanse the conscience or produce spiritual life, they pointed to Christ who could. The regulations under the old covenant were only regulations for the body. They provided ceremonial purity. The food, drink, and washings had beneficial effects for the body, but they could not bring liberty to the spirit. Only Christ can do this.

🅱 An Effective Remedy for Sin (vv. 11–28)

SUPPORTING IDEA: *Jesus offered a remedy for sin which cleansed the conscience, offered forgiveness, and never needed repetition.*

1. A Remedy Affecting the Conscience (vv. 11–14)

9:11. What did Jesus do under the new covenant? Jesus purifies believers for service. He supplied the real action which lay behind the symbols of the tabernacle and its ritual. Jesus' death had secured divine blessings for his people.

Christ came as high priest and accomplished **good things** for his people. The good things were the blessings Christ won for believers by his sacrificial death. Although Christ has provided these blessings, not all Christians have experienced them. Believers are urged to claim their heritage (Heb. 10:22–24).

Jesus came as high priest **through the greater and more perfect tabernacle.** This is a reference to Christ's ministry in heaven. That ministry was **not a part of this creation.** Jesus' ministry did not deal with shadows and copies of reality as did the Aaronic priests who served in the tabernacle. Jesus ministered in heaven before God and secured our acceptance.

9:12. Jesus' redemptive work consisted of offering **his own blood,** not **the blood of goats and calves.** Jesus had given himself. The blood of Jesus our High Priest was far more precious than the blood of animals. His was a **once for all** offering that never needed repeating. Christ's offering required no daily or even annual repetition. A single offering was eternally effective.

Some interpreters emphasize the idea that Christ took his blood into heaven as if our redemption depended on something which Jesus did after the cross. The statement that Jesus had obtained eternal redemption suggests that Jesus has accomplished redemption at the cross. It was by the blood shed at the cross that he entered heaven. All of Jesus' work for our salvation occurred at the cross, not subsequent to it.

9:13. What happened when Old Testament worshipers offered sacrifices? Did these offerings provide spiritual benefit for the offerers? These sacrifices sanctified the offerers so that **they are outwardly clean. Goats and bulls** probably spoke of offerings on the Day of Atonement (Lev. 16:1–19). The **ashes of a heifer** spoke of an offering which provided purification to the ritually unclean (Num. 19:1–10). These offerings were provisions for cleansing from fleshly defilement and provided temporary ceremonial purity. They could not give inner, spiritual cleansing. Only the blood of Christ could touch the conscience.

9:14. This verse argues from the lesser to the greater. If the blood of animals can provide external cleaning, how much more effective is the cleansing of Christ's blood. Three features made Christ's cleansing effective.

First, Christ made the offering **through the eternal Spirit.** This is probably not a reference to the Holy Spirit, but to Christ's own spirit. Christ made an inner spiritual response in which he offered himself. His response was not merely outward but inward and eternal. The Holy Spirit energized this response.

Second, Christ **offered himself.** Christ's offering was voluntary, and it represented an intelligent act of spiritual obedience to God.

Third, Christ offered his **unblemished** character to God. Jesus responded in perfect moral purity. The sacrifice was of infinite value.

This offering produces a cleansed conscience among those who commit themselves to Christ. Animal sacrifices cannot remove sin, but Jesus can. The cleansing produced a new aim and vision. Instead of producing **acts that lead to death,** it fostered service to the living God. Purity led to service and commitment to God.

2. A Remedy Offering Forgiveness (vv. 15–22)

9:15. Jesus secures forgiveness of sin. On the basis of giving himself, Christ became **a mediator of the new covenant** and a ransom to free captives from their sin. Christ's death was the price paid to liberate spiritual prisoners. The old covenant had no provision for removing offenses against God. In his death, Christ removed the consequences of human sin for those who trust him. The real cleansing from sin against God did not come from sacrificing animals but from the sacrifice of Christ.

The purpose of the new covenant Jesus established was to provide an **eternal inheritance** for believers. Because of Christ, sin no longer can bar believers from divine blessings.

9:16–18. The death of Christ not only set believers free from their sins, but it also activated the positive benefits of the new covenant. In the Greek language, the same word (*diatheke*) is used to indicate both a **covenant** and a **will.** A will became active only when the testator died. Christ died so believers might receive the benefits of the new covenant.

Verse 17 explains that a death was necessary for a will to take effect. Verse 18 refers back to Exodus 24:6–8 to describe Moses' act of ratifying the old covenant by sprinkling sacrificial blood on the people and on the altar. A further description of Christ's sacrifice is found in verses 23–28.

9:19. Moses proclaimed the commandments to the people and offered animals in sacrifice. Then he announced the symbolism of his actions in sprinkling the people. The acts of sacrifice and sprinkling were important in inaugurating the covenant between God and Israel. Exodus did not mention the use of **water, scarlet wool and branches of hyssop,** but we could deduce their usage from Leviticus 14:4–5; and Numbers 19:18. Exodus made no mention of sprinkling the book, but reading it was central to Moses' contact with the people. The initiation of the first covenant demanded the presence of blood or death.

9:20. The words here sound close to Jesus' words at the institution of the Lord's Supper (see Matt. 26:28). When we compare the words of Hebrews with the words of Moses in Exodus 24:8, we realize that the symbolism of Moses' sprinkling has found its fulfillment in Jesus' death at Calvary. Moses' action of sprinkling the blood confirmed God's covenant with Israel and called his people to obedience.

9:21. This verse contains additional details not found in Exodus. Jewish tradition suggested that Moses' dedication of the altar involved sprinkling blood on the tent and the vessels of worship. The use of blood confirmed the reality of the covenant and showed the importance of obedience. The use of the blood obligated both parties to be faithful to the covenant. If either party were unfaithful to a covenant, he or she experienced the fate of the sacrificial animal.

9:22. This verse draws the general conclusion that **the law requires that nearly everything be cleansed with blood.** Some Jewish rituals specified the use of water, fire (Num. 31:22–24), or flour (Lev. 5:11–13) to bring cleansing, but the use of blood was the norm. The concluding statement that **without the shedding of blood there is no forgiveness** comes from the ideas of Leviticus 17:11. The act of shedding blood referred to the death of the sacrificial animal and to the application of the blood to secure forgiveness of sin. Forgiveness did not become a reality until the death of Christ actually removed sin.

3. A Remedy Needing No Repetition (vv. 23–28)

9:23. Jesus' sacrifice never needs repetition. Verses 15–22 show that the old covenant demanded the use of blood for purification. Earthly things needed purification by external means. The hearts of believers demanded a special type of purification before God.

Heavenly things symbolizes the spiritual sphere in which believers enjoy atonement. Christians who have their consciences sprinkled with the blood of Christ can approach God in heaven. This does not imply that heaven itself needed cleansing. The idea of cleansing heaven is a symbol of the cleaning of believers before God.

The **better** sacrifice was the death of Christ. The plural **sacrifices** is used because the single sacrifice of Christ required a complete range of sacrifices to serve as copies.

9:24. This verse explains how Christ offered **better sacrifices** by pointing out the past and present missions of Christ. After his death at Calvary, Christ **entered heaven itself.** The term **heaven** referred to the presence of God rather than to a specific location. The presence of God was a reality of which the earthly tabernacle was only a copy. Christ accomplished salvation for believers before God.

Aaron's high priests could enter God's presence only annually. Christ now appears **for us in God's presence.** He has constant access to God. Christ represents us, prays for us, and accomplishes what we could never do (Heb. 7:25).

9:25. This verse emphasizes the finality and voluntariness of Jesus' death. The final three verses of this chapter provide additional explanation of these ideas.

The Aaronic high priest made annual trips into the Most Holy Place of the tabernacle. Each time he carried the blood of a fresh animal sacrifice. Christ had no need to offer himself repeatedly. One offering was final for all time.

The Aaronic high priests came with blood from animal sacrifices that had been slain involuntarily. No animal could consciously say, "I desire to do your will, O God." Christ voluntarily surrendered his life for the sins of the world (Luke 22:42).

9:26. Jews would be acquainted with a repetition of sacrifices. They would need to understand why the death of Christ was final and unrepeatable. This verse implies that a repeated offering would have involved Christ in continual suffering. If Christ's death were repeatable, it would need to begin with the dawn of history when sin entered the world and to last throughout the ages.

However, the death of Christ could happen only once in history. There was only one incarnation and death. The timing of this event occurred in God's perfect wisdom.

Several facts about Christ's death are presented. First, it happened in history when he **appeared** on earth. Second, it was **once for all** and never needed repetition. Third, the effect of the sacrifice was to **do away with sin.** Fourth, the death was voluntary. Christ offered himself.

9:27–28. These verses contrast the death of human beings and the death of Christ. The death of human beings was **destined,** and judgment followed after it. We cannot avoid death. God has appointed that death should visit every human being.

The fact that judgment follows death does not mean that it occurs immediately after death. An interval separates death and judgment. The mention of judgment after death does not suggest that no judgment occurs prior to death. These verses speak of the final judgment which clearly occurred after physical death.

The death of Christ was voluntary. We saw this expressed clearly in 9:14, but verse 28 also implies it. The death of Christ was not only voluntary, but the malice of the Jews and the plan of God demanded it.

Christ died **to take away the sins of many people** (see 9:26). At a time after his death, he will come again not to deal with sin but to bring salvation for his people. Jesus dealt completely with sin in his death. At his return he will usher his people into the experience of eternal life. The idea of Christ's appearance a second time reminds us of the reappearance of the high priest after he had completed his task in the Most Holy Place on the Day of Atonement (see Luke 1:21–22).

MAIN IDEA REVIEW: *Through Jesus, God has acted to destroy the effects of sin permanently.*

III. CONCLUSION

A Serious Ritual

I was playing tennis doubles. One of my opponents had played quite poorly. After contributing heavily to the loss of a game, the opponent exclaimed, "I hate myself." Both seriously and in jest, I said to him, "I forgive you." Then I thought. What I had done was a half-serious ritual. What Jesus had done was real. He has forgiven us though we have lived badly.

My friend's tennis game improved, and he went on to contribute to a victory in the set. I was still thinking about forgiveness. How important it is to receive real forgiveness which permanently changes our lifestyle. How meaningless it is to repeat a ritual which merely reminds us that we are sinful but cannot bring pardon.

Jewish Christians in the first century were acquainted with a system of worship which reminded them of their sin (9:1–10). Individual Jews could not come into God's presence. Once a year the high priest carried the blood of sacrifices into the Most Holy Place of the Jerusalem Temple (see v. 7). The fact that he could only approach God once a year demonstrated limited access to God. The annual offering of sacrifices only reminded the high priest and the worshipers that they had unpardoned sin. Sincere Jews could really hate themselves. They did not experience forgiveness!

The ministry of Jesus changed all of this, both for first-century Christians and for believers today. Jesus' death touched the conscience (vv. 11–14). The holy influence of his death developed in his people a desire to serve the living God. Jesus' death also brought permanent forgiveness (vv. 15–22). Jesus' death was permanently effective (vv. 23–28). It required no repetition. The single offering of his life removed the sins of all who trust in him. Jesus gives us permanent forgiveness which cleanses our conscience. God's grace richly blesses us.

PRINCIPLES

- The regular routine of sacrificing to God reminded the worshipers that they had unforgiven sin.
- The influence of Christ's death produces in his followers a desire to serve God.
- Christ's death removes the stain of sin.
- Christ's death is so effective it requires no repetition.

APPLICATIONS

- Don't trust modern religious ritual to remove your sin.
- Nurture in your heart a desire to serve God.
- Trust in Jesus Christ as your Savior to remove the guilt of sin.
- Look for the coming return of Jesus which will complete the salvation which began with our commitment to him.

IV. LIFE APPLICATION

Sacrifice—Effective but Deadly

On Wednesday, January 13, 1982, an Air Florida Boeing 737 jet left National Airport in Washington, D.C., during severely cold weather. Moments later it hit the 14th Street Bridge and crashed into the icy waters of the Potomac River. The tragic accident took seventy-eight lives.

Immediately after the crash six passengers held to a piece of the plane, trying to stay afloat in the icy Potomac. Helicopters from the Coast Guard and Park Police came to rescue these survivors. They lowered a lifesaving ring. One of the men caught the ring and handed it five times to his companions. All five made it to the helicopters.

As the helicopter returned for a final trip to rescue this man, he disappeared beneath the water. The survivors did not even know his name. He gave his life that they might live. His was an effective but deadly sacrifice.

Our rescuer has the name Jesus. He gave his life for our sins. His offering was effective because he has done **away with sin by the sacrifice of himself** (Heb. 9:26). His offering of himself needed no repetition. His offering was deadly because in doing God's will he surrendered his own life. Jesus now holds out a lifesaving ring to us. By taking his offer we can receive eternal life.

V. PRAYER

Jesus, thank you. You voluntarily died on the cross. You have done all that is necessary to take away my sins. I don't have to go through any rituals or look for any other act. I trust in you and know my sins are forgiven. I look forward to the time you return to complete my salvation. I love you and will always serve you. Amen.

VI. DEEPER DISCOVERIES

A. Atonement Cover (Mercy Seat) (v. 5)

In the Greek Old Testament (Septuagint) the Greek term (*hilasterion*) was used to refer to the atonement cover or mercy seat, a slab of gold covering the ark of the covenant in the tabernacle (Exod. 25:17–19). It served as the base for the golden cherubim. On the Day of Atonement the high priest sprinkled the blood of a sacrificial animal on the mercy seat as a request to God to forgive the nation's sins (Lev. 16:14–15).

The only other appearance of the Greek term in the New Testament is in Romans 3:25. There it describes the death of Christ. Christ became the person who shed his blood to secure forgiveness from God for the sins of the world.

B. Redemption (vv. 12,15)

The word (*lutrosis*) translated "redemption" in verse 12 appears also in Luke 1:68 and 2:38. The term was used to refer to the price paid for the liberation of a slave. When used to refer to Christ's sacrifice, it describes the death of Christ as the price paid to free sinners from the penalty and power of sin.

The word (*apolutrosin*) translated as **a ransom to set them free** in verse 15 is related to the word in verse 12 and has a similar meaning. It again refers to Christ's death as the price paid for the sinner's release.

The fact of Christ's redemption brings hope to sinners and true fellowship with the Father. The act of redemption demonstrates both divine love and righteousness. It makes possible a new life and genuine thanksgiving to God.

C. Ceremonial Cleansing (v. 13)

Hebrews 9:13 speaks of using the blood of bulls and goats and the ashes of a red heifer to give ceremonial cleansing to make people outwardly clean. How does ceremonial cleansing differ from spiritual cleansing? Leviticus 16:15–16 and Numbers 19:17–19 describe the ceremonies of cleansing. The sin removed by these rituals was ceremonial defilement. The cleansing offered by these ceremonies was only temporary. The conscience remained untouched. These Old Testament sacrifices could not remove guilt and provide inward cleansing.

By contrast, the shed blood of Christ affects the conscience (9:14). It removes moral guilt and gives forgiveness and peace to sinners. Christ's sacrifice allows believers to enjoy fellowship with God. Real spiritual cleansing provides forgiveness and an incentive to holy living. Believers enjoy this privilege through Jesus Christ.

D. Inheritance (v. 15)

Those who followed God under the regulations of the old covenant thought in terms of an earthly inheritance. By contrast, believers in Jesus receive the promise of an **eternal inheritance**. This inheritance involves an experience of divine grace both here and hereafter. It allows believers to experience the presence of God in their lives. It permits them to live with joy and delight in experiencing God's blessings. Believers enjoy an eternal inheritance because the salvation Jesus gives lasts forever.

E. Shedding of Blood (v. 22)

The uniform teaching of the Old Testament was that the forgiveness of sins demanded **the shedding of blood** (Lev. 17:11). The fact that Leviticus 5:11–13 described an exception to blood atonement did not nullify the general principle. The expression in the Old Testament describes the death of an animal and the outpouring of the blood on the altar. It involved both the death of the animal and the use of that blood to remove sin's defilement.

The death of Christ in the New Testament was the means of atoning for the sins of the world. The removal of sins required the sprinkling of Jesus' blood (1 Pet. 1:1–2) and provided forgiveness of sin (1 John 1:7) and cleansing of conscience (Heb. 9:14). The reference to the shed blood of Christ in the New Testament refers both to his violent death and also to the use of his blood as a means of reconciling sinners to God. Christians can rejoice that the shed blood of Christ has provided access to God.

F. The End of the Ages (v. 26)

The phrase **the end of the ages** in verse 26 reminds us of the phrase **in these last days** of Hebrews 1:2. The atonement of Christ was the climax of the age of the old covenant and the inauguration of a new era. The expression did not mean that the end of all time was near. It emphasized that Christ's death was the climax of the Old Testament age and the beginning of the New Testament era.

Christ's coming made the time of his death a time of fulfillment. His death on the cross removed or canceled the sin of those who respond in faith to him. The first coming of Christ brought in the final state of affairs. The new age of the Messiah has started. Whenever Jesus returns, he will conclude the age.

VII. TEACHING OUTLINE

A. INTRODUCTION

1. Lead Story: A Lesson from an Easy-Bake Oven
2. Context: This chapter draws comparisons and contrasts between the Levitical ritual and the priestly work of Christ. The rituals of the old covenant were temporary, inadequate, and ineffective. The work of Christ was permanent, thorough, and sufficient to remove sin permanently.

   An Ineffective Antidote for Sin (9:1–10). The physical layout of the tabernacle and the rituals which took place within its sanctuary were temporary and could not provide permanent forgiveness. The ceremonies could not remove sin or cleanse the conscience of the worshiper.

   An Effective Remedy for Sin (9:11–28). Christ's death was effective because it cleansed the conscience (vv. 11–14), provided full forgiveness (vv. 15–22), and needed no repetition (vv. 23–28).
3. Transition: Effective, eternal, encouraging. These three adjectives contrast the death of Christ with the ineffective animal sacrifices which the readers of Hebrews had seen and observed. Christ's death was effective because it removed sin permanently. It was eternal because it never needed repetition. It was encouraging because it provided hope to sinners struggling with guilt and weakness because of sin. Christ's death provides the power and forgiveness for godly living!

B. COMMENTARY

1. An Ineffective Antidote for Sin (vv. 1–10)
   a. An ineffective sanctuary (vv. 1–5)
   b. Ineffective ceremonies (vv. 6–10)
2. An Effective Remedy for Sin (vv. 11–28)

a. A remedy affecting the conscience (vv. 11–14)
b. A remedy offering forgiveness (vv. 15–22)
c. A remedy needing no repetition (vv. 23–28)

C. CONCLUSION: SACRIFICE—EFFECTIVE BUT DEADLY

VIII. ISSUES FOR DISCUSSION

1. Describe what you know about the Old Testament sacrificial system? Why was it inadequate to provide final salvation and forgiveness?
2. What did the Old Testament sacrificial system provide? How does studying that system help you as a Christian believer?
3. How did people in the Old Testament obtain eternal salvation?
4. How are salvation and forgiveness available now? Do you know that your sins are forgiven and that when Jesus returns you will experience final salvation?

Hebrews 10

The Power of Christ's Permanent Sacrifice

Quote

"If God were not willing to forgive sin,

heaven would be empty."

German Proverb

Hebrews

IN A NUTSHELL

Christ's sacrifice is permanent. It makes forgiveness possible, gives access to God, and produces people who can endure in righteous living and in love for one another. It develops followers who can face and overcome persecution. Receiving Christ's sacrifice is so important that anyone rejecting it will find no other means of paying for sins.

The Power of Christ's Permanent Sacrifice

I. INTRODUCTION

Producing a Superior Product

*A*uthentic Christianity produces people who live well. The devoted follower of Christ demonstrates love for the Lord, unselfishness, concern for others, stamina in trial, and hope for the future. Quite a superior product! Christianity is best known by the devoted people it produces.

In 1958, a young Korean student at the University of Pennsylvania finished a night of study and penned a letter to his parents in Korea. After sealing the letter, he left his apartment to drop it in a corner mailbox. When he turned away from the mailbox, a gang of teenage boys attacked him without speaking a word. They kicked him with their shoes and pummeled him with their fists. One beat him with a lead pipe. Another had a blackjack. When they finished their nasty work, they left him mortally wounded. When police found him in the gutter several hours later, he was dead.

Philadelphia citizens were shocked at the violence and cried out for vengeance. The district attorney obtained permission to try the offenders as adults so they could receive the death penalty. Then an incident occurred which changed the entire outlook of the trial.

A letter arrived from Korea, signed by the parents of the murdered student and twenty of his relatives. It read in part:

> Our family has met together and we have decided to petition that the most generous treatment possible within the laws of your government be given to those who have committed this criminal act. To give evidence of our sincere hope contained in this petition, we have decided to save money to start a fund to be used for the religious, educational, vocational, and social guidance of the boys when they are released. We have dared to express our hope with the spirit received from the Gospel of our Savior Jesus Christ, who died for our sins.

I do not know the outcome of this trial, but I know that the attitude of the parents and relatives of the deceased student surrounded the trial with a different outlook. Few of us will be challenged to practice forgiveness in such difficult circumstances as this Korean family. All of us will face situations in which we must forgive some who slander, threaten, abuse, injure, or steal from us. The marvel is that Christianity produces people who respond to these challenges. Christianity produces people capable of such forgiveness by the grace of God. Christ's sacrificial death has the power to produce people **who are being made holy** (Heb. 10:14). This is a superior product!

II. COMMENTARY

The Power of Christ's Permanent Sacrifice

MAIN IDEA: *Because the sacrifice of Christ is endlessly effective, it produces people with spiritual stamina, liberal love, and conspicuous commitment.*

A The Permanence of Christ's Sacrifice (vv. 1–18)

SUPPORTING IDEA: *Christ's sacrifice is permanent because it demonstrates a chosen obedience and true forgiveness.*

1. Permanent in Contrast to Old Testament Sacrifices (vv. 1–4)

10:1. The Old Testament law had impressive ceremonies supported by centuries of tradition. It preserved an awareness of divine holiness and revealed the need for atonement. Nevertheless, the repetition of offerings and sacrifices on the annual Day of Atonement never brought the worshipers into a permanent relationship with God. Why? Old Testament sacrifices reminded of sin but did not remove it.

Hebrews emphasizes that the Law was only a shadow of God's good blessings and not the reality. A shadow can never reveal its object, but it can provide an outline of reality. Whenever the reality comes, the shadow is irrelevant. Because the Law was only a faint outline of the glories of the coming gospel, it was a temporary element in God's plan.

10:2. This verse highlights the imperfection of the Law by asking a question, If the Law made the worshipers perfect, then wouldn't offerings cease because the worshipers would **no longer have felt guilty for their sins?** If the offerings had reached their goals, they would have stopped. These sacrifices dealt only with infractions committed since the last offerings. They left the root cause—sin—untouched. Their repetition showed their inadequacy.

10:3. Every offering announced the inadequacy of the previous offerings. It reminded the worshipers to get ready for the next annual offering. Only the sacrifice of Christ could abolish the consequences of sin permanently. An annual reminder of sin could only produce people who could say, "We've got to do something about this sin problem." But nothing was ever done. When Christ came to die for sin, believers were blessed by an experience with a God who no longer remembered their sins (Heb. 8:12).

10:4. Why were the animal sacrifices so ineffective in removing sin? Animal sacrifices could never remove sin because they were never intended to take away sin. They were intended to foreshadow Jesus, who would later come to die to take away the sins of believers. Only the death of the perfect God-man could take away sin. The psalmist had grasped centuries earlier that "the sacrifices of God are a broken spirit; a broken and contrite heart, O God, you will not despise" (Ps. 51:17). God accepted the perfect sacrifice of Christ because it represented a broken, contrite expression of obedience to his will.

2. Permanent Based on Obedience (vv. 5–10)

10:5–6. The failure of animal sacrifices to secure forgiveness led to the explanation of a better approach. The answer comes from Psalm 40:6–8 and applies to our situation. The words of the psalm express Christ's mission after he entered the world in the incarnation. Christ's sacrifice lasted because it showed a volitional commitment to do God's will. Jesus showed a continuous awareness that he was to do the Father's will, and he pursued it relentlessly.

God was not really seeking any type of animal sacrifice. What God desired was a person devoted to fulfilling his will. The thoughtless slaughtering of animals did not remove sin. God had no pleasure in specific sacrifices—**burnt offerings and sin offerings**—because they had become an end in themselves. Those who offered them had failed to do God's will. He was pleased only when the sacrifices were a demonstration of a broken and contrite heart. Wholehearted obedience was the only sacrifice God really wanted, and he found this response supremely in Jesus Christ.

10:7. When Christ came, he willingly committed his life to the plan of God. Doing God's will was his supreme goal. The **scroll** probably referred to what was written in the Old Testament Scriptures. Christ came to fulfill the promises of Scripture. In Psalm 40 the words appearing after the reference to the "scroll" describe someone who desires to do God's will because the divine law is in his heart. Surely these words describe the attitude of Christ. Christ came to earth with the passion of doing the will of God.

10:8–9. These verses repeat the chief ideas of verses 5–7. They contrast Old and New Testament means of approaching God. Christ came to give perfect obedience to the divine will. In so doing, he abolished the first covenant to establish the second or the new covenant.

10:10. The only complete fulfillment of the will of God appeared in Christ's perfect obedience. Because we who have trusted Christ are identified with him, we also have fulfilled the will of God. God received us on the basis of Jesus' complete fulfillment of God's will. **Once for all** showed the finality of the transaction.

In Christ believers receive complete cleansing of their sin. They are equipped to enter God's presence. They can offer acceptable worship to him. They are accepted!

3. Permanent Because It Secured Forgiveness (vv. 11–18)

10:11. Christ's sacrifice lasted because it offered permanent pardon to those who had offended God. Priests presided over an endless round of ineffective sacrifices. Some sacrifices were offered annually at the Day of Atonement. Priests also officiated at the daily sacrifices. The sheer futility of the whole process is evident in this verse.

Standing was a position of continuous work. Sitting was a position of accomplishment. The priests continued to stand because their work was never done. Christ sat (v. 12) because he had made payment for the price of sin.

The standing priest performed **his religious duties**, doing what he was commanded but without permanent results. **Again and again** translates a single Greek word which stands in contrast with Jesus' **once for all** work (v. 10).

The work of the priest was ineffective, offering repetitious sacrifices which could **never take away sins.** By contrast, Christ's single offering effectively removed sins **for all time.**

10:12. Two features showed the conclusive nature of Christ's sacrifice. First, Christ had offered only a single sacrifice, and this single offering did the job (v. 10). Second, Jesus' job as sacrificial lamb was finished. When Jesus exclaimed, "It is finished" (John 19:30), he really meant it. His enthronement **at the right hand of God** showed the completion of the task. His seat at God's right hand showed that God had exalted him to the position of highest glory. In Jesus, believers have access to unlimited grace and power.

10:13. The present era is a waiting period as Christ anticipates a final victory over his enemies. We have been living in this era since the time of Jesus' exaltation to heaven. Christ has already won the victory, but we do not yet see the complete defeat of Christ's spiritual enemies. Rather than complaining about the delay, we should see this time as a day of grace to allow outsiders to experience God's mercy and forgiveness. We have no doubt or question about the ultimate outcome.

Although this verse does not directly quote Psalm 110:1 (see Heb. 1:13), that passage is clearly in view. Jesus is portrayed as our High Priest, assuming the kingship. As a king, Christ will enjoy full victory over his enemies. He will make a final display of triumph over evil at the end of history (see 1 Cor. 15:22–28).

10:14. Returning to the work of Christ as our High Priest, this verse spotlights the effect of his single offering. (For the purifying effect of Jesus' death, see v. 10.)

On the cross Christ has already made a single offering so that in generation after generation he is continually making holy all who respond in faith.

To become **perfect** did not promise sinless perfection, but it promised believers the full realization of God's saving purpose.

10:15–17. Here we return to the new covenant (cf. 8:8–13), again quoting Jeremiah 31. The Holy Spirit was the author of this practical and relevant application.

God has written his law within us and will no longer remember our sins and lawless acts. The old covenant had provided for an annual remembrance of sin (v. 3). The new covenant promised no more remembrance of sin. We can receive complete forgiveness, for Jesus' death gives freedom from the penalty of sin.

10:18. These words close the doctrinal section of Hebrews. Christ's new covenant makes Old Testament sacrifices obsolete. When God erases our sins, we no longer need a sin offering. The entire sacrificial system is unnecessary. The single offering of Christ has wiped out the need for the old sacrificial system and has introduced a new era. Christ himself fulfilled the message which God intended the sacrifices to proclaim.

Anyone who wants forgiveness of sin can find access by placing a repentant faith in the completed work of Christ. Christ's sacrifice was God's final answer to the universal problem of human sin. God has no need to speak a word beyond Jesus.

🅑 The Power of Christ's Sacrifice (vv. 19–39)

SUPPORTING IDEA: *Our response to Christ's death provides power to love others and to demonstrate endurance in the Christian life.*

1. An Appeal to Experience Christ's Power (vv. 19–25)

10:19. The practical section of Hebrews begins by teaching us that we experience Christ's power by drawing near to God, maintaining our faith, and loving other believers. **Therefore** emphasizes that in view of what Jesus has done, believers can approach God with confidence. **Confidence** describes a boldness believers have because of our new relationship to God. The **Most Holy Place** was that part of the sanctuary which symbolized the presence of God (see 9:3). This verse uses the term not for the tabernacle but for the presence of God. All believers can come to God's presence. This privilege is no longer limited to the priesthood.

Believers can approach God because of the **blood of Jesus.** Not animal sacrifice but Jesus' sacrifice of himself has opened the door. All who have found a new relationship to God through Jesus can experience this privilege.

10:20–21. We have the boldness to enter into the holiest place because Jesus has opened for us **a new and living way.** He serves as our **great priest** to encourage us to enter God's presence. Christ's way to the Father is **new**

because he opened it by his death. The resurrection of the sacrificed One has made the way **living**, or effective and enduring. This stands in contrast with the weak, ineffective rituals of the priests with slain animals who remained dead. We don't walk up to God in halfhearted weakness but with the power of the risen, living Christ.

Jesus told his disciples he is the **way**. Early Christians found their movement described as "the Way" (Acts 9:2). In Hebrews 9:8 the term describes our access to God. Christ's atoning work has provided free access to God for believers.

Curtain (see 6:19; 9:3) refers to the veil that stood between the Holy Place and the Most Holy Place. In Hebrews it becomes a symbol of Jesus' human life. As a human being, Jesus opened up a new way to God. Jesus presented his human life to God to bring us to him (1 Pet. 3:18). Jesus' human life and sacrificial death have made the Most Holy Place wide open so believers can enter directly into God's presence. This was part of Jesus' high priestly service.

10:22. We can now approach God and have the mercy and grace of our High Priest standing over us. This blessing brings us many privileges. The next three verses contain three exhortations.

The first exhortation is for believers to draw near to God in an expression of personal devotion. Four conditions for approaching God are given.

First, we are to come **with a sincere heart.** This calls for genuine devotion rather than hypocrisy. Second, we are to come **in full assurance of faith.** This demands a bold confidence that God has provided full access to his presence through Christ alone. Third, we are to have our **hearts sprinkled . . . from a guilty conscience.** This demands constant confession of our sins and openness to God. Finally we are to have our **bodies washed with pure water.** This may be a reference to baptism as an outward commitment to Christ, or it might be symbolic as is the previous reference to hearts sprinkled with blood. If it is symbolic, the hearts sprinkled from a guilty conscience would picture our salvation, and our bodies washed would symbolize a righteous lifestyle. In this new state of purity made possible by Jesus, believers can come boldly to God and claim his grace and mercy.

10:23. The second exhortation appeals to us to maintain spiritual consistency. We are urged to hold firmly to **the hope** we profess. This hope offers glory which beamed more brightly than the glories of the old order. **Unswervingly** denotes an object which stands absolutely straight, not departing from the perpendicular. We are to lay hold of Christ and never let go, even in the slightest. No persecution, real or feared, was to lessen the ardor of these believers for Christ.

Is it really possible to live unswervingly? If holding on to the promises depended on personal commitment, we would all be in trouble. God is faithful to provide strength and stamina for endurance. His faithful character is beyond all doubt. In his strength we hold on unswervingly. We will read heroic examples of spiritual steadfastness in chapter 11.

10:24. The third exhortation calls us to responsibility to one another. The appeal to **consider** demands concentrated attention. The goal of this attention was to **spur one another on toward love and good deeds.** As Christians we have a corporate responsibility. We must help others who stumble and falter. We must concentrate on the needs of others and not on our individual salvation only.

We can **spur** people toward either good or bad works. Hebrews calls us to lead others to a practical expression of love and an attractive display of unselfish deeds.

The three important virtues of faith, hope, and love are mentioned in three consecutive verses (see 1 Cor. 13:13). Faith provides assurance. Hope promises an incentive to obedience. Love provides a foundation for prodding believers to godly living

10:25. To spur other believers forward in the Christian life, followers of Christ must meet together. Some of the readers of Hebrews were neglecting to meet together for worship, and this limited their ability to give and receive encouragement toward good works.

Christians who meet together with the aim of promoting godliness and love for one another can be remarkably successful in their ventures. Regular fellowship with believers is an essential ingredient in Christian growth. The readers of Hebrews knew that the **Day** of Christ's return was drawing near. The closeness of this day compelled them to stimulate one another in an outburst of energy and concern.

Persecution may have led some believers to drop out of the fellowship. The remedy they needed was to begin meeting again. The verses following in 26–31 showed the final outcome of neglecting to meet with other believers. Such careless living could produce a contempt for Jesus and a renunciation of Christianity.

2. A Warning to Avoid God's Judgment (vv. 26–31)

10:26–27. These verses contain a warning which resembles the words of Hebrews 6:4–6: Neglecting to fellowship with believers can lead to a rejection of Christ's sacrifice for sin. The act of sinning **deliberately** involved a willful sin for which the Law of Moses did not provide clear forgiveness (see Num. 15:30). The Law promised forgiveness for sins of ignorance, but willful sins had no remedy.

As believers, we have assurance that "if we confess our sins, he is faithful and just and will forgive us our sins" (1 John 1:9a). The New Testament is quick to offer forgiveness for all types of sins for people who confess and repent. Willful sins can receive divine forgiveness, but people involved in these sins often fail to seek God's forgiveness by repentance.

The sin against which these believers were warned involved a deliberate rejection of the truth of the gospel. Some were apparently considering leaving Christ to return to Judaism to avoid persecution. Anyone who rejected the sacrifice of Christ for sins would not find any other means of handling sin. Some of the readers of Hebrews were in danger of spurning the only way God had provided to remove sin. Thus the warning that they would find no other path to God open.

If they abandoned Christ, they would face **only a fearful expectation of judgment and of raging fire**. This describes eternal judgment on those who were not believers. No sinners should expect deliverance when they are guilty of trifling with the living God.

The author of Hebrews did not say that any of the readers had committed the sin he had described. He warned that if such a thing occurred, those who had sinned could anticipate judgment and divine wrath. Anyone who rejected the sacrifice of Christ would find no other answer to the problem of sin.

The issue addressed in Hebrews 10 resembles that in chapter 6. The present writer feels that the author of Hebrews addressed a message to those who professed to be Christians and urged them to show their genuine profession by their refusal to apostatize (see the discussion in ch. 6). Hebrews calls the readers, **brothers**. That means the author related to the readers as fellow Christians. He could not evaluate clearly their inward commitment. If the readers left Christ for Judaism, they would show that they had never responded in faith to Christ. The author of Hebrews spoke to them as Christians and urged them to show their real faith by endurance in their commitment. He probably suspected that all his readers would not respond in the same way. He assumed their continuance in commitment to Christ would demonstrate authentic Christianity. Any other response would show they had never become believers in Christ. He wrote those thinking of returning to Judaism, making sure they understood the serious nature of such action.

10:28–29. These verses cite an example of the kind of deliberate sinning which received divine wrath. Under the old covenant, anyone who rejected the Mosaic Law could not expect mercy. The outlook was for death (Deut. 17:6). Sinners of this type could not expect mercy.

More serious still was the judgment of someone who has trampled the **Son of God under foot**. This was a condition much worse than violating the Mosaic Law. The words used picture a strong antagonism toward Jesus. To treat **as an unholy thing the blood of the covenant** involved despising Christ's work. To insult **the Spirit of grace** involved an arrogant rejection of the truth which the Holy Spirit tried to communicate about Jesus. These phrases contain a warning to professing believers who were threatening to turn against Christ. Any who turned from Christ could expect divine judgment and eternal rejection.

10:30–31. When we come to God, we do not want to receive his judgment but his mercy. The result of falling into God's hands is fearful. The apostate who experiences God's hand in judgment should know that it would be a frightening experience. The anticipation of judgment by the living God should fill sinners with dread (see Heb. 12:29).

3. A Commendation to All Who Persevere (vv. 32–39)

10:32–33. These verses urged the readers to remember the days after their conversion when they stood their ground while they faced threats to their faith. They were to remember their previous record. What a positive record it had been!

They had refused to compromise when they faced persecution for their faith. Sometimes they had become **publicly exposed to insult and persecution.** They had endured scorn and threats from crowds. The words of 12:4 suggest that they had not yet suffered martyrdom.

Sometimes they **stood side by side** with friends who were insulted and abused. They suffered because of their association with others. They found it a privilege to share in the sufferings of others.

10:34. The general description of persecution in verse 33 becomes specific in this verse. Facing hardship involves two matters. First, they had **sympathized with those in prison.** It was common in those days for Christians to receive imprisonment for their commitment to Christ (note Paul's imprisonments mentioned in 2 Cor. 11:23). Probably at least some of the recipients of Hebrews had suffered imprisonment because of their Christian confession. Visiting these imprisoned believers openly identified some of the readers as Christians and made them subject to arrest and persecution. They had endured public shame because of their encouragement to imprisoned Christians.

Second, the readers had experienced the loss of their property. They took the loss with joy. They were so convinced of the truth of Christianity that they submitted joyfully to the loss of their possessions. How could they do this?

The readers had learned that in Christ they had **better and lasting possessions.** They could never lose their possessions in Christ because these possessions lasted (see Matt. 6:20). Heaven's treasures had greater appeal than the temporary blessings of earth.

10:35. The confidence of these believers had caused them to endure much suffering. They were urged, "Don't throw away your confidence which will bring you great reward." They were already receiving a reward in their present steadfastness. They could expect even greater reward in the future. God's goodness and faithfulness would make their rewards certain.

10:36. What did they need to endure? They needed stamina or staying power. **You need to persevere** described a persistence in the face of persecution and difficult circumstances. In James 1:2–4 we learn that God develops this trait in those who trust him through trying circumstances. Staying power comes through learning to trust God in trials.

Two events would happen if these believers showed staying power. First, they would do the will of God. Second, they would receive the benefit of God's promises. Mature Christians have learned that God's strength will take them through adversity. They trust that God will provide them his glorious promises because he is dependable and trustworthy.

10:37–38. These verses refer to a pair of Old Testament passages to encourage these believers to persevere.

First, some words of Isaiah 26:20 in the Greek Old Testament are quoted to show that in Isaiah's day Israel waited for God to act. No one should think that lack of action indicated a failure on God's part to keep his word. Believers can endure with confidence because God will come through! Christ would come to rescue and deliver his people.

Second, the thoughts of Habakkuk 2:3–4 are cited to express the certainty of God's coming intervention for those who trust him. Those who are righteous **will live by faith.** Their faith will support them as they wait confidently for God to act.

To those who wavered, a warning is issued. God has no pleasure in those who shrink back. These believers needed to maintain their confidence.

10:39. This chapter of Hebrews closes with an expression of blazing confidence. These believers were **not of those who shrink back and are destroyed, but of those who believe and are saved.** The stern warnings were an effort to prod the readers of Hebrews to faithful commitment.

MAIN IDEA REVIEW: *Because the sacrifice of Christ is effective, it produces people with spiritual stamina, liberal love, and conspicuous commitment.*

III. CONCLUSION

Power in Sacrifice

Imprisoned in Rome, Paul wrote his friends at Philippi one of his most joyous letters. Most inmates find a grim existence in confinement, but Paul announced to his Philippian friends that his confinement had actually contributed to the spread of the gospel (Phil. 1:12). Soldiers, ordinary servants of the king, and many other people learned that Paul's confinement came because of his commitment to Christ.

On the outside, some of Paul's Christian friends became bolder in their witness when they saw God's care of Paul. Others, who seemed to be Paul's opponents, tried to add misery to his affliction (Phil. 1:16). Whatever their motivation, Paul rejoiced at the preaching of Christ (Phil. 1:18). What caused Paul the inmate to have this joy? What prevented his issuing a chorus of complaints about his lot in life? Paul would say, "I find power in Christ to strengthen me" (Phil. 4:13).

The writer of Hebrews knew that Christians would find power in Christ's permanent sacrifice. He had seen the ineffectiveness of Old Testament sacrifices (Heb. 10:1–4), but he had also observed that Christ's sacrifice produced long-lasting changes which prompted new life in his followers. Christ's sacrifice demonstrated a chosen commitment to follow God's will (10:5–10). His sacrifice did the job because it obtained forgiveness for Jesus' followers (10:11–18), unlike the Jewish priests who regularly offered sacrifices which did not remove sin (10:11).

Because Christ's sacrifice had power to change people, three appeals were given (10:19–25). These believers were urged to draw near to God, to hold fast to their commitment, and to stir up fellow believers to love and unselfish deeds.

Some of these believers were considering turning away from Christ. They were reminded that abandoning Christ left them without any sacrifice for their sins. Those who left Jesus could expect judgment because they would turn away from the only solution to their sin, the death of Jesus (10:26–31).

The author of Hebrews had strong hope that his readers had made a commitment they would follow (10:32–39). They had faced public humiliation, imprisonment, and loss of property because they had followed Christ. They had endured in doing God's will. God would honor their faithfulness. Only Jesus could provide struggling believers the grace and strength to move forward in stalwart service to him.

PRINCIPLES

- The annual repetition of sacrifices reminded the Jews of their sin but did not remove it.
- Jesus' sacrifice represented a volitional choice to obey God.
- Jesus' sacrifice secured forgiveness of sin.
- Jesus' sacrifice provided Christians the privilege of entering God's very presence.
- Rejecting Jesus' sacrifice leads to judgment.
- Christians need stamina to endure in commitment to God's will despite hardship and persecution.

APPLICATIONS

- Freely choose to obey God even as you suffer.
- Live before God in the joy of forgiven sin.
- Trust God's faithfulness, and maintain your commitment to Christ without flinching.
- Let fear of God's judgment give you a healthy incentive to obey him.
- Claim from God the stamina to obey him even when you cannot understand what is happening.

IV. LIFE APPLICATION

The Power to Persevere

A few years ago Billy Graham's *Decision* magazine published an article entitled, "My Wife Pushes Me Around." Reading the title, I thought the article dealt with a husband being pushed around by an overbearing wife. Then I saw a picture of the writer beside the title. He was in a wheelchair, and his wife stood behind him. She literally pushed him around, and he was thankful.

Leslie K. Tarr was a pastor in Winnipeg, Manitoba. Tubercular meningitis left him paralyzed and confined to a wheelchair. He hoped for a miracle of healing, but it never came. Gradually, he realized he must live with his difficulty.

The support and prayer of his immediate family and church family were unfailing sources of strength as he faced his limitations. As he walked with the Lord along the path of the new adventure, he found God opening doors of ministry for him. He found opportunities for Christian writing, teaching in a seminary, and encouragement of others.

He testified: "As simply as I can express it, I contend that he worked a miracle inside me. He did not lift me out of the wheelchair, but he has given the grace and the strength to be thankful and contented in the wheelchair. To be grateful that someone cares enough to push me around." God's grace has met his needs. Leslie Tarr has found in Christ the power to persevere in the face of life's difficulties. God has given him stamina and the will to trust him. God makes this strength available to those who obey him and walk with him in the face of difficulty and hardship.

V. PRAYER

Lord, life is hard. The world never encourages my faith. It tries everything to make me forget you. Give me strength and faith to cling to you. Show me the joy of faith even in the darkness of hardship. Fill me with your love, so I may love others as you do. Hold my hand so I will have light in the darkness. Amen.

VI. DEEPER DISCOVERIES

A. Cleansing (v. 2)

When Christians trust Jesus as Savior and Lord, they receive permanent cleansing from sin. This cleansing does not require any repetition of animal sacrifices because Christ's sacrifice involved a perfect offering. Cleansing involves the forgiveness of sin and brings the privilege of perfect fellowship with God. Christians receive this cleansing by faith (Acts 15:9).

Christians who fall into sin and disobedience break their fellowship with God, but they never lose their position in his family. Confession of sin can restore this fellowship (1 John 1:9).

B. Sacrifice, Offering, Burnt Offerings, Sin Offerings (vv. 5–6)

Four different words are used to describe sacrifices that the Old Testament priests offered to God. **Sacrifice** (*thusia*) refers often to the Old Testament peace offering, but it may refer to any type of animal sacrifice. The peace offering knitted fellowship between God and the worshiper. **Offering** (*prosphora*) often refers to a cereal offering. This offering expressed consecration. **Burnt offerings** (*holokautoma*) describes a sacrifice which expresses worship. **Sin offerings** (*peri hamartia*) refers to an atonement for sin. All of these terms taken together provide a comprehensive picture of the complete range of sacrifices which the Old Testament priests offered before God.

C. Take Away (v. 11)

This vivid word (*periaireo*) describes the action of removing something which surrounds someone. It portrays the image of the peeling away of an unwanted coat or covering in a warm room. Hebrews teaches that Old Testament sacrifices could never peel away sin. Sin still lingered even after the priests offered sacrifices. Jesus' single sacrifice permanently removed the sin which hinders our fellowship with God.

D. Confidence (v. 19)

Confidence (*parresia*) also appears in 4:16. It describes boldness gained from our new freedom in relationship to God. Christians can approach God with a freedom of expression and a release from fear. This confidence allows believers to approach God with a hopefulness previously limited to the priests.

E. Curtain (v. 20)

The curtain mentioned here divided the Holy Place of the tabernacle from the Most Holy Place. This curtain symbolized the body or flesh of Christ. The author of Hebrews was probably relating this curtain to the incident in Matthew 27:51 which involved the tearing of the curtain of the Temple at the time of Jesus' crucifixion. This act symbolized the provision of direct access to God because of Jesus' death. The offering of Jesus' body in obedience to God has opened a **new and living way** to God's presence.

F. Spur (v. 24)

Spur (*paroxusmos*) is a word which describes the act of stirring up something. It can be used in the negative sense of stirring up disagreements (see Acts 15:39). Hebrews 10 uses it in the positive sense of urging the readers to consider how they could stimulate their Christian friends to produce love and good deeds. We must make it our object to nudge fellow Christians forward in love, service, and obedience.

G. The Day (v. 25)

The New Testament makes many references to the Day of the Lord (1 Thess. 5:2; 2 Pet. 3:10). The term is used here in Hebrews as a reference to a day of reckoning (Rom. 2:16), or the time of Jesus' return in the second coming.

An awareness of the nearness of the time of Jesus' return would prod Christians to wholehearted obedience (see 2 Pet. 3:11). Knowing that Jesus will return gives believers an eagerness to prepare for him by godly living.

H. Deliberate Sinning (v. 26)

People who sinned deliberately walked into sin with their eyes open. The Old Testament made provision for forgiveness for careless sins (Num. 15:30). It allowed no mercy for willful sins. Does this mean that no willful sin could ever receive forgiveness? Probably not, and here is why.

When New Testament saints sin deliberately before God, their sin does not break their legal standing before God (Rom. 8:1). Christ's death for our sins paid for all our sins—past, present, and future (1 Cor. 15:3; Rom. 6:23). Sinning Christians are still God's children.

Sinning Christians break their fellowship with God (Eph. 4:30), and they experience God's discipline in their lives (Heb. 12:10). Sinning Christians damage their usefulness in service for the Lord. They weaken their spiritual lives (John 15:4).

The reference to deliberate sinning in Hebrews probably describes a willful turning from Christ which could only lead to judgment and lostness. Those who returned to Judaism and abandoned Christ after having learned the truth of the gospel would find no forgiveness anywhere. They would show they had never made a personal commitment to Jesus Christ.

I. Perseverance (v. 36)

Perseverance involves endurance in the face of difficult circumstances. It is a spiritual grace developed by facing and overcoming hardship and adversity with divine strength (Jas. 1:2–4). Christians must endure to reap the benefits of God's promised blessings. Those who are believers will persevere. Those who are not believers will fall away in the face of persecution, life's difficulties, or the worries of life.

VII. TEACHING OUTLINE

A. INTRODUCTION

1. Lead Story: Producing a Superior Product
2. Context: Chapter 9 of Hebrews presents the rituals of the old covenant as temporary, inadequate, and ineffective. The work of Christ is described as permanent, thorough, and sufficient to remove sin permanently. Chapter 10 emphasizes the permanence and power of Christ's sacrifice. Many of the ideas in these two chapters complement one another.

   First, believers are reminded of the impermanence of Old Testament sacrifices. The constant repetition of the offerings demonstrated their ineffectiveness (10:1–4). The sacrifice of Christ was permanent because it represented an obedience chosen by Christ, who was following God's will (10:5–10). Christ's sacrifice was also permanent because it secured forgiveness and never needed repetition (10:11–18).

   Second, the power of Christ's sacrifice is emphasized (10:19–39). Christians should draw near to God, hold fast to their commitment, and consider how to stimulate one another to obedience (10:19–25). All who abandoned Christ could expect judgment, not mercy (10:26–31). Finally, these believers are commended for their endurance of hardship, and they are urged to develop perseverance so they might reach out to God's promises (10:32–39).

3. Transition: "Permanent" and "powerful" describe the effect of Christ's death. Christ's death was permanent because it had accomplished the task of obtaining forgiveness. It also represented a choice to obey God, a decision which God loved and desired. Christ's death was powerful because it could take people harassed and hounded by trials and transform them into people of endurance. This chapter

encouraged the readers of Hebrews to endure in their commitment until they received the goal of their salvation.

B. COMMENTARY
1. The Permanence of Christ's Sacrifice (vv. 1–18)
    a. Permanent in contrast to Old Testament sacrifices (vv. 1–4)
    b. Permanent based on Jesus' obedience (vv. 5–10)
    c. Permanent because it secured forgiveness (vv. 11–18)
2. The Power of Christ's Sacrifice (vv. 19–39)
    a. An appeal to experience Christ's power (vv. 19–25)
    b. A warning to avoid God's judgment (vv. 26–31)
    c. A commendation to all who persevere (vv. 32–39)

C. CONCLUSION: THE POWER TO PERSEVERE

VIII. ISSUES FOR DISCUSSION

1. How do you define a willful sin? Do you fear that you have committed willful, deliberate sins? Do you think Jesus will forgive you of these sins? What must you do?
2. What pleases God if sacrifices do not? In what way did Jesus please the Father? How does this bring benefits to you?
3. What conditions cause there to be "no longer any sacrifice for sin"?
4. What does it mean to draw near to God? Have you done so?

Hebrews 11

Learning Faith from the Champions!

I. **INTRODUCTION**
Living and Dying Well

II. **COMMENTARY**
A verse-by-verse explanation of the chapter.

III. **CONCLUSION**
I Will Try

An overview of the principles and applications from the chapter.

IV. **LIFE APPLICATION**
Accomplishing for God

Melding the chapter to life.

V. **PRAYER**
Tying the chapter to life with God.

VI. **DEEPER DISCOVERIES**
Historical, geographical, and grammatical enrichment of the commentary.

VII. **TEACHING OUTLINE**
Suggested step-by-step group study of the chapter.

VIII. **ISSUES FOR DISCUSSION**
Zeroing the chapter in on daily life.

"*The* great achievers in history have been the men and women who could see the invisible and strive to reach it. Explorers, inventors, liberators, and pioneers in every field have always been characterized by the steady eye that sees the invisible and strives for the seemingly impossible."

Warren W. Wiersbe

IN A NUTSHELL

Faith provides a certainty about things we cannot see. Many Old Testament saints exemplified this faith. Hebrews 11 applauds many of these, holding them up for an example. Included are Abel, Enoch, Noah, Abraham, Isaac, Jacob, Joseph, Moses' parents, Moses, Israel during the Exodus from Egypt, Gideon, David, Samuel, and Isaiah. Rahab is a surprising member on the list. All these lived by faith, placing their confidence in things they could not see.

Old Testament saints departed life without receiving God's promise. New Testament believers experience the **something better** which God made available through Christ. As we run the race of the Christian life, the champions of Hebrews 11 can encourage us to faith.

Learning Faith from the Champions!

I.   INTRODUCTION

Living and Dying Well

About A.D. 150, fierce anti-Christian persecution erupted in Asia Minor. One of the most famous examples of these trials occurred in Smyrna in A.D. 156. The rabble of the city demanded that Christian leaders swear obedience to Caesar by burning incense before his statue and affirming, "Caesar is Lord."

Polycarp served as bishop of Smyrna. His persistent devotion to Christ for decades had made him a highly visible local figure. When an unruly mob looked for Christians to humiliate, they called for Polycarp.

A police squad went to get the aged Christian leader. The captain, probably wanting to spare Polycarp from the coming hardship, said, "What harm is there in saying that Caesar is Lord? Swear loyalty to Caesar and save yourself." Polycarp refused the captain's request, and they hauled him to the city arena.

There the proconsul of Asia renewed the plea and said to him, "Consider your age. Swear by the divinity of Caesar. Just say, 'Away with the atheists.'"

Polycarp knew that the true atheists were those who denied the deity of Christ, not those who refused to acknowledge the divinity of Caesar. He waved his hand toward the pagan crowd and exclaimed, "Away with the atheists."

The proconsul still insisted, "Take the oath of loyalty to Caesar, and I will let you go. Revile Christ."

Then Polycarp made a noble confession: "Eighty-six years have I served Him, and He has done me no wrong; how then can I blaspheme my Saviour and King?" Further argument with Polycarp proved useless, and they sent him to the stake.

Polycarp's martyrdom did two things. It produced a temporary revulsion against martyrdoms among the pagan population. The pagan crowd had no stomach for burning old men at the stake. It also gave Christians a high level of credibility before their pagan neighbors. If Christianity could produce people like Polycarp, then even pagan people were interested in their source of conviction and commitment. Christianity produces people who both live well and die well. Polycarp's death provides powerful evidence of this truth as do the saints of Hebrews 11.

II. COMMENTARY

Learning Faith from the Champions!

> **MAIN IDEA:** *Faith in God's promises enabled the Old Testament saints to claim God's promises and experience salvation.*

A The Result of Faith (vv. 1–3)

> **SUPPORTING IDEA:** *Faith brings a confidence in God's promises and shows trust in his character.*

11:1. Eyesight produces a conviction about objects in the physical world. Faith produces the same convictions for the invisible order. Faith shows itself by producing assurance that what we hope for will happen. Faith also provides an insight into realities which otherwise remain unseen. A person with faith lets these unseen realities from God provide a living, effective power for daily life.

11:2–3. These verses present two illustrations of the use of faith. First, faith enabled the heroes of the Old Testament to receive a good standing with God. God gave his approval to the faith of these saints.

Second, believing that God created the world involves a leap of faith. Faith points to an unseen power who made the world we see. The **universe** involves more than the physical world. It includes the ages that God had planned, beginning with the act of creation and extending to the consummation of all things in Christ. By faith we know that all we see around us and all that takes place on earth came from one we cannot see.

By observing creation we may learn of God's power. We learn the manner of God's creation only by responding in faith to the statements of Scripture.

B Examples of Faith (vv. 4–38)

> **SUPPORTING IDEA:** *The actions of the Old Testament saints show that faith pleases God and that he rewards all who seek him.*

1. The Generations Before the Flood (vv. 4–7)

11:4. Genesis 4:3–7 and the rest of the Old Testament do not explain why Abel's offering was more acceptable than Cain's. Hebrews offers the explanation: Abel showed faith. The fact that God accepted Abel's sacrifice showed that he had an obedient attitude of mind. In some way Cain held back from God, perhaps in his heart. Abel's offering was an unrestrained response to

God, complete with lavish worship which pleased God. John tells us that Cain's works were evil, while those of Abel were righteous (1 John 3:12).

Even though Cain murdered Abel, the faith of Abel still spoke over the centuries. Even a violent death could not muzzle the message of faith. Abel's demonstration of faith allows him to speak a message of encouragement to us today.

11:5. Genesis 5:24 reports: "Enoch walked with God; then he was no more, because God took him away." Two comments on this statement are pertinent. First, Enoch's release from death was due to his faith. Second, before his translation to heaven he had lived a life pleasing to God. In an age of corruption Enoch stood out as a man of righteousness. He showed his faith by his walk with God. Faith in a God he could not see controlled Enoch's life.

11:6. Real fellowship with God cannot exist without faith. Two convictions must characterize the lives of believers. First, they must **believe that he exists.** Anyone wanting to commune with God must have the deep conviction that God is real. Second, God's servants must believe that **he rewards those who earnestly seek him.** Faith is not selfish; rather, faith has confidence in a God of love and goodness. These two convictions must provide a bedrock foundation for the lives of Christians. It would be foolish to look for a God who does not exist or for one who—if he did exist—would punish you if you found him.

11:7. Noah (Gen. 6–9) showed his faith in response to a specific warning from God. He took the warning to heart, built an ark, and saved his family. Noah's act of building the ark condemned the scoffing unbelief of his generation and provided visible evidence that Noah believed God. Noah's contemporaries must have been merciless in their ridicule of this "foolish" man who was building an ark so far inland.

In building the ark, Noah became an heir of faith righteousness, a theme echoing Paul's discussion of the subject (Rom. 9:30; 10:6).

2. Abraham and the Patriarchs (vv. 8–22)

11:8. Abraham's faith shined brightly out of a dark background. Paul spent an entire chapter (Rom. 4) commending the faith of this spiritual leader. Abraham received a call to follow God which he accepted without question. He left Haran by faith (Gen. 11:31–12:4) and let God supply the road map. He did not receive his inheritance at the time of his first call, and he did not even know the location of the Promised Land. His daring faith earned him the title of "father of the faithful."

Today Jews, Muslims, and Christians revere the name of faithful Abraham, but it is likely his contemporaries laughed at him when he left Haran. God can accomplish wonderful results in his followers, who walk with him as pilgrims on earth.

11:9–10. These verses add three facts about Abraham's faith. First, his faith extended to his family. Isaac and Jacob became linked as heirs with him of the same promise. Second, he showed a tenacious faith by living as a nomad in a foreign land without rights and privileges. Third, Abraham did not look primarily for a physical city in the Promised Land but for a spiritual city founded and built by God. Abraham wanted God to be the **architect and builder** of the city. The secret of Abraham's patient waiting was that he could see the invisible and move toward it.

11:11–12. Abraham's greatest demonstration of faith came when he showed faith in God's promise that he would have an heir. He was then one hundred years of age (Gen. 17:17; 21:5). Sarah at ninety (Gen. 17:17) embraced a promise which first caused her to laugh (Gen. 18:12–15). Both Abraham and Sarah shared the conviction that God was faithful to his promises.

From these two elderly Hebrews who were **as good as dead** came a nation teeming with life **as numerous as the stars in the sky and as countless as the sand on the seashore.**

11:13–16. These verses summarize the piety of the patriarchs, Abraham, Isaac, Jacob, and Joseph. Three features stand out.

First, these men **were still living by faith when they died.** Faith ruled their lives as they faced life and death. Second, **they did not receive the things promised.** They endured in their faith because they had seen the promises and embraced them. They trusted God to give future generations what they only hoped for. Third, they confessed that they were aliens and wanderers on earth. They did not try to return to the comforts and ease of Ur and Haran in Mesopotamia. They looked for a heavenly city prepared by God. What was the outcome of such sterling faith?

Despite the obvious failings of all these men, God was **not ashamed to be called their God.** He had prepared a spiritual city for them, and he was delighted to be known as their God.

11:17–19. These verses illustrate the faith of Abraham in his readiness to sacrifice Isaac (see Gen. 22:1–10). The test lay in the conflict between the divine promise that Isaac was the heir and the commandment of God to put him to death. Abraham chose to believe that God's promise could not fail and obeyed accordingly.

How could Abraham sacrifice Isaac when God had designated Isaac as the child of promise? Abraham could easily have questioned the guidance from God to offer Isaac. Even though he had never seen a resurrection, he came to the view that God was going to raise Isaac from the dead after the sacrifice had been completed (see Gen. 22:5). Abraham's faith ascended to the level of a resurrection, and God restored Isaac to him as one snatched unexpectedly from the dead.

11:20–22. These verses commend Isaac's faith in blessing both Jacob and Esau when he spoke of their future (Gen. 27:27–29,39–40) and the aged Jacob's faith in blessing the sons of Joseph (Gen. 48:15–20). Both Isaac and Jacob showed faith in recognizing that God intended to give the greater blessing to the younger son, and they accepted God's sovereign plans rather than resisting them.

Joseph showed his faith by giving directions concerning his future burial after the Exodus (see Gen. 50:24–25; Josh. 24:32). Believing in a future Exodus of Jews from Egypt involved considerable faith.

As different as these three men were from one another, each presented an example of faith. The ordinary Isaac, the scheming Jacob, and the exemplary Joseph showed a faith which death could not weaken or destroy.

3. The Faith of Moses (vv. 23–28)

11:23–28. Exodus 2 describes the hiding of Moses by his parents. Hebrews 11 mentions two features of the parents' actions (v. 23). First, they saw that Moses **was no ordinary child** (see Acts 7:20), sensing something in him which destined him for future spiritual greatness. Second, although Pharaoh had commanded death for the male children (Exod. 1:22), Moses' parents **were not afraid of the king's edict.** They trusted God to save Moses, and God rewarded their faith (Exod. 2:8–9).

These verses commend Moses' faith. When Moses became an adult, he made a deliberate choice to leave the comforts of living as **the son of Pharaoh's daughter.** Moses must have known that God had called him to a difficult task. Leaving the splendor of life in the Egyptian court, he chose to cast his lot with God's people in suffering. He refused the temporary pleasures which ease and sin could have provided (see Stephen's summary of Moses' life in Acts 7:20–44).

Why did Moses make this choice? He regarded abuse for Christ as preferable to the material treasures of Egypt (v. 26). Surely Moses' palace friends must have regarded his choice as stupid, but Moses **was looking ahead to his reward.** Moses knew that spiritual treasures would last while material advantages could wilt, disappear, or deceive.

In what sense can we say that Moses suffered **for the sake of Christ?** This could mean that he received the same type of persecution which Christ later received. More likely, however, the writer thought of Christ as being identified with suffering Old Testament saints. Isaiah could say that God was distressed when his people suffered distress (Isa. 63:9). In the same way Christ also identified with the sufferings of his people.

When Moses suffered, he suffered with the same Christ whom the writer urged his readers to identify. We do not know how much Moses understood about Christ. We can understand that the writer of Hebrews was calling his readers to identify with the attitudes and experiences of Moses.

The historical effects of Moses' choices are now summarized (vv. 27–28). Moses **left Egypt, . . . kept the Passover,** and preserved his people. The departure from Egypt was probably not a reference to his initial flight after killing the Egyptian, but to his act of leading his people out of Egypt in the Exodus. His faith overcame his fear of the king's anger. He lived by faith in a God he could not see. Moses kept the Passover in faith because he believed that the sprinkling of blood would banish the angel of death (Exod. 12:21–28).

4. The Faith of Israel (v. 29)

11:29. The nation Israel displayed faith as they safely journeyed through the Red Sea (Exod. 14:13). Moses' faith must have inspired their faith. Such faith did not endure, for they later fell into faithless bickering, quarreling, and disobedience (Exod. 17:1–7; 32:1–14). Their Egyptian pursuers had no such faith and drowned in an avalanche of water as they ventured into the murky sea basin.

5. Faith Throughout Jewish History (vv. 30–38)

11:30–38. Faith led God's people to win battles, endure persecution, and anticipate the life beyond. Joshua led his people to circle Jericho for seven days in what must have appeared to the pagan onlookers as an act of utter futility (Josh. 6). Faith steeled the Israelites with the conviction that their God could do the impossible.

The pagan prostitute Rahab had heard of the mighty exploits of Israel's God (Josh. 2:10–12), and her faith in God moved her to welcome the spies. Her faith enabled her to see them as divine agents rather than as enemies.

The list of faithful servants in Hebrews 11 consists of six names (v. 32) which were typical of the period of the Judges and the early monarchy along with some of the prophets. Included in the list are Gideon (Judg. 6–8), Barak (Judg. 4–5), Samson (Judg. 13–16), and Jephthah (Judg. 11–12). The faithful exploits of Samuel and David were engraved in Israel's history. Samuel was a link between the Judges and the monarchy. David was the most outstanding representative of the monarchy.

Verses 33–34 contain nine statements about the achievements of faith. The statements appeared in three groups of three commendations. The first group of statements marked such attainments as conquering kingdoms, establishing justice, and inheriting spiritual promises. In conquering kingdoms, weak people empowered by faith overcame Israel's enemies (Josh. 8:1–29). In establishing justice, Israel's leaders practiced righteousness rather than injustice (1 Sam. 7:13–17). In receiving promises, wavering human beings seized God's words and lived by them (see Heb. 11:17–19).

In the second triplet actions of endurance are rescue. Faith **shut the mouths of lions** in saving Daniel (see Dan. 6). Faith **quenched the fury of the flames** with Shadrach, Meshach, and Abednego in Daniel 3. Faith **escaped the edge of the sword** for David in 1 Samuel 23:19–26.

The third triplet focuses on positive achievements by believers. Hezekiah found his weakness turned to strength (Isa. 38). David became **powerful in battle and routed foreign armies** (2 Sam. 8:1–18).

The next four verses (vv. 35–38) present a remarkable sample of spiritual stamina and endurance. Elisha raised the Shunammite's son (2 Kgs. 4:18–37) as an example of a woman who received her dead raised to life again. To endure torture required an inner source of strength known only to people of faith.

In Jewish intertestamental writings one famous story of courageous martyrdom involved the death of a mother and her seven sons (see 2 Maccabees 7:1–42). Many scholars feel that the reference to enduring torture in Hebrews 11:35 has this incident in mind. All eight endured barbarous torture because they refused to disobey God's laws. One moving incident in the story occurred when the pagan king asked the mother to encourage the last of the seven sons to renounce his faith and eat swine's flesh. The mother, who had seen six other sons die, said to her son, "Fear not this tormentor, but, being worthy of thy brethren, take thy death, that I may receive thee again in mercy with thy brethren." The son refused to obey the king's command, and the king treated him with greater rage than all the other sons.

Joseph (Gen. 39:20) and Jeremiah (Jer. 20:2; 37:15) are among those who endured jeers, beatings, and imprisonments. Most scholars associate the reference to being **sawed in two** with Isaiah. Although this incident is not mentioned in the Bible, Jewish tradition held to this grisly manner of death for the prophet. (See Martyrdom and Ascension of Isaiah 1:1—3:12; 5:1–16.) In addition to violent death, we also find instances (v. 37) of prolonged hardship, including destitution, persecution, hunger, and severe abuse (1 Kings 18:13).

These instances of extreme difficulty led to the exclamation that **the world was not worthy of them** (v. 38). These people of faith lived in deserts, mountains, and caverns. They were banished from society without fellowship. Many of God's servants had to live like animals. Faith in God does not guarantee comfort in this world. Such faith does promise plentiful reward in the only world that matters.

C The Vindication of Faith (vv. 39–40)

SUPPORTING IDEA: *Faith led believers to experience God's better blessings.*

11:39–40. The promises for which believers eagerly waited appeared only in Christ. Old Testament saints did not experience the eternal inheritance. Their faith earned for them a remarkable reputation and favor with God. They lived and died in the hope of a fulfillment which none of them saw on earth. The reaping of the benefits did not occur until Christ opened the box of spiritual treasures.

Verse 40 may have been a warning to some Jewish Christians who exulted in Jewish heroes so that they forgot their own shortcomings. Such believers needed the finishing work which Christian believers could provide. No part of God's community can be complete without the rest.

Christ's revelation of God's redemption allows all believers to experience their eternal inheritance. Ultimately, all the redeemed from all the ages will be gathered under Christ (Eph. 1:9–10).

MAIN IDEA REVIEW: *Faith in God's promises enabled the Old Testament saints to claim God's promises and experience salvation.*

III. CONCLUSION

I Will Try

B. H. Carroll was an elderly but widely respected Baptist preacher in Texas in the early 1900s. Completely deaf, he sat silently on a train through the Texas Panhandle. His mind fell to the needs of the rapidly growing Baptist churches in Texas. The state had medical schools for doctors, law schools for lawyers, but no special school for training Baptist preachers. Carroll sensed that God was calling him to begin such a school, but he resisted because of his age and his plans to retire soon to devote time to his beloved books. Finally, a conviction that God was calling him to the task overpowered his resistance. Carroll found himself standing up on the train, his hands clutching the seat in front of him, and exclaiming, "Lord, it is clearly thy will; what is impossible with man is possible with God; go thou with me, and I will try."

Then he looked around and realized that his fellow passengers were staring at him with amusement and amazement. He sat down embarrassed but committed to the task. Armed with the determination of faith, Carroll founded Southwestern Baptist Theological Seminary in Fort Worth in 1908. He had responded to the call of a God he could not see. He had shown a faith that was pleasing to God. He lived by the conviction that God **rewards those who earnestly seek him.**

Faith consists of **being sure of what we hope for.** It carries the conviction of the reality of **what we do not see.** Abraham, Isaac, Jacob, Joseph, Moses, Rahab, Gideon, Barak, Samson, Jephthah, David, Samuel, and a host of other faithful followers showed their faith.

By faith they gained divine promises and conquered injustice. Through belief they faced torture and muzzled the mouths of lions. They endured jeers, threats, imprisonment, and death. They received God's commendation. They live as shining examples for us to follow. They challenge us when we waver. They call us to climb the mountains of difficulty which surround us.

When we believe God, we take him at his word and walk with him through whatever he places before us. With faith in God we can face sickness, loss of job, family difficulties, and uncertain futures. With faith in God we can glorify our Father in daily living, find and follow his will for our lives, and receive his commendation of "Well done, good and faithful servant" (Matt. 25:21).

PRINCIPLES

- Faith is a confidence in the reality of what we cannot see.
- Faith begins with a confidence in the existence of God.
- Faith provides a confidence that God rewards those who seek him with the whole heart.
- Faith enabled Abraham, the patriarchs, Gideon, David, Samuel, and a host of other followers of the Lord to honor him in daily life.
- Through Christ believers receive the rewards of their faith.

APPLICATIONS

- Trust God because of his faithfulness and reliability.
- Believe in God's promises, and trust in his character.
- Do not enjoy life on earth so much that you lose sight of your heavenly destination.
- Be willing to face threats, persecutions, and even death as you believe God's promises.
- Claim kingdoms for God as you trust him for the victory.

IV. LIFE APPLICATION

Accomplishing for God

In 1791, Baptist minister William Carey came to a meeting of the Nottinghamshire Baptist Association to urge his fellow ministers to send the gospel to foreign lands so that pagan people might "know the saving grace of the risen Lord." He introduced a resolution in support of foreign missions which stirred fierce debate among the strongly antimissionary Baptists. One of the elders jabbed at Carey and exclaimed, "Sit down, young man! If the Lord wants to convert the heathen he'll do it without your help—or mine!"

A few of the ministers present supported Carey's resolution and encouraged him to press forward. A year later Carey preached the annual sermon at the meeting and poured out his heart in a plea for missions. He emphasized the theme: "Attempt great things for God; expect great things from God."

A few months after his sermon, a small group of pastors and lay people, inspired by Carey's faith, met to form the "British Society for the Evangelization of the Heathen." Carey pledged to be the society's first missionary, and the group raised a small sum of money to support the work. In 1793 Carey and a medical doctor were appointed as Baptist missionaries to India. Carey's challenges were only beginning.

Carey's wife Dorothy at first refused to leave England, and she went only after her sister also promised to go and help with the family's five children. After arrival in India, Carey never received adequate support from his British friends. His wife was never a help to him, and she gradually fell into a state of insanity. Carey lovingly cared for her in this condition.

Carey labored seven years before he saw his first native convert. When news of the conversion of a native to Christianity became known to the Hindu population, a vicious mob formed, seized the convert, and put him in prison. Carey obtained his release and baptized him in a nearby river.

Slowly Carey and his fellow missionaries won a band of converts and established a church. Carey himself mastered numerous Indian languages, established a printing plant, translated the Bible into many languages of the people, and eventually joined the faculty of a government college. His influence helped to end the custom of burning widows alive on the funeral pyre of their husbands.

Through faith Carey overcame opposition from friends in his own country. He worked through the resistance of his wife and the failure to find adequate support from his British friends. He labored with confidence in the face of indifference and open opposition. Wherever Carey went, he attempted great things for God and expected great things from God.

You and I find strength from the indomitable courage of spiritual leaders such as William Carey. The same sources of faith which moved them to accomplish for God are available to us. May God enable us to respond to his promises with a faith that pleases him and a persistence which claims his heavenly rewards.

V. PRAYER

Father, you have gathered such a wonderful cloud of witnesses before us to show us the faith way. You have showered us with your promises. You have revealed your Son Jesus to us. We thank you for all you have done for us. Give us faith to trust you and obey you. May we join the cloud of witnesses so that our lives are examples for some one else. Amen.

VI. DEEPER DISCOVERIES

A. Faith (v. 1)

The Bible never presents a complete definition of faith. This verse provides the best explanation we can find. Practically, faith consists of taking God at his word and acting accordingly. Faith develops assurance about things which do not yet exist. The idea of **being sure** provides a conviction that what we hope for will happen, not because we can make it happen but because God has said it will happen.

Faith also provides a conviction of certainty of **what we do not see.** Just as physical eyesight provides evidence about visible things, faith provides evidence about the invisible. God has promised future blessings and eternal rewards. No one has seen these yet. Still, believers are certain God will deliver on his promises, and we will one day see and experience these blessings and rewards. Faith proves the reality of what we cannot see. Faith enables Christians to live obediently now in the light of what we know in faith will come. "Faith provides a platform for hope and a perception into the reality of what would otherwise remain unseen" (Donald Guthrie).

B. Architect and Builder (v. 10)

Architect (*technites*) appears elsewhere in the New Testament with the meaning of "craftsman" (Acts 19:24,38; Rev. 18:22). Here it refers to God as the designer of all things.

The term **builder** (*demiourgos*) does not occur elsewhere in the New Testament. Here it seems to convey the concept of maker or creator. The builder was someone who carried out the plans of the architect. God is both **architect and builder** of the eternal city in which we have our hope. We have not seen that city, but our faith keeps us obediently living for God until he reveals the eternal city to us.

C. The Faith of Sarah (v. 11)

In verse 11 the translation of the NIV emphasizes the faith of Abraham, but it does not attribute faith to Sarah. The King James Version reads differently: "Through faith also Sara herself received strength to conceive seed, and was delivered of a child when she was past age, because she judged him faithful who had promised."

In Genesis 18:12 Sarah laughed when she learned of the divine promise that she would bear a son. God's comment on her response makes it clear that she had felt that bringing about her conception would be too hard a task for the Lord (Gen. 18:13). It is certainly possible that Sarah later accepted a promise which she first rejected as an impossibility.

One difficulty in the translation of the text is that the words **enabled to become a father** refer to the father's part in the reproductive process, not the mother's. Sarah's name would not fit as the subject of a verb which emphasized the role of the father in child bearing.

Perhaps the best solution is to translate the difficult text with the words "By faith Abraham, together with Sarah, received power to beget a child when he was past age" (F. F. Bruce). This possible translation commends the faith of both Abraham and Sarah.

D. Promise, Promised (vv. 9,11,13,39)

These verses give different content to God's promise, referring to different Old Testament promises. Verse 9 focuses on the promise to Abraham of a land to call his own. Verse 11 speaks of the expectation that Sarah would bear a child. Verse 13 involves the anticipation of a future spiritual inheritance, life in a better country. Verse 39 also points to a spiritual inheritance which only Christ could provide.

The promises given to God's people began with visible, physical promises of a land. They became promises associated with a heavenly inheritance which only a Messiah could provide.

E. Suffering for Christ (v. 26)

Moses died centuries before Christ came to earth. In what sense can we speak of his suffering **disgrace for the sake of Christ?**

Whenever God's people suffer, these sufferings are linked with sufferings on behalf of the Messiah, who is God's perfect representative. All that Moses suffered was in the cause of God's plan of salvation for his people. This plan ended in the insults which Christ himself bore. Since there is a similarity between the sufferings of Moses and of Christ, we can understand that Moses' suffering was indeed for the sake of the work Christ was going to accomplish. The reproach Moses received from the Egyptians, Christ endured to the highest degree in the affliction he received from the Jews and the Romans.

F. Moses' Fear of Pharaoh (v. 27)

Exodus 2:14–15 describes Moses as fearing Pharaoh. A reader of Exodus would feel that fear drove Moses from Egypt to Midian. In what sense can we say that he did not fear **the king's anger** (Heb. 11:27)? There are two possibilities for interpreting these words.

First, the writer of Hebrews may have emphasized that Moses' flight from Egypt was not motivated by fear even though he did indeed fear Pharaoh. The author of Hebrews saw Moses' flight as an act of faith. Yes, Moses was afraid, but that fear did not drive him from Egypt.

Second, fear may have been the motivating factor driving Moses out of Egypt on his flight to Midian (Exod. 2:15). Hebrews 11:27 may refer, instead, to the Exodus departure when Moses led the Israelites out of the land in faith. The fact that Moses **persevered because he saw him who is invisible** could refer to Moses' experience at the burning bush (Exod. 3:1–6). God's revelation to Moses provided him the faith to overcome the fear which had gripped him on the earlier occasion.

G. "Sawed in Two" (v. 37)

Scholars have found a Jewish writing called "The Martyrdom and Ascension of Isaiah" which gives the gory details of Isaiah's martyrdom. The story narrates that Isaiah withdrew from Jerusalem to avoid the wickedness which ran out of control during the reign of Manasseh. He lived in Bethlehem surrounded by godly prophets until Manasseh's henchmen seized and falsely accused him. Manasseh's accusers gave Isaiah a chance to renounce his prophetic warning to the nation, and Isaiah answered, "There is nothing further that you can take except the skin of my body." With that answer Isaiah's enemies used a wooden saw to cut him in half. The account adds that he did not cry out or weep, but his mouth spoke with the Holy Spirit until he was sawed in two.

VII. TEACHING OUTLINE

A. INTRODUCTION

1. Lead Story: Living and Dying Well
2. Context: Hebrews 10:36 speaks of the **need to persevere**. Hebrews 10:39 commends **those who believe and are saved**. It was natural to

present next some examples of believers who showed faith and reaped eternal salvation from their trust.

The Result of Faith (vv. 1–3). Faith provided believers assurance of the reality of things they could only hope for. It provided a certainty of the existence of the invisible order. Those who have faith have received God's commendation. Faith enabled believers to accept God's creation.

Examples of Faith (vv. 4–38). Abel, Enoch, and Noah each demonstrated a faith which accepted God's existence and eagerly sought his reward. Abraham left a settled land armed only with the compass of divine guidance. He showed a willingness to offer Isaac, the child of promise, fortified with the certainty that God would bring him back from death. Moses showed faith by abandoning his privileged place in Egypt to identify with the suffering people of God. God's saints who demonstrated faith conquered their enemies, escaped persecution, and triumphed over tragedy.

Faith's Vindication (vv. 39–40). Old Testament believers received divine commendation for their faith, but they did not receive the inheritance which God had promised. Only with the coming of Christ did these followers of the Lord experience God's better blessings.

3. Transition: Our response in faith must take God at his word and seek to please him supremely. We will receive encouragement from our learning of the faith of God's Old Testament saints. Through Christ we have access to all of God's eternal inheritance. In Christ we have a better hope (7:19) based on better promises (8:6). In Christ we receive a better end in heaven (10:34), and we can long for a better country, a country in heaven (11:16).

B. COMMENTARY

1. The Result of Faith (vv. 1–3)
2. Examples of Faith (vv. 4–38)
   a. The generation before the flood (vv. 4–7)
   b. Abraham and the patriarchs (vv. 8–22)
   c. The faith of Moses (vv. 23–28)
   d. The faith of Israel (v. 29)
   e. Faith throughout Jewish history (vv. 30–38)
3. Faith's Vindication (vv. 39–40)

C. CONCLUSION: ACCOMPLISHING FOR GOD

VIII. ISSUES FOR DISCUSSION

1. Name heroes of faith whose example you have followed and continue to follow. What have you learned from each one?
2. How would you define faith?
3. What is the relationship between faith and perseverance?
4. What concrete results are necessary for a person to continue in faith with God? Explain your answer.

Hebrews 12

Encouragement and Warnings from a Loving, Powerful God

"Never give in! Never give in!

Never! Never! Never! Never!

In anything great or small, large or petty—never give

in except to convictions of honor and good sense."

W i n s t o n   C h u r c h i l l

Hebrews

I N   A   N U T S H E L L

*Find strength to follow the example of these faithful witnesses in chapter 11 by considering Jesus' example. He endured the **opposition from sinful men.** This will prevent your losing heart. Instead of growing faint over your hardship, regard your trials as divine discipline to produce holiness. Pursue holiness, for **without holiness no one will see the Lord.** God is **the judge of all men,** and you are heirs of **a kingdom that cannot be shaken,** so **worship God acceptably with reverence and awe.***

Encouragement and Warnings from a Loving, Powerful God

I. INTRODUCTION

Building Stamina for Life's Journey

*F*or many years Dr. Jeff Ray served as professor of preaching at Southwestern Baptist Theological Seminary in Fort Worth, Texas. He taught into the 1940s when he was more than eighty years of age. Trouble and tragedy etched their influence on the life of Jeff Ray.

Early in his adult life his first wife died, leaving Dr. Ray to serve as mother and father to his children. His sorrow was compounded when one day in the 1930s he received the news that a beloved son had died. This calamity, added to life's other burdens, threatened to drive the vitality out of Jeff Ray. For a time he quit teaching and preaching in area churches. Dejected and depressed, he was unable to develop interest in anything and was ready to say, "I cannot go on!"

Mrs. L. R. Elliott, wife of the Seminary librarian, sent her husband to visit Dr. Ray with a scrapbook filled with poems and articles which had encouraged her. After Dr. Elliott's departure the weary professor listlessly leafed through the pages of the scrapbook. A poem with the engaging title of "I Won't Let Go!" caught his attention. Realizing that he had been wanting to do just that, Dr. Ray read these words:

I want to let go, but I won't let go.
There are battles to fight,
By day and by night,
For God and the right—
And I'll never let go.
I want to let go, but I won't let go.
I'm sick, 'tis true,
Worried and blue,
And worn through and through,
But I won't let go.
I want to let go, but I won't let go.
I will never yield!
What! lie down on the field

And surrender my shield?
No, I'll never let go!
I want to let go, but I won't let go.
May this be my song
"Mid legions of wrong—
Oh, God, keep me strong
That I may never let go!"
—Author Unknown

After reading the poem, Dr. Ray closed the scrapbook, arose from his couch of grief and defeat, and put behind him any thought of giving up and quitting. He returned to the classroom to teach and to pulpits to preach. For many years he distributed copies of the poem to his students. Many of them found encouragement from Dr. Ray's testimony and from the poem so that they did not let go. The writer of Hebrews found the same encouragement from following the example of Christ and his faithful servants mentioned in Hebrews 11.

II. COMMENTARY

Encouragement and Warnings from a Loving, Powerful God

MAIN IDEA: *God explains his discipline to his discouraged followers and his holiness to his careless servants.*

A Encouragement from Jesus' Example (vv. 1–11)

SUPPORTING IDEA: *We gain strength to face trials by considering Jesus' endurance of hardship as well as the divine purpose of discipline.*

1. Jesus as Our Pioneer and Perfecter (vv. 1–3)

12:1. Believers find encouragement in being surrounded **by such a great cloud of witnesses** as the saints mentioned in Hebrews 11. Their triumph gives evidence of the possibilities of a life of faith. The figure of a cloud suggests a massive host of these exemplary servants. We receive much encouragement from knowing that others have faced obstacles in the Christian life and have gloriously triumphed.

Such encouragement should lead us to cast aside every hindrance and besetting sin. We are to rid ourselves of any thought, attitude, or practice which impedes our progress in the Christian life. Sin finds an easy victim in all of us, so we must reject its entanglement.

Rejecting sin's entanglement lets us run our race with staying power. **Perseverance** calls for stamina or staying power. The **race** is that path God has marked out for us. We cannot select our own program. We must faithfully follow the route God himself has marked.

12:2. Christian athletes must keep their eyes fixed on the goal. That calls us to focus attention on Jesus without being diverted to anything else. Our Lord's steadfast obedience provided a perfect example of commitment for struggling believers.

As the **author** of our faith (see the same word in 2:10), Jesus inspires action in believers of all ages. As the **perfecter of our faith,** Jesus takes harassed believers, develops our faith, and brings us to heaven's Promised Land (Phil. 1:6).

Three features about Jesus demand attention. First, Jesus **endured the cross** to seize the blessed joy set before him. The path to victorious joy led through the cross. Second, Jesus scorned the shame of the cross. Jesus recognized the humiliation and ignominy of the cross, but these threats were of no consequence to him as he considered the coming glory. Third, Jesus **sat down at the right hand of the throne of God.** From the pain and agony of the cross God exalted Jesus to the position of a throne.

12:3. As we reflect on our own hardships, we need to assess carefully the endurance of Jesus. Jesus endured hostility from sinners that reached its climax at the cross. When you tend to let go, you can avoid faintheartedness and weariness by keeping your attention riveted upon Jesus. Jesus endured hostility from stubborn sinners. You have never faced such intense evil as did Jesus. His sterling example can stabilize us in our fear and concern.

2. God's Discipline for His Children (vv. 4–11).

12:4. God uses discipline to produce holiness in his people. The statement of this verse puts the struggles of the readers of Hebrews in perspective. Although they had experienced intense hardship, they had not yet faced resistance **to the point of shedding . . . blood.** None of them had suffered martyrdom. Their sufferings had by no means reached the severity of those that Jesus endured. This implies that they had not truly shown serious commitment in their resistance to the sin of apostasy. Others had remained faithful to Jesus in the face of far worse sufferings than theirs.

12:5–6. Verse 5 asks a question, "Have you forgotten?" based on the quotation of Proverbs 3:11–12 in verse 6. Together these verses urge us not to belittle God's discipline and not to lose heart in the face of God's rebuke. We should not see trials as cause for discouragement, but as a sign of God's determined love. We must reflect on the long-term benefits of our trials and recognize that discipline represents God's method of developing our maturity. We must respond to afflictions by searching out the faults or failures that hinder our spiritual growth.

12:7–10. These verses compare and contrast God's discipline of his children with parental discipline of their children.

Good parents provide training and instruction for their children. Such training demonstrates that they were **true sons** and not **illegitimate children**. A good God, like a good parent, will show love by providing nurture, guidance, and direction for the child.

Children respect their human parents because of their discipline. Believers must also be submissive to **the Father of our spirits.** Instead of turning away from God in apostasy, we must turn to him in obedience.

Verse 10 turns from comparison to contrast. Earthly parents discipline their children only **for a little while.** Children grow up, leave home, and move beyond the discipline of their parents. God, however, never finishes with his children. God disciplines us for a lifetime. For this we should be thankful rather than complaining.

Earthly parents discipline their children as they think best. All of us have made dreadful mistakes in our efforts to discipline our children. Fortunately, God knows precisely what he is doing and **disciplines us for our good, that we may share in his holiness.** God will never commit an overkill, nor will he neglect to give discipline. The fact that we receive discipline from a wise, omniscient God who never errs in his work gives us cause for commitment to his loving discipline.

12:11. This verse contrasts a short-term and a long-term response to discipline. Whenever discipline hits us, it causes pain. We tend to complain under its burden. We find nothing pleasant about the experience. Later, for those who submit to its training, **it produces a harvest of righteousness and peace.**

Ｂ A Call to Action (vv. 12–17)

> **SUPPORTING IDEA:** *Believers must show fresh commitment and a renewed concern for one another.*

12:12–13. These verses radiate encouragement. Drooping arms and tired knees appear in people who are utterly exhausted. To lift up the hands and to strengthen the knees demands a renewal of hope. Looking at Jesus and understanding God's purpose in discipline invigorates people who have faced spiritual exhaustion.

With new vigor we can walk on straight paths. Spiritually, this demands that we understand the beneficial effects of discipline, pull ourselves together, and move forward. If we do this, then those who are weak won't receive further spiritual injury. The entire community must experience renewed vigor to provide an example for the weak among us.

12:14. This verse provides two indicators of the **level paths** that believers should follow. First, we are to **make every effort to live in peace with all men.** We must make every effort to maintain peace while we endure discipline. Widespread trials often destroy a sense of community and produce an attitude of "looking out for number one." This verse warns against this tendency.

Second, we must seek holiness, for **without holiness no one will see the Lord.** People who would fellowship with the Lord must detest evil and pursue purity (Matt. 5:8). To **see** the Lord involves communion with him, but it may also include an anticipation of Christ's return (see 1 John 3:2).

12:15. We should be alert to prevent two developments. Both appeals reflect a concern that the community of believers care for each of its members.

First, we are to be careful that no one misses out on sharing fully in God's grace. Believers must be vigilant to assist those among us who have stumbled in weakness. We must bear one another's burdens (Gal. 6:2).

Second, we must prevent the growth of any **bitter root.** These words reflect the influence of Deuteronomy 29:18 and warn against the development of any practice or attitude which may contaminate the minds or consciences of believers. Some individuals can act like a poisonous weed and utterly devastate believers around them. Concerned Christians must take actions to prevent this.

12:16–17. These verses show the bad effect of the bitter behavior we are warned to avoid. Esau is an example of a person who acted in an immoral, godless manner. Esau showed contempt for his religious heritage by selling his "inheritance rights" (see Gen. 25:33–34). The bartering of his privileges as the eldest son for a single meal was a senseless act, showing that Esau lacked any sense of spiritual values. He exemplifies anyone who values immediate gratification beyond spiritual heritage.

In Genesis 27:6–29 Jacob used trickery to win the patriarchal blessing from Isaac. When Esau later sought the blessing, Isaac knew that he could not reverse his actions. Esau wept when he recognized that he had squandered his birthright, but his tears were futile (Gen. 27:34). He became a memorable example of someone who failed to appropriate God's grace by wasting his opportunity.

The New Testament emphasizes that spiritual repentance is possible for those who desire it. Esau's tears appeared when he recognized that he had no chance to remedy his foolish actions. We are to realize that denying Christ is a serious act. We should never count on an easy route of return at a time of our own choosing. Just as Esau's tears did not earn a return to God for him, a deliberate turning away from Christ will lead to ruin and sorrow.

C The Supremacy of the New Covenant (vv. 18–24)

> **SUPPORTING IDEA:** *The greater privileges of the new covenant demand greater responsiveness from believers.*

12:18. The reference to **a mountain that can be touched** reminds us of the giving of the Law at Sinai (Exod. 19:12–22; 20:18–21). The Israelites and their animals were forbidden to touch Sinai. The descriptions of **fire; . . . darkness, gloom and storm** portrayed the giving of the Law so as to affect the senses of sight and sound. The awesome details inspired reverence.

12:19–20. These verses continue the majestic description of the giving of the Law at Sinai. The sound of the trumpet conveyed an authoritative command not to be ignored. The **voice speaking words** proved terrifying to the listeners. The communications which the people could receive filled their hearts with dread (Deut. 5:23–27). The fright of the people was such that they begged **that no further word be spoken to them.**

God communicated a moving reminder of the unworthiness of the people by prohibiting their approach to the mountain. Any human being or animal who touched the mountain would die. The glory of the experience thoroughly awed the people so that **they could not bear what was commanded.**

The separation of God from his people under the Law stands in contrast with his approachableness under the gospel. Believers receive a command to **approach the throne of grace with confidence** (Heb. 4:16). The consequences of rejecting a gospel which offers such privileges will be even more fearful than the effects of rejecting the Law.

12:21. The Israelites were filled with dread even though God kept them at a distance from the mountain. Moses, who was in the midst of the turbulent events, received revelation that was withheld from the people. We should not wonder that he said, "**I am trembling with fear.**" The description of Moses' fear may come from Jewish traditions about the giving of the Law and may not reflect the content of any single passage of Scripture, since these exact words do not appear in the Old Testament. Deuteronomy 9:19 does narrate Moses' fear.

These words conclude the comments on the old order. The next verses emphasize the added responsibilities of believers under the new covenant.

12:22. This verse begins the description of the superior spiritual approach available to believers. Dread and fear have vanished. Believers can worship God in full fellowship and joy!

The name *Mount Sinai*, where Israel received the Law, does not appear in verses 18–21. The location at which believers meet with God is called **Mount Zion.** The mount is identified as **the city of the living God** and as **the heavenly Jerusalem.** The picture is one of calmness as God and his people enjoy fellowship together. Mount Zion represents the true worship of God, and Jerusalem symbolizes God's people in community with him.

Thousands upon thousands of angels in joyful assembly surrounding God show that he is approachable. He lives among a society of followers who worship him. These angels were the **ministering spirits** presented earlier in 1:14. Christians do not come together to worship these angels but to worship and serve the God who sends them forth.

This verse does not refer merely to a communion which believers enter at death. At conversion Christians become members of a community of those who can worship the living God and receive from him grace for daily needs (Heb. 4:16). Christians already experience a fulfillment of fellowship with God. The future will bring a complete consummation of this fellowship.

12:23. This verse describes those in God's church and their relationship with God. Those in the church are **firstborn**, a reference to rebirth through Christ. This term refers to the entire fellowship of believers and not merely to those of pre-Christian days. The term might also designate Christ as the one who is firstborn (Col. 1:15). With their names **written in heaven**, believers are already members of the heavenly Jerusalem.

These members of the church come to God as **the judge of all men**. As the all-knowing God, he will carry out judgment one day in accord with his nature and in conformity to his truth. This phrase calls us to live in fear of falling into apostasy through rejection of the work of Christ.

The church also contains **the spirits of righteous men made perfect**. These are probably believers of pre-Christians days such as those mentioned in Hebrews 11. They have become just because of the work of Christ. Their perfection does not suggest flawlessness. They are perfected in the sense that they already enjoy fellowship with God in heaven.

12:24. The superior privileges of Christian believers allow us to come directly into God's presence and to fellowship with reborn believers. We come to Jesus, "**the mediator of a new covenant**" (cf. 8:10–13). Jesus protected the readers of Hebrews by standing between guilty sinners and a holy God. The **sprinkled blood** of Jesus had a better word to speak because it proclaimed forgiveness of sin, reconciliation with God, and spiritual power for believers.

For **mediator**, see "Deeper Discoveries" on Hebrews 8:6.

Ⓓ Paying Careful Attention to God (vv. 25–29)

> **SUPPORTING IDEA:** *Since God promises believers an immovable kingdom, we must serve him with reverence and devotion.*

12:25. This chapter concludes with a powerful message about God. He had spoken earlier to the Israelites at the giving of the Law through Moses. That generation had refused God's message on earth. They did not escape (see

Heb. 3:14–19). This should warn us not to turn our backs on God, who is still speaking.

God speaks to this generation from heaven in the work of Christ. Those who ignore Jesus' message will not escape God's wrath. Surely we must listen carefully to him.

12:26–27. These verses contrast the instability of the old covenant with the security of the new covenant. In giving the old covenant, God had shaken the earth with a mighty earthquake (Exod. 19:18). A quote from Haggai 2:6 now promises that God will shake not only the earth but also the heavens. This refers to the final judgment in connection with the concluding events of the age (see 2 Thess. 1:7–10).

This shaking of the earth in judgment involves the destruction of created things. This judgment will reveal the greater, spiritual realities which cannot be shaken or removed. Christian believers share in a kingdom which no amount of final judgment can destroy. The security of our position in Christ gives us an incentive to endure in faithfulness.

12:28–29. How should we respond to this word of security and comfort about a kingdom which will endure forever? First, we are to **be thankful.** We must be thankful that God has put an unchangeable possession in our grasp. Second, we must worship. We must worship God acceptably, in a manner pleasing to him. We must also worship with **reverence** for God's greatness and with **awe** for his mighty power.

Reverence and awe are linked with the fact that **our God is a consuming fire.** We must focus attention on this feature of God's character in addition to celebrating his grace. When Jesus returns in glory, the fire of God's holiness will consume all that is false and evil. Those with wickedness will be consumed by the fire of this judgment. Those who profess faith in Christ cannot expect mercy if they willfully turn from Jesus back to sin, disobedience, the Law, or a false god. We must show the reality of our confession by our obedience and worship. "Reverence and awe before His holiness are not incompatible with grateful trust and love in response to His mercy" (F. F. Bruce).

MAIN IDEA REVIEW: *God explains his discipline to his discouraged followers and his holiness to his careless servants.*

III. CONCLUSION

Fear of God Payback

Jeff Street was a sixteen-year-old parking lot attendant for an amusement park in New York City in 1969 when he stole $40 from the cash register.

Street thought little about the incident over the years, but in 1978 he became a Christian.

Six years later in 1984 Street sent the amusement park a check for $326, money to repay the original $40 theft plus $286 in interest. Interviewed by media officials, he explained his actions: "I was praying at my desk and reading the Word, and it just came to me. It wasn't the Lord's voice, but it came from within me—I had to pay back the money." Street explained that his response was "more like an act of obedience."

What happened to Jeff Street? The fear of God seized him. He had determined to be a follower of a God who desired holiness in his people. He renewed his commitment to serve God **with reverence and awe.**

Two spiritual truths are emphasized in this chapter. Those who faced discouragement from multiple trials and afflictions needed to "fix [their] eyes on Jesus." We can find encouragement from Jesus' refusal to compromise or turn away from God. Realize that God is permitting discipline in your life for a benevolent purpose so that you may share in his holiness.

Those who were presumptuous and careless in their actions were challenged to pursue holiness (v. 14), to take advantage of the privileges of the new covenant (v. 24), and to **worship God acceptably with reverence and awe** (v. 28).

Both discouraged and careless Christians need grace and instruction. Our gracious God has wisely provided for both needs.

PRINCIPLES

- Jesus has provided his people an example to follow in facing life's trials.
- God demands holiness in his people.
- Jesus provides forgiveness and strength for his people.
- God has provided his people an eternal kingdom never to be destroyed.

APPLICATIONS

- Respond to God's discipline with obedience to his good purposes.
- Avoid all actions that produce bitter fruit and contaminate the lives of others.
- Live like newborn people whose names are written in heaven.
- Respond to God with gratitude for his mercy and with reverence for his majestic character.

IV. LIFE APPLICATION

What Big Business Can Teach Us About Repentance

My first post-college and pre-seminary job was with IBM. In 1960 I moved to Dallas, Texas, to work with Big Blue for a summer. At that time it was still producing electric typewriters and dominating that market. Its computers were the rage of the world. Ross Perot was an employee of the Dallas office of IBM, but he was making plans to begin Electronic Data Systems, which became an IBM competitor. IBM was outracing its entire pack of competitors.

Times have changed. In the early nineties the value of IBM stock plummeted. IBM lost its position as the leading maker of personal computers. When IBM management realized that they were not heading in the right direction, they made a commitment to restructuring.

Restructuring involves reviewing your strategy. It involves a redeployment of resources. It often produces a smaller work force, new priorities for spending, and a sharing of power in the company organizational chart. It requires a clarification of goals and a relentless devotion to attaining the right goals. It expresses a willingness to change any needed activities to reach those goals.

Restructuring a company resembles personal repentance. Repentance demands restructuring your life around the new demands of Jesus Christ. This, however, is not the popular understanding of repentance. For some people, repentance means to feel sad about sin. They think that it means to weep, to express sorrow, and to feel glum about the past.

I have been an observer and participant in numerous experiences of public repentance in which waves of people have come forward to acknowledge their failures. Often they have detailed embarrassing personal failures and announced their intention to change. Copious tears accompanied their confessions. The real test did not come from measuring their tears but from observing their life change over the coming weeks. People who repent do not merely cry over their sins. They change their lives by God's grace. They do not continue to go over the same failures time and time again. They put these failures behind them and get on with the task of living in obedience to God.

Three features about repentance are important for us to consider. First, repentance involves a commitment to live as a follower of Jesus Christ. The biblical word for "repent" demands a change of mind about God, self, and sin which produces a changed life. People who truly repent will live out the life of Jesus in their bodies. They will tap into God's power to do what their own will power could never accomplish.

Second, repentance involves our relationship to other people and to society as a whole. If we repent, we will not merely withdraw into self-centered personal agendas, but we will work for bringing divine mercy and justice into society as a whole. We will also be concerned to see that no believer **misses the grace of God.**

Third, our repentance will involve some changes which don't at first seem to be spiritual. Yes, we will read the Bible and pray more. We will also change the way we spend our money and the time we spend with television. We will find ourselves some new friends and some new activities. We may give up some foods and change our hobbies. Repentance will affect the totality of our lives. Hebrews 12 calls upon believers to restructure their lives around the ongoing purposes of the living God.

V. PRAYER

Father, I acknowledge your holiness and accept your discipline. You want me to be holy as you are. You discipline me to bring me to repentance, to a new style of life like Jesus'. Today I repent. I confess my sins. I call on your power to help me turn away from my sins. Jesus, help me restructure my life so it will be all you desire. Amen.

VI. DEEPER DISCOVERIES

A. Everything That Hinders and Sin That Easily Entangles (v. 1)

This verse focuses on the preparation necessary for running the race of the Christian life. Athletic imagery shows that anything which adds weight to the athlete, such as excess body fat, is a hindrance. What hinders one may not hinder another, and obeying this command calls for individual discernment. Spiritually, this means we must choose priorities wisely. We are to avoid anything which weights us down and prevents our full spiritual freedom.

We must also be wary of letting our lives be hindered by the **sin that so easily entangles.** "Entangles" (*euperistatos*) refers to a habit which easily surrounded someone, a besetting sin. It describes a practice which was prone to hamper or impede spiritual progress. No specific sin was in mind. All sin is an entanglement in trying to serve God. Each of us needs to find the sin that entangles our lives and stifles our spiritual growth. With God's grace and power, we must cast off these besetting sins.

B. Discipline (v. 5)

This word (*paideia*) appears in Hebrews 12:5,7,8,11 with the meaning of instruction, education, or discipline. Ephesians 6:4 also uses this same word to describe the nurture or discipline which a parent gives to a child. In Hebrews the word describes the instruction God conveys to his children through severe discipline.

In both Hebrews and Ephesians the term refers to a system of training set up by the heavenly Father or an earthly father to communicate instruction to a child who needed to learn. God often uses hardship to teach righteousness to his children (Heb. 12:11).

God's use of discipline to teach spiritual realities should not be pushed to suggest that God deliberately causes natural and moral evil to produce spiritual changes in his children. God can use such tragedies as the death of a loved one for spiritual good (cf. Rom. 8:28). This passage (vv. 5–6), however, is not suggesting that God deliberately causes these tragedies in order to promote spiritual ends. No one passage of Scripture gives a comprehensive discussion of the interrelationship of God, Satan, and human sin in allowing and bringing about what we as humans call natural and moral evil.

C. Father of Our Spirits (v. 9)

This unusual title presents God as the one who trains and develops our spiritual nature. It does not so much designate God as the Creator of our souls as the designer of our spiritual lives. Earthly fathers will influence the earthly existence of their children, but only a spiritual being such as God can develop our spiritual existence.

We begin to grow spiritually when we recognize that our heavenly Father uses discipline to develop our spiritual life. We must submit to God because he is the author not only of physical life but also of our spiritual and eternal life.

D. Trained (v. 11)

The verb translated as **trained** (*gumnazo*) was used frequently to describe athletic training. Athletic training produces pain and exhaustion which are necessary to build stamina in champion athletes. Spiritual training develops spiritual stamina and produces **righteousness and peace** in those who learn from it.

E. Bitter Root (v. 15)

Bitter root comes from Deuteronomy 29:17–18, referring to practices which led individuals to turn their hearts away from God. Here in Hebrews the words describe any action whose influence corrupts and defiles others. The term is not a reference to a bitter, harsh, or critical attitude. It describes moral actions which produce any kind of bitter harvest which would turn others away from God. The spiritual lapse of someone in the Christian community would present a disastrous example to other struggling believers. Believers must avoid this behavior because of its infectious, contaminating effect on others.

F. Inheritance Rights, Blessing (vv. 16–17)

The inheritance rights referred to the birthright, the promise of a larger portion of the family inheritance which was given to the oldest son in the family. These verses refer to the incident in Genesis 25:29–34 in which Esau gave up the claim to this extra share in exchange for a bowl of tangy food. He thought so little of his rights and responsibilities in his family that he traded them away to satisfy his stomach.

In Genesis 27:34, Esau wept before Isaac, seeking to obtain a restoration of this birthright as the firstborn son. Isaac had already given the blessing to Jacob through a deceitful act by the younger son (Gen. 27:6–29). Despite Esau's tearful protests, God disqualified Esau from receiving the blessing his father had already given to Jacob. The principle established here is that willful rejection of God's privileges renders it impossible for sinners to receive divine blessings.

G. The Church of the Firstborn (v. 23)

Three features of this designation are important. First, in the Old Testament era each household had only one firstborn child. The firstborn was placed in a special, privileged position. In the church all believers are special people, and the privileges of being the firstborn are scattered among all of God's people (1 Pet. 2:9–10).

Second, it is also likely that the firstborn are those who have been "born again" through Jesus. The fact that their **names are written in heaven** suggests that they have experienced the only birth which is significant—a spiritual birth.

Third, for Paul only Jesus Christ was truly the firstborn (Col. 1:15). The use of the term in reference to Christ is not a statement that Christ, the uncreated one, was the first of God's creatures. Rather, it describes his majesty and dominion over all creation.

Which of these emphases did the author of Hebrews have in mind? Probably all three ideas contributed to his use of the term. The writer was probably emphasizing the new nature and privileges of believers along with their link with Christ, the true firstborn.

H. God as a Consuming Fire (v. 29)

These words pick up on the description of God in Deuteronomy 4:24. This awesome view of God was derived from the descriptions of God at Sinai (Exod. 19:16–25). The term shows that God is righteous and that he demands righteousness in his children. He will not change his demands for sinful human beings. Our reading and reflecting on these words should develop in us a sense of awe and reverence for God and a commitment to obey him.

These words bring out a feature of the divine character which we must accept along with the emphasis on God's grace and mercy. They remind us of the need to be prepared for God's all-searching judgment at the time of Christ's return (2 Cor. 5:10; 2 Thess. 1:6–10).

VII. TEACHING OUTLINE

A. INTRODUCTION

1. Lead Story: Building Stamina for Life's Journey
2. Context: Hebrews 11 presents a list of God's devoted servants who demonstrated their faith by their endurance and commitment. Hebrews 12 urges believers to imitate the faith of these servants by following the example of Jesus and by serving God **with reverence and awe.**

   Encouragement from Jesus' Example (vv. 1–11). As the **author and perfecter of our faith**, Jesus has given us an example of courage and commitment to imitate. The readers of Hebrews must endure their trials with a desire to apply the lessons which God is teaching and with a trust in God's purposes.

   Challenge to Action (vv. 12–17). God's people must show courage and follow holiness. They must avoid giving a bad example which will infect and harm the spiritual lives of fellow Christians.

   Comparison of Earthly Sinai and Heavenly Zion (vv. 18–24). Christians can rest in confidence because they have fellowship with the living God and because they are part of a body of believers who have been born again.

   Paying Attention to God (vv. 25–29). Christians have a part in God's kingdom, a kingdom which is eternal and unshakeable. We must claim God's grace to serve him **with reverence and awe.**

3. Transition: As we read and apply the truths of this chapter to our lives, we must be committed to walk in Jesus' footsteps as sharers in his suffering. We must trust the wisdom of God in allowing trials and discipline in our lives and must apply the lessons from the trial in our

daily experience. We must pursue God's will with a desire to experience his holiness and a confidence in his ability to protect and lead us.

As Donald Hagner has taught, Christians "are to be thankful for what is theirs in Christ and to put out of mind all thoughts of lapsing from their Christianity to their former way of life."

B. COMMENTARY

1. Encouragement from Jesus' Example (vv. 1–11)
   a. Jesus as Our Pioneer and Perfecter (vv. 1–3)
   b. God's Discipline for His Children (vv. 4–11)
2. A Call to Action (vv. 12–17)
3. The Supremacy of the New Covenant (vv. 18–24)
4. Paying Careful Attention to God (vv. 25–29)

C. CONCLUSION: WHAT BIG BUSINESS CAN TEACH US ABOUT REPENTANCE

VIII. ISSUES FOR DISCUSSION

1. How do you recognize God's discipline in your life? How do you respond to it?
2. Have you ever become a "careless servant" of God. What caused this to happen? What brought you out of this state and back into proper obedience to God?
3. What brings maturity to your Christian life? In what areas of life do you see spiritual maturity? In what areas do you have a lot of room for growth?
4. Can you recognize a besetting sin in your life that entangles you and prevents you from running the race God has set before you? How can you respond to the recognition of this habitual sin in your life?

Hebrews 13

The Sacrifices That God Loves

I. **INTRODUCTION**
Are All Sacrifices Acceptable to God?

II. **COMMENTARY**
A verse-by-verse explanation of the chapter.

III. **CONCLUSION**
Concluding Words Carry Weight
An overview of the principles and applications from the chapter.

IV. **LIFE APPLICATION**
Praising God in Difficulty
Melding the chapter to life.

V. **PRAYER**
Tying the chapter to life with God.

VI. **DEEPER DISCOVERIES**
Historical, geographical, and grammatical enrichment of the commentary.

VII. **TEACHING OUTLINE**
Suggested step-by-step group study of the chapter.

VIII. **ISSUES FOR DISCUSSION**
Zeroing the chapter in on daily life.

Quote

"*S*ometimes a man imagines that he will lose himself if he gives himself, and keep himself if he hides himself. But the opposite takes place with terrible exactness."

Ernest Hello

Hebrews

I N   A   N U T S H E L L

*H*ebrews concludes with directions for Christian living. Love other Christians with special needs. Be morally pure, and keep a right attitude toward money. Offer to God sacrifices of praise. Follow joyfully those who lead your churches. Pray for one another. Listen carefully to the words of Scripture.

The Sacrifices That God Loves

I. INTRODUCTION

Are All Sacrifices Acceptable to God?

Their names were Ananias and Sapphira, a husband and wife whose tragic deaths filled the early church with fear. Acts 5 tells the story of their crafty treachery. They sold a piece of land, pocketed some of the money, and gave the remainder to the church in Jerusalem. But there was a catch.

They pretended to give the entire amount, but they kept some of the money to enjoy themselves. They received praise from the church for their generosity, but this act of hypocrisy was an open declaration of greed and self-will.

These pious frauds had probably basked in the public adulation. Peter said first to Ananias, "How is it that Satan has so filled your heart that you have lied to the Holy Spirit and have kept for yourself some of the money you received for the land?" Ananias responded to Peter's stern rebuke by dropping dead on the spot. When Peter repeated the confrontation with Sapphira three hours later, she also died. A hushed reverence fell over the church and the community. Some might have called their gift a sacrifice, but it was obvious that God was not pleased with their actions.

Why was God displeased? Ananias and Sapphira had succumbed to greed and had trifled with the truth. They pretended to give the total amount of the sale. They gave only a part. Apparently their motive was not to please God and to help people but to receive public praise. God's heavy judgment showed his displeasure.

Today, people sometimes donate worthless tracts of property to churches, take a large tax write-off, and make money on the gift. Others give huge sums on single occasions, receive great public recognition at the time, and hardly give another cent in their remaining years. Their aim may be to honor a deceased parent or loved one, but does the practice honor God? What are the sacrifices which honor God? What types of sacrifices does God love to see among his children?

This chapter mentions three sacrifices God is always pleased to find. First is costly commitment (v. 13), a commitment to Christ capable of holding firm during trial and opposition. Second is praise and gratitude to God (v. 15). Such praise implies a trust in God and a submission to his will. Third is unselfish service to the needy (v. 16). Such service prevents greed, glorifies God, and meets the needs of the lonely and destitute.

II. COMMENTARY

The Sacrifices that God Loves

MAIN IDEA: *God's people must demonstrate actions, attitudes, practices, and sacrifices which please God.*

A A Right Response to Fellow Christians (vv. 1–9)

SUPPORTING IDEA: *Christians are to help the needy, practice purity in family life, and follow the faith of their leaders.*

1. To Believers with Special Needs (vv. 1–3)

13:1. What is Christian love? It involves showing special regard for the needs of fellow believers without concern for their social or racial position. The fact that the writer of Hebrews urged his readers to **keep on loving each other** suggests that some of them may have neglected this important response. Comments in 10:33–34 suggest that some had already taken the lead in showing Christian love. Showing "brotherly" love demanded treating fellow believers as esteemed family members. Verses 2–3 give two ways of demonstrating this special love.

13:2. One practical demonstration of love involves meeting the needs of Christian workers on the move. Facilities for travelers were often not available. Whenever they were, they were usually dens of immorality and danger. In the Middle East, demonstrating hospitality in the home provided an important basis for friendship. The practice of hospitality was a quality required in Christian leaders (1 Tim. 3:2).

A reference to Genesis 18–19 encourages the display of hospitality. Abraham entertained mysterious strangers who were in reality angels. The principle here teaches us that it is better to treat needy guests as messengers from God than to risk offending them by an inhospitable act. Messengers from God brought a greater blessing than they received. Whoever entertained a servant of the Lord entertained the Lord himself (Matt. 25:44–45).

13:3. This verse changes the focus to those imprisoned and abused for their faith (cf. 10:34). Imprisoned believers could easily be forgotten and neglected. We need to identify and help those imprisoned and mistreated for their Christian commitment. Such help could involve bringing food, providing warm clothing for life in damp, moldy cells, and making personal visits of encouragement. One day we could face the same experiences of suffering. Thus, we need to focus on the sufferers as if we ourselves were the victims of suffering.

2. To the Family (vv. 4–6)

13:4. Both Jewish and pagan marriages in the New Testament period were characterized by laxity and immorality. Christians have a different approach to marriage. Purity, contentment, and a trust in God are ingredients needed for developing strong Christian families. Two pro-marriage ideas appear in this verse.

First, marriage is to be honored by all. Even among believers today the stability of marriage faces strong challenges. Christians must honor marriage as divine in its origin and as right and good in its practice. This verse helps us to see that celibacy is not superior to marriage.

Second, those who are married must maintain moral purity. The fact that God will judge sexual promiscuity provides motivation for a holy lifestyle among believers. Violators of this command may be celebrated by some human beings, but they will reap eternal divine displeasure (Eph. 5:6).

13:5. Another threat to family stability is materialism. Obeying two features could control materialism. First, renounce **love of money.** Do not make the possession of money an end in itself. Second, **be content with what you have.** The presence of God in all of life encourages such contentment. Knowing the Lord will not abandon us gives us the stability to enjoy what he gives us (Deut. 31:6,8). Enjoying his unfailing presence is better than coveting glistening bullions of gold.

13:6. Another threat to family life is anxiety. Encouraging words from Psalm 118:6–7 remind us that God's presence in life banishes anxiety about personal needs. This is the only New Testament verse describing God as a **helper.** Hebrews 2:18 uses the verbal form of the word to picture Jesus as a source of help for the tempted (cf. Mark 9:22; 2 Cor. 6:2).

The question, **What can man do to me?** presumes the answer: "Nothing at all!" With God's presence, no event in life can shake believers from their foundation. Anxiety about life's needs or challenges has no place in the heart of the believer who has determined to make God his helper.

3. In the Fellowship of the Church (vv. 7–9)

13:7. Committed believers are to imitate the faith of their spiritual leaders and avoid unchristian doctrines. This chapter contains three references to leaders of churches (vv. 17,24). The reference in this verse appears to be to leaders who had completed their service in a congregation and had died. The readers were to reflect on both the words and deeds of these former leaders, from beginning to end, and **imitate their faith.**

Steady spiritual reflection on the life of a committed believer can teach us lessons of faith, commitment, and priority. Once we have seen the outcome of their ruling passion for God, we should follow steadfastly in their way.

13:8. Former leaders have died, but Jesus Christ remains the same. The constancy of Jesus enables us to follow the faith of great Christian leaders. The lives of the former leaders declared memorably the changelessness of Christ. Both the readers of Hebrews and believers today have access to the power and example of the unchanging Christ. Because of his past and present work, Jesus Christ can meet our every need.

Christ's work of **yesterday** was to suffer for our sins on the cross. His work of **today** is to serve as our High Priest (Heb. 4:14-16; 7:25). His future work is to return and conclude God's saving purposes (Heb. 9:28). Jesus never needs to be replaced, and his work needs nothing added to maintain its perfection.

13:9. In contrast to the constancy of Christ was the parade of **all kinds of strange teachings** from human beings. The reference to **ceremonial foods** suggests that some type of ritual observance was enticing these believers. God's grace and not some tantalizing ritual provides a secure foundation for relating to God.

Paul wrote that "food does not bring us near to God; we are no worse if we do not eat, and no better if we do" (1 Cor. 8:8). Divine grace and not some meaningless rule about food provides the spiritual strength needed for walking along the journey of the Christian life.

B A Right Response to God (vv. 10–16)

SUPPORTING IDEA: *Commitment, praise, and kind deeds to others are spiritual responses God loves.*

13:10. This verse uses much symbolism to contrast the privileges of those Jews who were believers with those who were not. Faith in Jesus provides an approach to God from which unbelief separates. Those Jews who had become Christians had access to a special **altar,** Christ's atoning death. Believing Jews had eternal access to all the spiritual blessings Jesus could provide for them. Unbelieving Jews **minister at the tabernacle.** These Jews had no access to the benefits Christ made available.

Unbelieving Jews may have eaten the material food of the Jewish altar, but they enjoyed no link with Christ. Believers contact Christ himself and live with a daily experience of his benefits. This subtle warning urged the readers not to turn away from Christ to the meaningless rituals of Judaism and so lose the privilege of access to Jesus.

13:11. This verse focuses on the offering of **the blood of animals** to God and the burning of the bodies of the animals **outside the camp.** Jewish high priests who brought sin offerings to God did not eat from the altar. The sacrifices were burned. The actions of the high priests symbolized the actions of unbelievers, for the priest was among those who ministered **at the tabernacle.** Again we see unbelievers do not have any real contact with Christ and the benefits he offers.

Christians do have spiritual access to the great sin offering Jesus presented. This offering is their food, nourishing and refreshing their souls as they feed on Christ by faith.

13:12–13. These verses build on the knowledge that Jesus died outside the walls of Jerusalem (John 19:20). Jesus died **to make the people holy.** He wanted to produce followers with pure consciences. Jesus' death outside Jerusalem represented his rejection by religious Jerusalem. Unbelieving Jews attached a stigma to Jesus' exclusion from Jerusalem and his crucifixion. Instead of complaining about the circumstances, believers commit themselves to Christ.

Thus, Hebrews urges us to go outside the **camp** of Judaism. We are to reject the fellowship and rituals of Judaism and cling only to Jesus. In so doing we surrender security and court danger. We must venture into new territory under the flag of Jesus without fearing ridicule from unbelievers. Bearing **the disgrace** of commitment to Jesus brings eternal reward.

13:14. This verse adds two features to the appeal for commitment to Christ. First, Christians live for the future, not the present. No matter how appealing life in the present is, believers **are looking for the city that is to come.** Christians look for a reward which lies ahead.

Second, Christians enjoy togetherness. We must not allow our practice of Christianity to degenerate into self-seeking individual choices. Believers who move forward for Christ like a mighty army find encouragement from common commitment and enthusiasm.

13:15. Christians must also present **a sacrifice of praise.** This praise is to be constant. We find no circumstances in which praise for God is inappropriate. Believers find no joy in dead animals, but in the living Lord. His glory, not our comfort, is to be our desire. God is not pleased by animal sacrifices, but by believers who acknowledge his goodness, greatness, and mercy (Ps. 51:15–17).

13:16. Hebrews calls us to commitment to Christ, to praise for God, and **to do good and to share with others.** This demands that we share our material plenty with the needy. We are to be on the lookout for occasions where we can give spontaneous help. Christians respond to Christ's atoning death with good deeds and praise, not with animals. God finds great pleasure in these responses.

🄲 A Right Response to Church Leaders (v. 17)

> **SUPPORTING IDEA:** *Submitting to church leaders enables them to do their work with joy.*

13:17. Already we have received an appeal to imitate the lifestyle of leaders who have passed off the scene. Now we see an appeal to give a proper response to present leaders. Some specific occasion of disrespect or discontent probably made this appeal necessary (see Heb. 10:25).

The response involves obedience and submission. Believers follow their leaders without grudging. The leader was to maintain a constant watchfulness over the souls of their flock and to give an account of their work. Leaders had responsibilities and not merely privileges.

Ⓓ Prayer for One Another (vv. 18–21)

SUPPORTING IDEA: *Our requests for the prayers of others should spark our earnest prayers for them.*

13:18. This verse requests prayer for the author of Hebrews and for those with him. Such prayer was appropriate because the writer had **a clear conscience** and a **desire to live honorably in every way.**

Perhaps someone among the readers of Hebrews had criticized him, and he needed to offer this personal defense. His conscience and his behavior worked in righteous harmony with one another. We find it easier to pray vigorously for others when we see unquestioned spiritual integrity in their actions.

13:19. The writer of Hebrews made a specific request for prayer. Some circumstances hindered a reunion between him and his readers. He felt convinced that their prayers could change those circumstances. We must bring into intercession the conviction that God can use our prayers to effect changes when, humanly speaking, change seems impossible.

His request **to be restored** did not suggest that he had been imprisoned. His statement of verse 23 suggested that he enjoyed liberty. He wanted the privilege of being restored to fellowship with his friends after an absence.

13:20–21. Now the author uttered a theologically packed benediction for his readers with statements about both the Father and the Son. He identified God as **the God of peace** seeking to promote peace among the readers. God's dynamic actions caused the resurrection of Jesus. (This is the only clear reference to the resurrection in Hebrews.) The resurrection presents clear evidence that God has accepted Jesus' sacrifice and that he has established a new covenant on that basis.

Jesus is presented as **that great Shepherd of the sheep.** He will lead us through any circumstances which threaten our peace with God.

The writer of Hebrews prayed that God would bring out the full potential of each believer. This might reconcile factions in the church, or it might produce individual believers who were fully developed and mature. The supreme desire of the prayer was that God would provide the readers with **everything good for doing his will** and to produce in their lives only **what is pleasing to him.** The work of God is necessary to make man's work a reality. If God produces in us what is pleasing to him, we will be supremely equipped to do his will.

The prayer concludes with a doxology. Grammar would let the praise be directed either to Jesus or to the Father. Likely the author calls for eternal glory to the Father. We can only give an **Amen** to thoughts about God as wonderful as these.

Ⓔ Genuine Affection Among Believers (vv. 22–25)

SUPPORTING IDEA: *Gracious words build fellowship among believers.*

13:22. Hebrews ends with two comments about the entire letter. First, it is a **word of exhortation.** Its message throbbed with encouragement and appeals for godly living. Second, it is **only a short letter**—brief at least in comparison with what was on the mind of the author (see Heb. 5:11; 9:5b). The letter covered a vast subject, but it could be read in less than an hour. Perhaps such contrast of a vast subject and a quick coverage of the subject led him to describe his letter as brief.

13:23. Good news is always welcome. The readers knew and loved Timothy and would have been overjoyed to know of his release from imprisonment. The readers must have known about Timothy's imprisonment, but the writer of Hebrews only wanted to assure them that he hoped to accompany Timothy on a visit to them. He was not sure of Timothy's travel plans, and we can learn no other information about Timothy other than the fact of his earlier imprisonment.

13:24. The greeting to the leaders and to the members shows personal interest and a desire to communicate with all the believers in the congregation. The writer presumed they would read his letter to the gathered church. His use of **all** twice in the verse suggested that not all leaders and members would be present at any one time. He wanted to be sure that he omitted no one from a happy hello. This verse contains the third reference in this chapter to church leaders (see also vv. 7,17).

We do not know where **those from Italy** were living. They could have been residing in Italy, or they may have been elsewhere. The writer may have been sending greetings to those living in Italy from some Italian residents who had moved away. He may also be writing from Italy (Rome) to believers living in another country and sending greetings from the homefolks. Settling the issue is impossible, and any attempted solution will not affect our understanding of the letter.

13:25. All people can conclude letters with a word of personal greeting and good will, but only Christians can understand the importance of God's grace. The writer of Hebrews filled this letter with a presentation of all that

God has done through Jesus. An appeal for an experience of God's grace is a fitting way to conclude the message.

> **MAIN IDEA REVIEW:** *God's people must demonstrate actions, attitudes, practices, and sacrifices which please God.*

III. CONCLUSION

Concluding Words Carry Weight

When our young adult children were college students, our letters to them were not frequent, but they were important. These letters often contained a recitation of family news and concluded with a few reminders and appeals which we regarded as meaningful and necessary. We may have appealed for more serious study, careful spending of money, or more time spent in serving God and others. Often the concluding remarks in our letters represented what we saw as very important.

The conclusion of Hebrews reflects that principle. The writer reminded his readers of the urgency of caring for needy believers, strengthening the family, and following the faith of church leaders. He appealed for commitment, praise, and unselfish service. He requested prayer and prayed for God to perfect his readers. He urged his readers to bear with his words and commended them to God's grace. Through all of his concluding words we see an emphasis on obeying and pleasing God and accomplishing his will. We find a passionate call appealing for us to produce **what is pleasing to him** in our lives. If we leave Hebrews with the emphasis that we must develop a passion for pleasing God, we will be prepared to live out its teachings with commitment and character.

Accomplishing God's will demands that we choose to obey God. We must make the right choices between those lifestyles which follow the Lord and those which turn away from him. We must accept the sovereign hand of God in our lives when we "face trials of many kinds" (Jas. 1:2). We cannot avoid our share of sickness, financial challenges, disappointing circumstances, and plain hardship. In these circumstances we must demonstrate a heart of praise for God, trust in his sovereign leadership, and desire that he be glorified.

Craig Barnes serves as pastor of the National Presbyterian Church in Washington, D.C. This two-thousand-member congregation has included presidents, senators, and powerful politicians among its worshipers. Week by week, Barnes presents to his congregation an appeal to trust God's grace and sovereignty.

The pastor had an opportunity to demonstrate his own acceptance of this challenge just nine days after coming to the church when he learned that he had metastatic cancer. He went through surgery and radiation therapy and enjoys many indications today that God has healed him. Later Barnes wrote of his experience, "It was a wonderful opportunity for the pastor to be a symbol of the truth that God's good sovereign faithfulness is our only hope."

Barnes has learned that devotion to doing God's will is the only important issue in life. The writer of Hebrews has called us to follow that same path, not only in this chapter but throughout the entire letter. May the prayer of our life be that God may equip us **with everything good for doing his will, and may he work in us what is pleasing to him** (v. 21)

PRINCIPLES

- God disapproves and judges all forms of sexual immorality.
- God promises never to leave or forsake us.
- God is pleased with our obedience, praise, and unselfish service to others.
- Only God is able to equip us with the needed attitudes and skills to accomplish his will.
- Prayer from and for others is an important element of the Christian life.

APPLICATIONS

- Love other believers as family members.
- Christian leaders must lead a lifestyle worthy of imitation by their congregations.
- Rely on Jesus to guard, protect, and encourage you.
- Make bringing glory to God the supreme aim of your life.
- Follow your church leaders.
- Pray constantly for your leaders, and ask others to pray for you.

IV. LIFE APPLICATION

Praising God in Difficulty

In 1981, J. D. Hughey retired as director of work in Europe and the Middle East for the Southern Baptist Foreign Mission Board. He envisioned a continued ministry in teaching and traveling in mission areas. In 1982 he left for Zurich, Switzerland, where he was scheduled to teach at the International Baptist Theological Seminary.

Soon after arrival there, he underwent surgery and learned that he had a malignancy. He returned to the United States for additional surgery and continued treatment with chemotherapy. In October 1982, he preached at the

First Baptist Church in Richmond, Virginia, with a message entitled "When It Is Difficult to Praise God."

Consider the challenge he faced. He had lived a full life, but he had planned for additional years. His future was uncertain with the discovery of cancer. How do people praise God in such circumstances? What do Christians do when it is difficult to praise God? Hughey gave three answers to the question.

First, he said, "We should praise him anyway." We must not wait until we feel like offering praise to God, but must praise him as a daily experience. We praise God, not for our circumstances, but for his nature. Whatever our circumstances, he is our help, guide, and rock. Hughey said, "I do not thank God for my illness, but I praise him in the midst of it and in spite of it. . . . I seem to have had just the right combination of prayer, tender loving care and chemotherapy."

Second, he said, "When praise is difficult, . . . remember the past." Hughey remembered the blessings of having Christian parents and the privilege of being raised in a church which encouraged and ordained him. He remembered the time and location of his baptism, and added, "The memory of God's blessings years ago helps me to praise Him today."

Hughey celebrated what God had done for others. He remembered the biblical event of the Passover and its celebration of deliverance. He recalled rescue from trying experiences and God's abundant supply of grace to endure difficulty.

Third, he said, "Plan for future praise." Sometimes all of us feel low emotionally and spiritually, and it is difficult to focus on the goodness and greatness of God. The Bible, however, provides a basis for us to hope, trust, and respond to God. Even in difficulty we can ask God to use our experiences for his glory. Then he concluded, "We pray for health, and sometimes God grants our requests. However, we cannot expect always to be healed of all our diseases. Death will eventually come to all of us. However, we can say with the Apostle Paul, 'I am convinced that neither death nor life, neither angels nor demons, neither the present nor the future, nor any powers, neither height nor depth, nor anything else in all creation, will be able to separate us from the love of God that is in Christ Jesus our Lord' (Rom. 8:38–39)."

The writer of Hebrews knew that his readers faced trial, persecution, and difficulty. He encouraged continual praise to God, even in difficulty (Heb. 13:15). We will face some of the same trials in life as J. D. Hughey. We must plan for the same response of praise by remembering God's nature, his past blessings, and his promise of hope which provides for future blessings.

V. PRAYER

God of peace, give me peace and hope in the midst of life's sorrows, pains, and frustrations. Let me experience your daily presence in such a way that I praise you no matter the outward circumstances or the inner turmoil. Lord, I will obey you no matter what the results seem to be. I am confident that you have eternal rewards for me beyond anything I can imagine. So I praise you for past memories, present hopes, and future blessings. Amen.

VI. DEEPER DISCOVERIES

A. Angels Without Knowing It (v. 2)

Offering hospitality to Christians on mission for the Lord was both a need and a commandment in the first century. The sparse supply of reputable guest houses and hotels made it imperative for Christians to host other believers who were traveling to bring the good news to others.

As an incentive to encourage this display of Christian hospitality, the writer of Hebrews reminded his readers that in hosting strangers some had **entertained angels without knowing it.** The reference was to Abraham's experience in Genesis 18 when he entertained three men on the plains of Mamre and found that one of them was the angel of the Lord. This angel promised that Abraham and Sarah would have a son the following year.

This angel remained behind to talk with Abraham, and the two angelic companions traveled to Sodom. Abraham interceded with the Lord for the preservation of Sodom from destruction and received the Lord's promise that he would not destroy the city if he found ten righteous people there.

The writer of Hebrews was not necessarily encouraging the readers to expect always to entertain supernatural visitors in disguise. He was suggesting that some visitors would be messengers from God, who would bring them a true blessing. The Old Testament also has other stories of visits from unexpected divine supernatural beings in Judges 6:11–24; 13:2–5.

B. God's Judgment (v. 4)

God's promise of judgment for those who practice sexual immorality becomes an incentive for the practice of purity by those who acknowledge divine sovereignty. Paul's warning to those practicing immorality and idolatry was that God's wrath comes on those who practice these things (Eph. 5:5–6).

This was a novel view in the first century, and it is equally surprising to many in the twentieth century, who feel that issues of right and wrong are to be determined by each individual. Those who practice sexual immorality may escape human disapproval, but in the end they will find that none other than God will judge them.

C. Altar, Tabernacle, Most Holy Place (vv. 10–11)

All of these terms refer to various aspects of the Jewish sacrificial system with which Christ's sacrifice is contrasted. The **altar** presented a figure of speech for the sacrifice of Christ.

The **tabernacle** was the Jewish tent of worship used by those who traveled under Moses through the wilderness. **Those who minister at the tabernacle** spoke of Jewish worshipers who had not relied on the sacrificial death of Christ. The **Most Holy Place** referred to the place to which Jewish high priests carried the blood of the sacrificial victim on the Day of Atonement. On that day the high priest carried the blood into this inner area of the tabernacle, but he left the bodies of the animals to be burned outside the camp (Lev. 16:14–15, 27).

Each of these three references illustrates the superior importance of Christ's sacrifice in comparison to Jewish sacrificial practices. Only the sacrifice of Jesus produced benefits which were blessing and changing the lives of Jewish Christians.

D. Camp, Gate, City (vv. 11–14)

Camp was a military expression applied to the assembly of the tribes of Israel as they gathered in the wilderness. Verse 11 reminds us that the bodies of those animals used in sacrifice were burned outside the assembly location of these tribes.

The New Testament records the fact that Jesus' death occurred outside the walls of Jerusalem (John 19:20). Hebrews understands this to symbolize the stigma of Jesus' death. These believers were encouraged to make a courageous commitment to follow Jesus, even though such an obedience assured hardship and trial.

City reminded the readers of Hebrews that Christianity involved a corporate relationship with other believers. The coming city which believers are to seek is heaven itself. By faith those who follow Christ are already citizens of this heavenly city, and it cannot be shaken (Heb. 12:27).

E. Non-Animal Sacrifices (vv. 15–16)

Many religions made a practice of offering animal sacrifices, but Christians had no need for the animal sacrifices of Judaism or of pagan religions. The Old Testament contains hints that the mere offering of animal sacrifices unaccompanied by a committed heart was not pleasing to God (Ps. 51:15–17). The sacrifice of Christ rendered animal sacrifices forever obsolete, but certain sacrifices still pleased God. All who had experienced the benefits of Christ's perfect sacrifice should offer those sacrifices which pleased God. Christians are to offer the sacrifice of praise continually, to offer tangible gifts such as money to those in need, and to delight in fellowship with other believers.

F. God of Peace (v. 20)

Paul used the phrase **the God of peace** several times in his writings (Rom. 15:33; 16:20; 2 Cor. 13:11; 1 Thess. 5:23). Here the term shows God as fully involved in the prosperity of the whole person. A life centered in God will be full of the experience of his peace and prosperity.

The term has significance in light of the persecution the readers of Hebrews faced. Such intense opposition tempted some to abandon Christianity. They may have wondered where they could find the strength and grace they needed for daily life. Hebrews points to God as the only source of real peace and prosperity. We will find no wholeness if we turn away from Christ.

G. Shepherd of the Sheep (v. 20)

Several times the New Testament applies the image of a shepherd to Christ. In John 10:11 Jesus called himself "the good shepherd." In 1 Peter 2:25 the apostle Peter described Jesus as "the Shepherd and Overseer" of our souls. In Mark 14:27 Jesus applied the shepherd imagery from Zechariah 13:7 to himself. Each of these presentations emphasizes Jesus' care for his own. The imagery also emphasizes the sovereign control of Christ as Shepherd over his own flock (see Rev. 2:27; 12:5).

The reference to Christ as Shepherd in Hebrews 13:20 relates to Christ as one who was raised from the dead. The idea seems to be that Christ experienced resurrection and is able to transfer the power of this resurrection to his own people.

H. A Short Letter (v. 22)

The phrase **a short letter** simply means "briefly." This comment probably referred to the entire letter, making many wonder how a book of thirteen chapters like Hebrews gains the description, "short." It is not short in its total length, but it is short considering the lengthy subject matter. The writer of Hebrews covered a weighty subject, dealing with the priestly work of Christ, the effects of the new covenant, and the effect of Christ's sacrificial death. He has moved deliberately through the discussion without using excess verbiage, and he may simply be saying that he has not labored his points at great length and is thereby deserving of their closest attention.

VII. TEACHING OUTLINE

A. INTRODUCTION

1. Lead Story: Are All Sacrifices Acceptable to God?

2. Context: In this final chapter the author of Hebrews has gathered together a group of miscellaneous commands and warnings. He has outlined actions, attitudes, and practices which please God.

   A Right Response to Fellow Christians (vv. 1–9). Christians are to show compassion to traveling Christians and to those imprisoned for their faith (vv. 1–3). Married believers must practice moral purity (vv. 4–6), and all believers must follow the faithful example and teaching of the leaders who have served them (vv. 7–9).

   A Right Response to God (vv. 10–16). Commitment, continuous praise, and unselfish service to others are spiritual sacrifices which please God. Although Christians no longer need material sacrifices, they must offer spiritual sacrifices to God.

   A Right Response to Church Leaders (v. 17). Submission to the leadership of church leaders makes it possible for them to do their jobs with joy and not with difficulty.

   Prayer for One Another (vv. 18–21). Mutual prayer for one another is foundational for accomplishing God's will.

   Genuine Affection among Believers (vv. 22–25). News about travel plans shows an interest among Christians in the challenges and difficulties believers face. All Christians need an abundant supply of divine grace.

3. Transition: Christianity has both a vertical and a horizontal dimension. Vertically we respond to **the God of peace**. Horizontally we love and relate to other believers. Hebrews calls us to show compassion for one another, purity in marriage, and respect for Christian leaders (vv. 1–9, 22–25). It also calls for prayer for one another (vv. 18–21). Each of these responsibilities relates to other believers and demonstrates the fact that genuine Christianity impacts how we live with our believing brothers and sisters.

   Vital Christianity also touches our response to the living God. He wants full commitment, praise, and an unselfish giving of ourselves to please him (vv. 10–16). A balanced Christianity will produce vertical and horizontal evidence of its reality.

B. COMMENTARY

1. A Right Response to Fellow Christians (vv. 1–9)
   a. To Christians with special needs (vv. 1–3)
   b. To the family (vv. 4–6)
   c. Within the church (vv. 7–9)
2. A Right Response to God (vv. 10–16)
3. A Right Response to Church Leaders (v. 17)
4. Prayer for One Another (vv. 18–21)
5. Genuine Affection among Believers (vv. 22–25)

C. CONCLUSION: PRAISING GOD IN DIFFICULTY

VIII. ISSUES FOR DISCUSSION

1. How do the elements and practices of Old Testament religion help you understand Jesus and the practice of Christianity?
2. Is there ever an acceptable reason for a Christian to practice sexual immorality? How do you explain your answer to unbelievers?
3. How are you related to money? In what ways does it tempt you away from total devotion to God? What can you do about this?
4. How are you relating to the leaders of your church? What qualities in them are you imitating? In what ways are you submitting to their authority?
5. What are you doing that shows love for other Christians and that shares your resources with those in need?

Introduction to

James

AUTHORSHIP

The author presented himself in 1:1 as **James, a servant of God and of the Lord Jesus Christ**. This brief identification showed two facts about him. First, he was well-known. He introduced himself only with his first name, assuming that his readers could identify him. Second, he showed great humility. He wanted to be known only as a follower of Jesus.

Four men named James appear in the New Testament. Two of these, James, the father of Judas (Luke 6:16) and James, the son of Alphaeus (Mark 3:18), are little-known figures who do not seem to qualify as possible authors of the letter. James, the son of Zebedee and brother of John, was a prominent leader among the apostles (Acts 12:2), but his early death as a martyr occurred at a time before the Book of James was written.

The most likely candidate among the New Testament Jameses for authorship of this letter is the Lord's brother (Mark 6:3; Acts 15:13). The letter contains several references showing possible influence by Jesus' words on the author (cf. Jas. 4:11 and Matt. 7:1–2). The early church also accepted the Lord's half brother as the author of the writing.

James was a younger half brother of Jesus and a child of Joseph and Mary. The fact that his name appeared first in a list of Jesus' brothers suggests that he was the oldest of the half brothers (Mark 6:3).

James was not a believer in the Lord during Jesus' public ministry (John 7:2–10). After seeing the risen Christ, he became his follower (1 Cor. 15:7). He was among those awaiting the coming of the Spirit on the day of Pentecost (Acts 1:14). At the Jerusalem Council he threw his support behind Paul's position that observance of the Law was not a condition for the salvation of the Gentiles (Acts 15:12–21).

The church historian Eusebius recorded the tradition that James spent so much time on his knees that they became like those of a camel. This statement has probably caught the spirit of James's piety, but we need not expect that Eusebius meant it as a literal description of his knees.

READER PROFILE

James addressed his letter to **the twelve tribes scattered among the nations** (Jas. 1:1). This does not identify a specific location of the readers, but it suggests a Jewish-Christian audience outside of Palestine.

In 2:2 he used the Greek word for *synagogue* to refer to the **meeting** of Christians. He also referred to the Old Testament and to information Jews would know well (4:6; 5:11,17).

It is possible that James wrote to some of the Jewish believers who left Jerusalem after persecutions (Acts 11:19).

DATE

The Jewish historian Josephus mentioned the martyrdom of James, and we can date his reference to some events occurring around A.D. 62. We must place the writing of James prior to this date.

James described economic conditions in Palestine which disappeared after the war with Rome. The unjust treatment of laborers by landowners (5:1–6) would more likely appear before the war rather than after it.

His use of the term **elders** in 5:14 supports a simple church organization. This encourages an earlier date for the book.

The use of the Greek word for "synagogue" (2:2) to describe the meeting place of Christians indicates a time early in the spread of Christianity.

These features point to an undetermined early date for the letter, probably in the fifties.

CHARACTERISTICS OF THE BOOK OF JAMES

The content of James moves quickly from one subject to another. James quickly covers such subjects as trials, hearing God's Word, the tongue, and the right use of wealth. This rambling style resembles the approach of Proverbs in the Old Testament.

James omits personal references, prayer requests, and travel plans. This may indicate that the letter was written to several Christian groups scattered over a large area.

James presents a series of messages sharing pastoral advice to groups of scattered Christians. He uses rebuke and exhortation to encourage new behavior in them (2:1–4; 3:9–12). Some scholars see James as presenting a loosely connected collection of moral warnings.

Martin Luther faulted James's emphasis on justification by works (2:24) He felt that Paul's emphasis on justification by faith contained stronger meat for Christians (Rom. 3:27–30). Luther's outlook on James shows that the writing had some difficulty in being accepted into the canon of Scripture.

James 1

Triumphing When Troubled

──────────────────── | Quote | ────────────────────

"*If* He governs all, then nothing but good can befall those to whom He would do good. . . . He will so govern all things that we shall reap only good from all that befalls us."

Presbyterian theologian B. B. Warfield, commenting on the meaning of Romans 8:28

I N A N U T S H E L L

*G*reetings! Be patient when you suffer, for your trials will produce a quality you must have—perseverance. If you lack insight into your suffering, ask God for it. You will get a crown of life after your trials are over. Don't blame God for your being attracted to evil. God is the source of everything good. Be sure you don't merely hear God's Word. Do it!

Triumphing When Troubled

I. INTRODUCTION

Getting Sick for the Glory of God

$\mathcal{D}$ottie and Ed Powell came to a small village in Burkina Faso, West Africa, as a part of their orientation to African culture. They were beginning translation and literacy work among largely animistic people. They lived in a village of fifty-five people, all members of an extended family. They were to remain there for a limited time as they learned the rigors of living at the tip of the Sahara Desert.

Two in the village could speak French. The rest only knew the local tongue. Daily temperatures reached above 100 degrees. The Powells kept the door of their house open for light and air. Livestock traffic and a stream of curious Africans poured through their living room.

Several days after arrival in the village, Dottie became ill with dysentery. The heat and the difficulty of adjusting to native food sapped her energy. Tears of anger and self-pity flowed frequently. Then one day, she asked the Lord in desperation, "Lord, what can I do?"

Back came the answer, "Be sick."

Dottie Powell felt relief in accepting that task because she judged that she could handle it. She was already sick, and she determined that she would do a fabulous job of performing that role. At the time she did not realize the excruciating events she would face in her sickness.

The day after determining that she would honor God in her sickness, she and her husband received a fax from America telling of trouble for her married daughter. Doctors could no longer pick up the heartbeat of her unborn child. When villagers learned of the concern the Powells had for their daughter, one man borrowed a motorbike, loaded Dottie Powell on it, sickness and all, and carried her to the nearest telephone. Dottie was relieved to talk to her daughter in a hospital delivery room and to learn that mother and child were doing well.

Back home in the village, Dottie Powell complained to God, "Lord, I want to go home. I want to see my daughter and hold my grandchild. I can't stay here." God's love responded to her during this outburst, and she stayed. She made the commitment, "Yes, Lord. I'll be sick for you."

The chief elder of the village grew concerned at Dottie's inability to retain her food. He called for two Christian men to come from an evangelical church nearby and pray for her. The elder was an animist. People in his village had actively persecuted the little church. The men came and prayed. She recovered. The Powells requested permission of the village elder to take the two French-speaking villagers with them to the church. Surprisingly, he agreed. That day the two villagers heard the gospel. One of them became a believer.

After the Powells completed their orientation time in the village, they still maintained contact with their friends. Letters frequently come from the two French-speaking villagers to them. One letter told of the conversion of the brother of the village elder.

Dottie Powell learned that God wanted her to be faithful to him in her sickness. He did not require that she be strong or effective. She was to live in complete faithfulness. He would compensate for her weakness.

She learned afresh her weakness. She also understood more richly God's provision. She learned that God only wanted her commitment. She was reminded that God himself had assumed a nature of weakness for the purpose of reaching the world with his saving message (Phil. 2:6–11). She learned how to be true even though tested and tried. She understood the truth that **the testing of your faith develops perseverance** (Jas. 1:3).

II. COMMENTARY

Triumphing When Troubled

MAIN IDEA: *God wants his people to triumph over their trials and to live in obedience to his commandments.*

A How to Be Tried and True (vv. 1–18)

SUPPORTING IDEA: *Christians are to develop perseverance in their trials and accept responsibility for their failures.*

1. A Word of Greeting (v. 1)

1:1. This verse identifies the author and the readers but does not give us enough information about either group to be crystal clear in our identifications.

James was a common name, but at least two well-known Jameses appeared in the early church. One was the son of Zebedee and brother of the apostle John, but he became a martyr around A.D. 44 (see Acts 12:1–2). Most scholars feel that the Book of James was written at a later date. The second James was the brother of Jesus (Mark 6:3). He started out in his contact with Jesus as an unbeliever (John 7:5), but an encounter with Jesus after the resurrection put him on the road to faith (1 Cor. 15:7). Paul identified him as a "pillar" in the early church (Gal. 2:9). He presented the decision of the Jerusalem Council in Acts 15:13–21. This is probably the James who wrote this letter.

James was the son of Mary and Joseph. He was thus younger than Jesus. He showed his humility by identifying himself as **a servant of God and of the Lord Jesus Christ.** James never mentioned his relationship to Jesus, a fact that most of us would quickly publicize if we had been James. His conversion allowed him to describe himself as a servant of someone who was his half brother. Normal sibling rivalry would make that a truly challenging task! James meant that he had installed Christ as Lord over every realm of his life and was committed to his service.

The readers of James were **the twelve tribes scattered among the nations,** probably Jewish Christians living outside of Palestine. Persecution might have driven some from their homeland (Acts 8:1). Some could have been among converts gathered in Jerusalem on the day of Pentecost (Acts 2:5–12).

Greetings was the normal first-century way of wishing joy for people you greeted on the street (Matt. 26:49; 27:29; 28:9; Luke 1:28; cf. 2 John 10) and for readers of letters you wrote (Acts 15:23; 23:26). The verb comes from a root suggesting "joy."

When we compare James's greeting with those in Paul's letters, we see one major difference. Paul did not use the common word for *greetings,* but gave distinctively Christian expressions such as "grace" and "peace." James omitted this type of greeting.

2. Outer Trials (vv. 2–12)

Verses 2–12 focus on calamities and sufferings which can suddenly surround Christians. These eleven verses begin and end with a discussion about **trials** (see vv. 2,12).Christians must seek wisdom from God to endure afflictions and difficulties which threaten to overpower us.

1:2–4. Trials are **of many kinds,** but believers can triumph over them. Verse 2 presents a command concerning trials: **consider it pure joy, . . . whenever you face trials of many kinds.** This does not suggest that we should seek out trials. Nor are we to pretend that enduring trials is pleasant. They cause pain and difficulty. Still, we should look at trials as an occasion for joy because of their potential for producing something good in us. This calls us consciously to develop a positive attitude toward trials, quite contrary to our normal response. Similarly, Hebrews regards trials as the discipline a Father gives to help us share in God's holiness (Heb. 12:10).

Verse 3 explains how believers can show **pure joy** as they face trials. We are to realize that God intends the testing of our faith to produce perseverance. Without these trials, some character would be undeveloped. God also uses trials to purge and remove defects from immature faith.

Perseverance suggests endurance or stamina. It does not refer merely to the ability to hold back the discouraging results of a bad temper or remorseful self-pity. It also includes staying power that believers can have because they trust their God. Tested faith becomes spiritually tough and rugged.

Verse 4 presents the spiritual outcome or result of a **perseverance** which attains its appointed role within the believer. A believer with perseverance is **perfect**. This does not mean sinlessness or moral flawlessness. It describes maturity, the state of being fully developed. **Complete** pictures someone who possesses all the spiritual traits needed for moral completeness. People who endure trials with faith in God can develop every trait needed for spiritual victory. Moreover, these traits can be ripened to a full maturity. An outlook like this naturally describes trials as an occasion for **pure joy**.

Joseph's brothers sold him into slavery in Egypt. Potiphar's wife betrayed him (Gen. 39:1–20), and Pharaoh's cupbearer forgot him (Gen. 40:23). Still, in God's plan he became the second most powerful leader in Egypt. After their father Jacob died in Egypt, Joseph's brothers asked for mercy and forgiveness for their past wrongs to him. Joseph's inspiring response was, "Don't be afraid. Am I in the place of God? You intended to harm me, but God intended it for good to accomplish what is now being done, the saving of many lives" (Gen. 50:19–20). Enduring affliction had produced in Joseph an ability to see God's greater hand in the malicious intentions of his brothers. God had used trials to make Joseph **mature and complete**.

1:5–8. These verses outline our resources for facing trials and explain how to get them. Christians need wisdom and faith as they encounter trials. We are encouraged to pray for wisdom and to pray with faith.

Jewish Christians should understand **wisdom**. To James and to Jews, wisdom was much more than knowledge and intelligence. Judaism emphasized that "the fear of the Lord" was the starting point of wisdom (Prov. 1:7). Wisdom was a spiritual trait which developed from a wholehearted love for God's ways. James will later contrast divine wisdom with earthly wisdom (3:13–18). Earthly wisdom is **unspiritual** and demonic. Divine wisdom is **pure; . . . peace-loving, considerate, submissive, full of mercy and good fruit, impartial, and sincere** (Jas. 3:17). With wisdom Christians can understand how their trials merged into God's plan for their lives. They have the commitment to his will necessary to assure that they follow God and not wander from the path of his plan. But how do Christians get this wisdom?

They must ask God for it. Four facts about God encourage us to ask for this wisdom. First, God is a giving God. Giving to those who ask from him is natural for God. Second, God gives **generously to all**. He has no favorite recipients of his gifts, but gives to all classes, races, and types of people. Third, God gave **without finding fault**. God does not give in such a way as to humiliate us. He does not chastise us for our failures or hold our unworthiness against us. He is always ready to add new blessings to old ones without finding fault in us for our many shortcomings. Finally, God promises to answer those who come seeking wisdom. A request according to his will receives his answer (1 John 5:14–15).

Such wisdom helps us understand how our troubles fit in with God's plan. It assures us that God has not forsaken us. God's gift of wisdom allows us to understand how God is involved in life's daily events. Instead of serving as a hindrance, trials present a marvelous opportunity to become wise!

Verses 6–7 deal with the need for faith in prayer. Whoever asks God for wisdom **must believe and not doubt.** Faith is a complete commitment to God in trusting obedience. Two reasons to encourage faith are presented. First, a doubting person is spiritually unstable like **a wave of the sea, blown and tossed by the wind.** Our prayers for wisdom must not alternate between faith and unbelief. We must endure in the confidence that God will answer our request according to his will.

Second, doubters should not even imagine that God will answer their prayers. Faith alone opens the door to God's limitless treasury of wisdom. Unbelief receives God's rejection slip which reads, "Request denied due to insufficient faith."

Let us be careful not to make light of our hesitant faith. Doubting God is serious business! Such doubt implies we have a low view of God. To receive answers from God, you must come to him with the conviction that he gives rewards to those who diligently seek him (Heb. 11:6). Diligence is a trait we all need desperately.

Verse 8 provides an additional description of the spiritual makeup of a doubter. The doubter is **a double-minded man, unstable in all he does.** Doubters display no stamina in their commitment to the Lord. One moment they are inclined to obedience; another moment, they follow their own ways. Failure to endure with faith in prayer is an indicator of the doubter's general character.

1:9–11. These verses give examples of trials for two different groups of people and call for both groups to show a right estimate of their trials. Poor people must not lament their poverty, but must rejoice at God's bounty in their lives. The rich people must not delight in their wealth, but must find joy in the humility which trials produce in their lives.

James wanted poor people to find delight in their spiritual position in God's kingdom and avoid the temptation to murmur about their material distress. **The brother in humble circumstances** is a Christian who lives in poverty. Depression, resentment, and selfish ambition may easily characterize their lives. Instead, they should glory in the prominent position to which God has elevated them as believers. Paul suggested that God has given the Holy Spirit as a down payment on all the good things he will do for believers throughout eternity (Eph. 1:14). Poor believers are to rejoice that they are "fellow citizens with God's people and members of God's household" (Eph. 2:19).

Verses 10–11 focus on wealthy people. The rich person faces the temptation of glorying in wealth. In one sense the possession of wealth is a trial because it tempts rich people to rejoice in earthly treasures (Matt. 6:19–21). The wealthy are encouraged to glory in the humbling of soul which life's trials can bring them. They can learn that worldly riches pass away, while God's wisdom lasts for eternity. Wealthy people should exult in the privilege of learning that true treasures are located only in heaven.

Since the possession of money often gives wealthy people a false sense of security, an illustration from nature demonstrates the brevity and uncertainty of life. The pageantry of wealth resembles the blooming of a wild plant which fades in the hot sun soon after it displays its beauty. Isaiah 40:6–7 uses a similar image to show that life is brief and uncertain. These verses warn that **in the same way, the rich man will fade away even while he goes about his business.** Rich people must recognize that the possession of wealth provides a challenge to overcome (cf. 1 Tim. 6:9). Possessing wealth without spiritual wisdom eventually brings only emptiness. Like the poor, the rich should revel in the spiritual privileges which the Lord has opened for them.

These verses also warn against the tendencies of both poverty and wealth. Poverty brings no joy, so many people feel that wealth provides joy. In reality the poor must find joy in their spiritual privileges despite their penury. The wealthy must avoid delighting in wealth, glorying instead in the spiritual privileges God makes available. James would doubtless have followed Paul in urging his wealthy listeners to be "rich in good deeds" (1 Tim. 6:18).

1:12. A double result is promised those who faithfully endure their trials. First is an inner reward of blessedness. **Blessed** is the same term which appears repeatedly in the Beatitudes (Matt. 5:3–12). It describes an inner quality of joy resting in God and unaffected by external events. It is not a wish or statement of fact but a joyous affirmation: "O the blessedness of the person who endures trials." In the New Testament it often describes people whom the world would never regard as blessed or fortunate in any sense—such as the persecuted (Matt. 5:11–12). Having the trial is not a blessing in itself, but the stalwart endurance of the trial brought blessing.

The second blessing is a gift from God, **the crown of life. Crown** did not refer to the ornament of a ruler but to a garland wreath given to the victor in an athletic contest. God's reward to us for faithfully enduring trials is not a position of royalty over others. Rather, it is recognition from God for spiritual victory. The crown is not a physical object but a spiritual privilege which gives a deeper, fuller life on earth (John 10:10) and an unending, joyous life in the world to come. Enduring trials for his glory shows that we love God. God has stored up marvelous blessings for those who love him.

Four features in this section provide encouragement for people caught up in trials. First, God uses trials to produce staying power in those who endure. Second, for those who seek it, God provides wisdom to understand trials. Third, believers, whether rich or poor, find encouragement to rejoice over their position in life. Fourth, God promises a reward to fill the believer with hope.

3. Inner Temptations (vv. 13–18)

Outward trials frequently provide an occasion for the development of sinful attitudes within. When you don't understand these trials, it is easy to revolt against God. Who is responsible when these trials appear? May we blame God? The Bible teaches that God sends trials (Gen. 22:1; 2 Chr. 32:31). However, we must not blame him for the evil effects of the trials. God does not call us to disobedience by enticing us to evil (1:13–16), but he is the source of everything good (1:17–18). He allows trials to produce holiness and stamina in his people. We hold the blame for any evil effects of trials in our lives.

1:13–16. People sometimes complain, **God is tempting me.** Two insights about God show that he is not responsible for evil. First, **God cannot be tempted by evil.** God has no weakness or tendency which temptation can exploit. God's holy character puts him out of reach of temptation. Evil has no appeal for God. Evil is repulsive to God.

Second, God does not use evil to tempt anyone. True, God sometimes places us in situations in which we can compromise (Gen. 22:1). However, he does not do this with a view to encourage our sin but to build us up.

Verses 14–15 outline the beginnings of sin in the human heart. First, openness to temptation develops from weaknesses in the human heart. **Dragged away and enticed** comes from the language of fishing. The first word described the act of luring fish from their hiding places. The second word pictured the enticing of fish as with a juicy worm on a hook. Evil desire is the bait which hooks the human being. The Bible will not let us blame heredity, an evil environment, or wicked companions for sin. The blame rests squarely on the individual, on you and me.

Verse 15 uses the language of childbirth to trace the development of evil desire. A conception occurs when persons surrender their wills to lust. The conception produces a child named **sin.** When sin becomes full grown, it produces **death.**

Practically speaking, sin occurs whenever a person's mind approves the performance of a sinful act. Whenever the person repeatedly approves the same sin, the result is death. This is death in all its terror—a total disintegration of the personality, physically, emotionally, and spiritually. It leads to a separation from God lasting for eternity. It all begins when an individual yields his will to evil. No one can blame God for this. I do it to myself.

The act of temptation itself is not sinful. Sin develops only when an individual assents to the deed and agrees that it is good or desirable. Our evil nature and disobedient wills provide an easy avenue along which temptation can stroll. Sin develops only when we invite temptation to leave the avenue and visit with us personally.

Verses 14 and 15 do not mention the role of Satan in temptation. The Bible pictures Satan as active in temptation (1 Pet. 5:8–9), but James was not presenting a complete analysis of all temptation. He only wanted to show that God was not the cause of sin. He laid the blame for sin upon human weakness and disobedience.

Verse 16 provides a solemn warning against being deceived by wrong thinking concerning the source of sin. We may apply the words either to what has immediately preceded (vv. 13–15) or the verses which follow (vv. 17–18). If we apply the words to the preceding statements, the warning is against excusing ourselves from responsibility for sin. If we apply the words to what follows, the warning is against a wrong view of God's character. Either interpretation provides truth.

Verses 2–12 urge us to endure the trials of life. Verses 13–16 urge us to resist temptations. We can ask God for the wisdom to know whether to endure the trial or to resist the temptation. God can supply both grace to endure and strength to resist. He uses our endurance and our resistance to give us spiritual maturity and growth in holiness and stamina.

1:17–18. Having learned God is not responsible for human sin, we now see that God is the source of all that is good. God shows his goodness in that he does not change (v. 17) and by giving the good gift of new life to believers (v. 18).

Every kind of good has its ultimate source in God. Gifts are perfect because they fully meet the needs of the recipients. **Gift** includes not only God's spiritual blessings, but also the many benefits which provide for the physical and emotional needs of human beings.

The last part of verse 17 makes three statements about God. The King James Version makes this clear, describing God as "the Father of lights, with whom is no variableness, neither shadow of turning." First, as the **Father of the heavenly lights** God is the Creator of the stars and other heavenly bodies. Second, God **does not change**. This term from astronomy frequently refers to the change in light intensity from sun and moon. The sun gives full light at midday, dim light at dusk, and no light at all in the night. In stark contrast to the sun, God's character does not change. The light of his truth and holiness remains constant.

Third, God does not undergo any "shadow of turning." This term also comes from astronomy, describing moving heavenly bodies that produce constantly changing shadows on the earth. God's purposes do not have such a variation or shifting. The movements of the sun, moon, and clouds regularly cause changes in light and shadows throughout the day. God's character is always constant, true, unchanging, reliable, good, and faithful. What a God we have! As the hymn writer has said: "Change and decay in all around I see. O Thou who changest not, abide with me."

Verse 18 looks at the new birth God has given his people. God chose to give the new birth. The means of the new birth was the **word of truth**, a description of the gospel, the good news about Jesus Christ (Eph. 1:13). The result of this new birth is that believers become **a kind of firstfruits of all he created.** The firstfruits represented that initial portion of the harvest offered to God before the rest of the crop was harvested. They were the pledge of a full crop to come (Lev. 23:9–11). These first-century Christians were a pledge of a vast harvest of saved people in the centuries to come.

Many years ago my father encouraged me to take my first jump from a diving board into his outstretched arms as he waited near the edge of a swimming pool. I stood at the end of the board with fear. The water was deep. I was small. I was not a good swimmer. Courage in the water was not my strong point. But my father was there waiting on me. So I took the leap. It was good that he was there. I put too much energy into the jump and nearly leaped over him to crash into a concrete bank. But my father reached for me and hurled me back into the water. I was safe. Dad had taken care of me.

In much the same way James encourages us to take a leap of faith in trusting God to lead us to endure through trials and to provide strength for temptations. We can trust him. He is faithful. His intentions are good. We have no excuse for falling away.

Ⓑ The Danger of Listless Listening (vv. 19–27)

SUPPORTING IDEA: *This passage warns against pretending instead of listening, deceiving instead of obeying, and talking instead of serving.*

As a college freshman, I sat through a semester-length course named "Orientation." The grade of pass or fail came from mere attendance and included no other requirement. Various college officials discussed such subjects as "Using College Services," "How to Study," and "Planning for the Future." We took no notes, completed no assignments, and endured no tests. The sole requirement was to sit through the lectures.

This course produced a lot of listless listeners. Since no one demanded anything from us, we did nothing. It was easy to hear the words and ignore the content. A listless listener is someone who can endure a speech, lecture, or sermon without purposing to do a thing. A listless listener can mistake hearing and learning for obeying God.

James warns us against listless listening. We have heard messages from God's Word, learned new truths, and even been "born again." James wants to know, Are we still learners who have not yet become doers?

God is not content when his people merely attend Christian lectures. He wants us to absorb his message and change our lives because of it. Listless listening which produces no change is a blight on a Christian's life. To prevent listless listening, this passage gives a warning (vv. 19–21), a contrast (vv. 22–25), and a demand (vv. 26–27).

1. A Warning Against Ignoring God's Word (vv. 19–21)

1:19. Christians can pretend to obey God without truly listening to his commands. The readers of James's letter knew the transforming power of God's Word, the gospel. James urged them to demonstrate this change, particularly in their speech. He began by courteously addressing them as **My dear brothers,** and then challenged them to **be quick to listen, slow to speak and slow to become angry.** The commands probably refer both to our relationships to one another and to God. We are to be quick to hear and slow to talk both toward other people and toward God.

The command to **be quick to listen** calls for an eagerness to hear and obey God's message. The appeal to be **slow to speak** demands silence until we have understood and applied the message. It is a call for restraint lest we produce hasty, ill-timed reactions. The challenge to be **slow to become angry** warns against hostile, bitter feelings. We cannot hear God if we remain distracted with resentment, hatred, or vengeful attitudes.

Our society encourages us to express our feelings, whether they be good or bad, peaceful or inflammatory, godly or ungodly. James 1:19, however, pictures the wise person as one who listens to God and others, deliberates a response carefully, and answers with cautious words.

1:20. This verse supports the command to be **slow to become angry. Man's anger does not bring about the righteous life that God desires.** The anger prohibited by this passage is not so much a flashing, destructive temper as a simmering pot of hostile, mean-spirited feelings.

Human anger wastes the energies of God's people, produces divisions, and often comes from selfish ambition. The righteousness that God desires includes deeds which are **pure; . . . peace-loving, considerate, submissive, full of mercy and good fruit, impartial and sincere** (Jas. 3:17). Angry words and deeds cannot produce purity and peace. Proverbs 29:22 warns that "an angry man stirs up dissension, and a hot-tempered one commits many sins." Moses' murderous anger in Exodus 2:11–15 resulted in his flight from Egypt and added forty additional years to the misery of the Jews in Egypt (Acts 7:27–32).

The mischievous works of angry Christians prevent the unsaved world from seeing that the God of all the earth does right (Gen. 18:25). It is impossible to look at the disorderly conduct of fighting believers and worship the God they profess to serve. This should make Christians cautious in our display of an angry spirit.

1:21. Believers can make a positive response instead of indulging in the hurtful anger which so easily hinders God's righteous designs. This verse issues a command and then provides a prerequisite for obeying the command, an incentive for obedience, and a description of our attitude in obedience.

The command is to **accept the word planted in you.** This calls for a warm, open welcome to the influence of God's message in our lives (1 Thess. 2:13). The prerequisite is to **get rid of all moral filth and the evil that is so prevalent.** To obey the command we must strip off like a dirty garment any moral indecency and malicious attitudes. Why do this? The incentive for obedience is that God's **word planted in you can save you.** Obedience to God's Word promotes holiness and develops godly character. We demonstrate a genuine likeness toward Christ as we get rid of the flaming desires for filth and evil. This shows the presence of a real experience of salvation.

In our obedience we must display humility. We must not quarrel or quibble with God as we receive his message. We must receive the spiritual medicine which our divine physician prescribes for us.

David committed adultery with Bathsheba and carried out a plan to murder her husband (see 2 Sam. 11). For some months he refused to acknowledge his sin until the prophet Nathan boldly said to him, "You are the man" (2 Sam. 12:7). In Psalm 51 we catch a glimpse of a David who has come to his senses and expressed repentance fully. David asked for mercy (Ps. 51:1–2), acknowledged his sin (Ps. 51:3–6), pleaded for cleansing (Ps. 51:7–9), and asked for divine renewal (Ps. 51:10–12). We should respond to the Lord with equal passion.

2. A Contrast of Responses to God's Command (vv. 22–25)

James 1:19–21 focuses on speech as an area for demonstrating obedience to God's Word. Here he calls for obedient action as the proper forum for demonstrating commitment to the Lord.

1:22. James's command is literally to "keep on becoming doers of God's Word." He insisted on an obedience which lasts. This does not minimize the importance of hearing God's Word. It does emphasize strongly the need for acting. Too often Christians view a sermon as an interesting moral or theological lecture. We need to do something other than sitting and listening. Jesus pronounced a blessing only on those "who hear the word of God and obey it" (Luke 11:28).

The command to **listen to** God's Word describes someone who attends a lecture. The hearer could nod agreeably to the message but do nothing as a result. God wants a listener to become a disciple, an obedient follower of Jesus. One who hears the message without doing anything is self-deceived. Such a listener has made a false estimate of the situation. Jesus warned against this error (Matt. 7:21–27).

1:23–25. James presented a negative and a positive illustration of a response to God's message. Via a vivid picture of listless listening, verses 23–24 compare those who only hear God's Word to people who gaze into a mirror and dash away with little memory of what they saw. Mirrors in New Testament times were made of polished metal. People used them to wash their faces, shave their beards, apply cosmetics, and comb their hair. Then they quickly left, giving little thought to the image they had seen. People can repeat this experience in the spiritual realm. We give a quick glance into God's Word, find a morsel of truth, and jump into another task without remembering or applying what we read.

Verse 25 uses the mirror metaphor with four verbs to picture the response of obedient listeners to God's message. First, obedient people look **intently into the perfect law that gives freedom.** This describes someone who gazes at God's message with a desire to learn. The same verb—translated as **bent over**—pictures the apostle John staring into Jesus' empty tomb (John 20:5). John's look led to an obedient faith (John 20:8).

Second, obedient people **continued to do** what God said. They put God's Word into practice and follow through with commitment. Third, obedient listeners do not forget what they hear. Spiritual amnesia never conquers their minds. Fourth, obedient listeners do what God's message instructs them to do.

Good listening, endurance, clear memory, and obedience characterize committed Christians. They are eager to receive and obey what God tells them to do.

God's Word is **the perfect law that gives freedom.** Obedience to Jesus' commands in Scripture brings freedom from sin and death. Whenever we submit to God's message, this law of liberty produces a disposition to obey God's will joyfully. We have freedom because we truly want to serve God. Jesus promised this freedom in John 8:31–32.

Obedient people are promised a blessing. We do not need to wait for a future blessing. We already have the blessing in our grasp. Doing what God requires brings a blessing with it.

Psalm 1:1–3 summarizes the blessings of obedience. Those who meditate on the Law of the Lord will be "like a tree planted by streams of water, which yields its fruit in season and whose leaf does not wither. Whatever he does prospers."

3. The Evidence of Good Listening to God's Word (vv. 26–27)

SUPPORTING IDEA: *Committed believers demonstrate their obedience with deeds of compassion and inner purity.*

1:26. This verse describes a person who considered himself to be **religious** but did not listen well to God's Word. The person focused on the externals of religious action such as public prayer, fasting, giving, and worship attendance. James did not belittle this action, but he added that inner control of the tongue must accompany outward performance.

Keep a tight rein on his tongue sometimes described the bridle used with a horse. The tongue is compared to an unmanageable horse which needed bit and bridle to tame its excesses. Controlling the tongue is so important that James devoted most of chapter 3 to its use.

James leveled two accusations at the person who practiced outward religion without inner control. First, **he deceives himself.** This repeats the idea of verse 22 in different words. What a pity to find after a lifetime of pseudo-religion that you have only been practicing self-deception!

Second, **his religion is worthless.** Peter used the same word—translated as *empty*—to describe useless pagan practices his readers had followed before they became Christians (1 Pet. 1:18). Religious practices without inner control have no more saving power than paganism.

1:27. Two evidences demonstrate pure religion: deeds of compassion and inner purity. This does not reduce Christianity to mere benevolence. True religion has more features than James has mentioned. The emphasis here is that for God to accept our worship it must be accompanied by loving ministry and a holy life. Both Christians and non-Christians could see and understand this type of evidence.

To **look after orphans and widows** demanded demonstrations of concern and active involvement. The psalmist pictured God as a defender of orphans and widows (Ps. 68:5). Christ used the word for **look after** in Matthew 25:43 to describe the ministry of caring for those in prison. Obeying this appeal calls for more than an occasional visit. It demands genuine compassion and true engagement.

(Not) polluted demands a freedom from contamination by the world. Peter used this word to refer to Christ as "without . . . defect" (1 Pet. 1:19). Christians are to model their purity after that of Jesus.

Some months ago I assembled a small playset with a sliding board and some climbing sections. I placed it in my backyard for my grandchildren to use. Although the process was not difficult, I constantly referred to the instruction book so I would know where to fit each piece. The writers of the book know how their product should fit together. I needed to follow their directions.

We must follow God's instructions devotedly if we want to produce a lifestyle honoring to God. Obeying God's Word demands control of the tongue, a compassion for others, and a separated life. These are the identifying marks of **pure and faultless** religion.

> **MAIN IDEA REVIEW:** *God wants his people to triumph over their trials and to live in obedience to his commandments.*

III. CONCLUSION

Sheer Memory Is Not Enough

Several years ago I spent a year's sabbatical leave in England. My daughter and son-in-law lived in our home while we were away. I left them detailed instructions about caring for the home and handling some financial matters in my absence. They followed them to perfection.

Suppose, however, that I had returned home to find my yard overgrown with weeds, windows broken out, my fence destroyed, and stacks of letters piled up in the living room. My response would have been, "Did you read any of my instructions? Did you get our letters? Did you do what I asked?"

They might have answered, "Oh, yes, we enjoyed your instructions and letters. We read all you wrote. We even memorized some of the instructions. The letters were great!"

How pleased would I be? The goal of my letters and instructions was not to entertain and inform but to provide guidelines for action. It would have been sheer folly to memorize my instructions without doing anything about them.

Christians make this same mistake in their spiritual lives. James called us to respond to God's commands with obedience. This obedience demands endurance in trial, resistance to temptation, and a reverent submission to God's commandments.

PRINCIPLES

- God permits trials to develop stamina in his people.
- God gives rewards to those who show their love for him by enduring trials.
- God does not use evil to tempt his children to disobedience.
- All good has its source in our God.
- Submission to God's demands brings a blessing in the act of obeying.

- Controlling what we say gives evidence of our obedience.
- Caring for the weak and needy shows we are following Christ.

APPLICATIONS

- Face the trials of life with faith in God.
- Ask God for insight whenever you fail to understand his ways in your life.
- Accept responsibility for your own sins and failures.
- Obey God's Word when you hear it.
- Be unselfish in service to others.
- Separate yourself from sin.

IV. LIFE APPLICATION

We Must Obey Our Lord

Ray Eitelman is a missionary serving in the African country of Togo. Some time ago he was driving his motorbike to a village preaching point. Suddenly a dog darted in front of him. He took a spill and ended up with arms, legs, and face scratched, scraped, and bleeding. A friend passed by and advised him to return home, but to Eitelman God said, "Go," and on he went.

He came to a gas station. The attendant took a look at the bleeding missionary and advised him to go to the hospital. For Ray Eitelman God still said, "Go," and on he went.

As he continued on his bike, a black cloud blanketed the horizon, extending its dark scowl for miles. Eitelman thought, "I'm hurting. I'm bleeding. Now I'll get wet. Maybe I should turn around." For Ray Eitelman God said, "Go," and on he went.

Arriving in the village, he preached a message of salvation on the sacrificial death of Christ. Doubtless, villagers who gazed at the bleeding missionary could better understand the shed blood of Christ. When Eitelman shared an invitation to follow Jesus in obedience, ten persons responded, four for salvation.

He returned home rejoicing, but the next morning the Lord did not tell Ray Eitelman to "Go." He was glad because he was too sore to get out of bed.

At multiple points along his ride to the village, he could have returned home, and no one would have questioned his commitment. For him it was more important to obey God than to seek immediate medical treatment. It was more important to obey God than to escape the downpour of a thunderstorm. It was more important to obey God than to avoid the humiliation of friendly questioners asking, "What happened to you?"

Each of us wants to feel healthy, to have others think well of us, and to avoid pain. We want to keep out of life's trials and avoid the discomfort of having to deny ourselves legitimate wishes. We like to speak what we think and want to show a little temper whenever we feel justified. We will be able to do some of these things in God's goodness, but we can't do all of them and should never do some of them.

What we must do is obey God. It may take us to a remote African village even though we are in pain and would like to be home. It may cause some to ridicule us. It may lead us to rein in our natural desires and say "Not now" to some goals we have made. Obeying God is the route to follow for triumph over the troubles and temptations of life. James has promised that whoever obeys **will be blessed in what he does** (Jas. 1:25). This is the way to live.

V. PRAYER

Father God, more than anything I want a religion you accept. I will endure trials. I will not complain about temptations. Help me to depend humbly on your wisdom and not on my own resources. Thank you for all your good and perfect gifts. Forgive me when I yield to temptation and sin. Put your bridle on my tongue so that it always praises and glorifies you. Teach me to hear and obey your word. This I pray in Jesus' name. Amen.

VI. DEEPER DISCOVERIES

A. Perseverance (vv. 3–4)

The KJV translates this majestic word as "patience." Today "patience" suggests reining in your temper. To many it involves holding back the anger at your car whenever it refuses to start on a cold winter morning. It is controlling your displeasure when a telephone conversation ties up your time and causes you to burn the main dish for the evening meal. Showing patience involves much more than merely holding back a foul temper.

The etymology of the word pictures a person under a heavy load and determined to stay there instead of trying to escape. It describes a frame of mind which endures trials and all the pressures which the trials produce (Rom. 5:3). It is the spiritual trait of remaining constant under trial and showing steadfastness, energy, and stamina. A person with perseverance holds up under pressure and looks to God to terminate the time or to offer a reward for endurance. The only route for developing patience involves trusting God through trials and nurturing our faith toward maturity.

B. Wisdom (v. 5)

Biblical wisdom involves much more than encyclopedic knowledge or subtle insights into life. Wisdom is a moral commitment which allows believers to endure life's trials with action which pleases God. Wise people are not merely experts on the stock market or victors in games of "Trivial Pursuit." They are people who have made a commitment to follow God and are living in the light of that commitment.

Proverbs discusses wisdom at length. It describes foolish behavior as talkative (Prov. 9:13; 13:16), destructive (Prov. 14:1), prideful (Prov. 14:3), and mocking (Prov. 14:9). By contrast, a wise person listens to instruction (Prov. 13:1), respects God's commandments (Prov. 9:10), and avoids immoral companions (Prov. 7:6–23).

Those who would have wisdom must ask God for it. Those who receive wisdom from God are able to see life with his understanding and can anticipate God's blessings as a life experience.

Some people must face situations of suffering, persecution, and hardship which seem beyond reason or rationale. James 1:5 promises wisdom to those who ask for it, but some ask and cannot hear a reason. What word would I have for them? Let me share my experience.

As I write these words, I have been dealing with cancer for three years. At present the disease cannot be healed medically, is not under control, but has not prevented my serving as a dean, preaching, and writing. I have good energy. Some people look at me and do not see any evidence of sickness.

I am in my late fifties. I come from a family in which many men have lived long lives. My father died in the summer of 1997 at the age of 95. I would normally expect many additional years of service and life. Why is my life threatened by cancer at this time? What understanding can God give me in his wisdom?

He hasn't chosen to let me know why I have the sickness. What he has done is to convince me more deeply of three truths to which I have become more dedicated. First, I am convinced that he is in charge of my life even in my sickness. He knows what he is doing and is moving toward accomplishing good in my life (Rom. 8:28). I accept this largely by faith and move forward with this conviction.

Second, he has given me grace in my time of weakness (2 Cor. 12:7–10). This grace comes in the form of people who encourage me, a loving wife, an assurance that God has not forsaken me, and a renewed sense of God's presence and guidance in my life.

Third, he has convinced me that my concerns should be focused on obeying him in my sickness rather than merely seeking healing. My prayers more and more have become requests that I might glorify him in my condition. He has given me evidence that he is answering these prayers.

Do you face suffering or hardship for which you can find no rationale? Let convictions such as those above provide guidance even as you remain faithful to God and seek to learn his wisdom.

C. The Seriousness of Doubting God (vv. 6–8)

These verses warn people who profess to have eternal life but who vacillate, waver, and wobble in their approach to God. Such persons will get no help from God in the midst of trials. Such persons will never grow toward spiritual maturity.

James was not demanding perfect faith. If he were, none of us would ever receive anything, for there is some doubt in all of us. Jesus honored the request of the distraught father of a demonized boy, who said to him, "I do believe; help me overcome my unbelief" (Mark 9:24). That father was radically honest. Jesus wants someone who comes to him with honesty, recognizes that he alone can provide strength for life's trials, and is willing to walk with him through those trials.

The person who utters a quick-fix-it type of prayer and, having finished, wonders aloud, "Did that do any good?" should not expect anything from God. Those kinds of people are only using God as a last resort to snatch them out of their misery. They have not honestly cast themselves in desperation into God's mighty hands. God honors the faith of desperate people and responds to their requests in his will.

D. James's Nature Illustrations (vv. 6,10–11,14,17)

James was a master at using illustrations from nature to clarify his point. In verse 6 he caught a picture of a succession of waves being swept along by the wind. He compared the doubter to the turbulent sea heaving under the force of a blustery gale. A wind-blown wave has no stability in any dimension. The doubter lacks the inner stability to attain God's goals.

Verses 10–11 speak of flowers being scorched by the burning heat. The verbs "rise," "wither," "fall," and "destroyed" show the vivid progression of a flower from breathtaking beauty to decadent destruction. The **scorching heat** can refer either to the burning Palestinian sun or to the sirocco, the oven-like wind blowing in from the Arabian Desert.

Verse 14 uses the language of fishing to show how lust draws persons toward their objects of desire and finally snares them with the bait of desire. **Enticed** conveys the idea of luring a fish from its lair with bait.

Verse 17 uses the language of astronomy to demonstrate the constancy and changelessness of God. The "shifting shadows" to which James refers describes the shadows produced when heavenly bodies moved from one place to another. The sundial captures the evidence of these shifting shadows.

Although sundials change, God does not, and believers can find great hope from the dependability and steadfastness of God.

James was a close observer of objects and events in the world of nature. We can be certain that he also carefully prepared his message to stimulate his readers toward godly living.

E. The Word Planted in You (v. 21)

Word describes the gospel as a living seed rooted into the human heart at regeneration. Although the message of the gospel is powerful and exerts great influence in the human heart, it grows best when believers welcome its message and cultivate its presence.

Accept this message indicates that believers must give a hearty welcome to the gospel message by obeying it and renewing their commitment to the Lord. The gospel has power because it actively roots itself in the human heart at regeneration. Welcoming this message provides a chance for it to change and transform individuals into committed followers of Jesus.

F. The Perfect Law That Gives Freedom (v. 25)

James may be referring either to the law as the revelation of God's will in general or to the gospel in particular. Ultimately we find both a declaration of God's will and the explanation of the gospel in Scripture. The law is perfect because it provides a full, complete disclosure of God through Jesus Christ.

It provides freedom in that it gives liberty to those who submit to its authority. This liberty provides a victory over the bondage of habits and attitudes which can overpower human will. It also provides freedom in that the power of the Holy Spirit becomes available to strengthen believers to a new quality of spiritual life (Gal. 5:22–23).

G. Pure Religion (v. 27)

"Pure religion" is worship of God free from any moral corruption or spiritual impurity. Pure religion is alive, vibrant, and committed to God through Jesus Christ. This is much more than someone who usually attends church, periodically gives money, and lives in decent morality. Pure religion demands self-control, self-sacrifice, and self-denial. The person with pure religion shows self-control by managing the tongue so that it praises the Lord and avoids the action of insulting and attacking human beings (Jas. 3:9–12).

A person practicing pure religion shows self-sacrifice by using time and money to care for others who are needy. Among the most needy groups in the first century were orphans and widows.

A committed believer shows self-denial by separation from the world. The **world** provides a system of values influenced by evil and antagonistic to

God. Wise, committed believers will identify worldly influences and avoid them.

VII. TEACHING OUTLINE

A. INTRODUCTION
1. Lead Story: Getting Sick for the Glory of God
2. Context: James provides insight enabling Jesus' followers to triumph over life's troubles. These troubles involve outward trials and inward temptations (vv. 1–18). They also include the danger of a listless listening which regards Christianity as primarily a spectator sport without team participation (vv. 19–27).

   James began with a word of encouragement for meeting external and internal trials. Trials of persecution and general hardship may produce endurance in committed believers (vv. 1–12). God does not use inward temptations to entice us to evil (vv. 13–18). We alone are accountable for a disobedient response.

   James also warned against a careless hearing of God's message. We are to be **quick to listen** and **slow to speak** (vv. 19–21), doers and not merely hearers of God's message (vv. 22–25). We will give evidences of **faultless** religion through self control, compassionate ministry, and inner purity (vv. 26–27).

   Whoever reads James 1 will emerge with the conviction that real Christianity produces stamina and obedience in the followers of the Lord Jesus Christ.
3. Transition: How then should James 1 cause us to live? Three responses to its message should take place. First, we should respond to trial with a development of hope, confidence in God, and new stamina because God can use them to make us **mature and complete**. Second, we should accept responsibility for our own failures and look to our unchanging God for strength. Third, we should drink in God's message and allow it to transform us into self-controlled, loving, holy followers of Jesus.

B. COMMENTARY
1. How to Be Tried and True (vv. 1–18)
   a. A word of greeting (v. 1)
   b. Outer trials (vv. 2–12)
      (1) Response to trials (vv. 2–4)
      (2) Resources for facing trials (vv. 5–8)
      (3) Making a correct estimate of trials (vv. 9–11)

(4) The result of trials (v. 12)
   c. Inner temptations (vv. 13–18)
     (1) Exonerating God from evil (vv. 13–16)
     (2) Involving God in the good (vv. 17–18)
2. The Danger of Listless Listening (vv. 19–27)
   a. A warning against ignoring God's Word (vv. 19–21)
   b. A contrast of responses to God's command (vv. 22–25)
   c. The evidence of listening to God's Word (vv. 26–27)

C. CONCLUSION: WE MUST OBEY OUR LORD

VIII. ISSUES FOR DISCUSSION

1. What trials trouble you most? Have you asked for Godly wisdom to endure them? What positive good can come to you out of these trials?
2. In what ways do you express doubt before God? What causes you to doubt? What can you do to put away these doubts and exercise faith?
3. Where does wealth fit into your priorities? Where would James have you place it? Are you ready and willing to set aside wealth as a major priority in life? What can you expect when you do?
4. What brings temptation into your life? How are you supposed to respond to temptation? What part does God play in your temptations?
5. Describe your own religious life. How does this description compare to James's definition of pure religion?

James 2

Displaying Pure Religion

Quote

"*H*e that prizeth the person of Christ prizeth all his relatives."

Puritan scholar
Thomas Manton

James

 I N   A   N U T S H E L L

*C*hapter 1 concluded with an appeal for us to practice pure religion. Chapter 2 presents two requirements of pure religion.

First, show no partiality. Cater to the poor and spiritually hungry rather than to the powerful. Live by **the royal law** and experience the **law that gives freedom.**

Second, produce obedient deeds, for true faith is obedient. Look to Abraham and Rahab for examples.

Displaying Pure Religion

I. INTRODUCTION

Caring for Life's Outcasts

Jim is blind. Helen has a mentally retarded daughter. Barbara is deaf. Bennett is an alcoholic. Judy, a mother with three children, survives on government checks and food stamps. Vanessa is divorced. Tom is retired, a widower, and lonely. Not all of these names represent specific people, but each need appears in growing numbers throughout our country and our world. Each of these persons has special needs. What can churches do for these people?

At one church the first member I met was Bill, a hearing-impaired person. I introduced myself to him. He smiled and gave his name. Chattering amiably as he led me along a church hallway, he took me to the church office and introduced me to a staff member. Later as I stood to teach the Bible to a group of members, I noticed that a husband and wife were signing for Bill. The wife had the greater skills, but the husband had begun to master the language of signing to communicate with Bill. During a break as I talked with the husband and Bill, I noticed that the husband signed everything for Bill as he talked with me. He included Bill in our dialogue. Little wonder that Bill felt at home in this church. He was surrounded by the love of a husband and wife who had learned how to communicate with him and to link him with others.

Another church holds a bimonthly meeting for blind people on Sunday afternoons. The church has three aims. First, they invite the blind to worship with them if they do not have their own church. Second, they offer to help them with tasks which need to be done. Third, they offer to make contact with community and government agencies that can help them in ways the church cannot.

Among these blind people they found one woman who wanted to play the piano. A man needed transportation to the dentist to get new dentures. A woman needed an escort to go shopping. A man needed a companion to go with him to the laundry. Several needed clothes, and others wanted talking books. Several needed jobs, and all needed friends.

This church assigned volunteers to each person to meet the specific need. The committee volunteers stay in touch with the blind person and seek to monitor the needs they learn. This same church has an exceptional ministry to retarded children, divorced people, alcoholics, and the poor.

Christians cannot compete with the financial resources of welfare agencies or government programs. We make our unique contribution by seeking to glorify Jesus Christ. We must make our ministries open to people of all races and backgrounds. We must continue these ministries even if they do not provide statistical church growth. We must find people we can help in the name of Jesus and seek to minister to their needs.

II. COMMENTARY

Displaying Pure Religion

MAIN IDEA: *God wants his people to demonstrate pure religion by overcoming the practice of partiality and by producing deeds of compassion.*

A Transcending Partiality (vv. 1–13)

SUPPORTING IDEA: *Christians are to show compassion for the poor and spiritually hungry rather than cater to the powerful.*

1. Rebuking Partiality (vv. 1–4)

2:1. This verse commends Jesus as **our glorious Lord Jesus Christ** and warns that partiality against the poor is inconsistent with faith in Jesus Christ. **My brothers** shows that James wrote to his readers as believers and urged them to show the reality of their profession. Who is this Jesus?

First, Jesus is the object of our faith. We have made a trust or commitment to him. We are **believers** in Jesus.

Second, Jesus is the Lord of Glory. The Greek literally reads, "our Lord Jesus Christ, who is the Glory." James gave the title of "Glory" to Jesus, using a term that represents the full presentation of God's presence and majesty. Jesus is the glorious God. This is a remarkable confession to come from Jesus' half brother.

The practice of favoritism involved giving benefits to people who had outward advantages such as money, power, or social prominence. The readers of James were courting the favor of these important people by showing preference for them over the poor. The Mosaic Law had forbidden giving respect to persons of prominence (Deut. 1:17). To these scheming readers James gave a sharp directive, "Stop it!"

2:2–4. These verses illustrate the discrimination. In a Christian assembly a rich man and a poor man appeared. Perhaps both were non-Christians. The meeting could have taken place in the home of a Christian. The rich man wore **a gold ring and fine clothes.** The poor man appeared **in shabby clothes.** The word describing the ring of the rich man indicated that he was "gold-fingered." He may have worn gold rings on several fingers. Wealthy people often wore more than a single ring. Shops rented rings to those wanting to give the appearance of wealth. **Fine**, used to describe the rich man's clothing, means "sparkling" or "glittering." Acts 10:30 uses the same word to describe the "shining" garments an angel was wearing. We would say he was a "smart" dresser.

Shabby, used to describe the poor man's clothing, pictured clothing which was dirty or filthy. The man may have come from work, his clothing stained with the evidence of his labor.

The handsome apparel of the rich man earned special treatment for him (v. 3). The greeter gave him a place of special honor. The soiled clothing of the poor man earned indifference to his comfort or feelings. He received the options of standing in some undesirable place or sitting on the floor near the greeter. The greeter showed no concern for his needs.

Verse 4 uses a question to accuse the readers of a pair of evil actions. An affirmative answer is expected. They had indeed **discriminated** and become evil judges.

First, they discriminated **among themselves**. They were guilty of creating divisions in their midst despite the fact that they had accepted the abolition of class distinctions (see Gal. 3:28). Second, they acted like evil-minded or prejudiced judges, regulating their conduct by blatantly false principles.

They practiced a favoritism toward the rich inconsistent with faith in the Lord Jesus Christ, who died for all people. If they continued to practice it, they could not claim to be followers of the Lord who abolished partiality. Deuteronomy 10:17 shows that God practices no partiality. Surely he could not tolerate such action among his own children. A wide difference separated the faith they professed from their partisan practices. We can apply this warning in our relationships with different races, social classes, or economic groups.

In 1982, the Rev. Nico J. Smith, professor of theology at the elite Stellenbosch University in South Africa, left his post to become pastor of a one-thousand-member church in Mamelodi, a black township outside Pretoria. He took a substantial salary cut, moved into a modest home in a whites-only section near his church, and began to relate to his congregation. Concerning the abrupt transition and change of lifestyle, Smith said, "I feel I am starting my life over again. I have a wonderful opportunity to get to know the black people, their hopes and their fears."

Nearly six years later Smith presided over a visit by 173 whites, who came to his church in Mamelodi to live for four days among the blacks. They slept in cramped homes, washed at backyard faucets, and tried to build bridges between the races. Concerning the visit, Smith said, "The whites of this country have got to see what pain there is under the black skin."

Smith's efforts represent an attempt to show that the gospel of Jesus Christ relates to people of all groups and backgrounds. His boldness and courage can help to overcome the evil results of the practice of partiality and discrimination.

2. Learning the Evil Results of Partiality (vv. 5–7)

2:5–6a. Partiality is contrary to God's plan and threatening to the best interests of believers. James contrasted God's exaltation of the poor with their abuse by his readers. Their practice of discrimination against the poor was contrary to the way God had purposed to treat them. Verse 5 shows how God views the poor. Verse 6a presents the contrasting practices of his readers. It is clear: Christians need to adopt God's outlook for the poor.

God chose the poor. Paul used "chose" to describe the election of believers to salvation (Eph. 1:4). In James 2:5 "chose" describes spiritual blessings God has reserved for the poor. God chose the poor **to be rich in faith and to inherit the kingdom he promised those who love him.**

The world may look on poverty-stricken people as insignificant and worthless. God sees them as abounding in the riches of faith. Their faith allows them to experience God's wealth—salvation and its accompanying blessings. This does not suggest all the poor are converted, nor does it mean God practices a bias against those who are not poor. The **poor** God blesses are those whose poverty is primarily to be "poor in spirit" (Matt. 5:3). Often those who are economically poor are better placed than the wealthy to understand God's purposes. They are more likely than the rich to be prospects for conversion.

The **kingdom** is the full manifestation of Christ's future kingdom at the end of the age. The poor may appear insignificant in this world, but they have the glorious hope of inheriting the kingdom with Jesus (see Matt. 25:34). God loves the poor more than their treatment by Christians indicates.

Verse 6a outlines the church's treatment of the poor. They had **insulted the poor** by asking them to stand in some uncomfortable location or to sit on the floor as the Christians gathered for worship. Such shabby treatment could convince the poor that Christianity was not for them.

2:6b–7. The actions of the Christians did not help their own interests. They were pursuing a path of folly. Their treatment of the rich and the poor resembled honoring an executioner while insulting a valued friend. The rich faced three charges.

First, they were **exploiting** the poor by social and economic mistreatment. James 5:4 accuses the wealthy of failing to pay past-due wages. It was a strange twist of circumstances to honor such abusive masters.

Second, the rich hauled believers into court and practiced judicial persecution. Notice the actions of the wealthy slaveowners who dragged Paul and Silas into court in Acts 16:19–21.

Third, they belittled the Lord Jesus by insulting his person and rejecting his claims. The Jews of Antioch showed this behavior in Acts 13:45. These whom the church welcomed were not Christians but wealthy, Christ-rejecting Jews. The readers of James belonged to Jesus, and their biased actions dishonored his honorable name.

Can we suggest a better way to respond to the poor? Several years ago unemployment in Pittsburgh, Pennsylvania, suburbs reached the heights of skyscrapers. St. Stephen's Episcopal Church in the suburb of Sewickley began a service called Help Offer People Employment (HOPE). It was a temporary job service for those experiencing layoffs. In its first year the service received 1,200 calls for food, housing, child care, and money. They found work for 130 people, and nine found permanent jobs.

Later the church developed Job Seekers, a course for the unemployed dealing with regaining dignity and self-esteem. Participants learned to use resumes wisely and to present their skills in an appealing way. Some fifteen to twenty clients accepted Christ. The pastor of the church said, "Social action is part of evangelism. What's great is when Christians tackle those issues with the love of Jesus, but with secular ingenuity."

3. Living by God's Law (vv. 8–13)

2:8. James designated the command to **love your neighbor as yourself** (Lev. 19:18) as the **royal law.** He may have used the term **royal** because Christ, the true king, set forth the law (Matt. 22:39).

In the parable of the Good Samaritan (Luke 10:25–37) Jesus defined a **neighbor** and discussed the demands of loving a neighbor. Jesus defined a neighbor as anyone in need. He urged us to show our love to neighbors by responding to their needs.

Some of James's readers felt they had been obedient to God in the matter of showing love for the poor and needy. Wherever that was true, James gave credit. If they were really putting God's law into practice, this was noble and commendable. The command to love our neighbor as we love ourselves is an impossible standard without the power of the living Christ (John 13:34–35). Whenever Christians have applied this standard, it has remade communities, societies, and homes. Whoever follows this life of service will receive the Lord's commendation at the final judgment (Matt. 25:21).

2:9–11. This section deplores the violation of the royal law. If the readers truly practiced favoritism, they committed sin and stood convicted as lawbreakers. Leviticus 19:15 had warned against the practice of favoritism, against either the poor or the rich. It appealed for fair treatment of our neighbors.

Lawbreakers describes persons who have stepped over a line or a limit. Lawbreakers had mockingly stepped over God's boundaries and performed a forbidden practice.

Verse 10 shows why those who practice partiality are lawbreakers. Some Jews saw God's law as containing many detached requirements forbidding such actions as murder, adultery, and robbery. They failed to see its unity. They may have felt that strict obedience at one point would compensate for disobedience elsewhere.

God's Law is not like a setup of ten bowling pins which we knock down one at a time. It more resembles a pane of glass in which a break at one point means that the entire pane is broken.

The primary application of verse 10 was to one who showed partiality for the rich over the poor. Violating this single commandment made a person a lawbreaker. We should apply the statement of verse 10 in other areas where we are tempted to praise ourselves for obedience at one point while neglecting to consider the points where we grievously disobey God's teachings.

The Bible does not say all sins are equal. Stealing a candy bar is not the same as committing adultery. Thinking about murder is not as bad as committing the act. Every sin does bring guilt. It takes only a single sin to make a person a sinner. No act of obedience can compensate for acts of disobedience.

It applies to a hit man for mobsters who prides himself on his marital fidelity while he ruthlessly murders mob enemies. It applies to a citizen caught running a red light who excuses his disobedience by claiming that he had previously stopped for ten thousand red lights. It applies to professing Christians who feel that giving $500,000 for equipping a new church facility will secure their salvation after years of indifference. Disobedience of one section of God's Law makes a person a sinner. No amount of imagined or actual obedience can compensate for that fact!

Verse 11 shows the unity of the Law lies in its origin in God. The commandments prohibiting both adultery and murder originated with God. To resist one requirement of the Law is to resist God, the authority beneath its requirements.

2:12–13. These verses conclude the discussion of partiality by appealing for obedience to the royal law in both speech and action. Those who judge others often forget that they must face God's judgment. The reality of God's coming judgment is an incentive for Christians to speak and act obediently.

The standard of judgment in that day will be **the law that gives freedom.** This is a reference to the gospel (see also James 1:25 and the discussion of the term under "Deeper Discoveries" in chapter 1). In John 8:32–36 Jesus had described the gospel as a truth which sets people free. James echoed these words in verse 12. Those who obey God by faith in Jesus Christ find freedom to serve God and escape from fear of future judgment. Faith in Jesus Christ provides freedom to escape hatred and self-love and to love our neighbors as ourselves.

James alluded to the words of Jesus in Matthew 5:7 to warn that those who show no mercy will receive none in the final judgment. Stated positively, this means **mercy triumphs over judgment.** This does not mean we receive mercy from God only when we show mercy to others. If that were true, it would make salvation a matter of God's payment for our good deeds. For those who have given themselves in faith to Christ, God's mercy triumphs over our guilt and judgment. If we have received God's grace, we will stand in the coming judgment. Mercy can rejoice in its victory over condemnation.

Christianity grew and developed in confrontation with an environment that breathed hostility to its doctrines and practices. A chief reason for its triumph was the superior moral practice of Christians. The lives of early Christians showed that accusations against them were lies (see 1 Pet. 2:15). They fed the needy, accepted outcasts, buried the poor, cared for orphans and the aged, encouraged prisoners and victims of disasters, and showered compassion on the persecuted. Their lives proved that Christianity produced a superior character. This is still the best proof of the reality of our faith. May God enable us today to make a bold demonstration of our mercy to others!

B Producing Obedient Deeds (vv. 14–26)

SUPPORTING IDEA: *Saving faith produces deeds of service to prove its reality.*

1. The Danger of Faith without Deeds (vv. 14–20)

Intellectual faith without deeds is an empty claim. Intellectual faith consists of giving assent or mental agreement to a series of propositions or doctrinal truths about Christianity. An individual can claim to have right beliefs about God, Jesus, and salvation but still lack real Christianity. Works, not intellectual statements, are the only acceptable demonstrations of your claim to have faith.

Verses 14–17 show that faith without deeds becomes an empty claim. Verses 18–20 denounce a faith which has become the mere acceptance of a creed.

2:14. Two rhetorical questions here expect negative answers. Three features of the questions are important. First, they accept the reader's claim to faith, but do not assume that the claim without works represents saving faith. The absence of deeds of obedience in this person's life makes the claim highly suspicious, if not outright wrong!

Second, the topic is not faith in general but a specific kind of faith, one which **has no deeds. Such** in the NIV text implies this focus. The question is not, "Can faith save the lost?" Of course, faith saves the lost. The question is,

"Can a faith without deeds save the lost?" The answer to that question is "no."

A verbal testimony alone is not an adequate evidence that true saving faith is present. Only works of obedience can prove the presence of genuine faith. Verse 15 provides an example of such **deeds.**

Third, **save** refers to acquittal at the final judgment. The question is, "What type of faith can guarantee a favorable verdict in the final judgment?" Only a faith that produces works can provide security in the final judgment.

Prospective drivers of automobiles and trucks must pass a written test on road rules and a skill test on the road. Lawyers must pass the bar examination, and accountants must pass the CPA exam. Students in all institutions must show their knowledge on examinations. It is only reasonable to realize that our profession of Christianity demands a test. That test is the production of works. Without works to demonstrate faith our claim becomes false, and we show our deception.

2:15–16. These verses offer a parable in miniature, illustrating the person who has the type of faith that cannot save. Verse 15 pictures people who needed clothes and food. Cold and hungry, these believers desperately needed the necessities of life!

Verse 16 shows how the person who claims to have faith approaches these needy people: with an offer of good wishes but no practical help. **Go, I wish you well** offers a good-bye to the needy person. Apparently, the speaker could have helped, but he chose to do nothing except offer kind expressions. Both John the Baptist (Luke 3:7–14) and Jesus (Matt. 7:15–27) condemned professions of piety without action.

Sympathy is valuable when this is all a person can give to the suffering. This speaker, however, had the ability to feed the hungry and clothe the needy. First John 3:18 gives us the proper response, "let us not love with words or tongue but with actions and in truth." James concluded his illustration by wondering aloud, "What good is a faith which can only give pious wishes but no practical help?"

2:17. Verse 17 concludes the matter. Good wishes consisting of mere talk are empty of all reality and lifeless. Offering only good wishes to the cold and the hungry serves to depress further those who are starving and chilled. They need more than good wishes. They need practical help.

A faith **not accompanied by action,** that is faith alone, having no works to distinguish it, is dead. Anything with life produces fruit. The living are the acting, creating things that reveal their nature and character. Faith in Jesus produces actions revealing the nature and character of Jesus. The dead lie still doing nothing. So faith that lies still, inactive, proves it is dead. True faith brings salvation and life, not death.

Christians should show works of love to prove their faith is real. When Paul warned that a person could not be saved by "works," he referred to the works of obedience to the Jewish law (Rom. 3:20). When James called for **deeds**, he was not suggesting that these deeds resulted in salvation. He was calling for Christians to do what living faith naturally does: show care and concern for those in need. Acts 6:1–4; 9:36–43; 20:34–35; Romans 15:25–27; 1 Timothy 5:1–16; and many other Scriptures show Christians and churches in action meeting needs. This type of loving, caring interest in others made early Christians distinctive. Likewise, today people who show loving, caring interest in others stand out as visible representatives of Jesus Christ.

2:18. James 2:14–17 warns that faith without works represents an empty claim. Beginning in verse 18, we are warned against a faith which merely accepts a creed. Here are the limitations of mere intellectual faith. Saving faith involves a commitment to Jesus Christ which produces works or deeds.

Verse 18 represents a dialog with an imaginary opponent. The opponent says: **You have faith; I have deeds.** James responded: **Show me your faith without deeds, and I will show you my faith by what I do.** In other words, the opponent claims, "James, you ought to let some people emphasize faith while others emphasize works." James insisted, "Real faith shows itself in deeds." You simply cannot find an example of real faith that does not show itself in works. We have no room for some people to emphasize faith while others stress deeds. You must have both. Genuine commitment to Jesus Christ demonstrates its presence by deeds. Faith produces works. You can't have one without the other.

2:19. Verse 19 speaks to the person claiming to have faith but lacking works. This kind of person merely gives intellectual assent to the creed of monotheism. This basic creed of Judaism appeared in Deuteronomy 6:4–5. The statement is intellectually true, but it doesn't proceed far enough. A person must believe in God to be a Christian, but not everyone who acknowledges the existence of God has made a commitment to Jesus Christ.

Even demons believe in the existence of one God. They shudder with fear at the thought of God (see Matt. 8:29). The behavior of demons demonstrated that someone can believe the right thing and still have an evil character. Verse 19 concerns intellectual faith, a faith that touches only the mind. Saving faith involves the will as well as the intellect (see Rom. 4:16–22).

2:20. Verse 20 calls on the objector to recognize that the conclusions of verses 18–19 are correct while also introducing verses 21–26. James appeals to us to become learners. We can rephrase the question as: "Are you willing to be taught that a barren faith is worthless?"

Foolish also appears in Mark 12:3, translated "empty-handed." The objector was spiritually foolish or willfully ignorant. The last word of the verse is different in important Greek manuscripts. King James follows the reading of many manuscripts in translating: "dead." Most modern versions follow Greek manuscripts with a word which means **useless** or "barren." The same Greek word in 2 Peter 1:8 is translated "ineffective."

Have you ever dealt with professing Christians who felt they could keep their faith to themselves and did not need to demonstrate their faith? We must lead these people to see that true faith shows itself in visible deeds, not merely by agreeing with a creed.

2. Examples of Faith That Works (vv. 21–26)

James selected Abraham and Rahab as examples of people who showed genuine faith by their deeds. Their examples stand in complete contrast. Abraham was the ancestor of both Jews and Gentiles. He provided a sterling example of faith (Heb. 11:8–12). Rahab was a Gentile and a prostitute (Josh. 2:1–24), but Matthew listed her in the genealogy of Christ (Matt. 1:5). Although they came from different backgrounds, both showed the reality of their faith.

2:21–23. Verse 21 picks up the Old Testament incident in which Abraham showed his willingness to offer Isaac as a sacrifice (Gen. 22:1–18). Verse 23 refers to the incident in which "Abraham believed the Lord, and he credited it to him as righteousness" (Gen. 15:6), which took place at least thirty years before that of Genesis 22.

Verse 21 concludes that Abraham showed his righteousness by his willingness to offer Isaac on the altar. KJV translates "justified" instead of NIV's **considered righteous.** Paul uses the same Greek word in Romans 3:28; 4:2,5; and 5:1 ("justified") to describe the righteousness God credits to a believer through faith in Jesus Christ. James uses the word to describe the righteousness we show to others as we obey Jesus. The saving faith of Abraham showed itself by his total obedience to God in the matter of offering up Isaac. The faith James commended moves the heart and controls the life. Again, James was demanding that true faith must be alive and vital.

Verse 22 states two facts about Abraham's faith. First, **his faith and his actions were working together.** Abraham's faith prompted his obedience. It prodded him on to do good works. Second, **his faith was made complete by what he did.** His obedience demonstrated the integrity of his faith. This is not to say that previously Abraham had a weak faith. His willingness to sacrifice Isaac vividly demonstrated the existence of true faith.

Verse 23 summarizes the entire process. Abraham's willingness to offer Isaac fulfilled the promise of Genesis 15:6. Abraham's obedience showed he was a righteous man. God declared Abraham righteous as a matter of grace. Abraham showed the reality of this righteousness by his actions in Genesis 22. As a result of this obedience, God drew Abraham into a closer fellowship with him and called him **God's friend.** Note that Abraham did not merely determine that God would be his friend. God initiated the action. God reached out to him and gave him the privilege of intimacy and closeness.

2:24. Verse 24 presents the conclusions about Abraham. Abraham had shown the reality of his faith by his willingness to offer Isaac in obedience to God's command. We are made right in God's sight through a faith which produces works. This does not claim that God justifies his people by our deeds. The Bible insists that saving faith must show itself by visible commitment to the Lord and compassion for others. Faith alone will bring salvation to anyone, but saving faith does not come alone. It is accompanied by works which show the genuineness of faith.

2:25. This section turns to the example of good works from the life of Rahab. Abraham was a man of prominent position and exemplary character. Rahab came from a background of degradation and insignificance. James insisted that these contrasting personalities showed deeds which demonstrated their righteousness.

Rahab (see Josh. 2) received into her home Israelites whom Joshua sent to spy out the city of Jericho. She hid them in her home and protected them from their pursuers. She deliberately misled the pursuers by sending them off in a different direction while she continued to hide the spies. Later, she guided the spies in making their escape. If residents—especially the rulers—of Jericho had known of her acts of disloyalty, they would likely have put her to death. Joshua 2:8–13 makes it clear that Rahab's faith in Israel's God caused her to protect his representatives.

2:26. In Genesis 2:7, God formed the first human being by breathing life into his body. The union of spirit and body produced a living human being. In death the spirit returns to God, and the body decays into dust. A body without the spirit is a corpse.

In the same way faith without works is also dead. A person claiming to have faith but lacking works is spiritually as lifeless as a corpse. An inactive faith, entombed in a creed affirmed by the intellect, has no more usefulness than a body with no heartbeat or breath. James did not intend to belittle correct doctrinal views, but he demanded practical holiness as an evidence of real faith.

MAIN IDEA REVIEW: *God wants his people to demonstrate pure religion by overcoming the practice of partiality and by carrying out deeds of compassion.*

III. CONCLUSION

The Evidence of Faith

James wrote to people whose barren lives distorted the doctrine of salvation by faith. James contrasted two types of faith. One was genuine and showed itself by works of compassion and obedience. Another was false, emphasizing correct belief but denying that belief by a life empty of good works. James insisted that saving faith must show itself in deeds. He denounced a partiality which favors the rich while abusing the poor. He condemned a profession of faith which emphasizes right belief but fails to care for the needy and obey the commands of God.

James also appealed for a faith which demonstrates its righteousness before others. Faith which never produces additional evidence is simply not credible. Faith can show its reality before others only by unselfish deeds of commitment and helpfulness.

We live in an age when many people limit faith to the mere verbal affirmation of "I believe." James's timely warnings remind us that people who have correct belief and an empty life are quite deceived. They must have a faith which produces visible evidence of commitment to Jesus Christ.

PRINCIPLES

- God demands obedience to his entire teachings, not just acceptance of a part of them.
- Those who hope to receive mercy from God must in turn show mercy to others.
- Saving faith produces works of compassion and obedience.
- Works of unselfishness and sacrifice for others prove the reality of our faith before a watching world.

APPLICATIONS

- Do not displease God by favoring the rich or abusing the poor.
- Treat people from all backgrounds as God does.
- Check your faith by your works.
- Draw closer to God through obedience.

IV. LIFE APPLICATION

Stories of Living Faith

Alex Hollub is a medical doctor who volunteers his time every Tuesday afternoon to staff the Christian Community Clinic in Arlington, Texas. On a typical Tuesday he may see more than fifteen patients in three hours.

A woman waiting to be seen at the clinic commended the staff by saying, "They are not here for themselves. They are not selfish." Hollub feels that God led him to volunteer his time at the clinic. He says, "We send missionaries all over the world, and right in our own backyard there are people in need."

In Indianapolis, Indiana, the Indianapolis Training Center has turned a former Stouffer Hotel into a juvenile detention center. In 1992 Indianapolis mayor Steve Goldsmith asked the organization, a part of Bill Gothard's Institute in Basic Life Principles, to help in reclaiming rebellious teens. Now a juvenile court judge offers young offenders a choice. They may serve their sentence at a government-run detention center, or at the ITC. In 1994 approximately 130 teens chose the ITC. Mr. Goldsmith, who is Jewish, commended the program by saying, "The [juvenile offenders] in the Gothard program have seen and adopted values that they never would have gotten in the court system." One juvenile sent to the center for robbery completed his stay, and on returning home he called every person he had robbed and asked for forgiveness.

During four years of bloody war in the former Yugoslavia province of Croatia, Southern Baptists have sent almost three million dollars worth of food, cooking supplies, and other help to victims on all sides. Croatian Baptists have set up aid organizations to channel food and help from Southern Baptists and other Christian organizations. In Karlovac, Croatia, pastor Ladislav Ruzicka distributed food parcels to people who trekked through snow to get food, cooking oil, and other basic supplies. Ruzicka has directed a major food distribution effort during the Yugoslavian war. A Karlovac newspaper survey named him as one of the city's best-known and most-admired persons, the first time a Protestant pastor had received this recognition. His food distribution work, along with active evangelistic programs, has helped his churches grow.

Denise was married to a prominent pastor, but after seventeen years of marriage he asked her for a divorce. She took her two children to Atlanta, Georgia, to be near friends and family. She found a job at Georgia Power Company, but affordable lodging was a problem. A friend brought her into contact with Beginning Anew, a family ministry which prevents families from becoming homeless. Established by Trinity Baptist Church and Ebenezer United Methodist Church in Conyers, Georgia, the ministry pays rent and most of the bills on an apartment or a duplex. Over a six- to twelve-month period, the client gradually assumes financial responsibility.

After some months in the program, Denise gradually began paying larger portions of the rent. Eventually she assumed the entire cost herself. She said, "Beginning Anew was the Lord's provision. It amazes me because it has enabled us to live like we always had."

A church, a pastor, a doctor, an organization—each of these has demonstrated that faith will produce works. Their actions leave us with the challenge of impacting our own world as they have influenced theirs.

V. PRAYER

Lord, I believe in you. You are my Savior and Lord. Show me how to demonstrate my faith. Open my blind eyes to opportunities to love others in your name. Excise favoritism and prejudice from my heart. Fill me with your Spirit of love and care. Amen.

VI. DEEPER DISCOVERIES

A. Lord of Glory (v. 1)

Modern versions differ in their translation of this phrase (*kuriou hemon Iesou Christou tes doxes*) at the beginning of James 2. The NIV refers to Jesus as **our glorious Lord Jesus Christ**. The NKJV designates Jesus as "our Lord Jesus Christ, *the Lord* of glory." The italics indicate that the phrase "the Lord" is absent from the best Greek texts.

Perhaps Curtis Vaughan makes the best suggestion for interpreting the phrase. He says that we should take **glory** as a name for Christ and should render the phrase as "our Lord Jesus Christ, who is the Glory" (*James: A Study Guide*).

Although the Old Testament did not use the term, Jewish rabbis used "Shekinah" to describe the glorious revelation of God to his people. In their writings the term became a reverent way of referring to God. James declared that Jesus was the Shekinah, the glorious presence of God. This bold declaration confesses that in his incarnate life Jesus reflected the nature of God himself. James, the half brother of Jesus, had originally refused to believe in Jesus (John 7:5), but an encounter with the risen Lord banished his doubts (1 Cor. 15:7). To use this phrase of someone with whom he grew up would indicate that God had given James a deep devotion to Christ as his Master.

B. Your Meeting (v. 2)

Meeting (*sunagogen*) in verse 2 is the Greek term usually translated as "synagogue." The usage of the term indicates that James wrote at a time before Jewish Christians consistently used the term *church* to refer to their places of meeting. The presence of the term **church** in James 5:14 showed that Jewish Christians at this time could use either the term **church** or the term **meeting** to describe their gatherings.

Your meeting shows the reference is to a Christian gathering and not to a meeting of non-Christian Jews in a synagogue. Probably the Christians met in the home of a believer.

C. Poor in the Eyes of This World (v. 5)

The "poor" were those who lacked the material benefits for living in this world. They are the special recipients of God's concern. Abusing them is an insult to God.

In Jewish thinking the terms *poor* and *pious* often meant nearly the same thing. The blessing on those who were poor in Luke 6:20 reflected this usage. Luke was equating the poor with the pious. Not all the poor were pious, but many were.

God's choice of the poor **to be rich in faith** does not suggest that God had chosen all the poor to receive his blessings. Neither does it mean that he had limited his concern to the poor. Christian history does demonstrate that poor people more often respond to the gospel than their wealthier counterparts. God's choice of the poor has presented them with great opportunities to enjoy faith in this present life and to anticipate sharing in God's kingdom in the life to come.

D. Favoritism (v. 9)

Favoritism (*prosopolempteite*) literally means "to receive the face." James applied it to the demonstration of partiality for the rich while showing contempt for the poor. The Mosaic Law prohibited this practice (Lev. 19:15) and called for fair treatment irrespective of economic standing.

James denounced the practice as more than discourtesy. He called it "sin" and described those who did it as **lawbreakers.** James knew that the readers were not showing love but favoritism. His words challenge us to show the reality of our religion as we face problems dealing with social, industrial, political, and racial issues.

E. James's Dialogue on Faith and Works (vv. 18–20)

Interpreters differ in their understanding of three features in these verses. Differences include: (1) the identity of the speaker referred to as **someone will say**. (2) the length of the statement of the speaker, and (3) the identity of the **You** and **I** of verse 18.

A common answer to these questions is that the speaker in verse 18 is an objector to the views of James. The first half of verse 18 contains the objection, and his comments end there. The use of the terms **You** and **I** represents the speaker's effort to introduce two imaginary persons. One person emphasizes the importance of faith, and the other stresses works. In the last half of verse 18 and in verse 19 James replied to the objector. In verse 20 James presented a challenging demand to the objector.

Using these guidelines, we can provide the following brief interpretation of the section. In the first part of verse 18 James introduced the words of an imaginary objector who argued that God had a place for some people to emphasize faith while others emphasized works. In the final part of the verse James challenged the objector to show his faith without works. For James the only way to show faith was by works.

In verse 19 James admitted that intellectual acceptance of God's existence was good, but it did not go far enough. Even the devil believes in the existence of God. In verse 20 James challenged his imaginary objector to realize that a faith which has no deeds is barren and empty.

F. Intellectual Faith (v. 19)

James commended the belief in God's existence mentioned in verse 19, but then he warned that mere belief in God's existence did not bring salvation. Believing in the existence of God can involve only assent to a creed. People who have only intellectual faith may uphold orthodox doctrines and support evangelical principles. The problem is that they have only made a mental commitment to the belief. They have not involved their wills, and they do nothing to demonstrate the reality of their faith.

We see intellectual faith when we hear someone say, "I believe that eight times eight is sixty-four," or when they say, "I believe that World War II ended in 1945." Both facts are true, but accepting them involves only the mind, not the will. Whenever someone sincerely says, "I believe in Jesus Christ as Lord and Savior," that person is claiming a commitment to Jesus Christ. Commitment to Christ involves a willingness to obey him, not merely the acceptance of right doctrines about him (John 3:36).

G. Considered Righteous (v. 21)

Both the KJV and the NKJV translate this phrase by the single word *justified*. Paul uses this word in Romans 3:24 ("justified") to describe the act by which God acquitted or declared righteous those who had formerly been seen only as sinners. For Paul this justification came by faith in Jesus Christ (Rom. 3:26).

James was not teaching that right standing with God comes by works. He was teaching that Abraham's faith was a proof of the faith that he professed. The actions of Abraham led those who saw him to consider him as righteous.

Paul was explaining how a lost sinner could receive righteousness with God. That came through faith in Jesus Christ. James was teaching how a person could show others the reality of faith. That came only by producing works of obedience and concern for others. Both were using the same word, but with a different meaning and emphasis. Paul wanted to urge self-righteous people to quit trusting in themselves and to trust in Jesus. James wanted to urge indifferent people to show their faith in Jesus by producing works as evidence.

H. Faith and Works According to James and Paul (v. 24)

James claimed that individuals were justified by works and not by faith only (Jas. 2:24). Paul insisted that people received justification by faith without the Law (Rom. 3:28). Apparently conflicting statements like these caused the Reformation leader Martin Luther to describe James's writing as a letter of straw. Luther felt that James did not correctly teach gospel content according to the rest of the New Testament.

Do Paul and James conflict? Absolutely not! James wrote to people whose barren lives distorted the doctrine of salvation by faith. He insisted that saving faith must show itself in deeds. Paul wrote to people who denied the doctrine of salvation by grace through faith. He refuted their insistence that a person must keep the requirements of Moses' law in order to be saved.

James was contrasting two types of faith, one which was genuine and another which was false. Paul was contrasting two plans of salvation, one which God approved, and another which human beings devised. James described the kind of faith which proved or demonstrated righteousness before human beings. Paul described the kind of faith which received God's approval. They were not opposing one another, but they fought against different enemies of the gospel.

VII. TEACHING OUTLINE

A. INTRODUCTION

1. Lead Story: Caring for Life's Outcasts
2. Context: James ended chapter 1 with an appeal for his readers to practice a pure religion. In chapter 2 he presented two examples of the practice of this pure religion.

   First, he showed that real religion did not cater to the rich and powerful but showed a concern for the poor and needy (2:1–13). He warned that real faith in Jesus excluded the practice of favoritism (2:1–4). He showed that favoritism was contrary to God's plan and a threat to the best interests of Christians (2:5–7). He appealed to his readers to love their neighbors and to lavish mercy on all (2:8–13).

   Second, James called for his readers to produce good works as a demonstration of their faith (2:14–26). He warned that faith without deeds becomes a meaningless claim and only involves giving mental assent to right doctrine (2:14–20). True faith involves a commitment of the will to Jesus, not merely assenting to correct doctrines.

James also presented Abraham and Rahab as people whose lives showed their faith by their works (2:21–26). Abraham showed obedience to God's command in his willingness to offer Isaac in sacrifice. Rahab showed her faith in God by her willingness to hide the Israelite spies at great risk to herself.

True religion will give mercy to all people. It will also give visible evidence of its presence by producing works which others can see.

3. Transition: We easily fall into the practice of mouthing pious words to others about our Christian faith and commitment. James reminds us that we must demonstrate our faith with deeds. Instead of showing favoritism, we must show genuine mercy to both rich and poor without favoring the wealthy over the poor. Instead of giving empty good wishes to the cold and hungry, we must show our faith by giving them something to eat and clothes to wear. James's words call us from contented slumber to unselfish obedience. They prevent our lapsing back into ease and comfort.

B. COMMENTARY

1. Transcending Partiality (vv. 1–13)
    a. A rebuke to partiality (vv. 1–4)
    b. The evil results of partiality (vv. 5–7)
        (1) Contrary to God's plan (vv. 5–6a)
        (2) Contrary to the Christian's best interests (vv. 6b–7)
    c. Living by God's Law (vv. 8–13)
        (1) Obeying the Royal Law (v. 8)
        (2) Violating the Royal Law (vv. 9–11)
        (3) Fulfilling the Law of Liberty (vv. 12–13)
2. Producing Obedient Deeds (vv. 14–26)
    a. The danger of faith without deeds (vv. 14–20)
        (1) The empty claim of faith without deeds (vv. 14–17)
        (2) The hypocrisy of a creed without conduct (vv. 18–20)
    b. Examples of faith which works (vv. 21–26)
        (1) Abraham (vv. 21–24)
        (2) Rahab (vv. 25–26)

C. CONCLUSION: STORIES OF LIVING FAITH

VIII. ISSUES FOR DISCUSSION

1. In what ways does your church show favoritism? What can you do to change this practice?
2. What does your church do to help the poor? In what other ways is your church demonstrating your faith?
3. How are you involved individually in demonstrating faith to people outside the church?
4. How do you explain the different statements about faith that James and Paul make?

James 3

A Warning to the World's Talkers

"*A* slip of the foot you may soon recover,

but a slip of the tongue you may never get over."

Benjamin Franklin

James

IN A NUTSHELL

Don't rush to be a teacher. It is dangerous, for everyone stumbles when he talks a lot. The tongue is small but powerful. Like a bit used to control a horse or a rudder to steer a ship, we control the whole person when we control the tongue. Tongues are virtually impossible to manage. We can tame all types of animals, birds, and reptiles; but our tongues are incorrigible. Only God's gracious power can supply the strength for change.

*One reason for our difficulty is the double-mindedness of the tongue. With the same tongue we praise God and curse people made in God's image. Show wisdom in speech and life. Demonstrate **humility. Envy and selfish ambition** are the evidences of false wisdom. True wisdom produces peace and **a harvest of righteousness.***

A Warning to the World's Talkers

I.   INTRODUCTION

Bubbagate

*I*t seemed like a harmless statement. A city councilman in Ft. Worth, Texas, was making a public announcement that a world-famous pianist would perform at the opening of the $110 million Texas Motor Speedway. A group of auto-racing fans would have an opportunity to hear renowned pianist Van Cliburn at the NASCAR Winston Cup race April 6, 1997. So, the city councilman notified the *Ft. Worth Star-Telegram* about the proposed event by saying, "Van Cliburn is going to play for Bubba."

The general manager of the Texas Motor Speedway, Eddie Gossage, took umbrage at the councilman's words and fired off a letter to him, saying, "Please do not refer to race fans as 'bubbas' or 'rednecks.' Race fans are supposedly tourists valued by the city of Fort Worth. The use of the term 'bubba' or 'redneck' can be considered a racial epithet."

The city councilman apologized by saying, "I'm sorry I called all those race fans Bubbas. I certainly didn't mean to offend them. These are valued people. I represent the Bubbas and the rednecks. They're good folks. They're not elite at all."

People who expressed their opinions lined up for and against the verbal choices of the councilman. Fort Worth's mayor said, "I wish he'd used a different set of words." The lieutenant governor of Texas described Bubbas as decent, hard-working Americans. A representative of the Center for the Study of Southern Culture in Oxford, Mississippi, shared the opinion, "Bubba is a Southern diminutive of brother, sort of like mama, papa, and bubba and sista. Within the working-class white world, 'Bubba' is a term of affection." The owner of a convenience store in Crowley, Texas, named "Bubba's No. 3" explained his choice of name for the store by saying, "We wanted them to know we were nice people. Bubba's nice, friendly, drives a pickup."

The councilman meant no harm, but the manager of a facility that will draw huge numbers of tourists to Fort Worth was irritated by his choice of words. What was humorous to the councilman was an insult to some of his constituency. People who talk need a warning. Our improperly chosen words can offend, wound, anger, and repel. Our tongues are powerful, potentially vicious, and woefully inconsistent.

Christians have an added factor to consider in their use of the tongue. We must not only avoid harming and insulting others with our tongues, but we must seek positive ways to use the tongue as a blessing. Our tongues must be an instrument to sow **a harvest of righteousness** (Jas. 3:18). As Christians we can use the tongue to teach the truth of God's Word, encourage the depressed, offer forgiveness to the sinner, and provide cheer and optimism for those who feel hopeless.

Curtis Vaughan in *James: A Study Guide* has warned, "A ready tongue without an informed mind, a devout character, and a holy life will hinder rather than advance the cause of Christ. It is extremely easy for vanity, self-conceit, and spiritual pride to creep in." James's instructions and challenges can provide us guidance in letting God regenerate our tongues for his glory.

II. COMMENTARY

A Warning to the World's Talkers

MAIN IDEA: *God wants his people to control their tongues and to display true wisdom.*

A The Need to Control the Tongue (vv. 1–2)

SUPPORTING IDEA: *Those who misuse the tongue receive God's condemnation.*

3:1–2. Verse 1 warns us not to **presume to be teachers** because of the stricter accountability God demands in the office. We should be more concerned about our fitness for teaching than with the benefits we might receive from the office. Those who teach **will be judged more strictly**. A teacher receives added prominence from the position, but also falls under stricter scrutiny from God. Teachers provide instruction in the practical duties of life and help to ground their hearers in the teachings and commandments of Jesus.

God's Word does not discourage people from assuming the position of a teacher. It raises the dignity of the position by pointing out the dangers and responsibilities of the office for those who might otherwise neglect these requirements. It seeks to restrain the rush into the office by those who lack spiritual qualifications for it.

Verse 2 explains the need to control the tongue. The concern is enlarged beyond the work of a teacher and includes **all**. Human beings stumble in many ways. **We** shows that James put himself in the category of those who made these "slips" of the tongue, an evidence of James's humility.

We show our imperfection and sinfulness by committing sins of the tongue. By the same measure we show our maturity by controlling the tongue. Two truths should encourage us to control our tongues. First, those who use the tongue, such as teachers, receive a stricter judgment. Surely the prospects of an intensive examination by God should prompt a desire to use our tongues rightly. Second, controlling our tongues provides evidence that we can control our personality. A person who can bring the tongue under control is able **to keep his whole body in check.** The verb used to describe the act of controlling the body refers in other contexts to the act of bridling a horse. Perhaps this word influenced James's decision to use the example of a **bit** in influencing a horse in verse 3.

One method of complying with the biblical warning about the tongue would be enforced silence. The Bible does not call for silence but for a tongue empowered by the Holy Spirit and used for the glory of God. Silence would not bring complete control of our thoughts. James wanted us to use divine power in bringing our thoughts into captivity to Christ (2 Cor. 10:5).

B The Power of the Tongue (vv. 3–6)

SUPPORTING IDEA: *The tongue is a small organ, but it can control and influence major events in life.*

This section uses three illustrations to show the power of the tongue. The first two illustrations picture the ability of a small object to control or influence a much larger object (vv. 3–4). The final illustration (v. 5b) illustrates the ability of a small item to destroy a much larger object.

3:3–5a. The rider of a horse can use a **bit** to control and govern a wild, unmanageable horse. Though the bit is small, its use gives riders the potential for turning the animal wherever they want.

In gales and violent winds, pilots use the rudder to guide the ship to safety or point it in the direction of intended travel. Compared to the size of a ship, the rudder was very small, but its importance in controlling the ship demanded careful attention in its use.

Verse 5a summarizes the point of these illustrations. Like the bit for the horse and the rudder for the ship, the tongue is small in relation to the body and yet has powerful potential to achieve great results, both good and bad. It can stir up violence or promote peace. It can crush the spirit or soothe the discouraged. If the tongue could personally express itself, it could legitimately boast of its great exploits.

3:5b–6. Verse 5b shows that an uncontrolled tongue is a source of great destruction. Just as a little flame can destroy a huge forest, a small misuse of the tongue can cause pain and agony to many.

The tongue can produce ruin and may represent the presence of a vast system of iniquity within our body. Within this body the tongue can produce three results. First, it can **corrupt the whole person.** It is a source of pollution and defilement for the entire personality. Second, it **sets the whole course of his life on fire. Course** may also mean "wheel." **Life** may refer to "birth," "origin," or "existence." A misused tongue may affect the cycle of life from birth onward! Third, the tongue **is itself set on fire by hell.** This describes Satan's influence on the tongue.

James 3:1–6 describes the tongue as it is by nature. By nature the tongue could serve as a divisive instrument of evil. By grace the tongue can become an instrument of positive blessing (Col. 4:6). We must not conclude that our tongue is doomed to be an instrument of discord and strife. God can mold an abusive tongue into a force for good and righteousness.

🄲 The Rebellion of the Tongue (vv. 7–8)

SUPPORTING IDEA: *We can tame all types of animals, but no one can tame the rebellious nature of the tongue.*

3:7–8. Verse 7 mentions four classifications of earthly animals men have subdued or tamed: animals which could walk, fly, crawl, or swim. Genesis 9:2 follows the same type of classification. These classifications represent a human observation about different types of animals rather than a scientific ordering.

Certainly no one has ever tamed a rhinoceros or an alligator, but in general wild animals can be brought under human control. Elephants, charmed snakes, and porpoises are examples of this principle. Although human beings can tame animals, they cannot tame their own tongues. The tongue is **a restless evil,** always busy creating more mischief. We must always keep the tongue under careful guard and never give it freedom to roam relentlessly, for it is **full of deadly poison.** Like the tongue of a serpent, the tongue deals out death (see Ps. 140:3).

Several years ago at the conclusion of a moving musical presentation, a man claiming to be Leonard Bernstein, Jr., son of the world-famous conductor, gave a check for twenty thousand dollars to the sanctuary choir of a large Baptist church. With tears in his eyes the man indicated that he and his father were Christian Jews and members of a New York City Baptist church. He asked that the church use the money to take the church choir to New York to perform with the New York Philharmonic Orchestra. Officials at the bank on which the check was drawn could not locate the account. The office of Leonard Bernstein in New York indicated that he had one son, whose name was Alexander. Neither father nor son had any connection with a Baptist church in New York. Someone had pulled a hoax. He had presented a picture of a tongue full of restless mischief.

The Bible's accurate picture of the tongue's destructive potential offers us no excuse for acquiescing to the tongue's evil potential (see Eph. 4:29). By committing our tongues to the power of God, we can see them used to build up and strengthen others rather than to tear them down.

Recently I spoke to a church in South Texas and focused during one evening on Paul's prayer in Ephesians 1:15–23. I urged my listeners to adopt the requests of Paul's prayer as they interceded for others. The next day one of the members pulled me aside to say that those words from Paul had changed her own prayer life. Her words of encouragement built me up and sent me back to my teaching with renewed enthusiasm. A tongue committed to God can be used as a positive tool for building hope and stamina in others.

Ⓓ The Double-Mindedness of the Tongue (vv. 9–12)

SUPPORTING IDEA: *We show our moral inconsistency by using the same tongue both to bless God and to insult his creatures.*

3:9–10. Verse 9 mentions both a positive and a negative use of the tongue. The positive use involved praise of God, the highest function of human speech (see Ps. 103:1–5). The negative use involved cursing human beings. Cursing refers to personal verbal abuse, perhaps arising from loss of temper in an argument or debate. It also involves the expression of angry wishes on enemies. It includes speech which is insulting as well as profane.

Verse 10 spotlights the inconsistency of this action. We are sinfully inconsistent when we bless God and then curse those made in God's likeness. When we curse those whom God has made, we are effectively cursing God. He is the object of both expressions. Such a double standard is outrageous: **My brethren, this should not be.**

3:11–12. These verses show the consistency of nature. Both verses ask questions to which the expected answer is "no." The illustrations from nature would have been familiar to inhabitants of Palestine. Areas around the Dead Sea contained many salty springs. Farther north of the Dead Sea travelers could find springs emitting fresh water. One spring could produce only one type of water.

The farmers of Palestine produced figs, olives, and grapes in abundance. James emphasized that a tree produced its own kind of fruit. We don't go to grapevines to find figs. We do not pluck olives from fig trees. Nature is consistent, but our tongues have never provided models of consistency.

The applications are so pointed they do not need to be made explicit. Colossians 4:6 provides a fitting conclusion: "Let your speech always be with grace, seasoned with salt, that you may know how you ought to answer each one" (NKJV).

In January 1917, the German Foreign Secretary Arthur Zimmerman sent a secret telegram to his country's ambassador in Mexico. The message announced the intention of the German government to begin unrestricted submarine warfare against all nations on February 1. It also urged the German ambassador to encourage both Mexico and Japan to support the German plans in order to keep America neutral and out of the war efforts.

British intelligence intercepted the message and saw that President Woodrow Wilson read the dispatch. Wilson released the telegram to the press. America had been a neutral nation in the First World War until this time. The disclosure of German intentions in the telegram led Wilson to ask for a declaration of war against Germany. The deceitful words of the German foreign secretary goaded America into war.

In the same way that printed words can inflame passions and tempers, the spoken word can arouse people to action, either good or bad. Paul called us to use our tongues positively: "Teaching and admonishing one another in psalms and hymns and spiritual songs" (Col. 3:16, NKJV). In seeking to control our tongues we must admit to God our weakness, seek his help, and place relentless guard on our tongues. God's grace can enable us to use our tongues and our words for blessing and encouraging others.

E The Need for Wisdom in Speech and Life (vv. 13–18)

SUPPORTING IDEA: *Believers with true wisdom avoid **envy** and **selfish ambition** and produce peace and **righteousness**.*

1. A Challenge to Demonstrate Wisdom in Behavior (v. 13)

3:13. James 3:2–12 presents shortcomings of the tongue to which teachers and all individuals are vulnerable. 3:13–18 reminds us of our need to demonstrate genuine wisdom. The words particularly apply to aspiring teachers, but they have relevance to all believers.

The opening rhetorical question asks how we can show that we have wisdom. **Wise** refers to someone with moral insight and skill in deciding practical issues of conduct. **Understanding** pictures someone with the knowledge of an expert. We are to show the presence of wisdom by good deeds practiced with humility. Only obedient deeds, not mere talk, prove the presence of wisdom.

Humility refers to a submissive spirit opposed to arrogance and self-seeking. The person with **humility** is not a doormat for the desires of others, but controls and overpowers the natural human tendency to be arrogant and self-assertive. Non-Christian Greeks felt that this type of humility was a vice. Christianity made meekness into a virtue. "Meek" in Matthew 5:5 is the adjectival form of the noun translated here as **humility**. Jesus promised the "meek" they would inherit the earth. Jesus meant a believer who relates to God with dependence and contentment will reap God's abundant blessings.

Even when you are involved in a disagreement, you must demonstrate a gentleness and kindness of attitude. You must banish all contentiousness and mutual accusation. The Bible calls on all Christians to show the presence of spiritual wisdom in their lives by deeds of humility and goodness.

2. The Wrong Response—False Wisdom (vv. 14–16)

False wisdom destroys unity and develops rivalry. This section discusses the demonstration of false wisdom (v. 14), the source of false wisdom (v. 15), and the results of false wisdom (v. 16).

3:14. Bitter envy and selfish ambition prove that a person is following the route of false wisdom. **Envy** describes a determined desire to promote one's opinion to the exclusion of the opinions of others. **Selfish ambition** pictures a person who tries to promote a cause in an unethical manner. This person becomes willing to use divisive means to promote a personal viewpoint. Bitter rivalries develop out of these practices.

James warned that people who had envy and selfish ambition could **boast about it or deny the truth.** Boasting describes the malicious triumphant attitude gained by one party over its opponents. Those who choose to deny the truth can end up rejecting the truth of the gospel. Envy of Jesus led the religious leaders to deny his person and power and to plot his death (John 11:47–53).

3:15. This verse uses three adjectives to describe the distinctive traits and source of false wisdom. First, negatively, false wisdom does not come **from heaven** or from God. Its source is **earthly.** It belongs to the way of life of this world. Second, false wisdom is **unspiritual,** belonging to the natural world and not to the supernatural world. It comes from the mental and emotional ideas of fallen human beings. Unfortunately, we Christians are too often guilty of using this twisted wisdom. Finally, this false wisdom is **of the devil.** Satan uses it to corrupt relationships.

3:16. The results of **envy and selfish ambition** are **disorder and every evil practice. Disorder** describes an experience of anarchy and disturbance. Such disarray affects private relationships between Christians and public meetings of believers. **Every evil practice** pictures an evil from which no good can come. People who cater to selfish ambition need never expect to develop any fruit which is godly, righteous, or helpful to others.

False wisdom promotes self-assertion and independence. It destroys a spirit of mutual concern. Where Christians "do their own thing" instead of caring for one another, a community of support and mercy can disintegrate (see 1 Cor. 1:10–17). Paul outlined a solution for this epidemic of selfish living, telling us to look out for "the interests of others" (Phil. 2:4).

3. The Right Response—True Wisdom (vv. 17–18)

3:17. True wisdom is free from self-interest and strife. This verse lists eight traits or characteristics of true wisdom. The first is purity. People with true wisdom are **pure** in that they have put aside the vices of a self-seeking nature and factionalism. This trait provides the secure foundation for all that follows.

The following five traits show the attitude of true wisdom toward other people. **Peace-loving** means it demonstrates a desire to promote peace between struggling factions. **Considerate** refers to being reasonable in the demands it makes on others. **Submissive** indicates a willingness to learn from others by being open to reason. **Full of mercy** is revealed by offering compassion to those in distress. **Full of good fruit** is shown by kind actions and helpful deeds to others.

The final two traits describe the essential nature of true wisdom in itself. It is **impartial**, without prejudice and unwavering in its commitments. True wisdom is **sincere**, genuine and open in its approaches to others. Jesus particularly showed his genuineness in his dialogues with Pilate (John 18:33–37).

3:18. Verse 18 concludes this section with a description of the effects of true wisdom. True wisdom results in **a harvest of righteousness**, that is, a conformity to God's will. True wisdom also lets one experience **peace**, the enjoyment of harmonious relationships between human beings.

Over the years Christians in various churches have developed wide differences in their social practices. American Christians from the South sometimes oppose mixed swimming, but they may offend a Christian from the North by their cultivation and use of tobacco. Christians differ in their preferences for English versions of the Bible. Some regard the use of certain modern translations as sure signs of compromise and moral apostasy. European Christians live in a culture which more readily accepts the use of alcohol by believers. Many American Christians find it hard to tolerate this acceptance. American women almost never feel compelled to wear a covering for their heads to worship services. Among many eastern European Christian groups it is expected that women will wear a covering, even if it is only a scarf. Each of these circumstances demands a response of peace and consideration to prevent strife, factionalism, and petty quarreling.

MAIN IDEA REVIEW: *God wants his people to control their tongues and to display true wisdom.*

III. CONCLUSION

Regenerated Tongues

Envy and selfish ambition can control our tongues. When we are in love with our own ideas instead of the Lord Jesus, we struggle to promote our ideas and our success rather than promoting him. We can easily slide into the habit of using our tongues to belittle others, work out our own agenda, develop pockets of strife, and promote our own policies. We can fail to love peace, respond in gentleness to others, produce righteousness, and demonstrate mercy.

James's words on the tongue provide information about its power, rebelliousness, and double-mindedness. He gives us warnings of the evil potential of the tongue which we must carefully observe. Though we are believers in the Lord Jesus, we do not automatically develop regenerated tongues. The potential for speaking evil with our tongues must drive us to let God search out our words and allow him to develop in us attitudes of grace and goodness.

James's words about wisdom warn against misplaced zeal and godless ambition. Some crusading zeal develops from Satan. Contentious words produce disorder and evil. God places a premium on peace.

We must seek God's grace to practice the words of Paul: "Do not let any unwholesome talk come out of your mouths, but only what is helpful for building others up according to their needs, that it may benefit those who listen" (Eph. 4:29). We can do no better than to commit our tongues to the Lord, ask him to develop true wisdom in us, and daily let him refine and purify our flashes of selfishness, anger, resentment, and pride.

PRINCIPLES

- God holds teachers more accountable for the words they utter.
- The tongue is a small object which can influence huge events with its words.
- Only the grace of God can tame the tongue.
- God values humility, peace, and righteousness more than self-centered zeal and ambition.

APPLICATIONS

- Control your tongue to show a mastery of your attitudes and impulses.
- Be consistent in the use of your tongue, not letting curses for people made in God's image come from the same tongue that praises.
- Do not treasure your goals and ambitions so much that you become prideful and deny God's truth.
- Cultivate an outlook that treasures the viewpoints and considers the needs of others.
- Ask God to help you develop true wisdom as the dominating characteristic of your life.

IV. LIFE APPLICATION

A Life of Deceit

In March 1805, Aaron Burr, vice president of the United States, delivered a farewell address to the Senate. After four years in office, he presented a valedictory to conclude his service. Burr said: "I shall, until I die, feel reverence for this house and the noble principles of which it is the primary guardian. In taking my leave of it and of you, I feel like the young man who leaves the dwelling of his parents to make his way into the world. This house is my mother, and has nurtured me; this house is my father, and has given me strength" (Philip Vail, *The Turbulent Life of Aaron Burr*).

After finishing his address Burr left the Senate chamber, receiving a standing ovation from his colleagues. His well-chosen words resembled the speech of a great patriot. They prompted the Senate to an outburst of affection and support. The picture of Burr we see in this speech is a complete distortion of this complex master of deceit. Burr was an accomplished liar!

When Burr reached the street after leaving the Senate chamber, he checked to see if bailiffs from either New York or New Jersey were waiting to arrest him. Not seeing any law officials in the streets, he left the Capitol on horseback, changed to another horse at the stable behind a small inn, and later transferred again to a coach with heavy, closed curtains. Then Burr disappeared from sight for two days.

At the time when he spoke Burr was wanted by officials in New York for murdering Alexander Hamilton, former secretary of the treasury, in a duel. He was also engaged in a plot to seize the Louisiana Territory and install himself as its emperor. He had shown nothing but contempt for the laws of the Senate. He adjusted his words to fit the occasion and felt no guilt about lying to protect himself or to arouse support. He used words as a tool to get people to act in his own ways.

Burr's speech showed two failures of the tongue. First, the tongue can deceive people. Aaron Burr was a first-class rascal, but his words resembled those of a pious prophet. Our words can deceive us and can mislead others. To be believable, our words must be supported by credible deeds. Second, we can use our tongues to advance our own agenda. Our ambition can drive us to distort the facts, present half-truths, and rationalize our failures.

James would have us use the tongue to produce **a harvest of righteousness.** We must claim God's grace to control our tongues, avoid using the tongue as an instrument of deceit, and instead use it for the purpose of encouragement, forgiveness, and mercy.

V. PRAYER

Lord, I have chosen to answer your call to teach. I know how much greater responsibility that places on me. I must rely on your guidance and wisdom every minute of each day. Forgive me when in moments of selfishness, I let my tongue paint false pictures and mislead people into following me rather than learning of you. Tame my tongue. Make it an instrument of your peace and grace. Amen.

VI. DEEPER DISCOVERIES

A. Teachers (v. 1)

"Teacher" appears fifty-nine times in the New Testament but only here in James. Most occurrences are in the Gospels. People addressed Jesus with this title (Matt. 12:38; 17:24; 22:16,36). Paul listed the office of teacher in a sequence following apostle and prophet (1 Cor. 12:28). Teaching is a chief function of the office of pastor (Eph. 4:11). The teacher remained in a specific location and provided instruction about Christian doctrine and spiritual living.

The work of a teacher was very visible before others, and this prominence attracted many who were unqualified and undeserving of the office. James urged aspiring teachers to show more concern about their qualifications for serving than with rushing into a position of high visibility. Verse 1 points out that the greater responsibility of teachers rendered them liable for a stricter standard of judgment. Today church leaders and would-be teachers of all types should heed this warning.

B. Perfect (v. 2)

Perfect is used to describe both God and human beings. It pictured God's moral perfection and completeness (Matt. 5:48). It describes maturity or complete development in people (1 Cor. 14:20; Eph. 4:13; Col. 1:28).

The word (*teleios*) does not describe sinless perfection, for no believer will reach that goal in this life. Rather, it presents someone who has moved toward spiritual maturity in the control of the tongue. James sought a maturity which showed the result of consistent growth in likeness to Christ. James even suggested that he himself had not reached the level in which he was **never at fault** in what he said. Such humility indicated growth toward maturity.

C. Course of His Life (v. 6)

This phrase (*trochon tes geneseos*) is part of a longer sentence reading, **It . . . sets the whole course of his life on fire.** Both the word **course** and the word **life** have multiple meanings, and it is difficult to know exactly what James intended to communicate.

Course may mean "wheel" or some sort of cycle of existence. **Life** may refer to "birth," "existence," or "nature." Some scholars have suggested that James was thinking of life as a wheel which began turning at birth and rolled along until death. They would place the tongue at the axle of this wheel and suggest that James was describing the tongue as an organ setting the entire wheel afire.

James probably intended his expression to show the broad social impact of an unruly tongue. His expression here seems to show that an undisciplined tongue can cause all of life's different relationships to burst into flames. A tongue out of control can stir up an entire household, neighborhood, community, or nation. James's vivid expression describes the potential of the tongue to inflame all of our existence.

D. God's Likeness (v. 9)

Sin has weakened the image of God in human beings, but despite human sin and evil every human being still bears a reflection of **God's likeness.** We see this likeness in the fact that human beings are personal, rational, and moral creatures. We have a conscience and an ability to reason. God has given us a will with which to choose. We have the privilege of knowing and worshiping the true God. Human beings still retain the marks of the original creation in holiness and purity.

James reasoned that it is inconsistent for human beings to offer praise to God and then to curse those who bear God's image. It is sin for God's creatures to offer blessing to God while they at the same time show contempt to those whom God has created in his image (1 John 4:20).

E. Bitter Envy and Selfish Ambition (v. 14)

Envy (*zelon*) comes from a word suggesting "zeal" and can have either a good or a bad sense. In Romans 10:2 the term describes a zeal for God. **Bitter** reveals the negative sense James had in mind as he described a determined desire to promote one's own opinion to the exclusion of others. Sinful human beings can pervert zeal for God into a bitter antagonism toward those who do not interpret God's message in the way they do. Our zeal for God may develop into a rivalry which reflects a certain ruthlessness and contempt rather than an earnest display of love.

Selfish ambition (*epitheian*) describes someone who promotes a cause in an unethical manner. Outside the New Testament the word described the pursuit of a political office by unfair methods. Paul used the word to say, "Do nothing out of selfish ambition or vain conceit" (Phil. 2:3). People in the Philippian church were divisively promoting their own viewpoints and running roughshod over their opposition. No fellowship or unity could survive such an attitude as this.

VII. TEACHING OUTLINE

A. INTRODUCTION
1. Lead Story: Bubbagate
2. Context: Chapter 2 of James calls for a demonstration of righteous living to show the reality of faith. Chapter 3 shows that a controlled tongue gives evidence of true faith.

   Verses 1–12 speak about the power, difficulty, and deceit of the tongue. Verses 13–18 describe the sources of strength which could empower the tongue to produce righteousness.

   Teachers who use the tongue in speaking will face a stricter judgment. The little tongue has power to create mighty mischief. Our extreme difficulty in managing the tongue reveals our need for divine power in controlling it. We can even use our tongues both to bless God and to curse his creatures, a dreadful inconsistency.

   The proper response is to show wisdom by humble behavior and to avoid envy and selfish ambition. Believers who practice true wisdom will emerge as **peacemakers** and produce **a harvest of righteousness**.
3. Transition: James's instructions concerning the tongue and true wisdom provide a pair of warnings and an expression of hope. An undisciplined tongue can wreck homes, destroy businesses, and send nations to war. On the other hand, wise behavior before God involves a love for peace supported by an attitude of mercy, gentleness, and approachability. Believers must make their impact in the church and society by working for unity, not for discord.

   A committed, disciplined tongue can inspire holiness, encourage forgiveness, and glorify God. May we seek to develop tongues committed to glorify God and to encourage his people.

B. COMMENTARY
1. The Need to Control the Tongue (vv. 1–2)
2. The Power of the Tongue (vv. 3–6)
3. The Rebellion of the Tongue (vv. 7–8)
4. The Double-Mindedness of the Tongue (vv. 9–12)
5. The Need for Wisdom in Speech and Life (vv. 13–18)
   a. A challenge to demonstrate wisdom by behavior (v. 13)
   b. The wrong response—false wisdom (vv. 14–16)
   c. The right response—true wisdom (vv. 17–18)

C. CONCLUSION: A LIFE OF DECEIT

VIII. ISSUES FOR DISCUSSION

1. Who qualifies to be a teacher of God's people? What message does James have for such people?
2. What temptations most beset you as you use your tongue day by day? What hope does James give you in this matter?
3. Define true wisdom. Give examples of people you have seen exercise true wisdom. Can you include your own conduct and speech among the examples?
4. How do envy and selfish ambition express themselves in your life? What are you doing to combat them?

James 4

The Danger of Living Without God

Quote

"*First* and foremost, I give all the glory to God.

He is the rock on which I stand,

and I would publicly like to ask him to forgive me

for my sins, of which there are many."

Danny Wuerffel upon accepting the 1996 Heisman Trophy

IN A NUTSHELL

People who live without God face five dangers. It stifles the prayer life. It makes them a friend of the world and an enemy of God. They neglect God's will in their lives. It produces insult and slander of fellow believers. It produces people who plan their lives without seeking God.

The Danger of Living Without God

I. INTRODUCTION

Should Christians Use Prayer "Hit Lists"?

"*P*rayer Hit Lists Forming" ran the title of the article. Christian leaders were urging their supporters to pray for the death of their political foes. On these prayer hit lists were state attorneys general and various Supreme Court justices. Usually the offending person had taken a political position which clashed with the religious beliefs of the other side. One religious leader who practiced these "prayers for death" ordered an airplane to circle overhead in Los Angeles as a Supreme Court justice who supported abortion spoke. The plane trailed the message: "Pray for Death" and then gave the name of the justice.

Those who explained the practice said their prayers first aimed at leading their foes to repent and reform their political positions. If they did not repent, then those involved in prayer would ask God to remove them from their position of authority. If all intercession failed, then they would pray for God to take their lives.

Scripture urges Christians to offer "requests, prayers, intercession and thanksgiving . . . for kings and all those in authority, that we may live peaceful and quiet lives in all godliness and holiness" (1 Tim. 2:1–2). It seems more in accord with Scripture for believers to pray for spiritual help and guidance for those who make political decisions than to seek their removal by death. Most Christians do not take imprecatory psalms such as Psalm 28:3–5 as their guide in prayer for their enemies. The prayer of the beleaguered disciples in Acts 4:24–30 for boldness and power to witness before their enemies sounds more in line with Christ's command to "love your enemies and pray for those who persecute you" (Matt. 5:44).

Using a prayer "hit list" sounds like unusual Christianity, but James's description of his readers in this section sounds equally strange. James pictured his readers in such dark terms that many interpreters have wondered whether he was describing a Christian audience.

James warned of people who wanted something and failed to get it. As a result they fought, coveted, quarreled, and killed over their desires. James warned these struggling warriors, **You do not have, because you do not ask**

God. When you ask, you do not receive, because you ask with wrong motives, that you may spend what you get on your pleasures (Jas. 4:2b–3).

James's readers claimed to be Christians, but they had the spirit of their unconverted neighbors in them. They were dominated by a self-will which pursued pleasure, power, and prominence rather than the will of God. James rebuked their sinful ways and urged his readers to turn to God with repentance and purity. His warnings apply to those who use "hit lists" in prayer as a means of removing those who take religious and political stands different from their own.

II. COMMENTARY

The Danger of Living Without God

> **MAIN IDEA:** *God wants his people to live with a conscious commitment to follow the divine will.*

A Self-Centered Living Stifles Prayer (vv. 1–3)

> **SUPPORTING IDEA:** *People who make their own desires the chief goal of their lives need not expect answers to prayer.*

4:1. Two rhetorical questions try to locate the source of struggles and **fights** among Christians. Such **fights and quarrels** come from **desires that battle within you.**

The **fights and quarrels** involved conflicts among Christians. The plural form of both words indicates the conflicts were chronic rather than a one-time incident. The disputes could have taken the form of arguments and controversies between teachers and factions in the churches. It could also have involved struggles about worldly affairs such as personal influence and financial gain.

The Greek word translated "desires" is related etymologically to the English word, *hedonism,* the philosophy that the chief purpose of living is to satisfy self. Jesus used the same word to describe people "choked by life's worries, riches and pleasures, and . . . do not mature" (Luke 8:14). There "pleasures" described any personal goal such as money, reputation, or success, which contributes to personal accomplishment rather than God's will.

These sinful desires lay within each Christian. Even believers find in themselves an alien army which seeks self rather than God. These desires express our pre-Christian nature still seeking to control our lives (see Rom. 7:14–25). Christians will never be freed from the evil influence of these subtle desires, but by God's grace we can escape their domination.

4:2. Verse 2 is difficult to interpret because punctuation was not an original part of Scripture. We must use our best interpretive skills to decide how to punctuate this verse. Compare the punctuation in NIV and NASB. The NIV lists three sentences before it concludes that **You do not have, because you do not ask God.** The NASB uses two sentences before it makes the same conclusion. Because it seems unduly harsh to join together "killing" and "coveting," we will use the NASB translation: "You lust and do not have; so you commit murder. And you are envious and cannot obtain; so you fight and quarrel. You do not have because you do not ask."

This translation suggests that murder is the result of desiring something and not getting it. It points out that fighting and quarreling are the results of having envy and being unable to obtain what you want.

"Lust" is frequently used in the New Testament in a bad sense to describe the act of coveting something belonging to someone else (see Matt. 5:28). "Envious" in this context refers to a quest for position, rank, or fame—an evil expression of personal ambition.

What type of "killing" did James have in mind? James was probably not thinking of physical murder. The Roman government would have executed murderers as criminals. Jesus linked an attitude of hatred and contempt with murder (Matt. 5:21–22). Hatred and jealousy produced by greed and worldliness are potential acts of murder because they can lead to actual murder. The inner attitude is wrong just as is the outward act of murder. Thus, James was not likely accusing his Christian readers of actual murder, but was showing them that their fights and disagreements were as offensive to God as killing.

At the conclusion of verse 2 James outlined the startling truth that his readers lacked what they sought because they failed to ask God. They hankered after satisfaction, but they looked in the wrong places. They did not ask God as Jesus had taught (Matt. 7:7). They allowed their lives to be governed by pleasure, selfishness, and greed. "There is, to be sure, no prayer that we all need to pray so much as the prayer that we may *love* what God commands and *desire* what He promises" (R. V. G. Tasker).

4:3. Here we see an additional reason these believers failed to gain their desires. When they asked, they asked with wrong motives. They may have made legitimate requests, but their purpose in praying was illegitimate. They only wanted to pursue their personal pleasures.

Scripture suggests that God listens to the prayers of the righteous (Ps. 34:15; 1 John 3:21–22). Those who are upright must voice their requests in accord with God's will (1 John 5:14–15). We will not receive prayer answers from the Lord unless we ask with the right motives in accord with God's will.

A cancer victim who had experienced healing wrote the following words to a denominational paper: "My family and I have become keenly aware of the value of prayer in the past few months. As a result of the prayers of people all over Alabama, God healed my body from cancer. . . . I am grateful to have been included in the prayers of so many people and grateful to the Lord for His healing power."

Experimental treatment removed all signs of the cancer in a few weeks, and the individual was able to return to an active ministry of pastoring. It is a legitimate prayer request to ask God for healing from sickness. Even that request may not be answered affirmatively because God may have another plan for an individual (see 2 Cor. 12:7–10). Our prayers can be a factor in bringing God's blessings to ourselves and to others.

Ⓑ Self-Centered Living Displeases God (vv. 4–6)

> **SUPPORTING IDEA:** *God demands complete loyalty from his people, and he provides the grace to achieve it.*

4:4. James harshly called his readers, **You adulterous people.** The Bible describes the act of turning away from God as spiritual adultery (see Isa. 57:3; Matt. 12:39). James charged his readers with spiritual adultery.

Friendship with the world describes a deliberate choice to follow the world. It is an act of defiance and rebellion against God. For a Christian, this type of response resembles entering the camp of the enemy and joining his army.

World can refer to the human race, the universe God made, or to a system of values separated from God. In this context it describes a society severed from God and pursuing its own godless agenda (see 1 John 2:15–17). A person cannot be loyal to God and controlled by worldliness at the same time. Christians cannot peacefully coexist with evil.

4:5. This verse confirms that friendship with the world and with God are incompatible. Two problems for interpretation appear in the text.

First, no verse in the Bible exactly states the words of the verse. Perhaps James was not quoting Scripture but was giving the general sense of a verse like Exodus 34:14 which pictures God as a jealous God.

Second, we must determine whether James was talking about the Holy Spirit or the spirit of a human being. The NIV translation sees James as referring to the human spirit, whereas the Holy Spirit is the interpretation of the Weymouth version: "The Spirit which He has caused to dwell in us yearns jealously over us." Galatians 5:16 describes the Holy Spirit as the opponent of "the desires of the sinful nature." This picture is consistent with the translation of the Weymouth version. James was saying that God's Spirit earnestly desired our undivided allegiance to the Lord.

James was probably asserting that God had placed his Holy Spirit within believers. The Spirit was intensely concerned about any rival in the Christian's heart. **Envy intensely** translates a strong word describing an intense longing or desire. It underscores the idea that God is a jealous God and allows no rivals. God refuses to share our commitment with any other so-called god. He wants our total loyalty and devotion. It is vitally important for us to remember that God makes great demands of his people.

4:6. If God makes heavy demands of his people, he supplies the grace to comply with the commands as the quotation from Proverbs 3:34 (quoted also in 1 Pet. 5:5) shows. The **proud** are those who turn their hearts away from God to another rival. The **humble** understand and practice total dependence on God. James assumed that believers, even though they might fall into temporary backslidings, are basically humble in that they recognize that salvation comes from God alone. Believers are recipients of the grace he is willing and able to give.

God resists the proud by opposing the life and practices of those who fail to follow him. He foils their plans and frustrates their dreams. God does not want our lives to be dominated by materialism, a search for prestige, selfish ambition, or deliberate forgetfulness of God. His aim is that we "seek first his kingdom and his righteousness" (Matt. 6:33).

Ⓒ Self-Centered Living Demands Repentance (vv. 7–10)

SUPPORTING IDEA: *Believers should submit to God by following basic steps which the text explains.*

4:7. These verses reflect the vigor of an Old Testament prophet as they express ten appeals to return to God.

Submit . . . to God calls us to subject our wills to his control. We can submit ourselves to the Lord only when we recognize that he is greater and worthy of more honor than we. The negative side of this command urges us to **resist the devil. Resist** is a military metaphor urging Christians to stand our ground against Satan's attacks. We resist the devil when we refuse to surrender to the impulse of sin.

If we obey these commandments, God promises that the devil **will flee from** us. Christ's resistance of Satan in his wilderness temptations provided the devil no foothold in his life and eventually forced the devil to flee (Matt. 4:1–11).

4:8. Come near to God involves approaching God in worship and commitment. Those who approach God in the obedience of worship find that he comes near to them. As our knowledge of the Lord deepens, we learn more fully his strength, power, and guidance for godly living.

Wash your hands uses the language of religious ceremony in a moral sense (see Exod. 30:19–21). We cleanse our hands by withdrawing them from all evil actions and compromises. Perhaps obedience to this command called more for cleansing the outward life, while **purify your hearts** called for an inner purification (see 1 John 3:3). The language here is soaked with words from Psalm 24:3–4 calling for believers to have "clean hands and a pure heart."

Double-minded people follow the practices of the world while they pretend to hold to God. Such people lack the purity of heart and focused purpose which the Lord wants in his disciples. The solution for this serious condition is a commitment of the entire personality to Christ and a fresh seeking of the power of the Holy Spirit.

4:9. This verse calls for open repentance. To **grieve** calls for sinners to experience a deep feeling of shame because of their disobedience. Mourning and weeping are the outward evidences of this sense of wretchedness. To change **laughter** and **joy** to **mourning** and **gloom** demands that we recognize the folly of our actions.

Laughter seems to describe the loud gaiety of worldly people. Their frivolity will become gloomy when they recognize their foolish choices. Laughter and joy are not evil. However, the particular moments when we meet God as sinners demand a serious repentance rather than hilarious celebration. Christians face times for serious repentance. Such times must not be laughed off.

Paul could write from a Roman prison cell for the Philippians always "to rejoice in the Lord" (Phil. 4:4). Under the burden of recognizing his disobedience, he could also cry out, "What a wretched man I am!" (Rom. 7:24). There is a right time to rejoice and a right time to mourn. James called his double-minded readers to recognize their moral unworthiness.

4:10. This final appeal contains both a command and a promise. To become **humble** before God demands a voluntary turning to God (see the words of Jesus in Matthew 23:12). The picture is that of a person who falls prostrate before a powerful oriental ruler, seeking mercy.

If we look at ourselves from our own perspective, we will invariably either be flattering or hopelessly pessimistic about ourselves. When we respond with insight provided by the Holy Spirit, we see our unworthiness; but we also sense God's ability to forgive us and receive us. Those who truly humble themselves before the Lord will experience his exaltation and elevation. This "lifting up" involves moral and spiritual power to live this life. It may also provide hopeful encouragement about our glorious future in heaven (1 Pet. 5:6).

Self-Centered Living Produces Slander (vv. 11–12)

SUPPORTING IDEA: *Human pride leads to disparaging criticism of others.*

4:11. Warnings in verses 11–12 grow out of the rebuke of pride and the call for humility in verses 7–10. Verse 11 prohibits slander and insulting language. Pride and the lack of humility are the chief causes of slanderous, insulting language. **Slander** is critical speech intended to inflame others against the person being criticized. It involves talking against people, perhaps attacking them behind their backs. In this instance Christians were slandering Christians. Christians are brothers and sisters in Christ. For Christians to malign other believers is a living contradiction of the close family ties which should bind them together.

A slanderous Christian must face two charges. First, one who practices slander speaks against the law. The law that a critical Christian misrepresents is the law of love (see Lev. 19:18). Christians are called to love our neighbors as ourselves. The slanderous Christian fails to do this.

Second, one who practices slander judges the law. With a fault-finding attitude I set myself up as a judge. I neglect God's law, thus declaring that it is a bad law and worthy of being removed. God calls Christians to keep the law, not to sit in judgment on it. When we slander our neighbors, we show our opposition to the law of love and imply that we are exempt from observing it.

4:12. God is the only **Lawgiver and Judge**, the one able both **to save and destroy.** Only God has the ability to enforce his laws and carry out his purposes. He allows no human being to share his role. A slanderous Christian attempts to play the role of God. God has no pleasure in those who practice slander.

Christians can easily come to the conclusion that we are free to show critical attitudes toward those who do wrong. The Bible warns us to leave this judgment with God. Only God has the competence to find and punish those who break his laws. Our calling is to respond in supportive love rather than biting criticism.

Ⓔ Self-Centered Living Produces People Who Ignore God's Will (vv. 13–17)

> **SUPPORTING IDEA:** *We must commit ourselves to discover the will of God as we make our plans for the future.*

It is easy for Christians to make plans and goals, expecting God to fall in line with them. It is easy to plan our lives as if we controlled the future and had unlimited authority over all factors affecting our life. It is quite simple to plan our lives as if God does not exist. This paragraph warns against such self-centered planning. Worldly living does not always show itself in hatred for God. Sometimes it appears in the form of disregarding God as we plan life's daily activities.

4:13–14. These verses rebuke our self-sufficient attitudes. Some interpreters feel James was describing non-Christian businessmen, who planned their lives without reference to God. Others point out that those rebuked could at least talk about **the Lord's will** and take this as a sign that those rebuked at least claimed to be Christians. Probably the original recipients were strong believers in the existence of God but lived as if he did not exist. They did not consider his will for their daily lives.

Trading was the surest method to make money in Palestine. Trading involved risk, but farming was even more uncertain. A person willing to take risks could become wealthy and live quite independently.

Verse 13 shows these businessmen planned the time of their departure, length of stay, and profit without reference to the will of God. The parable of the rich fool in Luke 12:16–21 warns against living such a self-sufficient lifestyle (see also Prov. 27:1).

Verse 14 mentions two features about daily life we often ignore. First, we have no sure knowledge of the future. We do not know whether tomorrow will produce a catastrophe or a visitation of God's grace. Even though we do not know the future, we so often act as if we are secure. We forget that we may be here for a moment and then gone. By failing to accept this fact, we demonstrate arrogant self-sufficiency.

Second, we do not understand the nature of human life which is like **a mist that appears for a little while and then vanishes.** Life is both uncertain and brief.

Many of us have busy schedules. It is easy to plan those schedules without considering the will of God. Many of us have visionary goals for our business, our job, our church, or our family. God wants us to work diligently in all of those areas, but we must consider his will first as we plan our goals.

4:15. Finally, we hear the proper attitude. We are to seek the will of God in all our plans. Doing the will of God demands an active listening for God's goals and plans. We must plan for the future, but we must plan with a deliberate seeking of the will of God.

As we discuss the will of God, we must not let his will become a strictly formal expression which lacks any spiritual meaning for us. We must remain spiritually alive to the necessity of building our plans around his desires. We must also avoid legalizing our own will under the disguise of seeking God's will.

Some years ago I was an avid collector of postage stamps. Often I received stamps from various companies on approval. This procedure allowed me to look at the stamps, select what I wanted, pay for them, and return the unwanted stamps to the company. Have you ever asked God to show you his will "on approval"? If we use this method of seeking God's will, it makes us the ultimate sovereigns over our lives. God desires that we obey his will unconditionally.

4:16–17. These verses reveal our disobedient attitude and rebuke our proud, boastful spirit. They call us to an humble dependence on God rather than priding ourselves on our independence.

James accused his readers of boasting and bragging. **Brag** describes the arrogant assumption they could handle the future as they wanted to do independently of God. Our boasting is to be in the Lord himself, in the blessings he gives us, and in the experiences which cause us to know him better. Paul boasted in his weaknesses that allowed the power of Christ to rest on him (2 Cor. 12:9). He gloried in the cross (Gal. 6:14) because it represented the action which brought the blessings of God's salvation to lost sinners.

Verse 17 states a specific principle applied to presumptuous planning about the future. It can also serve as a general principle applying to all areas of the Christian life: It is sin to know what is right and to fail to do it. These sins of omission refuse to make a right response to God. A sin of omission displeases God just as much as a sin of commission, that is, a blatant act against God's will. We know to make our plans in reliance on God's will. When we fail to follow this knowledge, we commit a sin of omission. God holds us accountable for more than merely knowing the right. He wants us to do the right.

God wants us to avoid acts of disobedience to his will. He also wants us to avoid the failure to live up to the truth he has given us. The response of the lazy servant which Jesus condemned involved burying his money and failing to increase it by hard work and effort (Matt. 25:14–30).

As Christians we must plan our lives in full commitment to the will and plans of God. We must also avoid omitting from our lives such important practices as prayer, Bible reading, helping the needy, and sharing our faith. To omit the latter is to commit a sin of omission. God wants our full and constant obedience.

MAIN IDEA REVIEW: *God wants his people to live with a conscious commitment to follow the will of God.*

III. CONCLUSION

Sadness—Getting What I Wanted

It was a large church. A member of the church called to inquire about my interest. My heart pulsed with excitement at the opportunity I could have as pastor of that congregation.

It was near a college, and I had children rapidly approaching their college years. It could be good for my family. Our entire family had been nurtured and helped by the churches I had pastored. It had been a family-friendly experience. We had loved the ministry of caring for the spiritual needs of people and seeing people trust Jesus, grow in him, and respond to his call.

I would have a high visibility in leading that church. Although I knew that this could produce pride and self-seeking, I realized that previous pastors of the church had been community and denominational leaders.

The church asked me to preach for them several times during the interim period. Each visit sent me away with prayer and excitement. I dreamed of what I might do if they were to call me as pastor. I dared to pray that God would see fit to call me there.

But they called someone else. I remained where God had called me, teaching New Testament in a seminary. I watched that church over the next several years as it experienced a time of trial. The church seemed to lose its focus. Discontent appeared. How hard it would have been to deal with this!

At the same time God confirmed that I was to stay where I was. He expanded my opportunities for writing, teaching, and ministry to others. I came to see that God knew what he was doing to keep me where I was. My wife and children came to the same conviction.

How sad it would have been if I had gotten what I wanted. I did not know what I needed. God knew better. If I had followed my own hopes and plans, I could have left a place of productive ministry for a location in which God did not want me. How important it was for me not to make and follow my own plans but genuinely to say, **If it is the Lord's will, we will live and do this or that** (v. 15).

The will of God must be the hub of our decision making. If we build our lives around any other plan, we will find ourselves saying, "How sad it is that God gave me what I wanted and not what he wanted."

PRINCIPLES

- We sometimes scheme and fight to obtain what God would give us if we would only ask.
- God yearns for us to give him our undivided allegiance.
- God exalts those who humble themselves before him.
- Only God has the ability to judge and evaluate our motives.
- Seeking the will of God must be the goal of our personal planning.
- We must beware of sins of omission as well as those of commission.

APPLICATIONS

- Don't ask with wrong motives, or you will not get your requests from God.
- Seek grace from God to love him with your whole heart.
- Resist temptation, and God will enable you to overcome it.

- Don't slander other believers, for in so doing you set yourself above God's laws.
- Be concerned not only about what you do but also about what you fail to do.

IV. LIFE APPLICATION

Humbling Yourself to Seek God's Will

Richard Greenham was a model English pastor from a Puritan background. From 1570 to 1590 Greenham served as pastor in the small village of Dry Drayton, five miles north of Cambridge. During twenty years of ministry, Greenham arose on most days of the week at 4 A.M. to begin to minister among his rural congregation. After delivering an early morning sermon, he tramped through the fields of his parish, talking with farmers in his congregation as they worked the fields. On Sundays he preached twice, and he held a meeting with children before the evening service. Regularly he prayed, visited, and wept over the needs of his small congregation.

He led farmers in his parish to store corn and barley in times of plenty for the needs of the poor in times of lean harvest. He freely gave money to impoverished prisoners. He was a skilled master at providing comfort for wounded consciences. Many who came to him weeping went away with joy in their souls. By nature he avoided controversy, although his age was a time of great agitation in the churches. He felt that personal religion was much more important, and he urged his listeners to make it their ambition to seek God.

Greenham's reputation for pastoral skill made him a legend among Puritans of his age. His location near Cambridge made it easy for travelers to beat a path to his door. Many of those who came wound up staying, spending the night, eating at his table, and participating in his times of instruction. His commitment and spiritual zeal became a source of encouragement and inspiration to godly pastors seeking a human model to imitate.

Despite his consistent zeal, Greenham did not reap much fruit among his people. The legend among Puritan pastors of his time was that "Greenham had pastures green but sheep full lean." Many in his parish remained so ignorant and stubborn that little spiritual progress was possible. Greenham left his parish in 1590 and commented that he could see no fruit from his ministry except in one family.

But fruit he did have. Many of those visitors who came to his home became leaders in the next generation of English ministers. They ate freely of the spiritual feast he gave them as they visited his home. Although he saw little fruit in his parish, God saw to it that Greenham's teaching and influence spread far abroad in the next generation. His faithful persistence produced among the next generation fruit which remained.

Many of us would find it easy to leave a task as difficult as Richard Greenham faced. We would seek more responsive ministries or people. Greenham stayed, taught those whom God sent him, and produced much fruit, chiefly in the next generation. He humbled himself to seek God's will.

Doing God's will is not always easy. It demands humility, repentance, discipline, and unflinching commitment. Not everyone wants to give this type of response to God. Doing God's will always brings good. The good may take time to appear. It may not always be good in the sense that the individual who does good receives honor and recognition. It will be good in that God will receive honor. It will be good in that you will see peace, righteousness, and purity appear. When we submit ourselves to do God's will, he will always produce a good result (Rom. 8:28).

To those who want to quit in the face of a hard task, James says, **Submit yourselves, then, to God. Resist the devil, and he will flee from you** (Jas. 4:7). Those who follow James's commands will find stamina to do God's will and will receive honor from the Lord (Jas. 4:10) for a job well done.

V. PRAYER

Lord, life seems so hard at times. So many things out there tempt me to seek them instead of seeking you. So often life seems meaningless and hopeless. I want to quit. The world seems so friendly. You seem so far away. Forgive me. I know I have moved. You have not. I will flee Satan. I will come back to you. Help me be humble in your presence. Help me see what you want me to do and never fail to do it. Show me your plans and how I can participate in what you are already doing. Amen.

VI. DEEPER DISCOVERIES

A. Desires, Pleasures (vv. 1,3)

The NIV translated the same Greek word (*hedone*) as **desires** (v. 1) and **pleasures** (v. 3). The Greek term stands behind our English derivative, *hedonism*. The word describes both the desire for pleasure (v. 1) and the pleasure itself (v. 3). The word appears only in three other New Testament passages, always carrying the suggestion of a self-centered, pleasure-filled lifestyle.

In Luke 8:14 it describes people "choked by life's worries, riches, and pleasures." In Titus 3:3 it pictures people "enslaved by all kinds of passions and pleasures." In 2 Peter 2:13 it portrays people whose "idea of pleasure is to carouse in broad daylight."

Christians can legitimately enjoy the pleasure of a moment of relaxation, listening to inspiring music. They can relish the joy of fellowship around a table with beloved family and good food given by God. However, the New Testament warns that Christians must not seek the pleasure which consists of self-indulgence, cheap thrills, and gains obtained by greed. Christians who seek these pleasures will forever live with unanswered prayers.

B. God's Conditions for Answering Prayer (v. 3)

God does not answer all prayers Christians address to him. Scripture specifies at least four conditions which we must meet to receive answers to our prayers.

First, we must come in an attitude of faith. **But when he asks, he must believe and not doubt** (Jas. 1:6).

Second, we must approach God with a commitment to obey him. "Dear friend, if our hearts do not condemn us, we have confidence before God and receive from him anything we ask, because we obey his commands and do what pleases him" (1 John 3:21–22).

Third, we must pray in accord with God's will. "This is the confidence we have in approaching God: that if we ask anything according to his will, he hears us. And if we know that he hears us—whatever we ask—we know that we have what we asked of him" (1 John 5:14–15).

Fourth, we must make our requests with a right motive as James tells us in 4:3. Self-centered motives prevent us from receiving God's answer to our requests.

Even though we may meet the above conditions, God is not obligated to meet our request in the way we ask. He still may answer as he answered Paul. Paul asked God to remove the "thorn in the flesh" (2 Cor. 12:7–10). God left the thorn with Paul but gave him a plentiful supply of grace so that he understood both his weakness and God's power.

C. The World (v. 4)

World (*kosmos*) carries several possible meanings, depending on its context. Sometimes it describes the inhabitants of the world whom God loved (John 3:16). In other contexts it can refer to the planet earth (Matt. 4:8) or to the universe (Rom. 1:20).

In James 4:4 it refers to the lifestyle of a world regulated by goals and aims contrary to God's commands. As Christians we live in this world, but we must not pursue its ideals. The Bible calls on believers not to "love the world" (1 John 2:15). We must never cultivate friendship with the world.

This does not suggest we must avoid contact with other human beings, and it does not indicate that we must live a monastic existence. We must not allow the goals and purposes of the world to become our goals and purposes.

In all our actions we must "seek first his kingdom and his righteousness" (Matt. 6:33).

D. Friendship with the World (v. 4)

When are we making friends with the world? How can we know if we are setting ourselves up to be at enmity with God? This is a condition we want to avoid. Here are some suggestions to help us discover when we are treading too closely to making friendships with the wrong people or institutions.

1. We make friendship with the world whenever we act in a way which is characteristic of the world such as displaying envy, strife, selfish ambition, jealousy, and hypocrisy (see Jas. 3:13–18).

2. We make friendship with the world whenever we tolerate a rival to the absolute lordship of Jesus Christ. What is most important to you? If it is job, pleasure, recognition, personal accomplishment, or personal gain, then you have set yourself at enmity toward God.

3. We make friendship with the world whenever we cherish a relationship with persons, institutions, or organizations which are indifferent to or hostile to God.

Above all, we must avoid making our friendship with the world and falling out of friendship with God. Our goal in life is to love God supremely and to permit our lives to be channels of obedience to him.

E. God's Jealousy (v. 5)

Human jealousy is reprehensible because it is fueled by envy, greed, and mistrust. When we develop jealousy of others, they usually have an appearance, possessions, or a position we want. Our envy of their appearance, material possessions, or public prominence comes from discontent with our situation and a desire to possess what they have.

In James 4:5, we read a description of the jealousy of God. The term *jealousy* does not appear in the NIV text, but it does appear in the NIV textual note. Jealousy is one characteristic of the God who is the only true and proper object of our worship. It became a part of a major confession of faith about God in the Old Testament (Exod. 20:5; 34:14; Deut. 4:24; 6:15; Josh. 24:19; Nah. 1:2).

God is jealous in that he will allow us to have no rivals for commitment to him. He is unapologetic in asking for our complete obedience (John 14:21). We sometimes speak of a jealous husband or wife. We recognize that it is entirely proper for a spouse to expect the complete commitment of a partner who has pledged to show love until "death do us part."

God's grace supplies us the strength to give him undivided allegiance. He provides us the strength to serve him with an obedient heart. As the followers of the risen Lord Jesus Christ, we should daily count it a privilege that we can render to him our full commitment.

F. Resisting the Devil (v. 7)

"Devil" (*diabolos*) literally means "slanderer." The word pictures the devil as one who misrepresents God to human beings (see his action in Gen. 3:1) and human beings to God (see his action in Job 1:9–11). The devil refuses to submit to God and is determined to prevent believers from obeying God. We must resist the devil incessantly and unrelentingly.

How do we **resist the devil?** We must surround ourselves with God's strength. Paul urged the Ephesians to "put on the full armor of God so that you can take your stand against the devil's schemes" (Eph. 6:11). The act of resistance includes our making a commitment to practice righteousness, live in truth, demonstrate faith, use God's Word, and exercise assurance of salvation. As we live in conflict with Satan, we must pray strongly for one another (Eph. 6:18).

The act of resisting the devil requires determined opposition to him. We must also submit to God and draw near to him. As we submit to God and live in obedience to him, we will experience his guidance, strength, and protection as we face temptations.

James promised that those who resist the devil will learn that **he will flee** from us. As we oppose Satan's strategies, we must not doubt or waver, but remain bold and confident in the Lord. As we confront him with a determined will and unflinching confidence in God, we will expose him as a coward. Jesus' death on the cross has made the devil a defeated foe (Heb. 2:14). As long as we draw our strength from the Lord and refuse to consent to Satan's temptations, we can remain victorious against the devil's deceitful deeds.

G. Christian Laughter (v. 9)

The Bible recognizes that laughter and good humor are a great gift from God. The Book of Job states approvingly that God will "fill your mouth with laughter and your lips with shouts of joy" (Job 8:21).

The Bible also recognizes that some laughter comes from flippant attitudes and from indecent jokes. Jesus pronounced a woe on those whose laughter showed a culpable ignorance of their true condition (Luke 6:25). Paul warned the Ephesians to avoid "obscenity, foolish talk or coarse joking" (Eph. 5:4).

In James 4:9, the Lord's brother saw some of his readers showing a casual, tolerant attitude toward sins and disobedience. Only those who mourned and wept over their sins would enjoy God's blessedness and laugh with a joy that was pure, satisfying, and blameless. His warnings have great application to people today who show a careless, accepting outlook toward disobedience when they should flee from it instead.

H. Judging Our Neighbors (vv. 11–12)

These verses warn us against slandering **one another**. They lead us to ask, Is any criticism of another person wrong? If any criticism were wrong, how could a church carry out the type of discipline advocated by Paul in 1 Corinthians 5:3–5?

What James denounced was critical, insulting speech intended to belittle someone else and to embarrass that person before others. The evil lay in the hostile intention of the speaker. The speaker wanted to destroy the character or position of the person being criticized.

James warned that such vicious insults violated the law of love. The speakers implied by their criticism that they were acting under higher principles than the one they criticized. They set themselves above the law as a judge. In their pride and arrogance they were acting the role of God.

The Bible calls on believers to remove evil from their midst (1 Cor. 5:6–8). This will demand clear exposure and confrontation of evil deeds and evil people. James, however, recognized that it is easy for Christians to lapse into a harsh, unjustified, self-promoting criticism of one another. He denounced this type of action.

I. The Will of God (v. 15)

The Lord's will involves God's plan for our lives, actions, and accomplishments. Christians must actively seek this will and do it. We must not merely mouth our obedience to the Lord's will as a device to mask our own plans. It is imperative for Christians earnestly to seek God's desires for their plans, goals, and actions. Paul wished farewell to the Ephesian Christians with the words, "I will come back if it is God's will" (Acts 18:21). He indicated to the Corinthians that he would visit them "if the Lord is willing" (1 Cor. 4:19).

To early Christians the sovereignty of God was a deeply personal reality. We who live today must make the seeking and doing of God's will our chief aim in life. We must not allow our advocacy of doing God's will to degenerate into a glib, formal expression empty of all spiritual reality.

Our recognition of our dependence on God for the future should not lead to inactivity, nor should it discourage future planning. We must plan our future with a zestful seeking of God's will. When we commit our plans to him and seek his will, we can proceed into the future with a conviction that God's grace sustains and empowers us. He will show us where he is actively at work and will draw us in to join him in that work.

J. Sins of Omission (v. 17)

This verse introduces us to a new category of sins, often called "sins of omission." This category emphasizes that what we fail to do in obeying God is just as important and significant as our acts of open disobedience.

The preceding verses warn us that God holds our future in his hands. Our life and prosperity are dependent on God and his grace. If we continue planning our lives without demonstration of dependence on God, we fail to know **the good** and are guilty of sin. Failing to seek God's will is a sin.

These words introduce the possibility of a broader application. Whenever we fail to follow a conscious commitment to Christ, we have omitted a deed of obedience and are involved in sin. Any action in which we reduce or omit obedience becomes sin in God's sight.

Our failures to seek God by prayer, Bible reading, and worship are sins of omission. Our omission of helpful acts of service to other human beings constitutes an act of disobedience. We must be people who confess to God our overt acts of disobedience. We must also ask him to show us those things we have forgotten to do.

VII. TEACHING OUTLINE

A. INTRODUCTION

1. Lead Story: Should Christians Use Prayer "Hit Lists"?
2. Context: Chapter 3 concludes the discussion of the tongue with an appeal for Christians to demonstrate heavenly wisdom which produces peace, purity, mercy, and righteousness. Chapter 4 provides some examples of the evil results of living in worldly wisdom rather than in heavenly wisdom.

   Verses 1–3 show that self-will leads to fights, quarrels, and a vitiated prayer life. God does not answer the prayers of those whose requests are motivated by a desire for pleasure rather than obeying God.

   Verses 4–6 show that self-will leads to friendship with the world and enmity with God. God's demand is for the unbroken commitment of his children.

   Verses 7–10 shoot out ten rapid-fire commands to call us to repentance. We need to respond to God with humility, submission, and steadfastness rather than with contentment, complacency, and compromise.

   Verses 11–12 warn of the prideful effects of slander. When we heap insults on Christian friends, we are guilty of setting ourselves above the law rather than submitting to it.

Verses 13–17 issue a concluding warning to those who practice a self-sufficient lifestyle. Such a lifestyle makes us guilty of attempting to plan life without seeking God's will. The Bible denounces this prideful behavior and calls it "sin."

3. Transition: Disobedience to God's will does not always produce immediate pain such as we see when people touch a bare hand to a hot stove. The burn warns you that a hot stove is dangerous. Disobedience to God's will often requires longer to "burn" us.

James has outlined the long-term results of self-centered living which does not seek to obey God. The descriptions are filled with tragedy. Disobedience to God produces fights, quarrels, enmity with God, compromise with Satan, backbiting insults, empty boastings, and habitual sin. These actions lead to misery, aimlessness, poor health, and deception about the future.

James's solution to this progressive problem is to call for submission to God, resistance to the devil, spiritual mourning, and humility before God. His promise to those who respond is fellowship with him, triumph over Satan, and honor from God.

The battle lines are drawn. The choices are clear. The outcomes are visible. The decision is ours. The benefits of obedience are indescribably good. May God give us the grace to choose wisely.

B. COMMENTARY

1. Self-Centered Living Stifles Prayer Life (vv. 1–3)
2. Self-Centered Living Displeases God (vv. 4–6)
3. Self-Centered Living Demands Repentance (vv. 7–10)
4. Self-Centered Living Produces Slander (vv. 11–12)
5. Self-Centered Living Produces People Who Ignore God's Will (vv. 13–17)
   a. A rebuke of a self-sufficient attitude (vv. 13–14)
   b. A description of the right attitude (v. 15)
   c. An explanation of their present evil attitude (vv. 16–17)

C. CONCLUSION: HUMBLING YOURSELF TO SEEK GOD'S WILL

VIII. ISSUES FOR DISCUSSION

1. Has your church been in a church fight recently? What are the causes? What are the solutions? Are you answering this from your own desires or from God's will?

2. Is something missing in your prayer life so that you do not seem to be receiving answers from God? What do you think is missing? What will you do about it?

3. What are your sins of omission? When will you begin doing what you know you should be doing?

4. In what ways are you a friend of the world? How will you break off this friendship so you can be sure you are a friend of God?

5. Are you guilty of slandering other believers? When will you repent? How will this repentance work itself out in your relationship to the other party?

James 5

A Call to Philanthropy, Patience, and Prayer

I. INTRODUCTION
Some Sources of Spiritual Numbness

II. COMMENTARY
A verse-by-verse explanation of the chapter.

III. CONCLUSION
Green Mamba Bites

An overview of the principles and applications from the chapter.

IV. LIFE APPLICATION
Changing Other People

Melding the chapter to life.

V. PRAYER
Tying the chapter to life with God.

VI. DEEPER DISCOVERIES
Historical, geographical, and grammatical enrichment of the commentary.

VII. TEACHING OUTLINE
Suggested step-by-step group study of the chapter.

VIII. ISSUES FOR DISCUSSION
Zeroing the chapter in on daily life.

"*T*here is nothing that makes men rich and strong

but that which they carry inside of them.

Wealth is of the heart, not of the hand."

J o h n   M i l t o n

James

I N   A   N U T S H E L L

*I*f you are rich, beware of the love of money and how you use your money. It will backfire on you! If you are not rich, be patient. Life's ledger will be tallied when the Lord returns. Be patient in suffering, as Jesus was. If you are sick, call the elders of the church to pray for you. The prayer offered in faith will make the sick person well. If you see anyone sinning, try to win him back. You will do him a great favor.

A Call to Philanthropy, Patience, and Prayer

I. INTRODUCTION

Some Sources of Spiritual Numbness

After the Revolutionary War many leading preachers from the original colonies migrated to Kentucky, where they pursued wealth and sometimes left active involvement in ministry. One of these was Elijah Craig, who moved to Kentucky from Virginia in 1787. He purchased one thousand acres of land, engaged in continuous land speculation, established the first saw and grist mill in Kentucky, and built a paper mill. An observer wrote about him that these business activities "impaired his ministerial usefulness."

Another preacher who left Virginia for Kentucky was John Taylor. He, too, became sidetracked from spiritual matters after his move. He wrote in his personal journal of the hard manual labor needed to make a successful living in Kentucky: "We had no time to pause and think, but go right on to work." After two years he was able to boast, "I was the richest man in the county where I lived." However, he had to admit that "through the course of this two years, I preached but little."

Both of these men had endured hardship, persecution, and had been relatively poor in Virginia. Building up wealth had not been their previous goal. In fact, one zealous minister in Virginia, Samuel Harris, had refused to take a man to court for money owed to him, money which he desperately needed. Harris's explanation was that he "didn't want to lose time in a lawsuit he could spend preaching saving souls." For some church leaders the new opportunity to seek material goals served as an anesthetic on the spiritual life.

Some zealous ministers showed a preference for political power rather than for spiritual power. James Garrard, a preacher who had moved to Kentucky, left his preaching in 1796 to become governor of the state. Historian Robert Semple sorrowfully wrote, "For the honours of men he resigned the office of God. He relinquished the clerical robe for the more splendid mantle of human power." Semple also spoke of another talented minister from the Roanoke Association in Virginia who, "misled by ambition," set himself up as a candidate for Congress. These words do not suggest that involvement in politics signifies automatic spiritual declension. Semple's words suggest that in the above instances a love for political power had replaced a pursuit for spiritual power.

A quest for wealth and power can consume all our energies. Those who have wealth and power face the additional temptations of pride, greed, and an attitude of self-sufficiency. The wealthy can also take advantage of their condition to practice injustice and dishonesty toward the poor and needy.

James saw wealthy people who were facing these temptations and yielding to them. He warned both the rich and poor—the majority of his Christian readers—of the numbing effects of wealth and the pursuit of power.

II. COMMENTARY

A Call to Philanthropy, Patience, and Prayer

MAIN IDEA: *Christians must flee the pursuit of wealth, demonstrate stamina in trials, and practice prayer at all times.*

A A Charge to People with Money (vv. 1–6)

SUPPORTING IDEA: *Divine judgment will come on wealthy people for their greed and misuse of wealth.*

1. Warnings to the Rich (vv. 1–3)

5:1. James 4:13–17 centers on the arrogance and pride involved in planning life without dependence on God, denouncing the worldliness of the self-centered businessman. James 5:1–6 indicts wealthy landowners for abusing the power of their wealth and for oppressing the poor. These landlords probably belonged to the same group whom James had mentioned in 2:6–7 as **the rich.**

These wealthy landowners were probably not believers, but they were making life miserable for Christians, who were their victims. Notice that James spoke to some readers as **brothers** (vv. 7,10), but he did not use this term in verses 1–6. We would not expect Christians to use their wealth to promote injustice as did the wealthy landowners in verses 1–6.

The possession of wealth is not evil. Abusing wealth by selfish living and by harming people dependent on you, is. These people seem to have used their wealth only for themselves.

Weep and wail represents the emotional outburst of those who ignore God's demands and are overwhelmed when they recognize what they will lose and suffer at God's final judgment. The same Greek verb appears in 4:9, calling sinful believers to repentance. Here the rich are not called to repent. Too late for that. They must cry out in fear and pain in view of the end.

Misery points to hardship, wretchedness, and difficult times which stood poised to strike at the wealthy people who had abused their financial power. This direct address to the wealthy oppressors represents a momentary shift of audience, yet James still wanted his oppressed people to hear what would happen to their oppressors. Rich non-Christian landowners who were oppressing poor believers probably would not hear the letter read. Christian readers would learn from the experience of the rich not to set too high a value on wealth.

James spoke with the passion of an Old Testament prophet (cf. Amos 5:11–27) as he sought to help oppressed Christians avoid the deceitful ways of wealth.

5:2–3. In the ancient world wealth took three primary forms: food (Luke 12:18), expensive clothing, and precious metals (Acts 20:33). When owners carelessly stored clothing, moths could cause extensive damage. Gold does not actually rust, but it can become corroded. James may have been using the corrosion of gold and silver as a symbol of the corrosive effects of greed on the human soul. James did not specifically mention food, but the **wealth** which had **rotted** could include food which had spoiled and wasted away.

The verb tenses picture destruction as if it had already occurred, another element of prophetic forcefulness, indicating that the events of divine judgment were so certain to occur that they could be pictured as fact.

The **corrosion** of gold and silver affects the wealthy in two different ways. First, it testifies against them, producing evidence of their greed and lack of concern. Second, it will consume their flesh as fire, a terrible image of divine judgment on those who had made money their chief aim in life.

Verse 3 concludes with the warning that the wealthy landlords had **hoarded wealth in the last days.** Instead of depending on God, these wealthy Scrooges collected wealth when they should have prepared for eternity. They resembled people in a burning house trying to save precious personal objects when they should flee for safety.

Last days could refer to the approaching death of the landowners or to the period of time preceding Jesus' return in judgment (Acts 2:17). In a sense Christians have been living in the **last days** since the outpouring of the Spirit at Pentecost (see Acts 2:17).

Jesus warned about the misuse of wealth (Matt. 6:19–21). Wealth can be destroyed by moths or rust or it can be stolen. So readily we place our affections on material items instead of trusting in God. Wanting to keep money for our own use is natural. The Bible does not discourage wise planning, but does denounce selfish, greedy living. God wanted money to be used to relieve the suffering of the needy (Eph. 4:28).

Basil the Great, a Christian leader in Caesarea of Asia Minor in A.D. 368, saw his country suffer first from floods and then from droughts. Many people starved to death. Basil thundered against wealthy hoarders of grain "who let their wheat rot, while men die of hunger." He sold property which he had inherited and used the money to feed the hungry. He interceded with the rich to give to the poor and with the poor to share with the poorer. He literally washed the feet of the poor and fed the starving with his own hands.

He wrote, "If you are reduced to your last loaf of bread and a beggar appears at your door, then take that loaf from your closet and lift your hands to Heaven, and say this prayer: 'O Lord, I have but this one loaf, which you see before you: Hunger lies in wait for me, but I worship your commandments more than all other things, and therefore this little I have I give to my brother, who suffers from hunger.'"

James thundered warnings of judgment on the stingy, greedy landlords who preferred to collect money rather than help the poor and needy. The generosity and unselfishness of early Christians provided visible solutions to the problems of hunger, need, and greed which they confronted (see Acts 4:32–37).

2. Charges against the Rich (vv. 4–6)

5:4. The sin of injustice occupies center stage here. The wealthy had failed to pay wages to their workers. In New Testament Palestine rich farmers hired day laborers to work their fields. Deuteronomy 24:14–15 demanded that an employer pay an employee his wages on a daily basis. The laborers lived a hand-to-mouth existence. They needed wages each day to purchase life's necessities. A wealthy employer might retain wages until the end of the harvest to prevent the workman from leaving him. If the worker protested, the rich man could blacklist him. If the poor went before judges, the rich had better legal representation. James's readers had mowed or reaped the fields, but the wealthy landowners withheld their pay. This injustice displeased God.

James personified the withheld wages. These unpaid wages cried out to God against the wealthy. Although the rich landowners might not hear the pleas of the poor, God would hear their prayers. One of the most majestic Old Testament names describes the God who hears prayers. He is termed **the Lord Almighty** or the Lord of Hosts. This pictures God as the head of Israel's armies (see 1 Sam. 17:45) and heaven's angels (see 1 Kings 22:19). It presents a powerful picture of God's mighty resources available for his people.

As we face hardship in daily living, we have the complete resources of almighty God protecting us. Ultimately, none of our hardships can vanquish us. Whatever needs we face, we can expect the Lord of Hosts to be our helper and source of strength.

5:5. The wealthy landowners lived in selfish luxury and waste as did the "rich man" in Luke 16:19. "Self-indulgence" pictures a pleasure-loving widow in 1 Timothy 5:6. These wealthy landowners lived in "high style."

Fattening themselves **in the day of slaughter** describes oxen being fed ample food in preparation for the kill. The oxen ate greedily, unaware of what awaited them. The wealthy should have known better, but they acted like senseless animals unaware. They were pampering themselves with their wealth while the **day of slaughter** or the day of divine judgment for their evil actions stood around the corner.

5:6. The final charge against the wealthy accuses them of violence against the poor or murdering **innocent men.** Jewish tradition taught that a person could murder another either by judicial murder or by depriving his neighbor of his living. The apocryphal book of Jesus ben Sirach or Ecclesiasticus declarared, "He that taketh away his neighbour's living slayeth him; and he that defraudeth the labourer of his hire is a blood shedder" (34:22). The wealthy landowners could have been guilty of murder in either sense. Probably the acts of violence were not limited to a single event but involved multiple occurrences.

The poor man made a subdued response to the injustice he suffered. As a committed Christian, he refused to respond with violence. He may have realized that violence would not assist him to do anything effective about his plight.

🄱 The Development of Patience and Reverence (vv. 7–12)

> **SUPPORTING IDEA:** *In persecution and trial Christians should show stamina and respect for God's name.*

1. An Appeal for Stamina in Trials (vv. 7–11)

5:7–8. James wrote these words to Christian readers, addressing them as **brothers.** His readers in these verses were the victims of mistreatment by the wealthy mentioned in 5:1–6. James presented an incentive to show stamina, a hindrance to stamina, and two positive examples of stamina.

Trials and afflictions often produce grumbling or complaints. James prohibited this response when he urged his readers to **be patient. Be patient** demands an attitude which shows long-suffering in the presence of affliction and injustice. Believers should show this stamina without complaining, giving up, or retaliating. They should be ready to endure affliction without complaint and to remain committed in their obedience to God.

Persecuted believers can develop stamina by looking to the coming of the Lord. At that time Jesus will bring judgment on the disobedient (see 2 Thess. 1:6–10). Instead of taking vengeance into our own hands, Christians are to trust God to perform justice and to bring punishment on those who may cause hardship for them (see Rom. 12:19). Such forward-looking waiting requires patience.

The hard-working farmer shows us an example of patience. The farmer can prepare the soil, plant the seed, and keep the field weeded. However, he must expect God to supply the conditions of rain and sunshine which encourage growth. For this he needs patience.

The **autumn rains** usually appeared in October and softened the ground for planting. The **spring rains** usually came in April or May and matured the crops for harvest. The fact that the farmer had to wait for these rains showed his stamina or patience. The farmer had learned to trust in the reliability of God to supply the needs for his crops. James called his readers to the same demonstration of trust as they faced persecution.

Verse 8 urges us to show patience and courage because of the nearness of Jesus' return. We should show a firm purpose and depend constantly on God's grace. We can find the strength to **stand firm** because the return of the Lord will bring salvation, eternal life, and spiritual health.

The blessed hope of the Christian is the personal, bodily return of Jesus Christ (see Titus 2:12–13). We must not allow events to dull our hope in Jesus' return. We must not reduce our hope for Jesus' return to something like the transformation of society by Christian values. Jesus will come personally!

The hope of Jesus' return gave the early Christians hope as they faced hardship (Heb. 9:28). We must look at time from the viewpoint of the God for whom a thousand years is only a day (2 Pet. 3:8; 2 Cor. 4:16–18). Though centuries have passed since Jesus promised to return, we serve a God for whom the length of time does not imply a failed promise. Our hope of Christ's return is an encouragement for us to obey him.

J. Hudson Taylor founded the China Inland Mission in the 1860s. He believed fervently in the impending return of Christ. His belief influenced him to make the evangelism of unreached areas of China his primary aim. His beliefs about Christ's return gave him direction and urgency in the establishment of the mission.

Our belief in the return of Christ can provide us courage to face difficulty. It can give us stamina to endure persecution. It can deepen our hope that God will provide us reward and recognition to vindicate our actions.

5:9. This verse points out that a complaining attitude hinders us from developing patience and long-suffering. "Grumbling" involves the development of criticism and faultfinding against one another. Hardship may have driven some believers to despondency. They may have blamed their troubles on one another. Some may have questioned the devotion of other Christians or faulted the way others had treated them. God will judge and punish "grumblers." Such a loveless attitude is a direct contradiction of the true spirit of Christianity.

Who can hold on to such attitudes when **the Judge is standing at the door**! How inappropriate it is for Christians to be fighting when the return of Jesus is a certain event. Jesus will bring with him a complete knowledge of our feelings, thoughts, and reactions. We should be living in readiness for his coming. Instead, too often we behave like a group of students fighting in a school classroom while the absent teacher walks rapidly toward the room. Jesus is coming! How are you living?

5:10–11. The Old Testament prophets and Job also exemplified patience in suffering. The prophets suffered because they spoke in the name of God. In suffering, they demonstrated incredible capacity for devotion without complaint.

Patience is related to the word for **patient** in verses 7–8 and refers to an attitude of long-suffering which does not complain or find fault under trial. In Jeremiah 38, King Zedekiah wrongly imprisoned the prophet Jeremiah in a muddy dungeon and left him to die. Jeremiah voiced no complaint toward God or his captors. When Zedekiah summoned him and asked for his advice in a matter, Jeremiah told him, "Obey the LORD by doing what I tell you. Then it will go well with you, and your life will be spared" (Jer. 38:20). Jeremiah spoke in the name of the Lord and showed obedience despite intense suffering. He showed long-suffering in that he neither complained nor found fault with God's treatment. We are to imitate behavior like that.

Job's consistent obedience under trial was legendary among the Jews. He endured abject misery and exhibited great perseverance. Christians considered those who endured like Job as happy. This viewpoint amounted to a reversal of the world's evaluation of such sufferers, for the world would pity such people.

The God who tested Job in the furnace of hardship finally brought him to an experience of compassion and mercy. Through enduring trials, Job received a more complete insight into the divine purpose, and he was able to show deeper repentance (see Job 42:5–6).

2. An Appeal for a Reverence for God (v. 12)

5:12. Here the appeal is for us to avoid using God's name disrespectfully. **Above all** does not suggest that this sin is more serious than other sins such as murder, immorality, or robbery. It is simply a common way of bringing a letter to a close, perhaps indicating that what follows in some way summarizes what has gone before.

Although these words prohibit profanity, they are not chiefly concerned about "taking the Lord's name in vain." They warn against the use of a hasty, irreverent oath involving God's name during a time of suffering or hardship. This logically follows the discussion of **suffering** in verses 10–11. **Above all** during our stress we should not resort to flippant oaths that communicate something about God to the world that we do not intend.

This prohibition bans the careless use of God's name to guarantee the truthfulness of a statement. Christians who face suffering can be easily tempted to make a frivolous appeal to God's name to bargain their way out of trouble or difficulty.

In the New Testament period, some Jews used oaths for frivolous swearing. They would make a statement such as "by my life" or "by my head" to bolster the truth of a promise or statement. They also used evasive swearing. If a person swore by the name of God, his oath was binding. If he swore by another object such as **heaven** or **earth,** his oath was not binding. Jesus condemned such false actions. He wanted the words of his followers to be so patently honest that they needed no additional confirmation. James affirmed what Jesus had already said. He wanted an individual's **yes** to mean **yes,** and the **no** to mean **no.** God would judge the words of an evasive or frivolous swearer (see Matt. 12:36).

ⓒ The Uses of Prayer (vv. 13–20)

> **SUPPORTING IDEA:** *Pray in all of life's situations, including sickness, confession of sin, seeking God's will, and reclaiming wanderers.*

1. Prayer in Life's Experiences (v. 13)

5:13. Christians pray both in times of trouble and in times of joy. In times of trouble Christians often fall victims to self-pity, anger, or morbid introspection. James directed Christians to pray rather than surrender to these wrong responses. **Trouble** includes physical and emotional stress arising from both ordinary trials and special spiritual difficulties. During such trouble we are to "keep on praying." Sufferers must not stop their prayers after a quick prayer for help. They must live in an attitude of prayer.

Happy describes a cheerful, elated mood. This is not a giddy, flippant outlook but a mood of cheer and optimism. Prosperity and pleasant experiences in life can cause a person to forsake God due to complacency or worldly contentment. Instead, life's good times should lead us to **sing songs of praise** to God as the author of the blessings. The same verb can be translated "make music" to the Lord (Eph. 5:19). This command does not demand the use of music but calls for the expression of words or thoughts to praise or thank God.

Christians who face trouble often lose their awareness of the presence of God due to gloom. Christians who have elation tend to forget God in the joy of their good success. Both darkness and sunshine should lead believers to a consciousness of God.

2. Prayer in Sickness (vv. 14–15)

5:14. Sickness includes all types of bodily weaknesses—physical, mental, or spiritual. Here the reference is primarily to physical illness. The sick person should take the initiative to call the elders of the church to pray for him. The elders were church leaders who had the task of pastoring and providing spiritual leadership for a congregation (Titus 1:5). We would normally expect them to be able to pray with effectiveness. These elders are called on to perform two tasks.

First, they pray **over him,** suggesting that they stand over the bed of the sick person. This is a special participation in prayer beyond the normal experiences of intercession. The fact the ill person was confined to a bed implied a serious or painful sickness. Second, they anoint him **with oil.** The act of anointing with personal touch and contact served to strengthen the faith of the sick person. This refers to olive oil, which served as a symbol of God's healing power. The oil had no healing power in itself. The experience of anointing with oil appears elsewhere in the New Testament in reference to physical healing (see Mark 6:13).

This practice had two benefits which encouraged more fervent prayer for the sick. The elders of the church would pray with more fervor because they had been at the scene of sickness. The sick person could become more aware of the encouragement which could come from their fervent prayer.

Roman Catholics have used this passage to justify the sacrament of extreme unction, a ceremony intended to prepare a sick person for death. The fact that in the next verse James spoke of restoring a person to health suggests that we must not understand the prayer of verse 14 as a preparation for death.

The word for "sickness" can refer to spiritual weakness (1 Cor. 8:11). Usually, however, the presence of spiritual sickness is noted by the appearance of a qualifying phrase such as "in faith" (Rom. 4:19). The absence of the phrase here lends support to the suggestion that physical sickness is the concern. The word for "sickness" was used to describe the physical sickness of Lazarus (John 11:2–3), the nobleman's son (John 4:46), and Dorcas (Acts 9:37).

5:15. The prayer offered in faith is a prayer based on confidence that God can and wants to heal. This does not imply that if a person has a sufficient degree of faith, God will automatically answer the prayer. Rather, it suggests that believers have a right to faith in all of life's situations.

Those who pray **in faith** receive two promises. First, these prayers will make the sick person well. Second, the statement about the forgiveness of sins suggests that in some instances illness may be due to the sins of the sick person. In such instances the healing provided a sign that God had forgiven the sins.

With these promises God still retains his freedom to do his will and work things out in the ways best for the kingdom. Prayer can bring healing, but lack of healing does not show that the one praying lacks faith. Neither does it show that the prayer is somehow invalid or God is somehow incapable of healing.

The promise of raising up the sick person refers to physical restoration to sound health and not to participation in the final resurrection. The verb for "making the sick person well" is sometimes used in the New Testament to describe "spiritual deliverance." The Gospels also use it for restoration to health (see Matt. 9:22). **Sick person** describes the experience of weariness (Heb. 12:3). **Raise up** describes the increased physical vigor of those who have experienced healing (Matt. 9:6; Mark 1:31). This seems to suggest that both verses 14 and 15 refer to physical healing and not to spiritual deliverance.

The Bible text here does not qualify the promise of healing in any way. It provides an absolute promise that **the prayer offered in faith will make the sick person well.** This poses a problem because it is obvious that believing prayer does not always produce bodily healing. Paul left Trophimus at Miletus sick (2 Tim. 4:20). We must always understand that this and other promises of the Bible (see Mark 11:24) contain an implied condition. God will grant the prayer whenever it accords with his will.

Thus, we cannot take this statement as a guarantee that every prayer offered with a sufficient degree of faith will be answered. The intercessor must approach God in an attitude of faith, but the request will be granted only if it accords with the will of God (1 John 5:14). Whenever God does not provide instant healing, the prayer is still useful because it provides encouragement and help for the person who is sick.

The concluding words of verse 15, **If he has sinned, he will be forgiven,** recognize that the sickness may be due to sin. When the sickness does come, the ill believer must examine himself before the Lord to determine if sin is the cause of the sickness. The grammatical construction shows that sin is not always the cause of sickness (see Jesus' teaching in Luke 13:1–4; John 9:3). Some sickness, however, is due to sin (1 Cor. 11:30).

If sin is present, the Bible offers hope. It assures the sick person that forgiveness is available. Sins are sent away because God no longer holds them against the sinner. He forgives completely.

Some interpreters have suggested that this passage discusses two types of healing: physical and spiritual. The reference to experiencing forgiveness seems to suggest this possibility. Such an interpretation would require that the action of making the sick person well in verse 15 also carries with it an additional meaning of spiritual wholeness. The meaning of the context is satisfied, however, when we see simply a reference to physical healing. We should not give the words of the text more meanings than they require.

3. Prayer in Confession of Sin (v. 16a)

5:16a. Because God hears the prayers of penitent people and forgives sin, Christians should confess their sins to one another and pray for one another. The mention of "healing" at the conclusion of this verse makes it likely that the sins to be confessed are those which have caused illness. The healing shows the purpose of the mutual confession and prayer.

Since the intent of the confession of sins is to experience physical healing, it seems best to refer the command to the confession of sins which may hinder healing. The confessor of sins is seeking healing by the act of admitting sins.

Two interesting observations come from this verse. First, the entire church is to be involved in this praying. It is not confined to the elders. Second, the power to heal appears in the act of praying, not in the elder or other one praying.

Confess means "to say the same thing." It suggests that in confessing, we must identify the sin by its true name and call it what it is. We must acknowledge and repent of specific sins, not merely offer a general confession of guilt.

Placed so close to the discussion of prayer for the sick, this verse likely has its primary application in confession of sin by people who are sick. However, the application is easily extended to confession of sin in any of life's situations.

This confession of sin seeks to secure faithful prayer support for stumbling Christians from trusted spiritual friends. It is not urging a careless confession to just anybody. Such a type of confession might cause more harm than good. It is confession to dedicated, trusted prayer warriors who will intercede for you with God.

Roman Catholics have used this verse to justify confession of sins to a priest. It is important to note that this verse discusses confession and intercession among Christians and not between a believer and a priest.

4. Prayer in Working Out the Will of God (vv. 16b–18)

5:16b. This verse concludes by showing the powerful effect of prayer. Translators have disagreed widely over the translation of the last half of this verse. Some translators emphasize that James was commenting on the effect of the prayers of righteous people. Other translators emphasize that James taught that righteousness and earnestness were requirements for uttering powerful prayers. The translation of the NIV emphasizes the former.

We learn two features of effective prayer in this verse. First, prayer must come from righteous people. A person must have a living faith shown by an obedient life. Second, effective prayer must have energy or persistence.

Effective prayer comes from the heart of a believer whose passion is to see the will of God worked out in life.

5:17. Elijah is spotlighted as one who prayed **earnestly** with power. **A man just like us** teaches us that Elijah had human weaknesses and frailties just like our own. The exact length of the drought in Elijah's time was not mentioned in the Old Testament (see 1 Kgs. 18:1). Jesus mentioned the same length of time as James (Luke 4:25).

5:18. Elijah knew the will of God so intimately that he could understand the exact time when the divine purposes were to occur. He was able to perceive when God wanted to begin and end the drought. The example of Elijah in determining God's will challenges us to seek a closeness in our walk with God so that we know and follow his will. Those prayers which accord with the will of God will always be answered (see 1 John 5:14–15). We must so walk in God's will that we love what God loves and reject what he rejects.

5. The Ministry of Reclaiming Wanderers (vv. 19–20)

The concluding section offers commendation for those who rescue straying believers.

5:19. This verse focuses on the spiritually sick and outlines how to reclaim and restore them. To **wander from the truth** describes someone who has made a serious error, either in doctrine or in Christian living. To **bring him back** describes someone who returned to Christ after having left.

The text here (vv. 19–20) discusses professing believers. The reference to **one of you** suggests that those involved claimed to be Christians. The fact that the professing believer wandered away indicated a serious spiritual lapse.

The act of bringing someone back is not a reference to conversion in the normal Christian sense. It is a description of reclaiming a professing Christian who has wandered into sin. God's grace has brought the wanderer home, and the backsliding is over.

Those who claim to know Christ but live in persistent disobedience show that their claim to know Christ is empty and wrong. They demonstrate that they were never believers at any time. Genuine believers will never lose their salvation. Some who are true believers may wander into sin. The Bible commends us when we exert our best efforts to bring wandering believers back to full commitment.

5:20. Those who work to return straying believers receive two promises. First, the wanderer is saved **from death**. The repentant wanderer avoided spiritual ruin. Sin destroys, and if people persist in following sin, they will experience eternal separation from God, that is, eternal death (see the clear statement in Jas. 1:13–15). Reclaiming such a person is worth the effort.

Some interpreters understand **death** to refer to physical death. They see this type of death as a punishment for sin. The text seems to go farther than this and speak of eternal death, permanent separation from God.

Some who wander away from the truth were never under its power. They professed faith in Christ, but they never experienced the power of the gospel in their lives. Their return is a real conversion to Christ. Although they previously professed to know Christ, they were deceived.

Others who wander are real Christians who have been enticed by Satan. Their return to Christ helps them to avoid the ruin and destruction of a life of disobedience. They enjoy God's blessing in their soul. Since James has described the person who wanders as **one of you,** he has pictured him as a professing Christian who has wandered from the truth. When the professing Christian returns to commitment to Christ, he avoids the spiritual ruin that would otherwise fall upon him.

Second, the wanderer is forgiven **a multitude of sins.** These are the sins of the person who returns. There is no thought here suggesting a way of atonement besides believing in Christ. People who successfully encourage straying believers back to commitment to Christ obey God and lead the sinner to forgiveness. Such encouragers do not atone for their own sins by their actions.

The text does not describe how a Christian should go about the work of restoring a wanderer. Certainly we would expect the starting point to be prayer for the repentance of wanderers and a ministry of love in supporting and encouraging them (John 13:34–35).

> **MAIN IDEA REVIEW:** *Christians must flee the pursuit of wealth, demonstrate stamina in trials, and practice prayer at all times.*

III. CONCLUSION

Green Mamba Bites

On October 16, 1996, John Dina, missionary to Mozambique, was bitten by a deadly green mamba snake as he walked in the Mozambican bush with coworkers. Dina drove himself home, a trip which required five hours. His wife and a missionary doctor stayed with him during the night as his pulse slowed and his breathing became more labored.

At dawn a medical evacuation airplane arrived to take him to Johannesburg, South Africa. Doctors at a hospital administered huge doses of antibiotics and anti-inflammatory drugs. They kept a ventilator on standby. Within days Dina had made a remarkable recovery. His doctor said that he would suffer no permanent damage from the bite. Dina's miraculous recovery from the bite left many villagers who knew of the incident amazed at the power of the God of Christians.

For his part, Dina thanked God for his recovery and acknowledged the prayers of God's people. Thousands of people prayed for him when his name appeared on a missionary prayer calendar on October 12, his thirty-fourth birthday. Thousands of others prayed when an urgent notice was posted on the toll-free prayer lines of the Mission Board and electronic prayer network.

This epistle concludes with an appeal to pray in trouble, in happiness, in sickness, at times of disobedience, and in working out God's will. We must bathe each event of life with prayer. No prayer uttered in faith is ever lost or ignored by God. It accomplishes a good and beneficial purpose.

God will answer the prayers of his people in ways that often differ from our expectations (see 2 Cor. 12:7–10), but the prayers of God's people are never wasted. God responds to the prayers of God's people to bring strength, encouragement, stamina, and healing.

PRINCIPLES

- God hears the prayers of his people as they cry out for justice.
- The fact of Jesus' return gives Christians the hope of eternal reward.
- The compassion and mercy of the Lord give Christians the stamina to endure.
- God hears the prayers of righteous people who pray with passion.

APPLICATIONS

- Recognize how wealthy you are, and use your wealth for the glory of God.
- Persevere in obedience.
- In all your actions be true to your word and keep your promises.
- Pray in strong faith to God both in times of trouble and in times of joy.

IV. LIFE APPLICATION

Changing Other People

In 1840, forty-seven year-old General Sam Houston, recently retired president of the Republic of Texas, married twenty-one-year-old Margaret Moffette Lea. She was the daughter of a minister from a staid south Alabama community. No one gave the marriage much chance due to the difference in age and previous lifestyles of the couple.

After the wedding Margaret Lea Houston began to work diligently at producing change in her husband. She remained at home, continually assuring him of her love and interest. Lovingly, but firmly, she insisted on his abstinence from the alcohol which threatened to shorten his life. Slowly but surely, his health improved, and his lifestyle mended.

After nearly a decade of marriage, Houston described his appreciation for Margaret in a letter to a cousin:

> It has been my lot to be happily united, to a wife that I love, and so far we have a young scion of the old stock. My wife is pious, and her great desire is that Sam [the newborn son] should be reared, in the fear and admonition of the Lord. It is likewise my desire. . . . You, have, I doubt not, heard that my wife controls me, and has reformed me, in many respects? This is pretty true. . . . She gets all the credit for my good actions, and I have to endure all the censure of my bad ones (William Seale, *Sam Houston's Wife*).

In 1854, Houston was baptized near Independence, Texas, by a pioneer preacher. After the baptism someone asked Houston if his sins were washed away. Houston reportedly replied, "I hope so, but if they were all washed away, the Lord help the fish down there."

Although we would have wanted Houston to give God the credit for the change, we can observe that his wife made the spiritual conversion of Sam Houston a goal of her life. Her actions helped to reclaim him **from the error of his way.** She provided for him a sense of security and encouragement which attracted him to her Savior. Peter's appeal to wives to live so that their husbands "may be won over without words by the behavior of their wives, when they see the purity and reverence of your lives" (1 Pet. 3:1) outlined Margaret Houston's method. We help best to bring change to others when we live to show the reality of our faith.

V. PRAYER

Lord, teach me to pray. In season and out of season, in joy or in sorrow, in sickness or in health, for my needs and for the needs of those around me, teach me to pray. Yes, I want to use my tongue to praise you, to talk to you, to love you, and to intercede for others. Let this not be a matter of pride but a matter of true faith dedicated solely to your will and for your glory. Amen.

VI. DEEPER DISCOVERIES

A. The Lord Almighty (v. 4)

The expression, **the Lord Almighty**, is a translation of a term meaning literally, "the Lord of Hosts." This was a popular term for Old Testament writers (see 1 Sam. 1:3,11; 4:4; 6:2; 17:45; 2 Sam. 5:10; 6:2; Ps. 24:10; 46:7,11; 89:8). The phrase pictured God as the commander of the armies of heaven. It shows that God has majesty and power both as ruler of the world and as the protector of his people. The phrase reminded the readers of James that the unlimited resources of God were available for the care of his people.

In this context it encouraged the poor and the helpless to believe that the one on their side was a God who could overpower the wicked deeds of unjust landlords and punish their evil.

B. The Day of Slaughter (v. 5)

This phrase carries at least two applications. First, it reminds us that God will correct injustices on the day of final judgment. The wealthy may think that God has overlooked their sins, but they face future judgment from God.

Second, it carries a vivid picture of the force feeding of cattle in preparation for their slaughter as food. The wealthy are as morally insensitive as beasts who eat greedily, not knowing their owners are fattening them for the kill. The entire picture is a vivid way of calling the wealthy to repentance before they experience God's judgment and more especially of calling believers to endure oppression from the wealthy in light of God's sovereign control of the future.

C. Innocent Men (v. 6)

The literal translation of the Greek (*dikaios*) is "the just one," a title used for Christ (Acts 3:14, "the righteous one"). Some interpreters see this as an accusation that James was accusing the wealthy of having murdered Christ. In this context, however, James was describing the tyranny of the rich against the poor. James pictured the poor believers as **innocent** people who responded to afflictions with meekness and obedience to Christ. The heartless actions of the wealthy only made their evil deeds more culpable.

D. Patient, Patience, Perseverance (vv. 7–11)

This section uses words with similar meanings to show the need for restraint and stamina in the face of persecution. **Patient** (*makrothumeo*, vv. 7,8) and **patience** (*makrothumia*, v. 10) both come from the same Greek root. **Patience** is sometimes translated as "long-suffering." Paul demanded this "patience" as a distinctive trait of believers (Col. 3:12). They must show it toward all (1 Thess. 5:14). Believers need the self-control which enables persecuted people to submit to insult and injury without using vindictive behavior.

Perseverance (*hupomone*, v. 11) denotes a consistent obedience to the Lord under trial. It calls for believers to show endurance in commitment and obedience as they face hardship. We cannot say that Job was free of complaint about his treatment. In Job 6:2–3; 7:11–16; and 10:1–2 he lamented his bitter treatment. Still, Job persevered in that he never gave up his obedience to God. He remained unswervingly loyal to God. James encouraged his readers by pointing out the encouraging outcome of Job's trials. He finally came to an experience of God's **compassion and mercy.**

Job's behavior becomes an example to us as we face trials, afflictions, and hardships. God's grace can develop a steadfastness which shows restraint under provocation and endures in commitment. Christians must not indulge in resentment against their persecutors. They must put aside all thoughts of retaliation and revenge.

To call for **patience** and **perseverance** does not rule out protesting a wrong. Christians must oppose evil in any form, but they must not be surprised by the hostile response of the world. They need a willingness to be a martyr without being recognized as one.

E. The Lord's Coming (vv. 7–8)

Believers are called to demonstrate our patience and restraint until **the Lord's coming.** This event will put to an end all forced subjection to injustice and mistreatment.

The term used to describe Jesus' coming (*parousia*), refers to a visit made by royalty to a city or geographical area. Usually in the New Testament it describes Jesus' return to bless and strengthen his people (1 Thess. 3:13). Here it describes our hope for the personal return of Jesus Christ. James gave few details about the chronology or effect of this return. His chief emphasis was that the hope of the Lord's return must promote holiness in each believer.

F. Oaths (v. 12)

The biblical prohibition of oaths does not ban their use to prove truthfulness. The frivolous use of an oath to be evasive or untruthful is wrong. Christians cannot follow the Jewish practice of taking a flippant oath and basing it on something other than God's name. Jews who did this felt that the only binding oaths were based on God's name. Oaths based on something other than God's name were not seen as binding. Thus, some Jews in Jesus' time used careless oaths to justify deception. The Bible prohibits this practice.

Christians today need not feel obliged to avoid an oath in a courtroom or in other legal procedures. Christians are to be known for their rugged commitment to truthfulness, and a courtroom oath is meant to establish this. They must not use an oath, however, to conceal deceit or to mislead others.

G. Praying for the Sick (vv. 14–15)

These verses contain great encouragement for offering prayer for the ill. However, we should not take his statements as a promise of sure healing if we pray with enough faith. John's statements in 1 John 5:14–15 remind us that all prayer is subject to the reservation that God's will be done. Sometimes God intends to leave the sickness with the ill person and allow that person to trust more deeply in God's grace (2 Cor. 12:7–10).

First John 3:22 teaches us that the obedience of the intercessor is a factor in receiving answers to prayer. Those who rush into prayer fresh from a disobedient lifestyle need not expect marvelous answers to prayer for healing the sick.

Sometimes remaining in sickness is God's plan for the individual. Paul advised Timothy about how to deal with his "frequent illnesses" (1 Tim. 5:23). The advice did not hold out hope for immediate healing, but contained information for treating the illness. In 2 Timothy 4:20, Paul announced that he had left "Trophimus sick in Miletus." Paul did not feel encouraged to expect immediate healing for his friend.

James's words encourage Christians to pray in all instances of sickness. In some instances God will provide the assurance that he intends to heal. As we pray, we must recognize that ultimate healing depends on God's will. This is an implied but unstated condition in the absolute promise for healing in verse 15. We can be assured that God uses all prayer for healing to accomplish good in the life of the sick person. Sometimes the good which God does will provide immediate strength and an experience of divine grace, but not instant healing.

H. Eternal Death (v. 20)

James promised his readers that **whoever turns a sinner from the error of his way will save him from death.** Some interpret **death** as a reference to physical death, but it seems better to understand the reference as a discussion of eternal death, separation from God for eternity.

The Bible uses "death" in at least three different ways. First, it uses the term in the way we normally do to talk of physical death. This is the condition of a person who is not breathing and has no heartbeat. Second, the Bible sometimes uses "death" in reference to spiritual death. This is the condition of being physically alive but without the life of God in the individual's personality. You are "dead in your transgressions and sins" until you accept Christ as Savior and are converted (Eph. 2:11).

Those who die physically in the condition of spiritual death pass into eternal death. This is the third usage of "death" in Scripture. It describes the condition of living in eternity without God. This is what the Bible calls existence in hell. James 5:20 warns against this eternal death.

James wrote persons who professed to know Christ. If they wandered from Christ, they would experience devastation and spiritual harm. Believers, however, cannot lose their salvation. They will not experience eternal death. "Through faith," God keeps them "until the coming of salvation" (1 Pet. 1:5). Though they wander, God will bring them back to himself.

Those who experience eternal death are those who have never confessed Christ in faith as their Lord and Savior and those who profess faith in Christ but have never truly come under the power of the gospel. With an empty profession devoid of saving experience with Christ, they continue in their waywardness and enter into eternity without a true relationship with Jesus Christ. They then experience eternal death.

Those who experience rescue from sin through faith in Jesus spend eternity in the presence of God. Those who succumb to sin's enticements remain eternally separated from God. This condition is eternal death.

VII. TEACHING OUTLINE

A. INTRODUCTION

1. Lead Story: Some Sources of Spiritual Numbness
2. Context: James 4:13–17 contains a word to self-confident Jewish businessmen, urging them to plan their lives around God's will rather their own selfish imaginations. James 5:1–6 cautions wealthy landlords who were abusing their tenants.

   The rich are warned (v. 1) and given a picture of God's coming judgments on those whose wealth has corrupted them (vv. 2–3). These wealthy people are charged with injustice, indulgence, and cruelty (vv. 4–6).

   James 5:7–12 calls for the development of patience and reverence toward God. **Patience** is restraint marked by willingness to bear insult and injury without retaliation. The coming return of Jesus provides us an incentive for this patience (vv. 7–8). Personal piques can hinder the development of the right attitude (v. 9). The prophets, Job, and industrious farmers are examples of people who showed restraint in face of hardship (vv. 7,10–11).

   In 5:12, James calls us to avoid an irreverent use of God's name to excuse our dishonesty. We are to practice verbal integrity so that we need not use God's name in oaths.

The Book of James concludes with a discussion of the uses of prayer (vv. 13–20). Believers should pray in times of joy as well as sorrow. Sickness calls for special prayer. We also need to practice confession of sin, prayer for accomplishing God's will, and prayer to reclaim wandering believers. James leaves us with the conviction that God will use all prayers to accomplish good both in the life of the intercessor and in the life of the one who receives prayer.

3. Transition: What should James's words cause us to do? First, most of us who read these words have enough wealth so that the rest of the world may regard us as "wealthy." We should use our wealth "to be rich in good deeds" (1 Tim. 6:18).

    Second, in times of trial and hardship we must put aside the human tendency to grumble and complain, commit ourselves to God's will, and "continue to do good" (1 Pet. 4:19).

    Third, we must be people who pray with praise, confession, and intercession. In Paul's words, we must be people who "pray continually" (1 Thess. 5:17).

B. COMMENTARY

1. A Charge to People with Money (vv. 1–6)
    a. Warnings to the rich (vv. 1–3)
    b. Charges against the rich (vv. 4–6)
2. The Development of Patience and Reverence (vv. 7–12)
    a. An appeal for stamina in trials (vv. 7–11)
    b. An appeal for a reverence for God (v. 12)
3. The Uses of Prayer (vv. 13–20)
    a. Prayer in life's experiences (v. 13)
    b. Prayer in sickness (vv. 14–15)
    c. Prayer in confession of sin (v. 16a)
    d. Prayer in working out the will of God (vv. 16b–18)
    e. The ministry of reclaiming wanderers (vv. 19–20)

C. CONCLUSION: CHANGING OTHER PEOPLE

VIII. ISSUES FOR DISCUSSION

1. How do you determine who is rich and who is poor? In what ways should you receive the warnings to the rich? What charges is God bringing against you for the way you use your financial resources?
2. What situations and circumstances test your patience? If you would begin exercising patience, what changes would come about in your

life? What motivation does God's Word give you to exercise patience and perseverance?

3. Do you have a habit of using certain words that really express an oath you do not intend to keep? What does God's Word say about such "unconscious" or habitual oaths?

4. What have you learned from the Book of James about prayer? What changes will you make in your prayer life? What will you do when your prayers do not seem to receive answers?

5. Do you know people who have professed faith in Christ but are not living the way Christ expects his followers to live? What can and will you do for such people? Why?

Glossary

1. **Angels**—supernatural beings created by God to care for believers (Heb. 1:14).
2. **Devil**—the personal agent of evil who leads the opposition to God's purposes in this world.
3. **Discipline**—instruction or training used by God to train his children in righteous living (see Heb. 12:11).
4. **Covenant**—God's agreement to complete the salvation of sinners based on Christ's saving work.
5. **End of the ages**—a reference to the death of Christ as the decisive event of world history and the event which begins the final age of time (Heb. 9:26). See also "last days."
6. **Faith**—a response which takes God at his word and acts upon it. Faith provides assurance of things we can only hope for and a certainty about things we cannot see.
7. **Firstborn**—Used in reference to Jesus, this term describes his majesty and dignity. It does not suggest that he is the first of God's creatures. Jesus has the dignity of the eldest son in a Hebrew family, and this shows his importance in the divine plan.
8. **Gospel**—In Hebrews 4:2,6, the term is used to refer to the message of deliverance preached both to Old Testament and New Testament hearers. For Old Testament believers the promise of deliverance appeared in Exodus 19:5–6. For New Testament believers the content of the gospel appeared in 1 Corinthians 15:1–4. The role of Jesus is a central feature of the gospel for New Testament believers.
9. **High priest**—official in charge of temple worship who represented human beings before God and once a year entered the Most Holy Place with sacrificial blood for the Day of Atonement.
10. **Hope**—an interest or desire in seeing a cherished goal fulfilled.
11. **Last days**—period beginning with the life, death, and resurrection of Christ. These are last days, not in a chronological sense, but because of their importance. The work of Jesus is God's last important act to reach lost sinners. See also "end of the ages."
12. **Melchizedek**—mysterious Old Testament king mentioned in Genesis 14:18–20. He offered blessings to Abraham and received a tithe of Abraham's possessions. Jesus' priesthood is patterned after that of Melchizedek (Heb. 7:1–4).
13. **Miracles**—events which show God's powerful actions and reveal his character or plans.
14. **Patience**—a response of persistence or stamina which endures in obedience despite difficulties.
15. **Perseverance**—the response of enduring even in the face of difficulty. Christians develop this trait by facing and overcoming hardship and adversity (Jas. 1:2–4).
16. **Redemption**—the act of releasing a captive by the payment of a price. Jesus' death provided our redemption from sin's power and penalty (Heb. 9:12).
17. **Repentance**—a spiritual and moral change of attitude toward God which turns people from their sin to God.
18. **Rest**—the provision of the strength of Christ for believers as they face hardships and persecution (Heb. 4:9–10).
19. **Sins of ignorance**—The Old Testament made provision for the forgiveness of sins done carelessly but offered no hope of forgiveness to those who were willful sinners (Num. 15:28,30).
20. **Son of Man**—Jesus' favorite term for himself, calling attention to his humanity and to his being an agent of God's judgment.

Glossary

21. **Temptations**—enticements to do evil which spring from our own evil desires. God is not responsible for sending them to us (Jas. 1:13).
22. **Trials**—afflictions and hardships permitted in our lives by God to develop stamina and endurance in us (Jas. 1:2–4).
23. **Typology**—a divinely intended correspondence between a person, place, or thing in the Old Testament and a person, place, or thing in the New Testament.
24. **Unbelief**—a deliberate unfaithfulness to God which leads to disobedience.
25. **Word of God**—This term appears in Hebrews 4:12 as a reference to God's message to human beings. This message appears in Scripture, but it also came in visions, dreams, and miraculous events.
26. **World to come**—either the new world order which Jesus began or the afterlife.

Bibliography for Hebrews

Barclay, William. *The Letter to the Hebrews*. 2d ed. The Daily Study Bible. Philadelphia: Westminster, 1957.

Brown, Raymond. *The Message of Hebrews*. The Bible Speaks Today. Downers Grove, Ill.: InterVarsity Press, 1982.

Bruce, F. F. *The Epistle to the Hebrews*. The New International Commentary on the New Testament. Grand Rapids, Mich.: Eerdmans, 1964.

Bruce, F. F. *Jesus: Lord & Savior*. Downers Grove, Ill.: InterVarsity Press.

Davidson, A.B. *The Epistle to the Hebrews*. Edinburgh: T & T Clark, n.d.

Ellingworth, Paul. *Commentary on Hebrews*. New International Greek Testament Commentary. Grand Rapids, Mich.: Eerdmans, 1993.

Ellingworth, Paul, and Eugene Nida. *A Translator's Handbook on the Letter to the Hebrews*. London: United Bible Societies, 1983.

Guthrie, Donald. *Hebrews*. Tyndale New Testament Commentaries. Grand Rapids: Eerdmans, 1983.

Hagner, Donald A. *Hebrews*. The New International Biblical Commentary. Peabody, Mass.: Hendrickson, 1990.

Hewitt, Thomas. *Hebrews*. Tyndale New Testament Commentaries. London: Tyndale Press, 1960.

Hughes, P. E. *A Commentary on the Epistle to the Hebrews*. Grand Rapids: Eerdmans, 1977.

Lane, William L. *Hebrews 1–8*. Word Biblical Commentary, Vol. 47a. Dallas: Word, 1991.

_____. *Hebrews 9–13*. Word Biblical Commentary, Vol. 47b. Dallas: Word, 1991.

Morris, Leon. *Hebrews*. The Expositor's Bible Commentary. Grand Rapids: Zondervan, 1981.

Westcott, B.F. *The Epistle to the Hebrews*. Grand Rapids: Eerdmans, 1970.

Bibliography for James

Davids, Peter H. *James*. A Good News Commentary. San Francisco: Harper & Row, 1983.

Hiebert, D. Edmond. *The Epistle of James: Tests of a Living Faith*. Chicago: Moody, 1979.

Hughes, R. Kent. *James: Faith That Works*. Preaching the Word Series. Wheaton, Ill.: Crossway, 1991.

Tasker, R. V. G. *James*. Tyndale New Testament Commentaries. London: Tyndale, 1957.

Vaughan, Curtis. *James: A Study Guide*. Grand Rapids: Zondervan, 1969.

HOLMAN REFERENCE

ALSO AVAILABLE:

THE HOLMAN COMMENTARIES SERIES – *Retail $19.99 ea.*

Old Testament

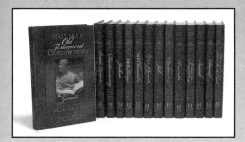

9-780-805-494-617	Genesis (Vol. 1)
9-780-805-494-624	Exodus, Leviticus, Numbers (Vol. 2)
9-780-805-494-631	Deuteronomy (Vol. 3)
9-780-805-494-648	Joshua (Vol. 4)
9-780-805-494-655	Judges, Ruth (Vol. 5)
9-780-805-494-662	1 & 2 Samuel (Vol. 6) *forthcoming*
9-780-805-494-679	1 & 2 Kings (Vol. 7)
9-780-805-494-686	1 & 2 Chronicles (Vol. 8)
9-780-805-494-693	Ezra, Nehemiah, Esther (Vol. 9)
9-780-805-494-709	Job (Vol. 10)
9-780-805-494-716	Psalms 1-75 (Vol. 11)
9-780-805-494-815	Psalms 76-150 (Vol. 12)
9-780-805-494-723	Proverbs (Vol. 13)
9-780-805-494-822	Ecclesiastes, Song of Songs (Vol. 14)
9-780-805-494-730	Isaiah (Vol. 15)
9-780-805-494-747	Jeremiah, Lamentations (Vol. 16)
9-780-805-494-754	Ezekiel (Vol. 17)
9-780-805-494-761	Daniel (Vol. 18)
9-780-805-494-778	Hosea, Joel, Amos, Obadiah, Jonah, Micah (Vol. 19)
9-780-805-494-785	Nahum-Malachi (Vol. 20)

New Testament

9-780-805-402-018	Matthew
9-780-805-402-025	Mark
9-780-805-402-032	Luke
9-780-805-402-049	John
9-780-805-402-056	Acts
9-780-805-402-063	Romans
9-780-805-402-070	1 & 2 Corinthians
9-780-805-402-087	Galatians-Colossians
9-780-805-402-094	1 Thessalonians-Philemon
9-780-805-402-117	Hebrews, James
9-780-805-402-100	1 & 2 Peter-Jude
9-780-805-402-124	Revelation

9-780-805-428-285   **NT Boxed Set Sale Price $179.97** (Reg. $239.88)
(*All Volumes Hardcover*)

1.800.233.1123   www.BHPublishingGroup.com